PSYCHOLOGICAL PERSPECTIVES ON THE SELF

Volume 1

PSYCHOLOGICAL PERSPECTIVES ON THE SELF

Volume 1

Edited by
Jerry Suls
*State University of New York
at Albany*

 LAWRENCE ERLBAUM ASSOCIATES, PUBLISHERS
1982   Hillsdale, New Jersey,   London

Lawrence Erlbaum Associates, Inc., Publishers
365 Broadway
Hillsdale, New Jersey 07642

Library of Congress Cataloging in Publication Data

Suls, Jerry M.
      Psychological perspectives on the self.

      Includes bibliographical references and index.
      1. Self.   2. Self—Psychological aspects.   3. Self—
Social aspects.   I. Title.   [DNLM: 1. Self-concept.
2. Ego.   BF697 P974]
BF697.S925   155.2   81-15108
ISBN 0-89859-197-X (v. 1)   AACR2

Printed in the United States of America

10 9 8 7 6 5 4 3 2 1

Contents

Preface

The self has been a subject of discussion and inquiry since antiquity. This is not surprising because self-reflection and self-evaluation are part and parcel of everyday life. But although the self is a central preoccupation, it eludes easy definition. Perhaps this is because the self is simultaneously a process and a structure, as William James so astutely observed. Gergen (1971) has noted, in the former sense it refers to the: "process by which the person conceptualizes or categorizes his/her behavior—both . . . external conduct and internal states." In the latter sense it refers to: "the system of concepts available to the person in attempting to define him/herself [pp. 22–23]."[1] William James brought the self to the center of psychological examination when psychology as a scientific discipline was in its infancy. Since his time there have been an untold number of attempts on the part of psychologists to grapple with this subject. Efforts have been made by all brands of psychologists from clinicians to experimental psychologists. Interest in this area may wax and wane, but the psychological study of the self has persisted for nearly 100 years and will, no doubt, continue for a long time to come.

Social psychology has had a critical role to play, as it seems clear that the self has significant social underpinnings. One major change in thinking brought in part by the work of social psychologists has been the appreciation that "to know thyself" means "to know one's fellows." Theoretical and empirical work reinforce the notion that self-knowledge stems from the reciprocal relationship between ourselves and our social group. Conceptions of our traits, abilities, and opinions grow out of the reactions of others, and how we compare to them. In short, the self is made of social cloth.

---

[1] K. J. Gergan. *The Concept of Self*. New York: Holt, Rinehart & Winston, 1971.

The present volume brings together a wide variety of social psychological views on the self. Whereas it is by no means a comprehensive survey, it does represent a diversity of current perspectives. There is a substantial mix of the theoretical and empirical, old themes and new ones. The chapters are organized into three major divisions. In the first section the contributions are concerned with the processes of self-appraisal and self-regulation. The second section deals with the question of the self as a unitary entity—is it consistent or inconsistent, single or multiple, stable or fluid? In the final section, the contributors consider the reciprocal interplay between the self and its social environment. Although some chapters could have been placed in more than one section, their final placement was determined by their primary emphasis.

Since the time the chapters in this volume were commissioned, an increasing number of psychologists have been pursuing significant new research on the self. To reflect these advances, a second volume of contributions is in preparation that will be coedited by the present editor and Anthony G. Greenwald of Ohio State University. The second volume will focus on personality and social perspectives.

Several individuals helped either directly or indirectly with the development of this book, for which I owe them much thanks. I am especially indebted to my colleague, Glenn Sanders, who provided needed advice and insight. Thanks also to Larry Erlbaum for his support and encouragement from the book's inception. I am grateful to Irene Farruggio for her valuable assistance in preparing the manuscripts. Finally, I dedicate this volume to my wife, Sue, and my son, Rob, with affection and thanks.

Jerry Suls
State University of New York
at Albany

PSYCHOLOGICAL PERSPECTIVES ON THE SELF

Volume 1

SELF-APPRAISAL
AND SELF-REGULATION

For some time scholars have been concerned with the processes by which persons appraise their traits, abilities, and level of personal agency. A related question is how these appraisals influence subsequent actions and evaluations of the social environment. Nearly all contemporary self-theories take the view that the self is a cognitive structure that is both *knower* and that which is *known*, processer and structure. This theme is carried either explicitly or implicitly by the chapters in this section in an attempt to understand how self-definition is developed.

Albert Bandura's chapter, "The Self and Mechanisms of Agency," is concerned with how people exert influence over what they do. He discusses the constituent processes of personal agency from an approach emphasizing that behavior, cognitive, personal factors, and environmental influences all operate as interlocking determinants of each other. In the chapter he integrates a wide range of theory and research, implicating the factors that determine feelings of personal agency.

In "The Self in Social Information Processing," Hazel Markus and Keith Sentis are concerned with how the self perceives the social world. Using cognitive psychology and information processing as a base, the self is conceptualized as a system of schemata. The authors then review empirical evidence that compares individuals assumed to have a schema in a particular domain, such as independence, with those without such a structure in that domain. Markus and Sentis demonstrate that variations in self-structure strongly determine the content and processing of self-relevant judgments and evaluations of social events.

William McGuire and Claire McGuire, in "Significant Others in Self-Space: Sex Differences and Developmental Trends in the Social Self," are concerned with the content that is available to the person when he/she reflects upon the self, the so-called, "self-space." To pursue this topic, the authors ask their subjects to "Tell us about yourself," a strategy that allows respondents to choose the dimensions of self-description. The first section of the chapter reviews the McGuires' past research on the effects of distinctiveness of personal characteristics on the self-space. The authors then discuss their more recent work concerning how the self-space is occupied by thoughts of significant others, and how contents of this social self vary with gender and age during childhood and adolescence.

In Chapter 4, "From the Cradle to the Grave: Comparison and Self-Evaluation Across the Life-Span," Jerry Suls and Brian Mullen outline a model of how modes of self-evaluation change in importance with age. Specifically, they propose that people make comparisons of present efforts with past ones (temporal comparisons) to evaluate important traits and abilities during the early and late phases of the life cycle, but rely principally on interpersonal comparisons for self-evaluation during the middle phases of life. The authors discuss the mechanisms underlying these changes and discuss relevant evidence from the social, developmental, and gerontological literatures.

1 The Self and Mechanisms of Agency

Albert Bandura
Stanford University

The self is a subject about which much has been written, although it is often so ill-defined as to mystify what it embodies. In examining the nature and functions of the self, any number of self-referent phenomena might be selected as the focus of attention (T. Mischel, 1977). However, most of the fundamental questions in this area of inquiry are concerned, directly or indirectly, with the problem of human agency. The matters of major interest center on whether, and how, people exert some influence over what they perceive and do.

The issue of whether people serve as partial causes of their own actions has received considerably greater attention in philosophical than in psychological analyses. This relative neglect is surprising considering that self processs are central to an understanding of human functioning. Moreover, it is around questions of personal causality that some of the major theoretical controversies in psychology revolve. This chapter therefore addresses itself to mechanisms of human agency as conceptualized within the framework of social learning theory.

Personal Agency in Triadic Reciprocality

Analysis of how persons might serve as agents of their own motivation and actions must address the broader issue of the causal model within which self processes operate. Theorists favoring one-sided determinism view persons mainly as conveyors of environmental stimuli, but they themselves cannot serve as a source of influence over their own behavior. Acts are the work of environmental forces and whatever residual products they lodge in the organism (Day, 1977; Skinner, 1974).

Most contemporary theorists subscribe to some form of interactional model that views behavior as a product of personal and situational influences (Bowers,

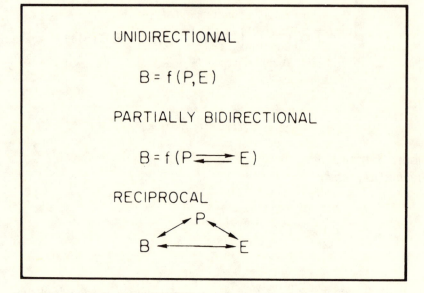

FIG. 1.1.   Schematic representation of three alternative conceptions of interaction. *B* signifies behavior, *P* the cognitive and other internal events that affect
perceptions and actions, and *E* the external environment (Bandura, 1978).

1973; Endler & Magnusson, 1975; Pervin & Lewis, 1978). However, interactive processes have been conceptualized in at least three different ways. These
alternative formulations are summarized schematically in Fig. 1.1.

In the unidirectional view of interaction, persons and situations are treated as
independent entities that combine to produce behavior. A major problem with
this view is that personal and environmental factors do not function as independent determinants; rather, they determine each other. People create, alter, and destroy environments. The changes they produce in environmental conditions , in
turn, influence their behavior and the nature of future life.

The partially bidirectional conception of interaction acknowledges that persons and situations affect each other. But it depicts influences relating to behavior as flowing in only one direction (i.e., the person–situation interchange is said
to produce the behavior, but behavior itself is not an influencer). A limitation of
this type of view is that, except for their social stimulus value, persons cannot be
considered causes apart from their actions. Their overt actions take the dominant
role in how people influence the situations that, in turn, affect their thoughts, affect, and behavior. It is hard to conceive of behavior as the offspring of an intimate meeting of person and situation. Behavior was an interacting influence on
the meeting and was active throughout events, rather than procreated by a union
of a behaviorless person and a situation. In short, behavior is an interacting determinant, not a detached byproduct that plays no role in the production process.

Social learning theory favors a conception of interaction based on triadic reciprocality (Bandura, 1977a, 1978). In this model, behavior, cognitive and other personal factors, and environmental influences all operate as interlocking determinants of each other. It would be exceedingly difficult to study all aspects of triadic reciprocality simultaneously. Hence, different research enterprises address different segments of reciprocality. Investigators who center their attention on the interaction between thought and action examine how conceptions, beliefs, self-percepts, and intentions give shape and direction to behavior. Both the natural and extrinsic effects of people's actions, in turn, alter their thought patterns and affective reactions (Bandura, 1977b; Bower, 1975; Neisser, 1976).

Consider next the segment of reciprocality between the person and the environment in the triadic system. Environmental influences can affect persons apart from their behavior, as when thoughts and feelings are modified through modeling, tuition, or by social persuasion (Bandura, 1977a; Rosenthal & Zimmerman, 1978; Zimbardo, Ebbesen, & Maslach, 1977). People also evoke different reactions from their social environment simply by their physical characteristics, such as age, size, race, sex, and physical attractiveness. People similarly activate different reactions depending on their socially conferred roles and status. For example, those who occupy high positions in prestige and power hierarchies elicit more deferential and accommodating reactions than do those of lowly status. Differential social treatments can alter recipients' self-conceptions and behavior in ways that either strengthen or reduce the environmental bias. Even erroneous information about a person's characteristics can set off social interchanges in directions that create behavioral validation for the initially erroneous conceptions (Snyder, Tanke, & Berscheid, 1977). The processes by which people's perceptions of each other influence the course of their interactions has been a subject of major concern to researchers working within the field of person perception (Schneider, Hastorf, & Ellsworth, 1979).

Of the various segments in the triadic interlocking system, it is the reciprocal interaction between behavior and environmental events that has received greatest attention. Indeed, some theories focus exclusively on this portion of reciprocity in the explanation of behavior (Skinner, 1974). Through their actions people alter their environment, and the changes produced in environmental conditions, in turn, influence the course of human behavior. Similarly, in the social transactions of everyday life, people reciprocally influence each other's behavior (Cairns, 1979; Patterson, 1976; Raush, Barry, Hertel, & Swain, 1974; Thomas & Malone, 1979). In such interactions, where persons largely serve as the environments for each other, the same act can be taken as behavior or environment depending arbitrarily on which side of the ongoing exchange one happens to look first in the flow of events.

Social interchanges are not governed solely by the immediate reciprocal effects of actions. While behaving, people entertain thoughts about where their actions are apt to lead and what they are likely to produce. Forethought can enhance, attentuate, or nullify the momentary effects of action. Hence, analysis of the interactive relation between behavior and environment must be extended temporally and broadened to include cognitive factors that operate in the triadic interlocking system.

In the model of triadic reciprocality, persons are neither autonomous agents nor mechanical conveyors of animating environmental forces. Rather, they serve as a reciprocally contributing influence on their own behavior in the interlocking system. An act therefore includes among its determinants self-produced influences. Within this process of reciprocal determinism lies the opportunity for people to exert some influence over the course of their lives as well as the limits of self-direction.

As already alluded to, there are innumerable ways in which self processes can enter interactively into the determination of behavior. In the perceptual realm, personal factors partly influence what people seek out, and how they select, organize, and transform the environmental stimuli that impinge upon them. In the realm of thought, people plan, create, and in other ways use their cognitive capabilities to guide their behavior. Rather than solve problems solely by enacting options and suffering the consequences, they usually test possible solutions symbolically and discard or retain them on the basis of calculated consequences before plunging into action. In the motivational realm, by anticipating outcomes of prospective actions and setting proximal goals for themselves, people generate motivational inducements and guides for given courses of behavior. Detailed analysis of interactive agency in each of these spheres falls beyond the scope of this chapter. Rather, the present inquiry centers on mechanisms of agency that figure prominently in a social learning view of the self.

MECHANISMS OF AGENCY: SELF-REGULATORY FUNCTIONS

Self-regulation is not achieved by a feat of willpower. It operates through a set of subfunctions that must be developed and mobilized for self-directed change (Bandura, 1977a; Kanfer, 1977). Neither intention nor desire alone has much effect if people lack the means for exercising influence over their own behavior (Bandura & Simon, 1977). The constituent processes in one of the major mechanisms of personal agency are summarized in Fig. 1.2.

Self-Observation

People cannot affect the direction of their actions if they are inattentive to relevant aspects of their behavior. Activities may vary on a number of dimensions, some of which are listed in the self-observation component. Depending on value orientations and on the functional significance of given activities, people attend

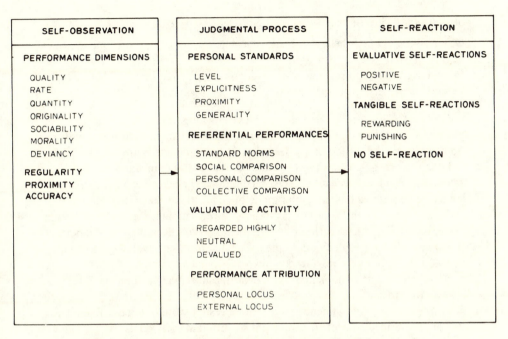

SELF-OBSERVATION	JUDGMENTAL PROCESS	SELF-REACTION
PERFORMANCE DIMENSIONS	**PERSONAL STANDARDS**	**EVALUATIVE SELF-REACTIONS**
QUALITY	LEVEL	POSITIVE
RATE	EXPLICITNESS	NEGATIVE
QUANTITY	PROXIMITY	**TANGIBLE SELF-REACTIONS**
ORIGINALITY	GENERALITY	
SOCIABILITY	**REFERENTIAL PERFORMANCES**	REWARDING
MORALITY		PUNISHING
DEVIANCY	STANDARD NORMS	**NO SELF-REACTION**
REGULARITY	SOCIAL COMPARISON	
PROXIMITY	PERSONAL COMPARISON	
ACCURACY	COLLECTIVE COMPARISON	
	VALUATION OF ACTIVITY	
	REGARDED HIGHLY	
	NEUTRAL	
	DEVALUED	
	PERFORMANCE ATTRIBUTION	
	PERSONAL LOCUS	
	EXTERNAL LOCUS	

FIG. 1.2.   Component processes through which people affect their own motivation and actions (Bandura 1977a).

selectively to certain aspects of their behavior and ignore variations on nonrelevant dimensions. For example, they monitor their work in achievement situations; and the sociability and morality of their conduct in interpersonal situations.

In the flow of transactions with the environment many factors compete for attention. People may attend most closely to what is going on around them, to the actions of others, to what they themselves are doing, or to the immediate or distal effects of their behavior. If they are to exert influence over their actions, they have to know what they are doing. Success in self-regulation therefore partly depends on the fidelity, consistency, and temporal proximity of self-monitoring.

Self-observation of ongoing behavior provides continuing information and thus the best opportunity for self-evaluative reactions to exert directive influence while the behavior is still in progress. When attention is focused on the more distal effects of actions, people may feel pleased or disappointed with their efforts, but such evaluative reactions cannot alter past behavior. Thus, for example, obese individuals are more successful in regulating their weight by monitoring their daily caloric intake than by keeping track of the pounds excessive calories have added (Romanczyk, Tracey, Wilson, & Thorpe, 1973). Intermittent self-monitoring, which is only partially informative, also produces less-effective self-regulation than does close attentiveness to one's own performances (Mahoney, Moore, Wade, & Moura, 1973).

Judgmental Subfunctions

Observing how one is behaving is the first step toward doing something to affect it, but, in itself, such information provides little basis for self-directed reactions. Behavior gives rise to self-reactions through a judgmental function that includes several subsidiary processes that are considered next.

Personal Standards. Self-directedness requires internal standards for judging and guiding one's actions. Such standards are developed from information conveyed by different modes of influence. People form standards for judging their own behavior partly on the basis of how significant others have reacted to it (Kanfer & Marston, 1963). Sociological perspectives on the self have tended to emphasize this particular mode of acquisition (Cooley, 1902; McCall, 1977). Standards can be promoted through direct teaching as well as through evaluative social reactions (McMains & Liebert, 1968; Rosenhan, Frederick, & Burrowes, 1968). People not only prescribe and teach self-evaluative standards; they also exemplify them in responding to their own behavior. Such modeling serves as an especially influential vehicle of transmission (Bandura, 1977a; Masters & Mokros, 1974).

In most social environments wide differences exist in the types of standards that are prescribed, modeled, and taught by different individuals or even by the same individuals in different activities and in different settings. People must therefore process the divergent information in forming generic personal standards against which to judge their own behavior (Bandura, 1976; Lepper, Sagotsky, & Mailer, 1975).

Social Referential Comparisons. For most activities there are no absolute measures of adequacy. The time in which a given distance is run or the number of points earned on an exam often do not convey sufficient information for self-appraisal even when measured against an internal standard. Thus, a student who scores 118 points on an examination and adopts a performance standard of *A* as the criterion of adequacy could make no meaningful self-appraisal without knowing the accomplishments of others. When adequacy is defined relationally, appraisals of one's own behavior require comparisons of three major sources of information: performance level, internal standards, and the performances of others.

The referential comparisons may take different forms for different tasks. For some regular activities, standard norms based on representative groups are used to determine one's relative standing. More often people compare themselves to particular associates in similar situations. This may involve either classmates, work associates, or people in other settings engaged in similar endeavors. Self-appraisals will therefore vary substantially depending on the level of ability of those chosen for social comparison (Simon, 1979b; Suls & Miller, 1977).

One's previous behavior is continuously used as a reference against which ongoing performance is judged. In this referential process, it is self-comparison that supplies the measure of adequacy. Past attainments affect self-appraisals mainly through their effects on standard setting. As a rule, people try to surpass their past performances (Festinger, 1942; Lewin, Dembo, Festinger, & Sears, 1944). After a given level of performance is attained, it is no longer challenging, and new satisfactions are sought through progressive improvement.

The referential performances against which one's own behavior is partly judged take other forms in societies organized around collectivist principles. In these social systems it is group performance rather than individual accomplishment that is evaluated and acclaimed (Bronfenbrenner, 1970). Comparison processes still operate under collective arrangements, but self-appraisal is primarily in terms of one's relative contribution to common goals and the level of group accomplishment.

Valuation of Activities.   Another important factor in the judgmental component of self-regulation concerns the evaluation of activities. People do not much care how they perform on tasks that have little or no significance for them, and little effort is expended on devalued activities. It is mainly in areas affecting one's welfare and self-esteem that performance appraisals activate self-reactions. The more relevant performances are to one's sense of personal adequacy, the more likely are self-evaluative reactions to be elicited in the activity (Simon, 1979a).

Performance Attribution.   Self-reactions also vary depending on how people perceive the determinants of their behavior. They take pride in their accomplishments when they ascribe their successes to their own abilities and efforts. They do not derive much self-satisfaction, however, when they view their performance attainments as heavily dependent on external factors. The same is true for judgments of failure and blameworthy conduct. People respond self-critically to inadequate performances for which they hold themselves responsible, but not to those they perceive are due to unusual circumstances or to insufficient capabilities (Weiner, Russell, & Lerman, 1978).

A number of factors influence causal judgments of performance. Some of these concern the circumstances under which activities are carried out. The greater the situational inducements, aids, and supports, the less likely are performances to be credited to oneself (Bem, 1972). Similarly, deficient performances ascribed to transitory internal conditions such as debilitating mood, fatigue, or maladies (Frieze, 1976) are unlikely to activate evaluative self-reactions. In addition to situational and personal factors, prior social learning experiences can create judgmental biases in how the determinants of one's behavior are viewed. Such attributional proclivities have been examined most intensively in investigations of depression and of sex differences in self-appraisal of achievement behavior (Dweck & Goetz, 1978; Parsons, Ruble, Hodges, & Small, 1976; Seligman, Abramson, Semmel, & von Baeyer, 1979).

Self-Reactive Influence

Development of evaluative standards and judgmental skills establishes the capability for self-directed influence. This is achieved by creating incentives for one's own actions and by applying self-consequences depending on how one's behavior measures up to internal standards. Thus, people pursue courses of action that produce positive self-reactions and refrain from behaving in ways that give rise to self-censure.

In the social learning view, self-regulated incentives affect behavior mainly through their motivational function (Bandura, 1977a). When people make self-satisfaction or tangible gratifications conditional upon certain accomplishments, they motivate themselves to expend the effort needed to attain the requisite performances. Both the anticipated satisfactions for matching attainments and dissatisfactions with insufficient ones provide incentives for self-directed actions.

In many areas of social and moral behavior, the personal standards that serve as a basis for regulating one's conduct are relatively stable; that is, people do not change from week to week what they regard as right or wrong, or as good or bad. However, in areas of functioning involving achievement behavior and the cultivation of competencies, the personal standard that is selected as the mark of adequacy is progressively raised as skills are developed.

Standards do more than simply provide a criterion of adequacy for maintaining a given level of behavior. As alluded to previously, they also represent aspirations that affect one's motivation when cast in the form of goals. Goals do not automatically activate the self-evaluative processes that affect performance. Certain properties of goals (Latham & Yukl, 1975; Locke, 1968; Steers & Porter, 1979) determine the likelihood that self-reactive influences will be generated in any given activity. The degree to which goals create incentives for action is partly determined by their specificity. Explicit goals foster accomplishments by designating the type and amount of effort required, whereas general intentions provide little basis for either regulating one's efforts or evaluating how one is doing.

The amount of effort and satisfaction that accompany variations in goals depends on the level at which they are set. When self-satisfaction is made contingent upon attainment of difficult goals, more effort is expended than if easy ones are adopted as adequate. For activities that are readily amenable to voluntary control, the higher the goals, the higher the performance level (Locke, 1968).

Success at affecting one's motivation and behavior depends heavily on the proximity of self-directed influence to the behavior being regulated. Self-motivation is best created and sustained by proximal subgoals that lead to larger future ones (Bandura & Simon, 1977; Jeffery, 1977). Proximal subgoals provide immediate incentives and guides for behavior, whereas subgoal attainments foster a growing sense of efficacy and self-satisfaction that sustains one's efforts along the way (Bandura & Schunk, 1981). By contrast, goals that are projected far into the future may provide some general direction, but they are too far removed in time to serve as effective incentives and guides for what one does in the here and now. Nor do distal goals provide sufficiently clear markers of progress along the way to build self-efficacy and interest.

Tangible Self-Motivators.   People get themselves to do things they would otherwise put off or avoid altogether by making tangible incentives conditional upon performance attainments. By making free time, relaxing breaks, recreational activities, and other types of tangible self-rewards contingent upon a certain amount of progress in an activity, they mobilize the effort necessary to get things done. The weaker the external demands for performance, the heavier is the reliance on self-regulatory influence. This is perhaps nowhere better illustrated than in the writing habits of successful novelists. They must depend heavily on their own self-discipline, because they have no resident supervisors issuing directives and overseeing their daily writing activities. As Wallace (1977) clearly documents, novelists influence how much they write by making pursuit of other activities contingent on either completing a certain amount of writing or writing for a designated length of time each day.

Numerous studies have been conducted in which children and adults regulate their own behavior by arranging tangible incentives for themselves. The results show that people who reward their own behavioral attainments achieve higher levels of performance than those who perform the same activities under instruction but without self-incentives, are rewarded noncontingently, or monitor their own behavior and set goals for themselves but do not reward their attainments (Bandura & Perloff, 1967; Bellack, 1975; Felixbrod & O'Leary, 1973; Glynn, 1970; Jeffrey, 1974; Litrownik, Franzini, & Skenderian, 1976; Mahoney, 1974; Montgomery & Parton, 1970; Speidel, 1974; Switzky & Haywood, 1974). Self-incentives prove to be as effective or better motivators than are externally arranged incentives.

Evaluative Self-Motivators.   Much human behavior is regulated through self-evaluative consequences in the form of self-satisfaction, self-pride, self-dissatisfaction, and self-criticism. The act of writing is an everyday example of a behavior that is continuously guided by evaluative self-reactions. Writers adopt a standard of what constitutes an acceptable piece of work. Ideas are generated and rephrased in thought before they are committed to paper. Provisional constructions are successively revised until authors are satisfied with what they have written. The more exacting the personal standards, the more extensive are the corrective improvements (Simon, 1980).

As the preceding example illustrates, evaluative self-incentives are heavily recruited in the service of behavior that reflects on personal competence. By making self-satisfaction conditional on performances that match an index of personal merit, people get themselves to put forth the effort necessary to accomplish what they value. When encouraged to respond self-evaluatively on neutral tasks, they boost their persistence and level of achievement (Masters & Santrock, 1976).

Evaluative self-sanctions also figure prominently in the self-regulation of conduct in the moral domain. The anticipation of self-reproach for behavior that violates one's moral standards provides a source of motivation to keep behavior in line with standards in the face of opposing inducements (Bandura & Walters, 1959).

In most instances, people exert influence on their own behavior by enlisting both evaluative and tangible self-incentives. Thus, novelists influence how much they write by making leisure-time activities contingent on completing a certain amount of work, but they revise and improve what they write by their self-evaluative reactions.

Alternative Conceptions of Agency

The manner in which human agency operates can be conceptualized in at least three different ways—as either *autonomous* agency, *mechanical* agency, or *interactive* agency. The notion that humans serve as autonomous agents of their own actions has few, if any, serious advocates, but it is often called forth by radical behaviorists who disavow self-influences in causal processes. Thus, for example, Skinner (1971) invokes the metaphor of "autonomous inner man" in dismissing theories contending that people can influence through thought what they will do.

A second approach to self processes is to treat them in terms of mechanical agency. In this view, people act mechanically without thinking under remote control of environmental forces. After the self-regulatory functions are established, the self system presumably operates in a wholly automatic fashion. Environmental stimuli trigger the self-regulatory machinery to produce predictable acts. Were this the case, functional relationships could be established between environmental stimuli and responses without considering the properties and processes of the self system. Because the agency resides in environmental forces, and the self system is merely a conduit for them, one can bypass the internal link in the causal chain (Skinner,1953).

The notion of mechanical agency rests on presuppositions that have not fared well empirically. An assumption that is crucial to the argument of external control is that environmental stimuli control behavior mechanically and automatically. One can dispense with the so-called internal link in causal chains only if persons are conceived of as mechanical respondents to external stimuli. In point of fact, most external influences operate through cognitive processes. Cognitive factors partly determine which external events will be observed, how they will be perceived, whether they leave any lasting effects, what valence they have, and how the information they convey will be organized for future use (Bandura, 1977a; Bower, 1975; W. Mischel, 1979; Neisser, 1976). The influence of thought, of course, is not confined simply to the processing of immediate environmental stimuli. In dealing with their environment, people engage in deliberative and reflective thought that culminates in particular courses of action.

The model of mechanical agency leans most heavily on the assumption of automaticity of reinforcement, which is disputed by several lines of evidence. During transactions with their environment, people are doing more than simply emitting responses and experiencing outcomes. They form expectations from observed regularities about the outcomes likely to result from actions in given situations. Contrary to claims that behavior is controlled by its immediate consequences, behavior is related to its outcomes at the level of aggregate consequences rather than momentary effects (Baum, 1973). People process and synthesize contextual and outcome information from sequences of events over long intervals about the action patterns that are necessary to produce given outcomes.

The notion that behavior is governed by its consequences fares better for anticipated than for actual consequences (Bandura, 1977a). In studies of the power of belief over consequent, the same environmental consequences have markedly different effects on behavior, depending on people's beliefs of how actions are related to outcomes and the meaning of the outcomes (Dulany, 1968; Kaufman, Baron, & Kopp, 1966). When belief differs from actuality, which is not uncommon, behavior is weakly influenced by its actual consequences until more realistic expectations are developed through repeated experience. But it is not always expectations that change in the direction of social reality. Acting on erroneous beliefs can alter how others behave, thus shaping the social reality in the direction of the initially mistaken beliefs (Snyder, 1980).

While undergoing reinforcing experiences, people are doing more than learning the probabilistic contingencies between actions and outcomes. They observe the progress they are making and tend to set themselves goals of progressive improvement. Investigators who have measured personal goal setting as well as changes in performance find that external incentives influence behavior partly through their effects on goal setting (Locke, Bryan, & Kendall, 1968). When variations in personal goals are partialled out, the effects of incentives on performance are reduced. Performance attainments also provide an important source of efficacy information for judging one's capabilities. As is shown in a later section, people's perceptions of their efficacy can influence their thought patterns, behavior, and emotional arousal (Bandura, 1981).

Because thought mediates reinforcement effects, to trace behavior back to environmental "reinforcers" by no means completes the explanatory regress. To predict how outcomes will affect behavior, one must know how they are cognitively processed. To understand fully the mechanisms through which consequences change behavior, one must analyze the reciprocally contributory influence of cognitive factors.

Psychocybernetic models of self-regulation, which emphasize goals and error correction based on feedback from ongoing performance, have been devised as analogues of human self-directedness. Such models also convey the impression that self systems operate with mechanical predictability. Behavior is compared with a target, and then the system takes whatever action is needed to reduce the discrepancy between these two aspects. But the automaticity with which the metaphoric system is thought to operate differs markedly from the manner in which human self-directedness actually works. Consider only a few of the complexities involved. At the first step, a self-regulatory system requires close and reliable monitoring of behavior. In reality, most performances are difficult to codify because, being multifaceted, they vary on many relevant dimensions. Consequently, one must rely on judgment rather than on preset mechanical sensors. In addition to complexities in the reading of behavior, self-observation is usually episodic rather than continuous. The poorer the quality of self-observation, the more difficult is the attainment of self-directed change (Kazdin, 1974a; Mahoney et al., 1973).

The demands on judgment are also heavy in the referential operations, which cannot rely solely on the preset properties of the system. Performances must be evaluated in terms of varying arrays of circumstances under which they occur and measured against reference standards that synthesize several sources of comparative information. Here we are dealing with evaluative and composite comparative judgments, rather than with a mechanical comparator that checks the readings from a sensor against a preprogrammed criterion as in the model of cybernetic control. Nor is there anything automatic about the strength, type, and timing of self-directed reactions.

To automate a self-regulation system one would have a preprogram: (1) an elaborate set of intricate sensors that could decipher instantly information contained in novel combinations of relevant factors that appear in multiform varieties; (2) a comparitor that contained all the possible referential standards derivable from the various comparative factors in the relational network and decision rules as to which combinations are appropriate in any given instance; and (3) a device whereby differential comparative signals would automatically select and trigger particular self-reactions from a wide variety of possible responses. The system would, of course, require precise and continuous self-monitoring. These conditions are achievable in mechanical and biological systems that perform specific routine functions that involve a limited number of possible responses regulated by a few factors. A thermostat is sensitive only to variations in temperature; it can only turn off or on, and it is ever watchful.

It is recalled from the earlier discussion that social learning theory treats self-regulatory processes in terms of *interactive agency*. Because behavior is subject to diverse perceptions, the referential comparitors against which perceived acts are judged can take different forms, and because there are many possible self-reactions to the same perceived discrepancy, thought must often serve in place of reflexive mechanics. How well self-regulatory functions operate, or whether they even become engaged in given activities, depends on judgment rather than solely on external prompts and negative feedback. The more complex the activities that are self-regulated and the less particularized the decision rules, the more judgmental factors enter the process and the more it departs from the mechanical servocybernetic metaphor. To use a simple analogy, a fully automatic camera system triggered by a release button cannot provide a sufficient model for the operation of a semiautomatic camera system in which, to achieve desired results, the photographer must select a lens of appropriate focal length, decide on whether or not to use certain filters, and set shutter speeds and lens openings based on judgments of light and movement conditions. The challenge for psychology is to explain how "semiautomatic" systems work.

Incomplete preprogramming has some decided benefits. A wholly automated psychocybernetic self system would produce completely predictable responsiveness, but at a heavy price of rigidity. When environmental demands vary widely across situations and time, as they typically do, what is functional under one set of circumstances becomes dysfunctional under different circumstances. An automaton that is self-guided by instant feedback to fixed internal referents would repeatedly direct itself into serious difficulties or even out of existence. In actuality, self-regulation operates in terms of basic preset properties, but it also relies on judgment in assessing behavioral events, in rendering referential comparisons, and in selecting self-reactions. To achieve full automaticity would require complete automation of judgment as well.

External Supports for Self-Regulatory Systems

In analyzing regulation of behavior through self-reactions, one must distinguish between two sources of incentives that operate in the process. Firstly, there are the conditional self-incentives that provide guides and proximal motivators for given courses of action. Secondly, there are the more distal incentives for adhering to internal standards. In this section we examine the issue of why people abide by internal standards, because it involves imposing performance requirements upon oneself and at least temporary self-denial of rewarding activities. A variety of external factors serve as reciprocal supports for the exercise of self-influence.

Personal Benefits.   There are a number of benefits for exercising influence over one's behavior. Some of these benefits are extrinsic to the behavior; others derive from changes in the behavior itself. People often rely on the aid of self-incentives in improving skills and competencies that serve them well in their everyday life. The personal gains accruing from improved proficiency make adherence to internal standards worthwhile. Given that they possess the necessary skills, people can do what needs to be done more effectively with self-incentives than without them though the external inducements remain the same. In these different ways self-directedness enables people to exercise better control over their lives.

People are especially motivated to employ self-directed influences when the behavior they seek to change is aversive or potentially so. Smokers are motivated to control their consumption of cigarettes by physical impairments and concern over its health hazards. Indeed, millions quit the smoking habit through their own efforts even though initially they have to suffer distressing withdrawal symptoms. Through personal prescripts they can reduce aversive behavior, thereby creating an intrinsic source of reward for their efforts.

Because self-regulation involves brief self-denial, it does not necessarily create an adverse state of affairs as might appear on first sight. Singling out self-privation from the total effects accompanying self-influence, as is commonly done, overemphasizes the negative aspects of the process. A different picture emerges if one compares the overall rather than only the momentary effects of self-influence. When rewards are used noncontingently, the likelihood of engaging in potentially advantageous behavior is reduced for lack of self-motivation. In addition to the lost benefits, there are the irritations and costs for failure to do what needs to be done. In contrast, self-directedness provides both the rewards that were temporarily withheld as well as the benefits accruing from increased proficiency. For activities that have potential value, self-directedness can therefore produce the greater overall advantages. Thus, on closer analysis, the exercise of momentary self-denial becomes less perplexing than it might originally appear. If, however, the behavior being self-regulated benefits others but is of little value to the performer, adherence to standards will require more in the way of extraneous supports.

Social Reward.   If societies relied solely on inherent benefits to sustain self-directedness, many activities that are tiresome and uninteresting until proficiency in them is acquired would never be mastered. Upholding standards is therefore socially promoted by a vast system of rewards including praise, social recognition, and rewards. Few accolades are bestowed on people for self-rewarding mediocre performances. Social encouragement fosters adherence to high performance standards. Direct praise or seeing others publicly recognized for upholding excellence aids emulation of high standards, even under social conditions that tend to undermine them (Bandura, Grusec, & Menlove, 1967; Brownell, Colletti, Ersner-Hershfield, Hershfield, & Wilson, 1977).

Modeling Supports.   Modeling is an excellent vehicle for transmitting knowledge and skills, but it has rarely been studied as a maintenance factor. Human behavior has been shown to be extensively regulated by the actions of others. There is every reason to expect that seeing others master tasks through self-directedness would make observers more inclined to abide by performance standards in their own pursuits.

Negative Sanctions.   When standards are being acquired or applied erratically, unmerited self-reward often produces negative social consequences. Rewarding oneself for inadequate or underserving performances is more likely than not to evoke criticism from others. And lowering one's standards is rarely considered praiseworthy. Occasional sanctions for unmerited self-reward aid adherence to standards.

Personal sanctions operate as well in fostering such adherence. After people adopt codes of conduct, when they perform inadequately or violate their standards, they tend to engage in self-critical and other distressing trains of thought. Anticipated thought-produced distress for faulty behavior provides an internal incentive to abide by personal standards of performance. In studies in which people are paid to sacrifice quality of work for quantity, those who subscribe to standards of excellence continue to strive for quality even though it reduces the prospects of monetary reward (Simon, 1980).

Contextual Supports. Situations differ in the standards of behavior they espouse. Self-leniency in settings favoring pursuit of excellence is likely to draw disapproval that eventually endows the situations with predictive significance. As a result, situational cues indicating that unmerited self-reward is frowned upon can, in themselves, bolster adherence to performance standards (Bandura, Mahoney, & Dirks, 1976).

Although self-regulatory functions are developed and occasionally supported by external influences, this does not negate the fact that exercise of that function partly determines how people behave. In the case of arduous tasks, environmental inducements alone often fail to produce change, whereas the same inducements with self-incentives prove successful. Competencies developed through the aid of self-incentives enable people to activate environmental influences that would otherwise not come into play. This is because most environmental influences are only potentialities until actualized by appropriate action. In still other instances, the behavior fashioned through self-directed effort transforms the environment.

Because personal and environmental determinants affect each other in a reciprocal fashion, attempts to assign causal priority to these two sources of influence reduce to the "chicken–or–egg" debate. Situational influences prompt self-generated influences that in turn alter the situational determinants. For example, overweight individuals who refrain, through self-regulatory aids, from buying an assortment of chocolates on a shopping tour create a different environment for themselves than those who head home with a generous supply of the high- caloric delicacies. A full explanation of self-regulatory processes must include the self-control determinants of environments as well as the environmental determinants of self-control. The quest for the ultimate environmental determinant of activities regulated by self-influence becomes a regressive exercise that can yield no victors in explanatory contests because, for every ultimate environmental cause that is invoked, one can find prior actions that helped to produce it. Promotion systems for occupational pursuits, grading schemes for academic activities, and reverence of slimness are human creations, not decrees of an autonomous, impersonal environment.

Selective Activation and Disengagement of Self-Reactive Influences.

Development of self-regulatory capabilities does not create an invariant control mechanism within a person, as implied by theories of internalization that portray incorporated entities (e.g., conscience, superego) as continuous internal overseers of conduct. Self-influences do not operate unless activated, and there are many factors that exercise selective control over their activation. Therefore, the same behavior is not uniformly self-rewarded or self-punished irrespective of the circumstances under which it is performed.

The processes by which self-reactive capabilities are acquired have been examined in some detail. However, the selective activation and disengagement of self-influences, which is of considerable theoretical and social import, has only recently received systematic study. These processes figure most prominently in patterns of behavior that serve the user in some way but are injurious to others.

After social and moral standards of conduct are adopted, anticipatory self-condemning reactions for violating personal standards ordinarily serve as self-deterrents against reprehensible acts. Individuals normally refrain from conduct that produces self-devaluative consequences and pursue activities that serve as sources of self-satisfaction and self-esteem. Self-deterring consequences are likely to be activated most strongly when the causal connection between conduct and its injurious effects is unambiguous. There are various means, however, by which self-evaluative consequences can be dissociated from censurable behavior. Figure 1.3 shows the several points in the process at which the disengagement can occur.

Moral Justification.   One set of disengagement practices operates at the level of the behavior. People do not ordinarily engage in reprehensible conduct until they have justified to themselves the morality of their actions. What is culpable can be made honorable through cognitive restructuring. In this process, detrimental conduct is made personally and socially acceptable by portraying it in the service of moral ends.

Over the years, much destructive conduct has been perpetrated by decent, moral people in the name of religious principles, righteous ideologies, and nationalistic imperatives (Ball–Rokeach, 1972; Kelman, 1973; Sanford & Comstock, 1971). Individuals espousing high moral principles are inclined to resist arbitrary social demands to behave punitively, but they will aggress against persons who violate their personal principles (Keniston, 1970). Because almost any conduct can be morally justified, the same moral principles can support different actions, and the same actions can be championed on the basis of different moral principles (Bandura, 1973; Kurtines & Greif, 1974).

Euphemistic Labeling.   Actions can take on very different appearances depending on what they are called. Euphemistic language thus provides a conven-

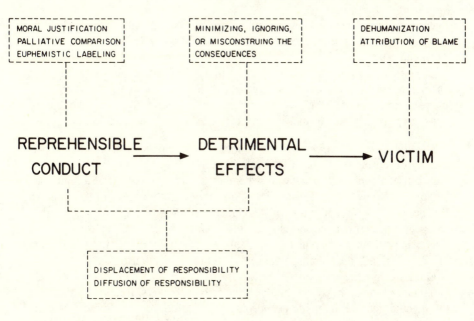

FIG. 1.3. Mechanisms through which behavior is disengaged from self-evaluative reactions at different points in the behavioral process (Bandura, 1977a).

ient device for masking reprehensible activities or even conferring a respectable status upon them. Through convoluted verbiage pernicious conduct is made benign, and those who engage in it are relieved of a sense of personal agency. The disinhibitory power of euphemistic language is clearly shown by Diener and his associates in a study on interpersonal aggression (Diener, Dineen, Endresen , Beaman, & Fraser, 1975). Adults behaved more than twice as aggressively when assaulting a person was called a game than when it was called aggression .

In an insightful analysis of the language of nonresponsibility, Gambino (1973) identifies the different varieties of euphemisms. One form, palliative expressions, is widely used to make the reprehensible respectable. The passive voice serves as a linguistic device for creating the appearance that culpable acts are the work of nameless forces rather than of people. It is as though they move with mechanical detachment but are not really the agents of their acts. The specialized jargon of a legitimate enterprise can be misused to lend an aura of respectability to an illegitimate one.

Advantageous Comparison.   Judgments of behavior depend in part on what it is compared against. Self-deplored acts can be made righteous by contrasting them with flagrant inhumanities. The more outrageous the comparison practices, the more likely are one's reprehensible acts to appear trifling or even benevolent.

In conflicts of power, injurious behavior usually escalates with each side lauding its own behavior but condemning that of their adversaries as heinous acts (Kelman, 1973).

Cognitive restructuring of behavior through moral justifications and palliative characterizations is the most effective self-disinhibitor, because it not only elimates self-generated deterrents but engages self-reward in the service of injurious enterprises. What was morally unacceptable becomes a source of self- pride.

Displacement of Responsibility.   Another set of dissociative practices operates by obscuring or distorting the relationship between actions and the effects they cause. People will behave in ways they normally repudiate if a legitimate authority acknowledges responsibility for the consequences of the conduct (Diener et al., 1975; Milgram, 1974). Under conditions of displaced responsibility, people view their actions as springing from the dictates of authorities rather than being personally responsible for them. Because they are not the actual agent of their actions, they are spared self-prohibiting reactions.

Obliging functionaries do not necessarily cast off all responsibility for their behavior as though they were mindless extensions of others. If this were the case, they would act like automatons and only when told to do so. In fact, they are much more conscientious and self-directed in the performance of their duties. It requires a strong sense of responsibility to be a good functionary. In situations involving obedience to authority, people carry out orders partly to honor the obligations they have undertaken (Mantell & Panzarella, 1976). One must therefore distinguish between two levels of responsibility—duty to one's superiors and accountability for the effects of one's actions. The self system operates most efficiently in the service of authority when followers assume personal responsibility for being dutiful executors but relinquish personal responsibility for the consequences of their behavior. Followers who disowned responsibility without being bound by a sense of duty would be quite unreliable.

Diffusion of Responsibility.   Deterring self-reactions are weakened when the link between conduct and its consequences is obscured by diffusing responsibility for culpable behavior. This is achieved through division of labor, group decision making, and collective action. Where everyone is responsible no one really feels responsible. Social organizations go to great lengths to devise sophisticated mechanisms for obscuring responsibility for decisions that affect others adversely. Any harm done collectively can always be ascribed in large part to the behavior or others. People therefore act more injuriously when responsibility is obfuscated by a collective instrumentality, then when they hold themselves personally accountable for what they do (Bandura, Underwood, & Fromson, 1975; Diener, 1977; Zimbardo, 1969).

Disregard or Distortion of Consequences.   Additional ways of weakening self-deterring reactions operate through disregard or misrepresentation of consequences of action. When people choose to pursue activities adverse to others for personal gain, or because of social inducements, they avoid facing the harm they cause or minimize it. Self-censuring reactions are unlikely to be activated as long as the detrimental effects of conduct are disregarded. Even high personal responsibility has weak restraining efficacy without feedback of the harm inflicted on others (Tilker, 1970). In contrast, when people can see and hear the suffering they cause (Milgram, 1974), vicariously aroused distress and self-censure serve as self-restraining influences.

Social systems typically involve hierarchical chains of command in which superiors formulate plans, intermediaries transmit them to executors, who then carry them out. The farther removed individuals are from the end results, the weaker is their restraining efficacy. Kilham and Mann (1974) provide empirical support for their thesis that disengagement of internal control is easiest for intermediaries in a hierarchical system—they neither bear responsibility for major decisions nor do they see the effects of the actions because they are not a party to their execution.

Dehumanization. The final set of disengagement practices operate at the level of the recipients of the consequences. The strength of self-evaluative reactions partly depends on how people toward whom the behavior is directed are viewed. To perceive another as human enhances empathetic or vicarious responsiveness through perceived similarity. This makes it difficult to mistreat humanized others without risking self-condemnation.

Self-sanctions against mistreatment of people can be disengaged or attenuated by divesting them of human qualities (Bernard, Ottenberg, & Redl, 1965; Zimbardo, 1969). Once dehumanized, they are no longer viewed as persons with feelings, hopes, and concerns but as subhuman objects. Subhumans are presumably insensitive to maltreatment and influenceable only through the more primitive methods. If dispossessing disfavored others of humanness does not blunt self-reproof, it can be fully eliminated by attributing bestial qualities to them.

The power of humanization to enlist self-restraint against injurious conduct is equally striking. Studies examining this process reveal that, even under conditions that weaken self-deterrents, it is exceedingly difficult for individuals to behave cruelly toward others when they are characterized in ways that personalize and humanize them (Bandura et al., 1975). The affirmation of common humanity can bring out the best in others.

Attribution of Blame. Attributing blame to those who are maltreated is still another expedient that can serve self-exonerative purposes. Detrimental interactions usually involve a series of reciprocally escalative actions in which the victims are rarely faultless. One can always select from the chain of events an instance of defensive behavior by the adversary and view it as the original instigation. At the societal level, adverse social practices breed human failings, which can then be used as self-confirming evidence of the victims' defects or badness. By blaming victims, one's own actions are excusable.

As the preceding discussion reveals, acquisition of self-regulatory functions does not create a fully automatic control system, nor do situational influences trigger mechanical control. Personal judgments operating at each subfunction preclude the automaticity of the process. There is leeway in judging whether a given behavioral standard is applicable. Because of the complexity and inherent ambiguity of most events, there is even greater leeway in the judgment of behavior and its effects. To add further to the variability of the self-regulatory process, most activities are performed under collective arrangements that obscure responsibility, thus permitting leeway in judging the degree of personal agency in the effects that are socially produced. In short, there exists considerable latitude for judgmental factors to affect whether or not self-regulatory influences will be activated in any given activity.

SELF-EFFICACY MECHANISM
IN PERSONAL AGENCY

Psychological theorizing and research tend to center on issues concerning either acquisition of knowledge or execution of response patterns. As a result, the processes governing the interrelationship between knowledge and action have been largely neglected (Newell, 1978). Some of the recent efforts to bridge this gap have been directed at the biomechanics problem—how efferent commands of action plans guide the production of appropriate response patterns (Stelmach, 1976, 1978). The relationship between knowledge and action is also significantly mediated by self-referent thought. The issues addressed in this line of inquiry are concerned with how people judge their capabilities, and how, through their self-percepts of efficacy, they affect their motivation and behavior.

The recent years have witnessed a growing convergence of theory and research on the influential role of self-referent thought in psychological functioning (DeCharms, 1978; Lefcourt, 1976; Perlmuter & Monty, 1980; Rotter, Chance, & Phares, 1972; Garber & Seligman, 1980). Although the research is conducted from a number of different perspectives under a variety of names, the basic phenomenon being addressed centers on people's sense of personal efficacy to produce and to regulate events in their lives.

Competence in dealing with one's environment is not a fixed act or simply a matter of knowing what to do. Rather, it involves a generative capability in which component cognitive and behavioral skills are organized into integrated courses of action in accordance with certain rules or strategies. A capability is only as good as its execution. Performance of a skill requires continuous improvisation and adjustment to ever-changing circumstances. Even routinized activities are rarely performed in exactly the same way. Thus, the initiation and regulation of transactions with the environment are partly governed by judgments of operative capabilities. Self-efficacy is concerned with judgments about how well one can organize and execute courses of action required to deal with prospective situations containing many ambiguous, unpredictable, and often stressful elements.

Function of Efficacy Judgment

In their daily lives people continuously have to make decisions about whether or not to attempt certain courses of action or how long to continue those they have undertaken. As we shall see shortly, such decisions are partly determined by judgments of personal efficacy. Accurate appraisal of one's own capabilities is therefore of considerable value in successful functioning. Misjudgments of personal efficacy in either direction have consequences. People who grossly overestimate their capabilities undertake activities that are clearly beyond their reach. As a result, they get themselves into difficulties and suffer needless failures, if not injuries.

People who underestimate their capabilities also bear costs, although these are more likely to take self-limiting rather than aversive forms. Such individuals typically avoid beneficial environments and activities that cultivate personal potentialities. By approaching tasks with strong self-doubts, they dwell on personal deficiencies and generate debilitating distress that creates internal obstacles to effective performance.

Relationship Between Efficacy Judgment and Action

Although efficacy judgments are functionally related to behavior (Bandura, 1982), the strength of relationship between these factors will vary under different conditions. Perceived efficacy alone will not produce desired performances if the component capabilities are lacking. Of course, people who lack the constituent skills for performing given activities are unlikely to judge themselves highly efficacious in those areas of functioning.

Individuals may possess the constituent skills and a strong sense of efficacy that they can execute them well but still choose not to perform the activities because they have no incentive to do so. Self-efficacy therefore will not come into play if there is little motivation to perform a behavior. Nor will efficacy be translated into corresponding action if people lack the equipment or resources needed to perform the behavior adequately. Physical or social constraints further impose limits on what people can do in particular situations. When performances are attenuated by disincentives, inadequate instrumental resources or external constraints, self-judged efficacy will exceed actual performance. In such discrepancies, it is not that people do not know their capabilities, but that performance of their skills is hindered.

The time elapsing between probes of self-efficacy and behavior is another factor affecting the relationship. People's competencies are continuously being tested in experience that might prompt reappraisals of self-efficacy from time to time. Strong self-percepts that are not readily amenable to change can predict actions over an extended period (Bandura, Adams, & Beyer, 1977). But weaker self-percepts of efficacy are sensitive to new experiences, and even firmly established ones are alterable through forceful experiences. Proximal self-percepts will bear a closer relationship to action than remote ones if they have been revised in the interim.

The seriousness of missteps can also influence the veridicality of self-efficacy judgments. Situations in which misjudgments of capabilities carry no consequences provide little incentive for accurate efficacy appraisal. When such judgments are made publicly, modesty or self-flattery can take precedence over accurateness because immediate concern over what others may think becomes more important than how well one performs on some future occasion. But when people have to choose between courses of action that have significant personal consequences, or to decide how long they will continue at a thwarting activity consuming their time, effort, and resources, then self-appraisals serve as important guides for action.

Performance tasks can vary widely in difficulty and in the subskills they require. Different activities make different demands on cognitive and memory skills, on manual facility, strength, endurance, and stress tolerance. Even the same activity may tap different abilities under different situational circumstances. Delivering a prepared speech requires less in the way of generative and memory skills than producing one spontaneously. The more knowledgeable and critical the audience, the heavier are the demands on skills in managing stress. Discrepancies between efficacy judgment and performance will arise when either the tasks, or the circumstances under which they are performed, are ambiguous. When performance requirements are ill-defined, people who underestimate the situational demands will display positive discrepancies between judged efficacy and performance attainments; those who overestimate the task demands will exhibit negative discrepancies.

In most of the situations discussed thus far self-appraisals of efficacy are reasonably accurate, but discrepancies arise between efficacy judgments and action because either people do not know fully what they will have to do, or they are hindered by external factors from doing what they can. However, discrepancies oftentimes arise from misjudgments of self-efficacy rather than from performance ambiguities or constraints (Bandura & Schunk, 1981; Schunk, 1981). Faulty self-judgments can result from a variety of sources. In new undertakings people have insufficient experience to assess the veridicality of their self-appraisals and hence must infer their performance capabilities from knowledge of what they can do in other situations, which may be misleading. Self-efficacy will also be misjudged when personal factors distort self-appraisal processes. The distortions may occur at the level of perceptual experience—at this initial point in the process people misperceive their failures and attainments. They may perceive their ongoing experiences accurately but introduce distortions in how they cognitively process their experiences—here they err in how they select, combine, and weigh the multiform efficacy information available to them. And finally, distortions in memory will produce faulty self-appraisals. We return to these issues later. Whatever the sources of distortion might be, when people act on faulty self-efficacy judgment they suffer adverse consequences.

In the case of habitual routines, people develop their self-knowledge through repeated experience to the point where they no longer need to judge their efficacy on each occasion they perform the same activity. They behave in accordance with what they know they can or cannot do without giving the matter much further thought. However, significant changes in task demands or situational circumstances prompt efficacy reappraisals as guides for action under altered conditions. There are decided benefits to suspending further efficacy appraisals in routinized performances that have proven highly successful. If people had to judge their capabilities anew each time they were about to drive their automobiles or to prepare a familiar dinner, they would spend much of their cognitive life in redundant self-referent thought. There are considerable personal costs, however, when self-judged inefficacy leads to routinized thoughtless avoidance of activities and situations that can enrich one's life. Langer and her associates (Langer, 1980) document the self-debilitating effects that result when people erroneously judge themselves as incompetent and begin to behave ineffectually without giving much further thought to their capabilities.

Diverse Effects of Perceived Self-Efficacy

Perceived efficacy can have diverse effects on behavior, thought patterns, and on affective arousal. With regard to behavioral effects, self-percepts of efficacy influence choice of activities and environmental settings. People tend to avoid situations they believe exceed their capabilities, but they undertake and perform assuredly activities they judge themselves capable of managing (Bandura, 1977a; Bandura, Adams, Hardy, & Howells, 1980). In studies in which different levels of self-efficacy are created, the higher the level of perceived self-efficacy, the greater are the performance accomplishments (Bandura, Reese, & Adams, 1982).

Self-judged efficacy also determines how much effort people will expend and how long they will persist in the face of obstacles or aversive experiences. The stronger the perceived self-efficacy, the more vigorous and persistent are the efforts. In the face of difficulties, people who entertain serious doubts about their capacities slacken their efforts or give up altogether, whereas those who have a strong sense of efficacy exert greater effort to master the challenges (Brown & Inouye, 1978; Schunk, 1981).

Self-percepts of efficacy not only affect ongoing behavior but also predict the future course it will take. The role of self-efficacy in the long-term maintenance of behavioral change is put to the most stringent test in addictive behaviors that are amenable to change but difficult to sustain. People who harbor self- doubts that they can exercise adequate control over their own behavior are more vulnerable to later relapses than are those who exhibit high self-regulatory efficacy (DiClemente, 1981; Marlatt & Gordon, 1979).

People's perceptions of their own capabilities can also influence their thought patterns and emotional reactions during anticipatory and actual transactions with the environment. People who judge themselves ineffectual in coping with environmental demands tend to generate high emotional arousal, become excessively preoccupied with personal deficiencies, and cognize potential difficulties as more formidable than they really are (Beck, 1976; Lazarus & Launier, 1978; Meichenbaum, 1977; Miller, 1979; Sarason, 1975). Such self-referent concerns undermine effective use of the competencies people possess.

In the social learning view of fear arousal, it is mainly perceived inefficacy in coping with potentially painful events that makes them fearsome (Bandura, 1982). To the extent that one can prevent, terminate, or lessen the severity of aversive events, there is little reason to fear them. Several lines of evidence from studies of the effects of perceived controllability on human stress are consistent with this formulation (Averill, 1973; Miller, 1979, 1980). Being able to wield behavioral control over aversive events reduces autonomic arousal even though the control is unexercised. It is the self-knowledge of coping efficacy rather than its application that reduces arousal. Moreover, people who are led to believe they can exercise some control over aversive events display less autonomic arousal and performance impairment than those who believe they lack personal control, even though they are all subjected to the same aversive stimulation.

That perceived efficacy may operate as a cognitive mechanism by which controllability reduces fear arousal receives support from microanalysis of level of arousal as a function of varying strengths of coping efficacy (Bandura et al., 1982). The findings show that perceived inefficacy is accompanied by high anticipatory and performance arousal, but as strength of perceived self-efficacy increases, fear arousal declines.

Sources of Self-Efficacy Information

Self-knowledge about one's efficacy, whether accurate or faulty, is based on four principal sources of information. These include performance accomplishments; vicarious experiences of observing the performances of others; verbal persuasion and allied types of social influences that one possesses certain capabilities; and states of physiological arousal from which people partly judge their capableness and vulnerability.

Performance Accomplishments.   Enactive attainments provide the most influential source of efficacy information because it is based on authentic mastery experiences (Bandura, Adams, & Beyer, 1977; Biran & Wilson, 1981; Feltz,

Landers & Raeder, 1979). Successes raise efficacy appraisals; repeated failures lower them, especially if the failures occur early in the course of events and do not reflect lack of effort or adverse external circumstances. After a strong sense of efficacy is developed through repeated success, occasional failures are unlikely to have much effect on judgments of one's capabilities. Indeed, failures that are overcome by determined effort can instill robust percepts of self-efficacy through experience that one can eventually master even the most difficult obstacles.

Vicarious Experience. Self-efficacy appraisals are also partly influenced by vicarious experiences. Seeing or visualizing similar others perform successfully can raise self-percepts of efficacy in observers that they too possess the capabilities to master comparable activities (Bandura et al., 1980; Kazdin, 1979). They persuade themselves that if others can do it, they should be able to achieve at least some improvement in performance. By the same token, observing others perceived to be of similar competence fail despite high effort lowers observers' judgments of their own capabilities and undermines their efforts (Brown & Inouye, 1978).

There are several conditions under which self-efficacy appraisals are especially sensitive to vicarious information. Amount of prior experience is one such factor. Perceived efficacy can be readily changed by relevant modeling influences when people have little previous experience on which to base evaluations of their personal competence. Lacking direct knowledge of their own capabilities, they rely more heavily on modeled indicators (Takata & Takata, 1976).

Although vicarious influences are generally weaker than direct experiences, they can produce significant enduring changes through their performance effects. People convinced vicariously of their inefficacy are inclined to behave in ineffectual ways that, in fact, generate confirmatory behavioral evidence of inability. Conversely, modeling influences that enhance perceived self-efficacy can weaken the impact of direct failure experiences by sustaining performance in the face of repeated failure (Brown & Inouye, 1978). A given mode of influence can thus set in motion processes that augment its effects or diminish the effects of otherwise powerful influences.

Verbal Persuasion. Verbal persuasion is widely used to get people to believe they possess capabilities that will enable them to achieve what they seek. Although social persuasion alone may be limited in its power to create enduring increases in self-efficacy, it can contribute to successful performance if the heightened appraisal is within realistic bounds. Persuasory efficacy attributions therefore have their greatest impact on people who have some reason to believe that they can produce effects through their actions (Chambliss & Murray, 1979a, b). To the extent that persuasive boosts in self-efficacy lead them to try hard enough to succeed, such influences promote development of skills and competencies.

Emotional Arousal.   Stressful and taxing situations elicit emotional arousal that provides another constituent source of efficacy information. People rely partly on their state of physiological arousal in judging their capabilities and vulnerability to stress. Because high arousal usually debilitates performance, individuals are more likely to expect success when they are not beset by aversive arousal than if they are tense and viscerally agitated. Fear reactions generate further fear through anticipatory self-arousal. By conjuring up fear-provoking thoughts about their inpetitude, people can rouse themselves to elevated levels of distress that produce the very dysfunctions they fear. Treatments that eliminate emotional arousal to subjective threats heighten perceived efficacy with corresponding improvements in performance (Bandura & Adams, 1977; Barrios, 1980).

Cognitive Processing of Self-Efficacy Information

The discussion thus far has centered on the different sources of information—enactive, vicarious, persuasory, and emotive—that people use in judging their capabilities. A distinction must be drawn between information conveyed by environmental events and information as selected, weighted, and integrated into efficacy judgments. The impact of different experiences on perceived self-efficacy will depend on how they are cognitively appraised. The cognitive processes in efficacy judgment involve two separable aspects: The first concerns the types of cues people use as indicators of personal efficacy; the second concerns the inference rules or heuristics they employ for integrating efficacy information from different sources in forming their self-efficacy judgments.

Enactive Efficacy Information.   Many factors can affect level of performance that have little to do with ability. Efficacy evaluation is therefore an inferential process in which the relative contribution of ability and nonability factors to performance successes and failures must be weighted. The extent to which people will alter their perceived efficacy through performance experiences will depend on, among other factors, the difficulty of the task, the amount of effort they expend, the amount of external aid they receive, the situational circumstances under which they perform, and the temporal pattern of their successes and failures.

To succeed at an easy task is redundant with what one already knows, whereas mastery of a difficult task conveys new efficacy information for raising one's efficacy appraisal. Successes achieved with external aid carry less efficacy value because they are likely to be credited to external factors rather than to personal capabilities. Similarly, faulty performances under adverse situational conditions will have much weaker efficacy implications than those executed under optimal circumstances.

Cognitive appraisals of effort expenditure may further affect the impact of performance accomplishments on judgments of personal efficacy. Success with minimal effort fosters ability ascriptions, but analogous attainments gained through heavy labor connote a lesser ability and are thus likely to have weaker impact on perceived self-efficacy. The rate and pattern of attainments furnish additional information for judging personal efficacy. Individuals who exprience periodic failures but continue to improve over time are more apt to raise their perceived efficacy, than those who succeed but see their performances leveling off compared to their prior rate of improvement.

Studies conducted within the attributional framework (Bem, 1972; Frieze, 1976; Weiner, 1979) have examined how some of the preceding variables affect performance. In a social learning analysis, these types of factors serve as conveyors of efficacy information that influence performance largely through their intervening effects on perceptions of self-efficacy, as when people infer their level of efficacy from effort and task difficulties.

Similar inferential processes operate in efficacy appraisal based on performance failures. Deficient performances are unlikely to lower perceived efficacy much, if at all, when failures are discounted on the grounds of insufficient effort, adverse situational conditions, despondent mood, or debilitated physical state. People who hold a low view of themselves are prone to the opposite judgmental bias—crediting their achievements to external factors rather than to their own capabilities (Bandura et al., 1980). Here the problem is one of inaccurate ascription of personal competency to situational factors. In such cases, stable boosts in self-efficacy require mastery experiences on challenging tasks with minimal external aid that verify personal capabilities (Bandura, 1977b).

Perceived efficacy is affected not only by how performance successes and failures are interpreted but also by biases in the self-monitoring of the performances themselves. In any given endeavor, some performances surpass, others match, and still others fall below one's typical attainments. Such variations allow some leeway in what aspects of one's performance are observed and remembered. People who selectively attend to the more negative aspects of their performances are likely to underestimate their efficacy even though they may process correctly what they remember. In such instances the problems reside in faulty attentional and memory processes, rather than in the inferential judgments made about the causes of one's successes and failures.

Selective self-monitoring can also magnify percepts of self-efficacy if it is the personal successes that are especially noticed and remembered. Research on self-modeling provides suggestive evidence bearing on this enhancement effect (Dowrick, 1977). In these studies children exhibiting gross deficits in psychomotor and social skills are helped, by a variety of aids, to perform at a level that exceeds their usual attainments. The hesitancies, mistakes, and external aids are then selectively deleted from the videotape recordings to show the children performing much more skillfully than they are normally capable. After observing their videotaped successes, they display substantial improvement in performance compared to their baseline level or to other activities that are filmed but not self-observed. Seeing oneself perform errorlessly can enhance proficiency in at least two ways: It provides further information on how to perform appropriately, and it strengthens self-beliefs that one can succeed.

Vicarious Efficacy Information.   The cognitive processing of vicariously derived information will similarly depend on efficacy indicants conveyed by modeled events. We noted earlier that people judge their capabilities partly through social comparison with the performances of others. Similarity to the model is one factor that increases the personal relevance of modeled performance information for observers' perceptions of their own efficacy. Persons who are similar or slightly higher in ability provide the most informative comparative information for gauging one's own capabilities (Festinger, 1954; Suls & Miller, 1977). Neither outperforming those of lesser ability nor being surpassed by the vastly superior convey much information about one's own level of competence. In general, modeled successes by similar others raise, and modeled failures lower, self-appraisals.

In gauging personal efficacy through social comparison, observers may rely on similarity to the model either in past performances or in attributes presumably predictive of the ability in question. The influential role of prior performance similarity on vicarious efficacy appraisal is revealed in a study by Brown and Inouye (1978). Observers who believed themselves to be superior to a failing model maintained a high sense of personal efficacy and did not at all slacken their efforts despite repeated failure. In contrast, modeled failure had a devastating effect on observers' self-judged efficacy when they perceived themselves of comparable ability to the model. They expressed a very low sense of personal efficacy and gave up quickly when they encountered difficulties.

Some writers have commented on the apparent paradox that social comparison is used to judge one's performance capabilities, yet prior knowledge that one is similar serves as the basis for the judgment (Goethals & Darley, 1977). The paradox exists only if past and new activities are identical and situational demands remain invariant. But it is often the case that activities and the situations in which they are performed vary. Therefore, in arriving at a self-efficacy appraisal observers must extrapolate from past performance similarities and knowledge of the model's attainments in new situations.

Efficacy appraisals are often based, not on comparative performance experiences, but on similarity to models on personal characteristics assumed to be predictive of performance capabilities (Suls & Miller, 1977). People develop preconceptions of performance capabilities according to age, sex, educational and socioeconomic level, race, and ethnic designation, even though the performances of individuals within these groups are extremely varied. Such preonceptions usually arise from a combination of cultural stereotyping and overgeneralization from salient personal experiences.

Attribute similarity generally increases the force of modeling influences even though the personal characteristics may be spurious indicants of performance capabilities (Rosenthal & Bandura, 1978). Indeed, when model attributes irrelevant to the new task are salient and overweighted in predictive value, irrelevant model characteristics (e.g., age or sex) exert greater sway on observers than do more relevant ability cues (Kazdin, 1974b). When the successes of models who possess similar attributes lead others to try things they would otherwise shun, spurious indicants have beneficial social effects. But comparative efficacy appraisals through faulty preconceptions often lead those who are uncertain about their abilities to judge valuable pursuits to be beyond their reach. In such instances, judging efficacy by social comparison is self-limiting.

Vicariously derived information can alter perceived self-efficacy through ways other than social comparison. Competent models can teach observers effective stategies for dealing with challenging or threatening situations. This contribution is especially important when perceived inefficacy reflects behavioral deficits rather than misappraisals of the skills one possesses. In addition, modeling displays convey information about the nature of environmental tasks and the difficulties they present. Modeled transactions may reveal the tasks to be more or less difficult, and potential threats more or less manageable than observers originally believed. Adoption of serviceable strategies and altered perceptions of task difficulty will alter perceived efficacy.

The influence of modeled strategy information can alter the usual efficacy effects of social comparative information. Seeing a superior other fail through means clearly insufficient can boost self-efficacy in observers who believe they have more suitable strategies at their command. Conversely, observing a similar other barely succeed through the most adroit tactics may lead observers to reevaluate the task as much more difficult than they had previously assumed. To shed new light on vicarious self-efficacy appraisals research should concern itself with strategy exemplification and task evaluation as well as with comparative-ability indicants.

Persuasory Efficacy Information.   People do not always believe what they are told concerning their performance capabilities. Skepticism develops from personal experiences that often run counter to what one has been told. Were this always the case, performers would eventually turn a deaf ear to their persuaders. But there are many occasions when individuals are persuaded to try things they avoid, or to persist at tasks they were ready to discontinue, only to discover, much to their surprise, that they were capable of mastering them. Consequently, persuasory efficacy appraisals have to be weighted in terms of who the persuaders are and their credibleness. The impact of persuasory opinions is apt to be only as strong as the recipient's confidence in the person who issues them.

People often voice opinions of what others can do without being thoroughly acquainted with the difficulty of the tasks, or with the circumstances under which they will have to be performed. Therefore, even the judgments of otherwise credible persuaders may be discounted on the grounds that they do not fully understand the task demands.

Arousal Efficacy Information.   The information conveyed by physiological arousal similarly affects perceived efficacy through judgmental processes. A number of factors, including appraisal of the sources of arousal, the level of activation, the circumstances under which arousal is elicited, and past experience on how arousal affects one's performance are likely to figure in the cognitive processing of emotional reactivity. Activities are often performed in situations containing varied evocative stimuli. This creates ambiguity about what caused the physiological reactions. The efficacy value of the resultant arousal will therefore vary, depending on the factors singled out and the meaning given to them.

The self-efficacy implications of arousal derive from past experiences with how labeled arousal affects performance. For people who generally find arousal facilitory rather than debilitating, arousal will have different efficacy value than those for whom arousal usually portends marred performances. The judgmental process is complicated by the fact that it is not arousal per se, but its level, that usually serves as the performance indicator. As a general rule, moderate levels of arousal facilitate performance, whereas high arousal disrupts it. This is especially true of complex activities requiring intricate organization of behavior.

What constitutes an optimal level of arousal depends not only on the nature of the task but on causal inferences concerning the arousal. People vary in their judgmental sets. Those who are inclined to perceive their arousal as stemming from personal inadequacies are more likely to lower their perceived efficacy than those who regard their arousal as a common transitory reaction that even the most competent persons experience.

Integration of Self-Efficacy Information

The preceding discussion explored the efficacy implications of single dimensions of information within each of the four modalities. In forming their efficacy judgments people have to deal, not only with different configurations of efficacy-relevant information conveyed by a given modality, but to weigh and integrate efficacy information from these diverse sources. There has been little research on how people process multidimensional efficacy information. However, there is every reason to believe that efficacy judgments are governed by some common judgmental processes.

Studies of judgmental processes show that people have difficulty weighting and integrating multidimensional information (Slovic, Fischhoff, & Lichtenstein, 1977; Slovic & Lichtenstein, 1971; Tversky & Kahneman, 1974). As a result, they tend to rely on simple judgmental rules. This often leads them to ignore or to misweigh relevant information. When subjective descriptions of their judgmental processes are compared with their actual judgments, the findings show that people tend to underestimate their reliance on important cues and overweigh those of lesser value.

Although common cognitive processes probably operate in both efficacy and nonpersonal judgments, forming conceptions of oneself undoubtedly involves some distinct processes as well. The persons are rare who are entirely dispassionate about themselves. Self-referent experiences are more likely than experiences involving other persons or objects to pose threats to self-esteem and social valuation. Such threats can produce self-exaggeration or self-belittlement of personal capabilities. Activation of self-protective processes may distort self-monitoring, retention, and processing of multidimensional efficacy information.

Interrelatedness of Mechanisms of Agency

There is every indication that internal standards and perceived efficacy operate as interrelated rather than as separate mechanisms of personal agency. Standards affect self-efficacy. We saw earlier that self-motivation through proximal standards serves as an important vehicle in the development of self-percepts of efficacy (Bandura & Schunk, 1981).

People's perceptions of their capabilities, in turn, affect their aspirations and how they respond to discrepancies between their performances and what they seek to achieve. The self-assured are much more likely than are self-doubters to set themselves challenging standards by which they affect their motivation. It is recalled from the earlier discussion that cognitive self-motivation operates through comparison between performance and internal standards. Whether negative discrepancies are motivating or disheartening will be partly determined by perceptions of personal efficacy. People who have a low sense of efficacy are easily discouraged by failure, whereas those who are assured of their capabilities intensify their efforts when their performances fall short and persist until they succeed.

Self phenomena lie at the very heart of causal processes because, not only do they often function as the most immediate determinants of behavior, but they also give shape to the more distal external influences arising in transactions with the environment. Nevertheless, self processes have yet to receive the systematic attention in psychological theorizing and research they deserve. Explorations of mechanisms of personal agency should go a long way toward clarifying how people make causal contributions to their own motivation and behavior.

ACKNOWLEDGMENT

Preparation of this chapter was facilitated by Public Health Research Research Grant M-5162-18 from the National Institute of Mental Health. The revised substance of some of the material on self-regulatory functions in personal agency was published in the *American Psychologist* (1978), under the title, *The self system in reciprocal determinism*.

REFERENCES

Averill, J. Personal control over aversive stimuli and its relationship to stress. *Psychological Bulletin*, 1973, *80*, 286–303.

Ball–Rokeach, S. J. The legitimation of violence. In J. F. Short, Jr. & M. E. Wolfgang (Eds.), *Collective violence*. Chicago: Aldine–Atherton, 1972.

Bandura, A. *Aggression: A social learning analysis*. Englewood Cliffs, N. J.: Prentice–Hall, 1973.

Bandura, A. Self-reinforcement: Theoretical and methodological considerations. *Behaviorism*, 1976, *4*, 135–155.

Bandura, A. *Social learning theory*. Englewood Cliffs, N. J. : Prentice–Hall, 1977. (a)

Bandura, A. Self-efficacy: Toward a unifying theory of behavioral change. *Psychological Review*, 1977, *84*, 191–215. (b)

Bandura, A. The self system in reciprocal determinism. *American Psychologist*, 1978, *33*, 344–358.

Bandura, A. Self-referent thought: The development of self-efficacy. In J. H. Flavell & L. D. Ross (Eds.), *Social cognitive development: Frontiers and possible futures*. Cambridge University Press, 1981.

Bandura, A., Self-efficacy mechanism in human agency. *American Psychologist*, 1982, *37*, in press.

Bandura, A., & Adams, N. E. Analysis of self-efficacy theory of behavioral change. *Cognitive Therapy and Research*, 1977, *1*, 287–308.

Bandura, A., Adams, N. E., & Beyer, J. Cognitive processes mediating behavioral change. *Journal of Personality and Social Psychology*, 1977, *35*, 125–139.

Bandura, A., Adams, N. E., Hardy, A. B., & Howells, G. N. Tests of the generality of self-efficacy theory. *Cognitive Therapy and Research*, 1980, *4*, 39–66.

Bandura, A., Grusec, J. E., & Menlove, F. L. Some social determinants of self-monitoring reinforcement systems. *Journal of Personality and Social Psychology*, 1967, *5*, 449–455.

Bandura, A., Mahoney, M. J., & Dirks, S. J. Discriminative activation and maintenance of contingent self-reinforcement. *Behaviour Research and Therapy*, 1976, *14*, 1-6.

Bandura, A., & Perloff, B. Relative efficacy of self-monitored and externally imposed reinforcement systems. *Journal of Personality and Social Psychology*, 1967, *7*, 111–116.

Bandura, A., Reese, L., & Adams, N. E. Microanalysis of action and fear arousal as a function of different levels of perceived self-efficacy. *Journal of Personality and Social Psychology*, 1982, in press.

Bandura, A., & Schunk, D. H. Cultivating competence, self-efficacy and intrinsic interest through proximal self-motivation. *Journal of Personality and Social Psychology*, 1981, *41*, 586–598.

Bandura, A., & Simon, K. M. The role of proximal intentions in self-regulation of refractory behavior. *Cognitive Therapy and Research*, 1977, *1*, 177–193.

Bandura, A., Underwood, B., & Fromson, M. E. Disinhibition of aggression through diffusion of responsibility and dehumanization of victims. *Journal of Research in Personality*, 1975, *9*, 253–269.

Bandura, A., & Walters, R. H. *Adolescent aggression*. New York: Ronald Press, 1959.

Barrios, B. A. *The role of self-efficacy in the reduction of heterosocial anxiety: A microanalysis*. Unpublished manuscript, University of Utah, 1980.

Baum, W. M. The correlation-based law of effect. *Journal of the Experimental Analysis of Behavior*, 1973, *20*, 137–153.

Beck, A. T.   *Cognitive therapy and the emotional disorders.* New York: International Universities Press, 1976.

Bellack, A. S.   Self-evaluation, self-reinforcement, and locus of control. *Journal of Research in Personality, 1975, 9* 158–167.

Bem, D. J.   Self-perception theory. In L. Berkowitz (Ed.), *Advances in experimental social psychology* (Vol. 6). New York: Academic Press, 1972.

Bernard, V., Ottenberg, P., & Redl, F.   Dehumanization: A composite psychological defense in relation to modern war. In M. Schwebel (Ed.), *Behavioral science and human survival.* Palo Alto, Calif.: Science and Behavior Books, 1965.

Biran, M., & Wilson, G. T. Cognitive versus behavioral methods in the treatment of phobic disorders: A self-efficacy analysis, *Journal of Consulting and Clinical Psychology,* 1981, 886–899.

Bower, G. H.   Cognitive Psychology: An introduction. In W. K. Estes (Ed.), *Handbook of learning and cognition.* Hillsdale, N. J.: Lawrence Erlbaum Associates, 1975.

Bowers, K. S.   Situationism in psychology: An analysis and a critique. *Psychological Review, 1973, 80,* 307–336.

Bronfenbrenner, U.   *Two worlds of childhood: U. S. and U. S. S. R.* New York: Russell Sage Foundation, 1970.

Brown, I., Jr., & Inouye, D. K.   Learned helplessness through modeling: The role of perceived similarity in competence. *Journal of Personality and Social Psychology, 1978, 36,* 900–908.

Brownell, K. D., Colletti, G., Ersner-Hershfield, R., Hershfield, S. M. , & Wilson, G. T.   Self-control in school children: Stringency and leniency in self-determined and externally imposed performance standards. *Behavior Therapy,* 1977, *8,* 442–445.

Cairns, R. B. (Ed.).   *The analysis of social interactions: Methods, issues, and illustrations.* Hillsdale, N. J.: Lawrence Erlbaum Associates, 1979.

Chambliss, C. A., & Murray, E. J.   Efficacy attribution, locus of control, and weight loss. *Cognitive Therapy and Research,* 1979, *3,* 349–353. (a)

Chambliss, C. A., & Murray, E. J.   Cognitive procedures for smoking reduction: Symptom attribution versus efficacy attribution. *Cognitive Therapy and Research,* 1979, *3,* 91–95. (b)

Cooley, C. H.   *Human nature and the social order.* New York: Scribner's, 1902.

Day, W. F., Jr.   On the behavioral analysis of self-deception and self-development. In T. Mischel (Ed.), *The self: Psychological and philosophical issues.* Oxford, England: Basil Blackwell, 1977.

DeCharms, R.   *Personal causation: The internal affective determinants of behavior.* New York: Academic Press, 1978.

DiClemente, C. C.   Self-efficacy and smoking cessation maintenance. A preliminary report. *Cognitive Therapy and Research,* 1981, *5,* 175–187.

Diener, D., Dineen, J., Endresen, K., Beaman, A. L., & Fraser, S. C. Effects of altered responsibility, cognitive set, and modeling on physical aggression and deindividualtion. *Journal of Personality and Social Psychology,* 1975, *31,* 328–337.

Diener, E.   Deindividuation: Causes and consequences. *Social Behavior and Personality,* 1977, *5,* 143–156.

Dowrick, P. W.   *Videotape replay as observational learning from oneself.* Unpublished manuscript, University of Auckland, 1977.

Dulany, D. E.   Awareness, rules, and propositional control: A confrontation with *S–R* theory. In T. R. Dixon & D. L. Horton (Eds.), *Verbal behavior and general behavior theory.* Englewood Cliffs, N. J.: Prentice–Hall, 1968.

Dweck, C. S., & Goetz, T. E.   Attributions and learned helplessness. In J. Harvey, W. Ickes, & R. Kidd (Eds.), *New directions in attribution research* (Vol. 2). Hillsdale, N. J.: Lawrence Erlbaum Associates 1978.

Endler, N. S., & Magnusson, D. (Eds.).   *Interactional psychology and personality.* Washington, D. C.: Hemisphere, 1975.

Felixbrod, J. J., & O'Leary, K. D.   Effects of reinforcement on children's academic behavior as a function of self-determined and externally imposed contingencies. *Journal of Applied Bahavior Analysis,* 1973, *6,* 241–250.

Feltz, D. L., Landers, D. M., & Raeder, U.   Enhancing self-efficacy in high-avoidance motor tasks: A comparison of modeling techniques. *Journal of Sport Psychology,* 1979, *1,* 112–122.

Festinger, L.   A theoretical interpretation of shifts in level of aspiration. *Psychological Review,* 1942, *49,* 235–250.

Festinger, L.   A theory of social comparison processes. *Human Relations,* 1954, *7,* 117–140.

Frieze, I. H.   Role of information processing in making causal attributions for success and failure. In J. C. Carroll & J. W. Payne (Eds.), *Cognition and social behavior.* Hillsdale, N. J.: Lawrence Erlbaum Associates, 1976.

Gambino, R. Watergate lingo: A language of nonresponsibility. *Freedom at Issue,* 1973, No. 22, *Nov.-Dec.,*7–9,15–17.

Garber, J., & Seligman, M. E. P. (Eds.).   *Human helplessness: Theory and applications.* New York: Academic Press, 1980.

Glynn, E. L.   Classroom applications of self-determined reinforcement. *Journal of Applied Behavior Analysis,* 1970, *3,* 123–132.

Goethals, G. R., & Darley, J. M.   Social comparison theory: Attributional approach. In J. M. Suls & R. L. Miller (Eds.), *Social comparison processes: Theoretical and empirical perspectives.* Washington, D. C.: Hemisphere, 1977.

Jeffery, K. M.   *The effects of goal-setting on self-motivated persistence.* Unpublished doctoral dissertation, Stanford University, 1977.

Jeffrey, D. B.   A comparison of the effects of external control and self-control on the modification and maintenance of weight. *Journal of Abnormal Psychology,* 1974, *83,* 404–410.

Kanfer, F. H.   The many faces of self-control, or behavior modification changes its focus. In R. B. Stuart (Ed.), *Behavioral self-management.* New York: Brunner/Mazel, 1977.

Kanfer, F. H., & Marston, A. R.   Determinants of self-reinforcement in human learning. *Journal of Experimental Psychology,* 1963, *66,* 245–254.

Kaufman, A., Baron, A., & Kopp, R. E.   Some effects of instructions on human operant behavior. *Psychonomic Monograph Supplements,* 1966, *1,* 243–250.

Kazdin, A. E.   Self-monitoring and behavior change. In M. J. Mahoney & C . E. Thoresen (Eds.), *Self-Control:Power to the person.* Monterey, Calif.: Brooks, Cole, 1974. (a)

Kazdin, A. E.   Covert modeling, model similarity, and reduction of avoidance behavior. *Behavior Therapy,1974, 5,* 325–340. (b)

Kazdin, A. E.   Imagery elaboration and self-efficacy in the covert modeling treatment of unassertive behavior. *Journal of Consulting and Clinical Psychology,* 1979, *47,* 725–733.

Kelman, H. C.   Violence without moral restraint: Reflections on the dehumanization of victims and victimizer. *Journal of Social Issues,* 1973, *29,* 25–61.

Keniston, K.   Student activism, moral development, and morality. *American Journal of Orthopsychiatry,* 1970, *40* 577–592.

Kilham, W., & Mann, L.   Level of destructive obedience as a function of transmitter and executant roles in the Milgram obedience paradigm. *Journal of Personality and Social Psychology,* 1974, 29, 696–702.

Kurtines, W., & Greif, E. B.   The development of moral thought: Review and evaluation of Kohlberg's approach. *Psychological Bulletin,* 1974, *8,* 453–470.

Langer, E. J.   The illusion of incompetence. In L. C. Perlmuter & R. A. Monty (Eds.), *Choice and perceived control.* Hillsdale, N. J .: Lawrence Erlbaum Associates, 1980.

Latham, G. P., & Yukl, G. A.   A review of research on the application of goal setting in organizations. *Academy of Management Journal,* 1975, *18,* 824–845.

Lazarus, R. S., & Launier, R.   Stress-related transactions between person and environment. In L. A. Pervin & M. Lewis (Eds.), *Perspectives in interactional psychology.* New York: Plenum Press, 1978.

Lefcourt, H. M. *Locus of control: Current trends in theory and research.* Hillsdale, N. J.: Lawrence Erlbaum Associates, 1976.

Lepper, M. R., Sagotsky, J., & Mailer, J.   Generalization and persistence of effects of exposure to self-reinforcement models. *Child Development,* 1975, *46,* 618–630.

Lewin, K., Dembo, T., Festinger, L., & Sears, P. S.   Level of aspiration .In J. McV. Hunt (Ed.), *Personality and the behavior disorders* (Vol. 1). New York: Ronald Press, 1944.

Litrownik, A. J., Franzini, L. R., & Skenderian, D.   The effect of locus of reinforcement control on a concept-identification task. *Psychological Reports,* 1976, *39,* 159–165.

Locke, E. A.   Toward a theory of task motivation and incentives. *Organizational Behavior and Human Performance,* 1968, *3,* 157–189.

Locke, E. A., Bryan, J. F., & Kendall, L. M.   Goals and intentions as mediators of the effects of monetary incentives on behavior. *Journal of Applied Psychology,* 1968, *52,* 104–121.

Mahoney, M. J.   *Cognition and behavior modification.* Cambridge: Ballinger, 1974.

Mahoney, M. J., Moore, B. S., Wade, T. C., & Moura, N. G. M.   The effects of continuous and intermittent self-monitoring on academic behavior. *Journal of Consulting and Clinical Psychology* 1973, *41,* 65–69.

Mantell, D. M., & Panzarella, R.   Obedience and responsibility. *The British Journal of Social and Clinical Psychology,* 1976, *15,* 239–246.

Marlatt, G. A., & Gordon, J. R.   Determinants of relapse: Implications for the maintenance of behavior change. In P. Davidson (Ed.), *Behavioral medicine: Changing health lifestyles.* New York: Brunner/Mazel, 1979.

Masters, J. C., & Mokros, J. R.   Self-reinforcement processes in children. In H. W. Reese (Ed.), *Advances in child development and behavior* (Vol.9). New York: Academic Press, 1974.

Masters, J. C., & Santrock, J. W.   Studies in the self-regulation of behavior: Effects of contingent cognitive and affective events. *Developmental Psychology,* 1976, *12,* 334–348.

Mc Call, G. J.   The social looking-glass: A sociological perspective on self-development. In T. Mischel (Ed.), *The self: Psychological and philosophical issues.* Oxford, England: Basil Blackwell, 1977.

Mc Mains, M. J., & Liebert, R. M.   Influence of discrepancies between successively modeled self-reward criteria on the adoption of a self-imposed standard. *Journal of Personality and Social Psychology,* 1968, *8,* 166–171.

Meichenbaum, D. H.   *Cognitive-behavior modification: An integrative approach.* New York: Plenum Press, 1977.

Milgram, S.   *Obedience to authority: An experimental view.* New York: Harper & Row, 1974.

Miller, S. M.   Controllability and human stress: Method, evidence and theory. *Behaviour Research and Therapy,* 1979, *17,* 287–304.

Miller, S. M.   Why having control reduces stress: If I can stop the rollercoaster I don't want to get off. In M. E. P. J.Garber & Seligman (Eds.), *Human helplessness: Theory and applications.* New York: Academic Press, 1980.

Mischel, T. (Ed.).   *The self: Psychological and philosophical issues.* Oxford, England: Basil Blackwell, 1977.

Mischel, W.   On the interface of cognition and personality. Beyond the person–situation debate. *American Psychologist,* 1979, *34,* 740–754.

Montgomery, G. T., & Parton, D. A.   Reinforcing effect of self-reward. *Journal of Experimental Psychology,* 1970, *84,* 273–276.

Neisser, U.   *Cognition and reality: Principles and implications of cognitive psychology.* San Francisco: W. H. Freeman, 1976.

Newell, K. M.   Some issues on action plans. In G. E. Stelmach (Ed.), *Information processing in motor control and learning.* New York: Academic Press, 1978.

Parsons, J. E., Ruble, D. N., Hodges, K. L., & Small, A. W.   Cognitive-developmental factors in emerging sex differences in achievement-related expectancies. *The Journal of Social Issues,* 1976, *32,* 47–62.

Patterson, G. R. The aggressive child: Victim and architect of a coercive system. In E. J. Mash, L. A. Hamerlynck, & L. C. Handy (Eds.), *Behavior modification and families.* New York: Brunner/Mazel, 1976.

Perlmuter, L. C., & Monty, R. A. (Eds.). *Choice and perceived control.* Hillsdale, N. J.: Lawrence Erlbaum Associates, 1980.

Pervin, L. A., & Lewis, M., (Eds.). *Perspectives in interactional psychology.* New York: Plenum Press, 1978.

Raush, H. L., Barry, W. A., Hertel, R. K., & Swain, M. A. *Communication, conflict, and marriage.* San Francisco: Jossey-Bass, 1974 .

Romanczyk, R. G., Tracey, D. A., Wilson, G. T., & Thorpe, G.   Behavioral techniques in the treatment of obesity: A comparative analysis. *Behaviour Research and Therapy,* 1973, *11,* 629–640.

Rosenhan, D., Frederick, F., & Burrowes, A.   Preaching and practicing: Effects of channel discrepancy on norm internalization. *Child Development,* 1968, *39,* 291–301.

Rosenthal, T. L., & Bandura, A.   Psychological modeling: Theory and practice. In S. L. Garfield & A. E. Bergin (Eds.), *Handbook of psychotherapy and behavior change: An empirical analysis* (2nd ed.). New York: Wiley, 1978.

Rosenthal, T. L., & Zimmerman, B. J.   *Socal learning and cognition .* New York: Academic Press, 1978.

Rotter, J. B., Chance, J. E., & Phares, E. J.   *Applications of a social learning theory of personality.* New York: Holt, Rinehart, & Winston, 1972.

Sanford, N. & Comstock, C.   *Sanctions for evil.* San Francisco: Jossey-Bass, 1971.

Sarason, I. G.   Anxiety and self-preoccupation. In I. G. Sarason & C. D. Spielberger (Eds.), *Stress and anxiety* (Vol. 2). Washington, D. C.: Hemisphere, 1975.

Schneider, D. J., Hastorf, A. H., & Ellsworth, P. C. *Person perception* (2nd ed.). Reading, Mass.: Addison-Wesley, 1979.

Schunk, D. H.   Modeling and attributional effects on children's achievements: A self-efficacy analysis. *Journal of Educational Psychology,* 1981, *73,* 93–105.

Seligman, M. E. P., Abramson, L. Y., Semmel, A., & von Baeyer, C.   Depressive attributional style. *Journal of Abnormal Psychology,* 1979, *88,* 242–247.

Simon, K. M.   Self-evaluative reactions: The role of personal valuation of the activity. *Cognitive Therapy and Research,* 1979, *3,* 111–116. (a)

Simon, K. M.   *Effects of self-comparison, social comparison, and depression on goal setting and self-evaluative reactions.* Unpublished manuscript, Stanford University, 1979. (b)

Simon, K. M.   Relative influence of personal standards and external incentives on complex performance (Doctoral dissertation, Stanford University, 1979). *Dissertation Abstracts International,* 1980, *40,* 4542–B, (Order No. 8006354, 115).

Skinner, B. F.   *Science and human behavior.* New York: Macmillan, 1953.

Skinner, B. F.   *Beyond freedom and dignity.* New York: Knopf , 1971.

Skinner, B. F.   *About behaviorism.* New York: Knopf, 1974.

Slovic, P., Fischhoff, B., & Lichtenstein, S.   Behavioral decision theory. In M. R. Rosenzweig & L. W. Porter (Eds.), *Annual review of psychology* (Vol. 28). Palo Alto, Calif.: Annual Reviews, 1977

Slovic, P., & Lichtenstein, S. Comparison of Bayesian and regression approaches to the study of information processing in judgment. *Organizational Behavior and Human Performance,* 1971, *6,* 649–744.

Snyder, M.   Seek, and ye shall find: Testing hypotheses about other people. In E. T. Higgins, C. P. Herman, & M. P. Zanna (Eds.), *Social cognition: The Ontario symposium on personality and social psychology.* Hillsdale, N. J.: Lawrence Erlbaum Associates, 1980.

Snyder, M., Tanke, E. D., & Berscheid, E.   Social perception and interpersonal behavior: On the self-fulfilling nature of social stereotypes. *Journal of Personality and Social Psychology,* 1977, *35,* 656–666.

Speidel, G. E.   Motivating effect of contingent self-reward. *Journal of Experimental Psychology,* 1974, *102,* 528-580.

Steers, R. M., & Porter, L. W.   *Motivation and work behavior* (2nd ed.). Hightstown, N. J.: McGraw-Hill, 1979.

Stelmach, G. E. (Ed.).   *Motor control: Issues and trends.* New York: Academic Press, 1976.

Stelmach, G. E. (Ed.).   *Information processing in motor control and learning.* New York: Academic Press, 1978.

Suls, J. M., & Miller, R. L. (Eds.).   *Social comparison processes: Theoretical and empirical perspectives.* Washington, D. C.: Hemisphere, 1977.

Switzky, H. N., & Haywood, H. C.   Motivational orientation and the relative efficacy of self-monitored and externally imposed reinforcement systems in children. *Journal of Personality and Social Psychology,* 1974, *30,* 360–366.

Takata, C., & Takata, T.   The influence of models on the evaluation of ability: Two functions of social comparison processes. *The Japanese Journal of Psychology,* 1976, *47,* 74–84.

Thomas, E. A. C., & Malone, T. W.   On the dynamics of two-person interactions. *Psychological Review,* 1979, *86,* 331–360.

Tilker, H. A.   Socially responsible behavior as a function of observer responsibility and victim feedback. *Journal of Personality and Social Psychology,* 1970, *14,* 95–100.

Tversky, A., & Kahneman, D.   Judgment under uncertainty: Heuristics and biases. *Science,* 1974, *185,* 1124–1131.

Wallace, I.   Self-control techniques of famous novelists.   *Journal of Applied Behavior Analysis,* 1977, *10,* 515–525.

Weiner, B.   A theory of motivation for some classroom experience. *Journal of Educational Psychology* 1979, *71,* 3–25.

Weiner, B., Russell, D., & Lerman, D.   Affective consequences of causal ascriptions. In J. Harvey, W. Ickes, & R. Kidd (Eds.), *New directions in attribution research* (Vol. 2). Hillsdale, N. J.: Lawrence Erlbaum Associates, 1978.

Zimbardo, P. G.   The human choice: Individuation, reason, and order versus deindividuation, impulse, and chaos. In W. J. Arnold & D. Levine (Eds.), *Nebraska symposium on motivation, 1969.* Lincoln: University of Nebraska Press, 1969.

Zimbardo, P. G., Ebbesen, E. B., & Maslach, C.   *Infuencing attitudes and changing behavior.* Reading, Mass.: Addison–Wesley, 1977.

The Self in Social Information Processing

Hazel Markus
University of Michigan

Keith Sentis
Young & Rubicam, USA*

THEORETICAL OVERVIEW

An Historical Perspective

The self is a key element in perceiving the social world. Even rudimentary discriminations among social stimuli may implicate the self in important ways. For example, Karen may only notice that Barbara is fatter than Jean if she believes herself to be fat. And our judgments of whether Martha is attractive, honest, or wealthy depend on our internal standards for these qualities—standards that are very much integral parts of the self. The self participates in social perception as an anchor, a target, a referent, and as an antecedent.

The crucial role of the self in social perception was unambiguously acknowledged by the early psychologists. For Hall (1898), James (1915), and McDougall (1921), the self was seen as the focal element that organized the perception of the individual's social world. It was generally represented as a cognitive or perceptual structure containing powerful emotional components, and numerous concepts ranging from aesthetics to xenophobia were linked to the concept of the self. There was a sharp break in the study of the nature and development of the self-concept occasioned by the rise of behaviorism, but the postbehaviorist view of the self was even more emphatic in its affirmation of the critical role of the self-structure in understanding the world. Krech and Crutchfield (1948) flatly asserted that:

> the self is the most important structure in the psychological field, and it is likely, under normal conditions to be one of the strongest structures. It has, therefore, a role of unparalleled significance in the determination of the organization of the

---

*This Chapter was written while Keith Sentis was at Bell Laboratories, Murrary Hill, N.J.

field. The nature of the relationship of the self to other parts of the field—to other objects, to people, to groups, to social organization—is of critical importance in understanding the individual's perception of a connection between various objects, individuals, and groups, and himself [p. 69].

With equal conviction, Combs and Snygg (1959) wrote: "As the central point of the perceptual field, the phenomenal self is the point of orientation for the individual's every behavior. It is the frame of reference in terms of which all other perceptions gain their meaning [p. 145]."

Given this historical perspective, it is hardly radical to suggest today that the self is deeply implicated in social information processing. A substantial number of self theorists have viewed the self as an integrating structure, and some, such as Kelly (1955), Sarbin (1962), and more recently Epstein (1973), Reykowski (1975), and Kernberg (1977), have considered the self as a set of *cognitive structures* that organize, modify, and integrate functions of the person. Thus, Sarbin (1962) wrote that: "Behavior is organized around cognitive structures, the result of responses of the organism to stimulus objects and residual stimuli. The self is one such cognitive structure ... When a person uses the term'I' the referent is a cognitive structure or inference, the internal organization of which is characterized by substructures with varying properties of strength and breadth [p. 12]." A similar view of the self was taken by Kernberg (1977), a more traditional psychodynamically oriented clinical psychologist. He described the self as affective-cognitive structure that consists of multiple self-representations and their related affect dispositions.

Although this cognitive view divests the self of some of its mystical qualities, it makes it no more accessible to direct observation. However, "cognitive structure" has the ring of a concept that can be understood and empirically investigated. We can begin to pose a variety of relatively focused questions about the self. We can ask, for example, how is the self represented in memory? Or, what type of cognitive structure is the self assumed to be? How does it influence the way we process information about the social world? Is the self-structure just one of many structures that may be engaged to handle incoming information, or is it unique in some ways? And where in the information-processing sequence is the self-structure likely to be implicated? The purpose of this chapter is: (1) to explicate the concept of the self as a cognitive structure; (2) to review recent empirical work that has taken this approach, and (3) to examine when and how the self is implicated in social information processing.

Some rudimentary answers to the questions posed above can be found in the work of the later self theorists. For example, Sarbin (1962) argued that the self-structure should be seen as similar, in large part, to other structures. "The human animal can regard itself as an object in the same way as it regards objects in the external world [p. 13]." Rogers (1951) also thought that the self-structure was one of a set of cognitive structures but implied that it was the first structure to be activated in processing social information. He claimed that: "As experiences occur in the life of the individual, they are either a) symbolized, perceived, and organized into some relationship to the self, b) ignored because there is not a perceived relationship to the self-structure, or c) denied symbolization or given a distorted symbolization because the experience is inconsistent with the structure of the self [p. 503]." The theorizing of Sarbin and of Rogers, as well as that of Kelly (1955) and of Combs and Snygg (1959), all stopped short of suggesting *how* the self-structure might perform its referencing, channeling, or distorting functions, or how the hypothesized operations of the self might be empirically validated. With the advent of the information-processing approach and its more recent emphasis in social cognition, it now seems fruitful to inquire more specifically about how the self might function in social information processing. The next section outlines several general concepts that are essential to developing a more detailed cognitive view of the self.

An Information-Processing Approach

The central tenet of the information-processing approach to psychology is that the organism actively seeks out information in the environment, operates on this information, and adjusts its behavior according to some internal representation of this knowledge. The prototypical information-processing model of Miller, Galanter, and Pribram (1960) assumes: "that any correlations between stimulation and response must be mediated by an organized representation of the environment, a system of concepts and relations within which the organism is located. A human being—and probably other animals as well—builds up an internal representation, a model of the universe, a schema, a simulacrum, a cognitive map, an image [pp. 6–7]." In the two decades since *Plans and the Structure of Behavior,* information-processing research has rapidly advanced our understanding of those cognitive processes that constitute mental life. The idea that if we are to understand behavior we must know how we represent or organize the world has been readily assimilated by psychologists, especially by those in social and developmental psychology.

In their everyday social experience, individuals engage a multitude of cognitive resources. A significant component of the cognitive apparatus activated in social perception is implicit real-world knowledge, or what Miller et al. (1960) call "an organized representation of the environment." This knowledge enables perceivers to detect features of their surroundings and higher-order stimulus structure to which they would otherwise be insensitive. The term *schemata* is used in reference to this crucially important collection of structured knowledge. Schemata are the central cognitive units in the human information-processing system (Neisser, 1976; Rumelhart & Norman, 1978). We view schemata as memory structures of conceptually related elements that guide the processing of information. They are conceptual frameworks for representing relationships among stimuli that are built up on the basis of experience with reality. They are active in the categorization, interpretation, and comprehension of social events and behavior. Social schemata guide an individual in organizing the social world by: (1) simplifying when there is too much (helping reduce an enormously complex environment to meaningful categories); and (2) filling out when there is too little (allowing the perceiver to fill in gaps in the stimulus material and, according to Bruner [1957], to go "beyond the information given".

An important characteristic of schemata is their dual nature: A schema is at once a *structure* and a *process*. A number of theorists have recognized the importance of both the content and function of schemata. For example, Rumelhart and Norman (1978) assert that schemata are: "interrelated knowledge structures, actively engaged in the comprehension of arriving information, guiding the execution of processing operations [p. 41]." Or as Neisser (1976) puts it, the: "schema is not only the plan but also the executor of the plan [p. 56]." Thus, one cannot consider the effects of schemata on behavior without reference to their content and vice versa.

Schemata are involved in both "bottom-up" and "top-down" modes of processing (Rumelhart & Ortony, 1977). The former refers to data-driven processing in which the incoming stimuli suggest which schemata ought to be invoked to account for the data. This mode of operation, also termed event-driven processing, amounts to finding the appropriate memory structures in which to embed the incoming data. In contrast, the second type of processing is schema-driven. With this type of processing, a strong hypothesis or model (a schema) exists for the incoming stimuli, and the processing system uses the model to operate on the input data. In essence, top-down processing fits the input to expectations. Of course, these two processing modes are not mutually exclusive. In novel situations where no strong hypothesis exists, selection from among the possible alternative models can be appropriately directed by bottom-up processing of details in the stimuli. Conversely, top-down operations probably influence the selection of areas in which subsequent phases of bottom-up processing will occur.

A key concept in the chapter is that of "representation." Representation refers to forming an internal model of portions of the world. Despite being the object of a great deal of theorizing by psychologists, the representation concept is ill-defined and not well-understood (Palmer, 1978). The basic idea of a cognitive representation is that there exists a correspondence or mapping from objects in the real world to objects in the mental world such that certain relations extant in the real world are structurally preserved in the mental world. Given this conceptualization, there can exist many different cognitive representations of the same set of real-world objects. As more fully discussed by Palmer (1978), individuals can differ in their cognitive representations of the same segment of the real world in at least two ways. Firstly, their internal models can represent different subsets of the relations among a group of objects in the world in the same manner, or secondly, their models can represent the same subset of world relationships in different manners. For the most part, we refer to the former class of differences in our discussion of individual variation in cognitive representations.

The Self as a System of Schemata

From our perspective, the self can be conceptualized as a system of *self-schemata*. These schemata are knowledge structures developed by individuals to understand and explain their own social experiences. They serve to integrate a wide range of stimulus information about the self. A schema integrates all the information known about the self in a given behavioral domain into a systematic framework used during processing (Neisser, 1976; Palmer, 1977). A schema is a conceptually advantageous analog for the self because it can potentially represent what James (1915) called the two distinct aspects of the self—''the self as the *knower* and the self as that which is *known*.'' Self-schemata, then, are assumed to be structures of knowledge about the self that engage in a process of ongoing interpretive activity.

More specifically, self-schemata are generalizations about the self derived from the repeated categorizations and evaluations of behavior by oneself and by others. The result is a well-differentiated idea of the kind of person one is with respect to a variety of domains of behavior. Individuals only develop schemata about those aspects of their behavior that are important to them in some ways. Over the life course, we become increasingly aware of the distinctive characteristics of our appearance, temperament, abilities, and preferences. As we accrue knowledge about ourselves and achieve cognitive representations of our experience in various behavioral domains, we become "experts" about ourselves in these domains. We may come to understand that we are shy, or creative, or fat, or stubborn, or intimidated by large groups, or pathologically late for appointments, facile with numbers, a good cook, a rotten child, or a loving parent. And at the same time we come to know a great deal about what it means to be "shy," "creative," "fat," etc. These generalizations about the self function as selective mechanisms in further processing. The expertise that accumulates as we organize the knowledge about the self in a given area affects the processing of information relevant to that domain. Self-schemata search for information that is congruent with them and direct behavior so that it is commensurate and consistent with them. As Boden (1979) put it: "if a person's self-image represents herself to herself ... [as a particular type of individual] ... then it can be used to generate choices and guide her actions accordingly. ... the internal representations of the possible roles of action that are available to the system can be crucial in directing the performance actually carried out [p. 455]."

Representation of the Self in Memory.   The schema approach to the self carries with it a particular view about how the self can be represented in memory—a view that can be contrasted with at least two other distinctly different perspectives. These views are sketched in Fig. 2.1. One of the opposing views assumes that the self is not represented separately in memory at all. As indicated in Panel A of Fig. 2.1, knowledge about the self is distributed throughout memory and stored with other relevant structures. Thus, the knowledge that you have just completed your seventh marathon, or that your new running shoes seem to ease the pain in your knees, will be organized with a general structure relevant to running or jogging, and not as part of a self-structure. Another view, sketched in Panel B, suggests that everything the individual processes is self-relevant, and thus *all* information in memory is part of the self-structure. This extreme view, though a logical possibility, does not leave much room for an empirically distinct investigation of the self.

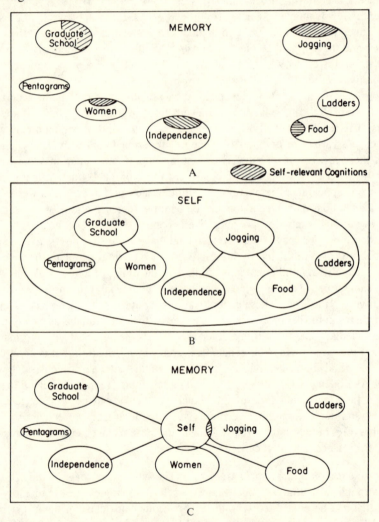

Fig. 2.1. Views of the role of the self in memory.

The conceptualization of the self that we present here suggests, as did Sarbin (1962), that the self is represented in thought and memory as a separate structure, or set of structures, in the same manner as other individuals, and aspects of the social environment are represented in memory (see Panel C). This view of the self posits that all general self-representations are connected, and that they are stored together in one distinct self-concept, linked with other concepts. Most concepts are joined with the self-concept because most things are experienced with reference to the self. Concepts that are very seldom self-relevant such as "ladders" and "pentagrams" are not shown as connected to the self, yet obviously they can be, should the need arise. This view allows for temporary connections between the self with other objects and also for more permanent, enduring connections.[1] Through repeated associations of the self-structure with other concepts and structures, new information will be linked with the self. Thus, for example, "wine" may constitute a conceptual area that consists of some vague elements having to do with grapes, alcohol, France, vintage, bottle shapes, etc. Such a cognitive structure is likely to exist for a person who is indifferent to wine. But for an oenophile, there will be a close contact between the "wine-structure" and the "self-structure." Some wines will become part of the self-structure as preferred ones, some experiences of drinking particular wines will stand out in memory, and the "ME" may evolve into a "ME" who prefers St. Emillion to St. Julien, or a "ME" who had a rare opportunity of tasting a 1959 Chateau Lafite. This incorporation of particular cognitive representations into the self-structure occurs when a large number of their elements become self-relevant, or when the elements of the self-structure become relevant for these cognitive representations. A self-structure for a particular behavioral or stimulus domain is just such an intersection between the representations of these behaviors or of these stimuli and the representations of the self. These types of structures become parts of the self-structure and are activated when the self-structure is accessed. In effect, these structures become the self and become the ones most salient, central, or important in organizing information about the self and perhaps the social world in general.

There is not yet any compelling evidence that argues for a distinct or separate structure of the self; yet there is a diverse variety of theoretical and empirical work that assumes or directly implies such a structure. In psychoanalytic theories of the self, a distinct structure of the self is virtually a given. The differentiation of self from others is assumed to be fundamental to healthy individual functioning (Guntrip, 1971). It is only through a separation of self from the mother

---

[1] In panel C of Fig. 2.1, two types of connections with the self are indicated. Relevance to the self is indicated by lines connecting a particular domain and the self. Increased relevance or involvement may lead to a merging of the self with some domain of knowledge, and then a *self-schema* may be said to exist. This is indicated by overlapping circles. For example, with respect to jogging, some aspects of one's cognitive representations of the self may now become associated with jogging, and in turn, some representations of jogging may engage representations of some aspects of the self. Some part of knowledge structure of jogging becomes part of the self-structure and is activated when the self-structure is accessed. Obviously, only a limited number of the domains of past, present, or future relevance for the self can be incorporated into the self in this manner.

that the child can begin to experience the social world and relate to other persons and objects. Given this perspective, it seems quite likely that a separate self-structure would develop to organize the new affective and cognitive representations of the self that accompany separation from the mother (Sherif & Cantril, 1947). Hall (1898) described this process quite vividly: "children of four and five months are described as attentively feeling of one hand with the other, each at the same time feeling and being felt, each subject and object to the other, and thus detaching them from the world of external things and labeling them with a mark which will enable the soul later to incorporate them into the plexus which forms the somatic ego [pp. 351-352]." Without dwelling on the specific role or attributes of the soul, the general nature of this self-labeling process seems quite reasonable, and it is plausible, then, that the cognitive and affective products of this marking process will be incorporated in a rudimentary memory structure relevant to the self. In fact, Sarbin (1962) regarded these somaesthetic sensations as part of the "infant's first reference schema [p. 18]."

Virtually all the theorizing about the development of the self-concept is based on anecdotal and intuitive evidence. The most directly relevant empirical research is on the ontogeny of self-recognition in infants (Bertenthal & Fischer, 1978). These studies indicate that children between 18 and 24 months can recognize and correctly identify themselves in a mirror. Whereas mirror recognition is probably only an indirect indicator of self-concept development, it can hardly be disputed that in order to make a correct identification the child must somehow match the mirror image to the cognitive representation of the self. Later in the course of development, linguistic pressure probably induces the child to elaborate upon the concepts "I" or "me" or "mine." For example, the least complicated way to organize the cognitions "My name is Eric," "I am a boy," "I am a brother," "This is my dog," "I like ice cream,' "and "This house belongs to me" is with a single "me" structure in memory that is associated with the memory structures "boy," "brother," "house," etc.

Content of the Self-Structure.   We assume that the core of the self-structure is comprised of the fundamental or most important self-representations. The self becomes increasingly differentiated with experience, and it evolves into a large and complex knowledge structure. Included in the core self may be representations of the basic identifying features of the self such as one's name, the representation of one's physical appearance, representations of other distinctive features of the self such as sex and kinship roles, and, perhaps following Kernberg (1977), representations of one's relationships to highly significant others. These are *universal* schemata that probably everyone will develop to one degree or another. One's general affective evaluation of the self is also represented in the core self.

Beside these universal self-schemata that comprise the core of the self-system, most individuals probably have a wide range of more *particularistic* schemata or structures that are likely to be developed by some individuals and not by others.

These might include, for example, schemata associated with characteristics of the self such as independence, friendliness, or financial standing. Some people think of themselves as rich and independent people, and they structure their thoughts about themselves and others around these central dimensions. Not all people, however, have self-schemata in these domains, and consequently they may not encode social behavior in these terms. Finally, the self-structure may also include a great deal of peripheral knowledge of the type, or "I work best when the sun is shining," or "Scotch gives me a headache."

Is the Self-Structure Unique?   As we develop the concept of the self as a system of knowledge structures, we are faced with the question of how much similarity there is between the self-structure and other structures. Is the self just one of many structures that may be activated in social information processing, or does it require some special status. Although research on the specific effects of processing information with reference to the self is quite recent, the idea that making information self-relevant can produce unique effects is a time-worn one, and one that has been heavily traded on by teachers, politicians, and lawyers. Advertisements in educational journals claim that to teach a child to read, or to help him or her learn faster, better, and with more enthusiasm, it is helpful to insert the child's name in the story and thereby make the events self-relevant. And of course, attorneys and advertisers have always realized the power of "bringing it home" by making their plea or messages self-relevant.

Besides the anecdotal evidence, there is also some research, of it much relatively old and not done with reference to cognitive structures, which suggests that the self can have a profound influence on information processing. It has been demonstrated repeatedly that one's personal record of one's past accomplishments may not be a perfect match with a observer's record of the same behavior. When concerned with memory for events about the self, it seems that the good, the correct, the responsible, the consistent, and the successful aspects of one's activities are much more likely to be recalled than the bad, the incorrect, the irresponsible, the inconsistent, or the unsuccessful (Bradley, 1978; Cartwright, 1956; Wallen, 1942; Wortman, 1976; Zeller, 1950). Although this literature is fraught with ambiguities and inconsistencies (Miller, 1978; Miller & Ross, 1975), it does seem that under some conditions we are quite likely to take the credit for success and put the blame for failure elsewhere. We tend to take much more credit for a joint project than a partner would accord us (Greenwald, 1980; Ross & Sicoly, 1978), or to judge a higher payment for ourselves to be as fair as a lower payment for another (Messick & Sentis, 1979). This research, however, has not been specific about how the self functions to produce these self-enhancing or self-protecting biases.

In an effort to develop an initial theory about how the self-structure influences information processing, where it should be implicated in the information-processing sequence, and whether it should be considered a unique structure, the next section reviews research specifically aimed at evaluating the role of self-structures in information processing.

EMPIRICAL RESEARCH

There are now a number of studies on how self-structures influence social cognition. These studies can be classified into three general categories: (1) those concerned with processing information about the self; (2) those focusing on processing information about others; and (3) those examining the role of the self in structuring social interaction.

Processing Information About the Self

To assess the influence of cognitive structures about the self on processing self-information, a series of studies have compared individuals assumed to have a schema in a particular domain, *schematics,* with those assumed to be without such a structure in that domain, or *aschematics.* The assumption of these studies is that differences in the response characteristics of schematics and aschematics should allow inferences about the nature of the cognitive structure mediating the processing. These studies have investigated self-schemata about independence, creativity, extraversion, dominance, body weight, gender, and social sensitivity. Each behavioral domain under study has been represented by a number of indicative and counter indicative trait adjectives. Thus, the dimension of independence is linked to ratings on the indicative adjectives—independent, leader, individualist—and to the counterindicative adjectives—dependent, follower, conformist. The domain of masculinity is linked to ratings on the indicative adjectives—aggressive, dominant, leader—and to ratings on the counter-indicative adjectives—sensitive, emotional, gentle. Prior to the experimental sessions, each trait adjective is rated on bipolar scales for its degree of self-descriptiveness and its importance in the individual's overall self-concept.

It is assumed that *schematic* individuals habitually categorize and code their behavior along the dimension in question and as a consequence will rate trait adjectives that are indicative of the dimension as both self-descriptive *and* important to their self-concept. In addition, schematic individuals will rate counterindicative trait adjectives as *not* self-descriptive. On the other hand, it is assumed that *aschematic* individuals will not categorize themselves along the dimension, and this will be manifest on the questionnaire by moderate to low self-descriptiveness ratings on trait adjectives that are indicative of the dimension, *and* by moderate to low self-descriptiveness ratings on trait adjectives that are counterindicative. Aschematic individuals also rate these trait adjectives as moderate to low in importance.

Content and Latency of Judgments about the Self. In an initial study, Markus (1977) showed that variations in the self-structure could have a marked impact on both the content and the processing time of self-relevant judgments and decisions. People with schemata about independence and dependence were compared with individuals who were aschematic with respect to these domains. In one task, trait adjectives associated with dependence (e.g., tolerant, conforming, obliging) and adjectives associated with independence (e.g., independent, individualistic, assertive) were presented on a screen one at a time. Individuals were instructed to press a "me" button if an adjective was self-descriptive and a "not-me" button if the word was not self-descriptive. The response and response latency were recorded for each judgment.

The assumption was that most people would respond "me" to an adjective like "independent," but that they would do so for a variety of reasons that could be differentiated with a response latency measure. Some people may respond "me" because a given characteristic is indeed part of their self-structure but others may respond "me" because independence is a socially desirable quality. If individuals have differentiated themselves in the domain of independence, such that the attribute of independence became part of their self-structures, they should be able to make "me" decisions relatively quickly. However, if a charac-

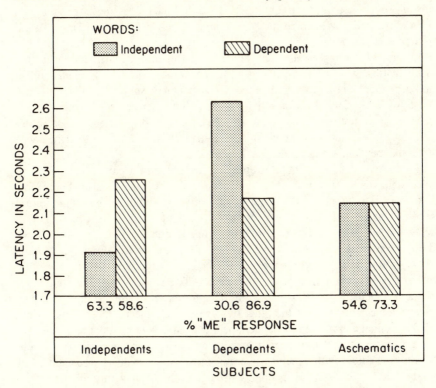

FIG. 2.2 Mean response latency for dependent and independent adjectives judged as self-descriptive.

teristic is really inconsistent with, or contradicts a self-schema about independence but a "me" judgment is made anyway, this will be indicated by a relatively longer latency. If an individual makes judgments in this domain that are not mediated by an underlying self-structure, this should be revealed by greater variance among the "ME/NOT ME" responses.

As shown in Fig. 2.2, the group of individuals who thought of themselves as "independent" responded "me" to a larger proportion of independent adjectives (see percentages below bars) and required a much shorter amount of time to make their judgments than they did for judgments to the dependent adjectives. This pattern of judgments and response latencies is to be expected of individuals who habitually evaluate and categorize their behavior with respect to its independence. The group of individuals who thought of themselves as "dependent" showed the same pattern of results, except that they responded much faster to the dependent adjectives than they did to the independent adjectives. Dependent Schematics are used to thinking of themselves as "conforming" and "obliging" and could make these judgments quite quickly. In contrast, these individuals are probably not so used to thinking about themselves as "assertive" and "individualistic" (even though they might like to), and thus the processing associated with a "me" response was more time consuming for the words that were inconsistent with the self-schema.

In marked contrast to the Independent and Dependent Schematics were the Aschematics, who did not differ at all in their processing time for independent and dependent words. It is evident that the Aschematic subjects do not really use these two sets of words differentially in describing themselves. Presumably because they do not have a cognitive structure for their own independence or dependence, Aschematics expend equal cognitive effort in labeling their behavior with independent or dependent adjectives.

To the extent a self-structure represents expertise in a particular domain of one's behavior, a schema ought to enhance recall of schema-consistent behavior. Likewise, a schema should increase subjective probabilities regarding future schema-related activities. This expertise also ought to allow for consistency in schema-relevant judgments over time, and in addition, ought to provide a backdrop against which to evaluate the validity of self-relevant information. Markus (1977) showed that the performance of Schematic subjects in a variety of other tasks evinced each of these aspects of schema-driven processing. The same Independent Schematic subjects were able to supply more specific examples of past independent behavior than the other two groups of subjects, thought they were likely to engage in future independent behavior, and were resistant to the acceptance of information that implied they were not independent. A parallel pattern of results was found with dependent stimuli for those individuals who thought of themselves as "dependent" people. Once again, the Aschematics did not differentiate in their handling of independent and dependent information; they thought they were as likely to engage in independent as dependent behavior and were relatively accepting of information about themselves in this domain. They also showed considerable inconsistency in their responses across the various tasks. Aschematics exhibited, on the average, only a .20 correlation between self-categorization responses in two different tasks, whereas Schematics exhibited an average correlation of .66. A schema then provides for consistency in response and provides a framework for evaluating the validity of information about the self.

In a recent study concerning self-schemata about social sensitivity, Sweeney and Moreland (1980) confirmed the role of a self-schema in resisting counterschematic information. Subjects were given feedback about their ability to identify authentic suicide notes (a procedure previously used by Ross, Lepper, & Hubbard, 1975). Sweeney and Moreland found that Schematics who thought the task was relevant to social sensitivity would not accept the false feedback when it was inconsistent with their self-image and, thus, did not exhibit the perseverance effect displayed by individuals in the study by Ross et al.[2]

Markus, Crane, and Siladi (1978) replicated the findings about independence with respect to self-schemata about gender. Individuals who thought of themselves either as stereotypically feminine or masculine were compared with those who were androgynous. Following Bem's view of androgyny (1977), it was reasoned that androgynous individuals were those who do not partition their self-concept into masculine and feminine components, and thus who are essentially aschematic with respect to both masculinity and femininity. Those three groups of subjects performed the "me/not me" self-categorization task using the 60 adjectives from the Bem Sex Role Inventory (1974). The Masculine Schematics were much faster at endorsing masculine adjectives than they were at endorsing feminine adjectives, although they responded "me" to a large number of feminine adjectives. They also were much more confident that the masculine adjectives described them than they were about the feminine attributes. Feminine Schematics exhibited the same pattern of results with respect to the feminine adjectives. The androgynous individuals displayed the same lack of differentiation with respect to latency as did those subjects who were aschematic with respect to independence.[3]

The general pattern of latency findings exhibited in the studies by Markus (1977) and Markus et al. (1978) was also reported by Kuiper and Rogers (1979),

---

[2] Unless otherwise indicated, the term *Schematic* in both the text and figures is used for those subjects who are extreme on the high end of the domain being examined. Thus, Social Sensitivity Schematics are those who think they are very socially sensitive and feel that being socially sensitive is important to their overall evaluation of themselves. Similarly, Masculine Schematics are those who feel they are very masculine, and who think that masculinity is very important to their self-evaluation.

[3] Based on Bem's (1977) procedure, two types of androgynous subjects were included in this study. Those who thought both masculine and feminine adjectives on the self-rating scale characterized them, and those who thought neither masculine or feminine adjectives characterized them. The endorsement and latency results were comparable for both groups.

who found that self-referent judgments about adjectives that were extremely like or extremely unlike the self could be made relatively quickly, but that judgments of moderately self-descriptive items took somewhat longer.

In general, response parameters of individual's self-descriptions,such as confidence and latency, have proved particularly useful in speculating about self-structures and potential differences between them and other structures. In a study by Markus, Crane, Bernstein and Siladi (1982), an optimal scaling technique (Lingoes, 1968) was used to assign a common metric for different combinations of endorsement, latencies, and response confidence. This analysis revealed four distinct groups—Masculine Schematics, Feminine Schematics, and two androgynous groups—those who think both masculine and feminine attributes are extremely characteristic of them (what has been called in the androgyny literature High Undifferentiated) and those who think neither masculine or feminine attributes describe them (Low Undifferentiated). The two androgynous groups appear to have quite different structures for gender information, even though they are similar in their lack of overall differentiation between masculine and feminine stimuli. Thus, the Low Undifferentiated group appeared to be essentially aschematic with respect to gender, whereas the other group seemed to have a structure containing information about both genders, that is, a structure that integrates knowledge both about masculine and feminine domains.

Similarly, in studies on self-schemata relevant to body weight by Markus, Hamill, and Sentis (1979), the latency measures provided the basis for a clear differentiation among subjects. These distinctions would have been obscured had the categorization been made on the basis of their self-description responses or their actual body weight. This study used four groups of subjects to explore differences in articulation of body-weight schemata. Two schematic groups were comprised of either overweight or normal-weight individuals who thought body weight was important to their overall self-image. Two aschematic groups consisted of overweight or normal-weight individuals who did not think body weight was important. On the self-categorization task using trait adjectives, all four groups differentiated "fat" words from "thin" words with respect to both response latency and endorsement rate. These findings were consistent with the idea that a body-weight schema is in some respects a universal schema; probably everyone has some type of knowledge structure or simple schema about this aspect of the self. Even if the individual does not characteristically attend to his or her body weight, others will do so, and thus even Aschematics are likely to develop some concept or organization of information relevant to their body weight that allows them to differentiate "fat" from "thin." The Schematics differed from the Aschematics, however, in their response to stimuli from two other domains related to body weight. Only the Schematics differentiated between fat- and thin-body silhouettes and between "fat" and "thin" foods. For these individuals, the body-weight schema is relatively articulated and allowed them to integrate (form associations or interconnections between) information that is conceptually related to the fat–thin dimension. The Aschematics do not seem to possess a broad-based knowledge structure related to body weight and thus did not exhibit differentiation in their response to stimuli from these other two domains.

Differences between Schematics and Aschematics in processing time for decisions and in confidence for these decisions imply clear differences in the knowledge structures mediating the judgments. The fact that judgments about the self in areas where an individual is an expert, or Schematic, can be made relatively quickly and confidently suggests that information about the self is organized in such a way that it can be readily accessed for efficient processing. Given that there probably is an elaborate network of knowledge about the self in schematic areas, it is evident that the knowledge in a schema must be organized in such a way that it is not necessary to search through all the confirming evidence before making judgments about the self. Information or knowledge in a self-schema may be integrated into a large unit that is activated in an all-or-none fashion (Sentis & Burnstein, 1979; Smith, Adams, & Schorr, 1978). The more a particular self-schema is used, the more the associations among the elements may be strengthened and the more available for future use it will become (Hayes-Roth, 1977).

Memory for Self-Related Information.   In addition to influencing the responses and latencies of self-relevant judgments, self-schemata ought to exert considerable influence on memory for personally relevant information. We can reasonably expect a self-structure to provide a memorial framework during the initial processing of self-relevant information that will be quite useful for subsequent retrieval of the material. Rogers (1977) explored this idea by instructing subjects to refer to themselves as they memorized personality items, and he found substantial improvement in recognition-memory performance following self-referent instructions. Sentis and Markus (1979) investigated the effects of self-schemata on recognition memory for self-relevant stimuli and found that Schematics showed superior recognition memory for schema-relevant material than for irrelevant material. The Aschematics, however, did not exhibit a difference for the two types of material. In addition, Schematics made fewer errors and were faster at recognizing schema-relevant material than were Aschematics. These results also indicated that Schematic subjects were significantly faster in correctly recognizing schema-relevant words they had endorsed than schema-relevant words they had not endorsed; that is, the prior me/not me judgments had an effect on the speed with which Schematics were able to recognize traits they had seen before. Reaction times for Aschematics did not differ according to whether or not the word was judged as self-descriptive. In a similar vein, Rogers, Rogers, and Kuiper (1979) found that highly self-descriptive adjectives were associated with "false alarms." Thus, the number of adjectives falsely identified as having been presented previously was found to increase as the adjectives became more self-descriptive. As noted by Kuiper and Derry (1980), this pattern

was identical to the false-alarm effect that has been found in the cognitive literature on prototype development.

Additional tests of the idea that self-schemata facilitate memory for self-
relevant material have employed an incidental recall paradigm. Markus, Crane,
and Siladi (1978) asked individuals who were classified as Feminine, Masculine,
or Androgynous, on the basis of their responses to the Bem Sex Role Inventory,
to recall as many adjectives from the scale as possible immediately after
completing the scale. They found that Masculine subjects recalled significantly
more masculine words than feminine words, and that Feminine subjects recalled
significantly more feminine words than masculine words. Androgynous subjects,
however, showed much less differentiation in the number of masculine and feminine words recalled. These results were interpreted by assuming that the Feminine Schematics, for example, have a self-schema about their gender, or their
femininity, which organizes information relevant to this domain. The schema
imposes structure on the relevant trait adjectives that accentuates the associations
among them, and this in turn enhances free recall.

Using a somewhat different approach, Rogers, Kuiper, and Kirker (1977)
compared encoding via self-reference to three other types of judgments—structural, phonemic, and semantic. They found that their subjects recalled substantially more of the words for which they had previously made
self-referent judgments when compared to words for which they had made other
types of judgments. These findings were explained by assuming that self-referent
judgments necessarily produce much richer, more elaborate encoding of the adjectives than do other types of judgments.

These studies clearly indicate that self-structures have a powerful effect on
memory processes. However, the question arises as to whether the self was necessarily implicated in these findings, or whether it was merely the "social" nature of the judgments that facilitated memory performance. In other words, are
self-schemata unique cognitive structures that are distinctive from knowledge
structures about other social phenomena, and do they have a unique impact on
social information processing? Scattered throughout the psychological literature
are a handful of studies indicating that memory for one's own performance is better than the memory for the performance of others (Brenner, 1973; Cartwright,
1956; Greenwald, 1980; Jarvella & Collars, 1974; Wallen, 1942). It is only recently, however, that investigators have studied why memory for information
about the self may be enhanced relative to information about others. To determine whether self-reference per se was responsible for their earlier findings on
incidental recall, Kuiper and Rogers (1979) compared recall of items following
judgments made about the self, to those made about a complete stranger, and to
those made about a person known for some time. Recall of words judged in reference to the self was enhanced relative to recall of words judged in reference to a
complete stranger, but *not* relative to words used in judgments about a person
known for a while. Lord (1980), however, found that self-referent decisions did

produce greater recall than other decisions including "Does this word describe your father?," "Does this word describe Walter Cronkite?," and "Does this word describe a tree?." Similarly, Kendzierski (1980) compared self-referent judgments to judgments about scripts for particular situations or other people and found that recall for self-judged words was superior to that for words judged relative to other people in particular situations. Overall, the empirical data, although somewhat equivocal with respect to the specific effects of self-reference, indicates that memory for a stimulus is enhanced if it is made self-relevant. This enhancement is probably a function, in large part, of the size and complexity of the self-structure.

Kuiper and Rogers (1979), in extending their earlier work, related recall of an item following a judgment to a latency for that judgment. They showed that the adjectives recalled from the self-referent task were those with a very short processing time, whereas the adjectives recalled from the judgment of strangers were those with the longer latencies. They believe this pattern of results is obtained because judgments about the self are mediated by a schema that enables efficient processing, whereas judgments about a stranger require a search for potentially relevant information and then a consolidation of the information, all of which consumes processing time. This same pattern was reported by Keenan and Baillet (1979), who compared recognition memory following judgments in reference to people of varying closeness to the self, raging from "best friend" to "your boss" to "Jimmy Carter." They found that the more personally significant the referent individual, the faster judgments in reference to that person were made and the better the subsequent recognition-memory performance. More generally, they noted that the more information associated with a schema, the faster the response.

These findings on memory about the self can be productively explained if it is assumed that self-reference judgments are mediated by a structure of knowledge about the self that contains the summarized and integrated past information about the self and consequently that can generate a rapid and rich encoding of the stimulus. The structures mediating self-reference judgments are different from those structures mediating judgments about Walter Cronkite or a tree.

The Influence of the Self on the Perception of Others

Given the substantial influence that variations in the self-structure appear to have on processing information about the self, it is reasonable to ask what is the influence of the self on processing information about others. The relationship between the self and the perception of others is a central concern for theories of identification, role taking, social comparison, and attribution. Yet the relationship has not been systematically investigated. We have lacked both a clear definition of the self-system and some notion about what components or aspects of the perception of others are likely to be influenced by the self-system.

The studies that have examined the influence of self-schemata on processing information about others have assumed that when we have little information about others it is likely that we will use our self-structure to elaborate or embellish the encoding of the available information. Hamill (1980) explored the impact of self-schemata on other perception when only minimal information about the other is available. In her study, Independent Schematics and Aschematic subjects were shown a series of slides of faces and were asked to make a judgment about each face, either with respect to a physical trait ("Does this person have wide-set eyes?") or regarding independence ("Does this person look like the independent type?"). Following an intervening task, subjects participated in a standard recognition memory test that included some faces viewed earlier and some faces not previously seen. Recall that the self-referent studies described previously (Keenan & Baillet, 1979; Kuiper & Rogers, 1979; Lord, 1980; Rogers et al., 1977) showed that encoding via a self-schema led to enhanced memory performance, an effect ascribed to the greater degree of articulation and richness of self-schemata relative to other cognitive structures. Hamill reasoned that Schematics should have a much richer and more articulated structure for independence than do Aschematics. During the processing involved in judging whether a face looks like an "independent type," a Schematic's structure for independence should

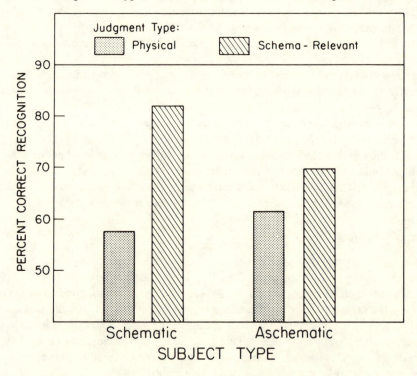

FIG. 2.3   Percent correct recognition for physical and schema-relevant judgments.

lead to a more elaborated encoding of the face relative to an Aschematic. This difference in schema richness and the concomitant difference in degree of elaborated encoding ought to enhance a Schematic's memory for faces judged for independence as compared to an Aschematic's memory under the same conditions. As indicated in Fig. 2.3, the results of Hamill's study showed that Schematics exhibited higher hit rates (correctly identifying old faces) for faces judged along the schema-relevant dimension of independence than for those judged along a physical dimension. The performance of the Aschematics did not differ according to the type of judgment. Moreover, between-group comparisons showed that Schematics exhibited higher hit rates than Aschematics for faces judged with respect to independence. These results suggest that when making a self-relevant judgment Schematics were able to develop a number of associations and connections between the stimulus and their schema, which resulted in a rich encoding and enhanced memory for the face. In contrast, the Aschematics did not perform differently on the two tasks because their schema for independence is not more articulated than their structure for physical features and thus did not result in differential encoding of the stimulus.

Other research in this direction has inquired into the role of self-schemata in the perception of others under conditions where we have access to more information about others than just physical appearance. A study by Markus and Fong (1979) explored the effects of self-schemata for independence on judgments and evaluations of other individuals' independent behavior. One would expect a schema to provide a clearly defined model of schema-consistent (i.e., independent) behavior. This model will delineate the behavior indicative of "independence" and thus provide a baseline for comparison in judging social behavior. In the parlance of early-attitude theorists, the schema is expected to establish a fairly restricted "latitude of acceptance" for independence. Markus and Fong had groups of Independent Schematics and Aschematics read different versions of a story in which the central character engaged in varying amounts of independent behavior. Analysis of the subjects' ratings of the central character along several dimensions indicated that Independent Schematics were decidedly more sensitive to variations in independence than were Aschematics and thus gave more extreme evaluations of a target's independent and dependent behavior. Markus and Smith (1981) argued that the self provides an anchor or frame of reference for the perception of others. It cannot be precisely specified, however, how this frame of reference will influence judgments and decisions about others without knowledge of the nature and the goal of the social situation or interaction.

Having seen that self-schemata influence perception of others in situations where minimal information about the other is available (e.g., physical appearance) as well as in situations where descriptions of behavior are available, one can inquire into the role of the self in the perception of ongoing behavior. In one such study, Markus, Smith, and Moreland (1979) had Masculine Schematics (those who had a self-schema for masculinity) and Aschematics (those without a masculinity self-schema) perform a unitizing task (Newtson, 1973) while viewing a film of an actor engaging in behavior that was either stereotypically masculine or irrelevant to gender. In this task subjects were instructed to push a button when they perceived one meaningful action to end and another to begin, that is, to break the behavioral stream into significant units. It was predicted that Schematics would divide the schema-relevant segments of the film into larger units than would Aschematics. This is consistent with the reasoning of Sentis and Burnstein (1979), who argue that one function of social schemata is the integration or chunking of stimuli into meaningful units. Schematics should segment schema-relevant behavior into larger units than Aschematics, in the same manner that experts in chess and Go (Chase & Simon, 1973; Reitman, 1976) perceive larger patterns of pieces on the game board than do novices. The results of Markus et al. indicate that Masculine Schematics made fewer button presses during the stereotypical masculine behavior than did Aschematics, but there was no difference between the groups on the schema-irrelevant segments of the film. The self-schema seems to allow individuals to organize the schema-relevant behavior into larger units that presumably correspond to their conceptual framework in this domain. These results, as well as those of Sentis and Burnstein (1979), indicate that one way in which a schema facilitates processing of relevant information is by integrating the material into relatively large units. This chunking operation obviates the need to cognitively contend with smaller details, thereby increasing processing efficiency. In labeling larger behavioral sequences as unitary events, Schematics seem to direct less cognitive effort toward the individual constituent acts comprising these events and, consequently, might have available more capacity for other cognitive processes such as evaluation and inferencing.

The Self in Social Interaction

If self-structures have an important influence on processing information about others, as the previous studies suggest, it is quickly evident that these structures must also influence the course of social interaction. In exploring how the self influences social information processing, recent studies considered the role of the self within social interaction. The self-structure can shape social interaction in at least two ways. Firstly, it influences how information about the self and others is handled (i.e., encoded, categorized, monitored, retrieved, stored, and evaluated). Secondly, it also determines the type and nature of information about the self that will be managed and presented to others in the course of a social interaction. Recent studies have attempted to develop paradigms that eventually may be used to study the role of self-structures in social interaction.

A study by Fong and Markus (in press) sought to investigate one of the ways in which a schema could channel social interaction. They hypothesized that subjects' self-schemata would influence strategies used to learn about others. The design of the study was based on one conducted by Snyder and Swann (1978), in which subjects were given hypotheses about the personal attributes of a target person they were about to meet. In one condition of the Snyder–Swann research, subjects were told that the target person was an extravert; in the other condition, subjects were told that the target person was an introvert. Each subject was then asked to test the hypothesis by choosing a series of questions to ask the target person in a forthcoming interview. It was found that subjects chose their questions by using an hypothesis confirming strategy; that is, they chose questions that tended to confirm the hypothesis rather than disconfirm the hypothesis. In this study, as well as in other studies performed by Snyder and his colleagues (Snyder & Swann, 1978; Snyder & Uranowitz, 1978; Snyder & Cantor, in press), subjects were given an hypothesis about a target person and then asked to judge its validity. In their study, Fong and Markus assumed that an individual's self-schema would provide the hypothesis about others, or the anchor against which information about the target could be evaluated. Thus, subjects were not given any explicit hypotheses about the target person. Instead, three types of subjects were used: Extravert Schematics, Introvert Schematics, and Aschematics. Subjects were presented with the list of questions used in the Snyder and Swann study and asked to choose those questions that they would want to ask a person they were about to meet. The prediction was that the Schematic groups would choose to seek out information about a target person that was related to their self-schema. This prediction was confirmed—Extravert Schematics chose to ask more extravert questions than Introvert Schematics, Introvert Schematics chose to ask more introvert questions than Extravert Schematics, and Aschematics chose to ask more neutral questions than either Extraverts or Introverts. This study indicates that self-schemata influence and direct what type of information one chooses to seek out about others. It is plausible then that these differential information-seeking strategies will have a substantial impact on the nature of social interaction. In further studies, it should be possible to determine whether schemata also influence the interpretation and evaluation of the information that is gathered.

Recent work by Sentis and Geller (1979) also has focused on the role of self-structures in social interaction. The framework of this research is Goffman's (1959) theorizing about the importance of self-presentation in the structuring of social interaction. Sentis and Geller explored the effects of self-schema in a particular domain on an individual's ability to discern the type of impression others were attempting to convey in a social interaction. Subjects in this study viewed a video tape of individuals in an interview situation who were engaged in impression management. The people on the video tape had been told that it was in their best interest to come across in the interview as either a dominant and independent person or as a submissive and dependent person. The impression managers were given independent ratings that indicated high or low success in conveying the desired impression to their interviewers. This success factor represents the extent to which the impression-management attempt was consistent with normative expectations about dominant and submissive behavior. The subject's task was to watch a short segment of the interview and to determine which type of impression the interviewee was attempting to convey.

The subjects' responses were analyzed in a signal-detection framework. The sensitivity analysis examined differences in the ability of Schematics and Aschematics to discriminate between dominant and submissive behavior. For the taped segments in which the impression managers were successful in their task and seemed to be using appropriate cues to convey their desired impression, the Schematics exhibited better discrimination than the Aschematics. However, when the impression managers were not successful in coming across appropriately to their interviewers, the Schematics were less sensitive than the Aschematics to differences between dominant and submissive impression-management attempts. This may be interpreted as indicating that the Schematics have a more well-defined conception of what constitutes dominant behavior than do the Aschematics. Schematics appear to have a limited latitude of acceptance for what is a relevant behavioral cue for dominance and seem to attend more closely to this restricted range of cues. They appear to be more sensitive to the normatively appropriate behavioral cues and less sensitive to the inappropriate cues than are their Aschematic counterparts. These findings imply that self-schemata enhance an individual's accuracy in social perception under conditions where schema-consistent information is predominant (such as the high success segments in the present study).

Summary of Empirical Results

Together, the studies reviewed in the last three sections strongly indicate that cognitive structures about the self have a pervasive impact on processing information about the self and about others. With respect to the *self*, individuals with self-schemata in particular domains: (1) can process information about the self efficiently (make judgments and decisions with relative ease and certainty); (2) are consistent in their responses; (3) have relatively better recognition memory and recall for information relevant to this domain, (4) can predict future behavior in the domain; (5) can resist information that is counter to a prevailing schema; and (6) evaluate new information for its relevance to a given domain. With respect to processing information about *others*, these individuals: (1) make accurate discriminations in the domain in question; (2) categorize or chunk schema-relevant information differentially; (3) are relatively more sensitive to variations in this domain; (4) select and prefer information that is relevant to this domain; and (5) make confident attributions and inferences about behavior in this domain.

These conclusions, of course, vary tremendously in their level of specificity, in the amount of supporting data, and in the conditions that qualify their validity.

Nevertheless, the existing research justifies the assertion that the self can be reasonably viewed as a system of cognitive structures. It appears that cognitive structures about the self—self-schemata—enable perceivers to detect features and higher-order structure in their own behavior and in that of others to which they would otherwise be insensitive. These schemata appear to be focally active in the interpretation and comprehension of social events and behavior. We posit that if schemata are central structures or processing units in the human information-processing system, and if memory is comprised of these schemata, then some of these structures, the richest and perhaps the most important ones, must be about the self.

It is certainly the case that any of the individual findings presented here can have explanations other than those offered. Some of the findings thus could be explained by a combination of arguments that involve recency and frequency. For example, demonstrations that certain items are more likely to be retrieved from memory, recognized more accurately, or endorsed more quickly and more confidently are not, in and of themselves, direct evidence for the existence and operation of schemata. Nevertheless, when considered in totality, the whole package of results seems to imply the existence of some organization of knowledge that directs the individual to process relevant information differentially and selectively. This concept could, or course, be given other names such as expertise, experience, values, ego-involvement, etc. But the schema language commands a heuristic parsimony that the other concepts do not have.

TOWARD A THEORY OF THE SELF
IN SOCIAL INFORMATION PROCESSING

The nature of the organization of knowledge about the self still needs to be determined and clearly must be determined if the concept is to have continued utility. However, some informed speculations can be made on the basis of the data in hand. Schemata about the self appear to be relatively stable, enduring, and well-articulated knowledge structures. By structure, we mean only at this point a package of knowledge in memory whose elements are interdependent such that they are likely to be evoked jointly. We are likely to have these knowledge structures for most of the important aspects of our social environment. From studies that have compared structures related to the self to structures about well-known others, however, it seems plausible to assert that schemata about the self, although similar to other schemata in many aspects, may be importantly different. There are at least four features that may distinguish the self-structure from other structures: size and complexity, connectedness, frequency of activation, and affect.

Size and Complexity.   For even the most selfless among us, the self is likely to be quite extensive and elaborate, with diverse substructures and connections and thus is quantitatively different from other structures, including those associated with the most significant others in our social environment. Its complexity results from the fact that all the significant events, objects, and situations that have been self-relevant (as well as all the attendant evaluations and interpretations) may be represented here in some form. Even a life-long, bosom buddy could not have a structure about a friend that rivals the friend's own self-structure in extent and articulation. The elaboration or embellishment of a stimulus that appears to result from encoding it within the self-structure can probably explain many of the findings summarized in the section on memory for information about the self. The fact that the self is a large complex structure that makes available an extensive, organized network of representations of past thoughts and feelings can account for differential recognition and recall of self-relevant material, for accurate discrimination along a self-relevant domain, and for the ability to make confident predictions and attributions about one's self and others.

Connectedness. A second difference that is difficult to explicate, but that could have important structural consequences, is that an individual "knows" what the connections or relationships are among the elements or components of the self-structure. The individual can provide the integrative thread that binds together particular ideas and concepts. In representing another person in one's own memory, however, this thread must be woven from repeated associations, inferences, or information provided by the relevant individual. Again, even a life-long friend (who is probably quite certain about many of the relevant connections in our self-structure) cannot have the same degree of certainty as we do about the relationships among the elements that characterize our self. Here, of course, some will be quick to argue that we are really no more accurate about the interconnections in our own self-structures than others are about these interconnections (Bem, 1972). And although this may be true, just the fact of thinking or feeling we are more certain is sufficient to make a difference in how the self is represented in memory. In addition, only the individual can know what aspects of the knowledge represented in his or her self-structure are contrived, or false, or distorted in the service of one or another self-presentational or interpersonal goals. This greater interconnectedness among the elements of the self might account for consistency of responses that are mediated by self-schemata, as well as the demonstrated resistance of the self-structure to contradictory or incongruent information.

Frequency of Activation. A third potentially important difference between self-structures and other structures has to do with the frequency of activation. Any model of the self will probably take as a given that the self (or some aspect of it) is activated very often. As a consequence of this frequent activation, the self-structure may become more articulated and more focused, and thus less malleable. This change in the structure's character may result from its elements becoming more integrated and more unitized (Hayes-Roth, 1977). Thus, frequent activation of a structure results in an increase in the probabilities that certain cognitive elements will be activated jointly. Once the probability that a component of the self-structure will be activated reaches a certain level, there may be a qualitative difference in the processing that results from the activation of this structure. Frequently activated self-structures may engage in conceptually driven, or top-down processing, and search for particular types of confirming evidence. As a consequence, when thinking about the self in certain domains, we may do a great deal of assimilating to the schema, and relatively less accommodating of the schema to fit the constraints of social reality. In contrast, the activation of other types of social structures is more likely to be event driven and result in relatively more accommodation. The idea that the self is more likely to assimilate rather than accommodate incoming information may explain the apparent resistance of the self-structure to change.

Affect   A final, but potentially most important difference between self-schemata and other-schemata has to do with the role of affect. Affect is a central component of our structures about the social world. Recently Zajonc (1980) has suggested that the primary discrimination to be made about all stimuli is an affective one, a good/bad, like/dislike distinction. And this is probably markedly so with respect to the self. It may be, for example, that any event or object that is invested with affect will be relevant to the self. Alternatively, it may be that the self embraces other concepts (see Fig. 2.1) when the concept has a large number of affective bonds. The affect associated with the self may be related to egocentric bias, the pervasive tendency to remember the good, the correct, the responsible, and the successful of our actions relative to their negative counterparts. If we assume that for most people the majority of structures in the self-system are those that promote a positive view of one's self and engender positive affect, then negative information about the self may not be retained, because there will be relatively few structures to assimilate it. Negative information, then, is likely to be encoded with some other knowledge structure. For example, a particularly frightening or threatening childhood incident, such as feeling you were about to drown when a sailboat overturned in a lake, may be associated with fear, failure, and inherently negative views of the self. This incident will not be easily assimilated into the prevailing system of self-structures. Instead, the incident may be encoded and stored with knowledge structures about "sailboats" or about "lakes" that do not have as strict criteria for category inclusion as does the self-structure. The result of this alternative organization may be a very infrequent rehearsal or rethinking of the incident. The incident may then appear to be repressed and will only surface through a directed probing of episodic memory.

We suggest that the self-structure is not only different from other structures, but that it can be viewed as the central structure and the first structure through which all information flows. It is the largest and most available structure (or set of structures) in memory. Attempts are first made to represent incoming data with the self-structure, and then other relevant structures are activated to account for the input. As a result of the top-down processing that characterizes the self,

all stimuli are likely to be at least minimally evaluated or encoded for correspondence with the self-structure. If we are not focusing on the self, or are in
some way outwardly directed, this process may proceed quite automatically or
with little conscious awareness until there is a mismatch such that some input
does not correspond with the prevailing self-structure. If there is a mismatch or a
lack of correspondence between the schema and the input, the individual may become more focally aware of the flow of information and engage in some active,
controlled processing.

The self-structure can be seen as a system of substructures, as a hierarchy of
universal, particularistic, and idiosyncratic knowledge structures about the self
that are embedded within each other. These structures will be activated as processing units depending on the nature or goal of the processing act or task and the
nature of the external stimuli. The repeated activation of some self-structures
causes them to become strong and well-articulated. They structure new input according to their constraints and thus influence the course of information processing. Stimuli that are inconsistent with knowledge stored in the self-structures
will have little chance of representation. For example, if a person who views
himself or herself as extremely concerned and considerate engages in behavior
that may be interpreted as inconsiderate (i.e., being 15 minutes late for an appointment), there are several possible outcomes. The behavior may be ignored (I
didn't realize I was late), or the behavior may be reinterpreted to be seen as consistent with the prevailing self-generalizations (I was late for this appointment
because I was so involved and concerned with another person and her problem).

We have suggested that the self is the "primary" memory structure in the
sense that the self is apt to be the first structure invoked in attempts to account for
input. A majority of stimuli thus are evaluated for self-relevance. This idea is
similar to observations made about a characteristic feature of expertise, namely
the automaticity of an expert's pattern recognition capability. As noted by
DeGroot (1966): "We know that increasing expertise and knowledge in a specific field [chess, for instance] has the effect that things [properties, etc.] which,
at earlier stages, had to be abstracted, or even inferred are apt to be immediately
perceived at later stages. To a rather large extent, abstraction is replaced by perception [p. 33]."

Evidence for automatic processes in cognition have been obtained in a number
of tasks (Schneider & Shiffrin, 1977). These processes are characterized by difficulty of suppression and by absence of capacity requirements. If the self-
structure is automatically processing the input for relevance, this should be
manifest in situations where unattended self-relevant material is picked up or attended to. The so-called "cocktail party phenomenon" is a well-known example
of this type of situation. At a crowded and noisy party, it is often difficult to
make sense of the conversation you are directly involved in. Yet, when your
name is mentioned in a neighboring discussion, you are quite likely to hear it and
orient toward that conversation. In Moray's (1959) dichotic listening studies of

this phenomenon, the subject's name proved to be a very powerful grabber of attention even in the laboratory.

This finding is consistent with the idea that incoming data are automatically processed for self-relevance. In recent studies, Shaffer and LaBerge (1979) found that unattended words in a Stroop-type paradigm were subject to automatic semantic processing. In a Stroop (1935) paradigm, subjects are instructed to respond to one class of stimuli and to ignore another class. For example, subjects might be asked to say the name of an object drawn in outline and to ignore the word written in block letters at the center of the drawing. The typical dependent measure in this paradigm is the amount of interference (e.g., elevated reaction times) associated with the type of to-be-ignored stimuli. Current efforts in the program of research reported here involve an attempt to use the Stroop paradigm to evaluate the idea that stimuli are ''automatically processed for self-relevance'' as they enter the information-processing sequence. The study uses a procedure similar to that of Shaffer and LaBerge and seeks to compare the magnitude of interference caused by self-relevant material with the amount of semantic interference that Shaffer and LaBerge (1979) report. The results bear on the viability of our hypotheses concerning the ubiquitous nature of self-relevant processing.

With these and related research efforts, it should be possible to develop an understanding of the nature of the self-structure and to implicate it more specifically in the information-processing sequence. At the very least, an explicit cognitive model of the self in social information processing will allow us to pose and begin to answer, with some degree of refinement, a wide range of questions about the nature of self-structures or the self-system. At the same time, theorizing and research about the specific nature of self-structures will provide evidence about rich, highly articulated, affect-laden knowledge structures, and how they structure the course of social information processing.

ACKNOWLEDGMENT

The authors wish to thank S. Dumais, V. Geller, R. Hamill, and R. B. Zajonc for their comments on an earlier draft.

REFERENCES

Bem, D. J.   Self-perception theory. In L. Berkowitz (Ed.), *Advances in experimental social psychology* (Vol. 6). New York: Academic Press, 1972.

Bem, S. L.   The measurement of psychological androgyny. *Journal of Consulting and Clinical Psychology,* 1974 *42,* 155–162.

Bem, S. L.   On the utility of alternative procedures for assessing psychological androgyny. *Journal of Consulting and Clinical Psychology,* 1977, *45,* 196–205.

Bertenthal, B. I. & Fischer, K. W.   Development of self-recognition in the infant. *Developmental Psychology,* 1978, *14,* 155–162.

Boden, M. A.   *Artificial intelligence and natural man.* New York: Basic Books, 1979.

Bradley, G. W.   Self-serving biases in the attribution process: A reexamination of the factor fiction question. *Journal of Personality and Social Psychology,* 1978, *36,* 56–71.

Brenner, M.   The next-in-line effect. *Journal of Verbal Learning and Verbal Behavior,* 1973, *12,* 320–323.

Bruner, J. S.   Going beyond the information given. In H. Gruber (Eds.), *Contemporary approaches to cognition.* Cambridge, Mass.: Harvard Press, 1957.

Cartwright, D.   Self-consistency as a factor affecting immediate recall. *Journal of Abnormal and Social Psychology,* 1956, *52,* 212–219.

Chase, W. G., & Simon, H. A.   Perception in chess. *Cognitive Psychology,* 1973, *4,* 55–81.

Combs, A. & Snygg, D.   *Individual behavior* (2nd ed.). New York: Harper, 1959.

DeGroot, A. D.   Perception and memory vs. thought. In B. Kleinmutz (Ed.), *Problem-solving: Research, method, and theory.* New York: Wiley, 1966.

Epstein, S.   The self-concept revisited: Or a theory of a theory. *American Psychologist,* 1973, *28,* 404–416 .

Fong, G., & Markus, H.   Self-schemas and judgments about others. *Social Cognition* (in press).

Goffman, E.   *Presentation of self in everyday life.* Garden City, N. Y.: Doubleday Anchor Books, 1959.

Greenwald, A. G.   The totalitarian ego: Fabrication and revision of personal history. *American Psychologist,* 1980, *25,* 603–618.

Guntrip, H.   *Psychoanalytic theory, therapy, and the self.* New York: Basic Books, 1971.

Hall, G. S.   Some aspects of the early sense of self. *American Journal of Psychology,* 1898, *9,* 351–395.

Hamill, R.   *Selective influences of the self on social perception and memory.* Unpublished dissertation, University of Michigan, 1980.

Hayes-Roth, B.   Evolution of cognitive structures and processes. *Psychological Review,* 1977, *84,* 260–278.

James W.   *Psychology, a briefer course.* New York: Holt, 1915.

Jarvella, R. J., & Collars, J. G.   Memory for the intentions of sentences. *Memory and Cognition,* 1974, *2,* 185–188.

Keenan, J. M., & Baillet, S. D.   Memory for personally and socially significant events. In R. S. Nickerson (Ed.), *Attention and performance* (VIII). Hillsdale, N. J.: Lawrence Erlbaum Associates, in press, 1979.

Kelly, G. A.   *The psychology of personal constructs.* New York: Norton, 1955.

Kendzierski, D.   Self-schemata and scripts: The recall of self-referent and scriptal information. *Personality and Social Psychology Bulletin,* 1980, *6,* 23–29.

Kernberg, O.   *Borderline conditions in pathological narcissism.* International University Press, 1977.

Krech, D., & Crutchfield, R.   *Theory and problems of social psychology.* New York: McGraw-Hill, 1948.

Kuiper, N. A., & Derry, P. A.   The self as a cognitive prototype: An application to person perception and depression. In N. Cantor & J. Kihlstrom (Eds.), *Cognition, social interaction, and personality.* Hillsdale, N. J.: Lawrence Erlbaum Associates, 1980.

Kuiper, N. A., & Rogers, T. B.   Encoding of personal information: Self-other differences. *Journal of Personality and Social Psychology,* 1979, *13,* 119–124.

Lingoes, J. C.   *The Guttman-Lingoes nonmetric program series.* Ann Arbor, Mich.: Mathesis Press, 1968.

Lord, C. G.   Schemas and images as memory aids: Two modes of processing social information. *Journal of Personality and Social Psychology,* 1980, *38,* 257–269.

Markus, H.   Self-schemata and processing information about the self. *Journal of Personality and Social Psychology,* 1977, *35,* 63–78.

Markus, H., Crane, M., Bernstein, S., & Siladi, M.   *Self-schemas and gender. Journal of Personality and Social Psychology,* 1982, *42,* 38–50.

Markus, H., Crane, M., & Siladi, M.   *Cognitive consequences of androgyny.* Paper presented at the meeting of the Midwestern Psychological Association, May, 1978.

Markus, H., & Fong, G.   *The role of the self in other perception.* Unpublished manuscript, University of Michigan, 1979.

Markus, H., Hamill, R., & Sentis, K.   *Thinking fat: Self-schemas for body weight and the processing of weight-relevant information.* Paper presented at the meeting of the American Psychological Association, Montreal, 1980.

Markus, H., & Smith, J.   The influence of self-schemas on the perception of others. In N. Cantor & J. Kihlstrom (Eds.), *Personality, cognition, and social interaction.* Hillsdale, N. J.: Lawrence Erlbaum Associates, 1981.

Markus, H., Smith, J., & Moreland, R. L.   *Self-schemas and other perception.* Paper presented at the meeting of the American Psychological Association, New York, August, 1979.

McDougall, W.   *An introduction to social psychology.* Boston: Luce, 1921.

Messick, D. M., & Sentis, K.   Fairness and preference. *Journal of Experimental Social Psychology*, 1979, *154*, 418–434.

Miller, D. T.   What constitutes a self-serving attributional bias? A reply to Bradley. *Journal of Personality and Social Psychology*, 1978, *36*, 1221–1223.

Miller, D. T., & Ross, M.   Self-serving biases in the attribution of causality: Fact or Fiction? *Psychological Bulletin*, 1975, *82*, 213–225.

Miller, G. A., Galanter, E., & Pribram, K. H.   *Plans and the structure of behavior.* New York: Holt, Rinehart, & Winston, 1960.

Moray, N.   Attention in dichotic listening. Affective cues and the influence of instructions. *Quarterly Journal of Experimental Psychology*, 1959, *12*, 56–60.

Neisser, U.   *Cognition and reality.* San Francisco: W. H. Freeman, 1976.

Newtson, D.   Attribution and the unit of perception of ongoing behavior. *Journal of Personality and Social Psychology*, 1973, *1*, 28–38.

Palmer, S. E.   Hierarchical structure in perceptual representation: *Cognitive Psychology*, 1977, *9*, 441–474.

Palmer, S. E.   Fundamental aspects of cognitive representation. In E. Rosch & B. Lloyd (Eds.), *Cognition and categorization.* Hillsdale, N. J.: Lawrence Erlbaum Associates, 1978.

Reitman, J. S.   Skilled perception in GO: Deducing memory structures for interresponse times. *Cognitive Psychology*, 1976, *8*, 336–356.

Reykowski, J.   Position of self-structure in a cognitive system and prosocial orientation. *Dialectics and Humanism*, 1975, *4*, 19–30.

Rogers, C. R.   *Client-centered therapy.* Boston: Houghton Mifflin, 1951.

Rogers, T. B.   Self-reference in memory: Recognition of personality items. *Journal of Research in Personality*, 1977, *11*, 295–305.

Rogers, T. B., Kuiper, N. A., & Kirker, W. S.   Self-reference and the encoding of personal information. *Journal of Personality and Social Psychology*, 1977, *35*, 677–688.

Rogers, T. B., Rogers, P. J., & Kuiper, N. A.   Evidence for the self as a cognitive prototype. The "false alarm effect." *Personality and Social Psychology Bulletin*, 1979, *5*, 53–56.

Ross, L., Lepper, M., & Hubbard, M.   Perseverance in self perception and social perception: Biased attributional processes in the debriefing paradigm. *Journal of Personality and Social Psychology*, 1975, *37*(4), 322–336.

Ross, M., & Sicoly, F.   *Egocentric biases in recall and attribution.* Manuscript submitted for publication, 1978.

Rumelhart, D. E., & Ortony, A.   The representation of knowledge in memory. In R. C. Anderson, R. J. Spiro, & W. E. Montague (Eds.), *Schooling and the aquisition of knowledge.* Hillsdale , N. J.: Lawrence Erlbaum Associates, 1977.

Rumelhart, D. E., & Norman, D.   Accretion, tuning, and restructuring: Three modes of learning. In J. Cotton & R. Klatsky (Eds.), *Sematic factors in cognition.* Hillsdale, N. J.: Lawrence Erlbaum Associates, 1978.

Sarbin, T. R.   A preface to a psychological analysis of the self. *Psychological Review*, 1962, *59*, 11–22.

Schneider, W., & Shiffrin, R. M.   Controlled and automatic human information processing: I. Detection, search, and attention. *Psychological Review,* 1977, *84,* 1–66.

Sentis, K., & Burnstein, E.   Remembering schema-consistent information: Effects of a balance schema on recognition memory. *Journal of Personality and Social Psychology,* 1979, *37 ,* 2200–2211.

Sentis, K., & Geller, V.   *Effects of self-schemas on impression formation.* Unpublished manuscript, Bell Laboratories, 1979.

Sentis, K., & Markus, H.   *Self-schemas and recognition memory.* Unpublished manuscript, University of Michigan, 1979.

Shaffer, W. O., & LaBerge, D.   Automatic semantic processing of unattended words. *Journal of Verbal Learning and Verbal Behavior,* 1979, *18,* 403–426.

Sherif, M., & Cantril, H.   *The psychology of ego-involvement.* New York: Wiley, 1947.

Smith, E. E., Adams, N., & Schorr, D.   Fact retrieval and the paradox of interference. *Cognitive Psychology,* 1978, *10,* 438–464.

Snyder, M., & Cantor, N.   Testing hypothesis about other people: The use of historical knowledge. *Journal of Experimental Social Psychology,* in press.

Snyder, M., & Swann, W. B., Jr.   Hypothesis testing processes in social interaction. *Journal of Personality and Social Psychology,* 1978, *36,* 1202–1212.

Snyder, M., & Uranowitz, S. W.   Reconstructing the past: Some cognitive consequences of person perception. *Journal of Personality and Social Psychology,* 1978, *36,* 941–950.

Stroop, J. R.   Studies of interference in serial verbal reactions. *Journal of Experimental Psychology,* 1935, *18,* 693–662.

Sweeney, P., & Moreland, R. L.   *Self-schemas and the perseverance of beliefs about the self.* Paper presented at the meeting of American Psychological Association, Montreal, 1980.

Wallen, R.   Ego-involvement as a determinant of selective forgetting. *Journal of Abnormal and Social Psychology,* 1942, *37,* 20–39.

Wortman, C. B.   Causal attributions and personal control. In J. H. Harvey, W. J. Ickes, & R. F. Kidd (Eds.), *New directions in attribution research* (Vol. I). Hillsdale, N. J.: Lawrence Erlbaum Associates, 1976.

Zajonc, R. B.   Feeling and thinking: Preferences need no inferences. *American Psychologist,* 1980, *35,* 151–175.

Zeller, A.F.   An experimental analogue of repression: I, Historical summary. *Psychological Bulletin,* 1950, *47,* 39–51.

Significant Others in Self-Space: Sex Differences and Developmental Trends in the Social Self

William J. McGuire
Claire V. McGuire
Yale University

"Self-space" is used here to denote the content that is available to the person when he/she reflects upon the self. Operationally, it is the material that the person reports when asked in a nonspecific context, "Tell us about yourself." The more recent work reported in this chapter focuses on the extent to which this self-space is occupied by thoughts of significant others and tests hypotheses about how the extent and contents of this "social self" vary with gender and age during childhood and adolescence. In this introductory section we discuss the "spontaneous self-concept" strategy used in our research program, summarizing previous work we did on distinctiveness of personal characteristics as a determinant of their salience. The remainder of the chapter describes our current "social self" research on sex differences and developmental trends in the way that children define themselves in terms of significant others.

The Spontaneous Self-Concept Approach

For some years (McGuire, 1973, 1981) we have been advocating a "contextualist" philosophy of science, one of whose basic tenets is that empirical research actually is (and ought to be) a hypothesis-constructing rather than hypothesis-testing process. We have argued that psychology would advance more quickly and gracefully if this contextualist process were stressed rather than suppressed in the design and reporting of research. A corollary of the contextualist position is that the researcher should adopt a low-profile approach to the participants, using low-structured measuring procedures that leave the participants room to provide more informative data than is possible in the usual reactive approach that constrains the participant to respond within the structured categories of a dimension selected a priori by the researcher.

About 95% of all self-concept research, as reported in Wylie's (1974, 1979) review of the topic, uses the "reactive" rather than "spontaneous" self-concept approach; that is, in almost all this work the experimenter specifies the dimension on which the participant is to define him or herself, leaving for the participant only the reactive option of indicating where he or she would conceptualize the self as falling on the researcher-selected dimension if he or she ever happened to think of that dimension. The reactive approach yields no new information on how often one thinks of oneself in terms of that researcher-selected dimension but only the as-if information about where one would perceive the self on the dimension if one ever thought of the self in terms of it. A researcher using our spontaneous self-concept approach, on the other hand, presents a much lower profile to the respondent, using a relatively low-structured probe (such as "Tell us about yourself") and so obtains information, not only on how the participant would conceptualize the self as falling on some preselected dimension, but also as regards the extent to which the various dimensions are salient when one thinks about the self.

This information loss entailed by the narrow channeling of most contemporary self-concept research within the reactive approach is further aggravated by the fact that most researchers converge on the same dimension, self-evaluation. Preoccupation with this evaluative dimension has been so prevalent that Wylie's two-volume review of the literature could as accurately have been called "Self-esteem" as "Self-concept." Self-evaluation is indeed an important and salient aspect of people's self-concepts, but it seems excessive that 95% of all research supposedly studying how people think about themselves focuses only on their self-esteem. Our own spontaneous self-concept research indicates that when one allows the participant to choose the dimensions of self-description (by permissively asking "Tell us abour yourself"), fewer than 10% of the responses are explicitly self-evaluative (McGuire, McGuire, & Winton, 1979; McGuire & Padawer–Singer, 1976).

Our position might give an exaggerated appearance of lonely advocacy of the spontaneous self-concept approach if we did not make two qualifications explicit. Firstly, we are not insisting that the reactive self-concept approach is always inferior to the spontaneous self-concept strategy. When an investigator's guiding ideas do focus the predictions on an a priori specifiable dimension of the self, then the reactive approach is more cost-effective in eliciting relevant data. What we are urging is a better balance, that the currently almost exclusive use of the reactive approach be balanced by more work that uses the spontaneous self-concept approach, thus allowing the investigation of theories, not only about how people would think of themselves on certain dimensions if the dimensions ever occurred to them, but also on the more interesting questions regarding which are the dimensions on which people actually do think of themselves.

A second qualification is that our advocacy of the spontaneous approach, although lonely, is not completely isolated. Two other traditions in the self-concept literature have used this low-profile approach. One is the W–A–Y (Who

Are You) approach used by Bugental, Zelen, and their colleagues (Bugental, 1964). The other tradition, employing the T–S–T (Twenty Statement Test), derives from the symbolic interaction theory of Manford Kuhn (Kuhn & McPartland, 1954). A useful summary of the work on these two instruments can be found in Spitzer, Couch, and Stratton (1971). The reader is also referred to Montemayor and Eisen (1977) and Keller, Ford, and Meacham (1978) for developmental work employing a spontaneous measure.

The next section summarizes our already published spontaneous self-concept research on the distinctiveness postulate that predicts that one tends to define oneself in terms of one's peculiarities. The remainder of the chapter then reports our new spontaneous self-concept research on the "social self," the extent and manner in which children define themselves in relation to significant others when asked nondirectively to "Tell us about yourself."

Attribute's Distinctiveness and Its Salience in Self-Space

The distinctiveness postulate asserts that when one is confronted by a complex stimulus whose aspects one cannot fully encode, one tends to notice selectively its more peculiar aspects. Behind this distinctiveness postulate lies a more basic assumption that humans' cognitive processing is selective, such that their senses take in more information than they can effectively register.

That humans have evolved with an information-encoding economy such that their senses and memory present them at any instant with more information than can be centrally processed into awareness can be demonstrated by a "thought" experiment. Consider that one is contemplating a roomful of people and then suddenly closes one's eyes and is asked specific questions about what one has just been observing. Often one cannot answer questions about parts of the scene that were just impinging on foveal vision, for example, the hair color of the person in the center of the front row, or whether he was wearing a sweater or a jacket. Among the various ways that humans cope with this information overload— chunking, parallel processing, diverting cognitive capacity from other functions, temporary storage for later processing, etc.—we discuss here only one, selectively noticing some aspects while ignoring the others.

This selective perception can be based on any of a number of factors, for example, the more energy-intense aspects of the stimulus may be selectively noticed, or the aspects we have been reinforced for noticing in the past, or the aspects most relevant to our enduring values or our transient need states, etc. (McGuire et al., 1979). The basis of selectivity stressed by the distinctiveness postulate is that we tend to notice those aspects of the stimulus that are most peculiar in our current (or habitual) environment. For example, as regards the perception of persons, one notices another individual's hair color, height, or whatever, in direct proportion to how peculiar the individual is in each of these physical characteristics. One perceives a person in terms of his/her height if the person is tall or short, but not if of average stature.

The distinctiveness postulate is appropriately applied to one's self-perception because the self is a complex stimulus, the human individual being intrinsically complicated and one being relatively knowledgeable about the self. Hence, when suddenly asked to "Tell us about yourself," there has to be a great deal of selectivity in what comes to consciousness and is reported. The distinctiveness postulate predicts that when one is given this spontaneous self-concept probe, one describes the self in terms of a given individual-difference dimension to the extent that one's position on that dimension is peculiar in one's usual social environment. For example, left-handers would be more likely than right-handed people to describe themselves in terms of their handedness; a blond person from a Mediterranean country is more likely to describe him/herself in terms of hair color than is a blond from Scandinavia. Distinctiveness can also be affected by the momentary, as well as chronic, social environment; for example, in a racially mixed crowd, people of the minority ethnicity will be more likely to think of themselves in terms of their race than will people of the majority ethnicity. Furthermore, by changing the person's social environment so that different characteristics become peculiar, we can change what is salient in his/her spontaneous self-concept: For example, when a black woman is asked to describe herself while sitting in a room with 12 black men, she is more likely to describe herself as a woman than as a black; but when she is in a room with a dozen white women, she is more likely to describe herself as a black than as a woman. In technical terms, we tend to notice aspects of ourselves to the extent that they have high information value (i.e., their atypicality makes them unpredictable). In the following sections, we describe a series of studies designed to test predictions derived from the distinctiveness postulate regarding what is salient in the spontaneous self-concept.

Salience of Physical Characteristics in the Self-Concept

The distinctiveness postulate implies that, when asked to "Tell us about yourself," a person will describe him or herself in terms of a given physical characteristic such as height or hair color to the extent that his/her height or hair color is peculiar in his or her usual social milieu. Several studies have confirmed these implications (McGuire & McGuire, 1980, 1981; McGuire & Padawer-Singer, 1976). The procedure in these studies called for students to participate in two sessions at their school, during the first of which we elicited their spontaneous self-concept by asking the question, "Tell us about yourself," and allowing 5 or 7 minutes for oral or written responding, depending on the experimental condition. These spontaneous self-descriptions were subsequently analyzed for mention of physical characteristics by coders unfamiliar with the hypotheses. In the second session, the students were asked to complete a structured questionnaire that asked them to indicate their specific physical characteristics, such as their height, weight, etc. From these second-session data on actual physical characteristics, we calculated the atypicality of each child on each physical trait, as compared to the other students in his/her class. The more peculiar the person is on a given characteristic, the greater the predicted probability that he/she would have spontaneously mentioned it in describing the self in response to the first-session "Tell us about yourself" question.

In the most elaborate study to test the physical characteristics prediction (McGuire & McGuire, 1981), we elicited the spontaneous self-concepts of 1000 school children in a medium-sized industrial city in the Northeast, representatively selecting 100 boys and 100 girls at each of five grade levels, the fifth, seventh, ninth, eleventh, and twelfth. The children participated while in their intact classrooms, so that we could use the child's classmates as his/her social environment for defining which of the child's physical characteristics were typical and which distinctive. Because the "Tell us about yourself" spontaneous self-concepts were elicited in this group classroom situation, we used written responses in this study (and thus did not study children younger than fifth graders). We tested the distinctiveness prediction in terms of the four physical characteristics that prestudy showed to be mentioned by 10% or more of the children in 5-minute written responses to the "Tell us about yourself" question. These were height (19% of the children spontaneously defining themselves in terms of their height), weight (11%), hair color (14%), and eye color (11%). The original publication (McGuire & McGuire, 1981) gives further details about the method and other aspects of the results.

The results lend significant support to three of the four hypotheses derived from the distinctiveness postulate. The analyses for all four physical characteristics were similar, so we describe them in detail only for height. Children's self-report of their height when they were explicitly asked in the second session allowed us to classify each of them as short, average, or tall. The "average" group included those within one inch of the mean height of children of their own sex at their grade level; the "tall" and "short" groups included five inches above or below, respectively, of this mean height. For the children of average height, only 17% had spontaneously described themselves in terms of their height in response to the "Tell us about yourself" question, whereas 27% of the tall and short children had spontaneously mentioned their height (a difference significant at the .05 level by a chi-square test). The 17% spontaneous mention of height by children of average height was exceeded both by the short children (25% of whom spontaneously mention their height) and the tall children (31% mention).

Comparable analyses were done for the other three commonly mentioned physical characteristics: weight, hair color, and eye color. The prediction was confirmed for weight as it was for height. For children of average weight (within 6 pounds of their grade's mean weight for own gender), only 6% spontaneously mentioned their weight in their spontaneous self-concept, whereas 12% of the heavy and light children (defined as those 14 pounds above or below their class's mean weight) spontaneously mentioned weight. The distinctiveness prediction received less strong support from the data on salience of more subtle physical characteristics of hair color and eye color. It was confirmed, though just slightly above the .05 level, for hair color: Only 13% of the children with the majority (black and brown) hair color spontaneously mentioned their hair color in the first session as part of the spontaneous self-concept, whereas 17% of those of atypical blond-and red-haired children had spontaneously described themselves in terms of their hair color. There was a slight trend in the confirmatory direction for eye color, but it did not reach the conventional .05 level of significance for this dimension: 11% of the brown-eyed majority spontaneously mentioned eye color as part of their spontaneous self-concept, only trivially less than the 13% mention by the blue-eyed minority.

In another set of studies we tested the distinctiveness postulate prediction about a low-salient physical characteristic, handedness. Because it is the left-handers who are peculiar in this regard, we would predict that they are more likely spontaneously to describe themselves in terms of their sinistrality than are right-handers to mention their dexterity. Analysis of the self-descriptions of 1732 respondents from first graders through college students confirms this prediction. Only one-half of 1% of the right-handers mentioned this as part of their self-descriptions, as contrasted with 3% of the left-handers, a difference significant at the .01 level (McGuire & McGuire, 1980).

Distinctiveness and the Spontaneous Salience of Ethnicity

The distinctiveness postulate has implications for the salience in self-concept not only of physical characteristics but also for socially sensitive characteristics such as ethnicity and gender. For example, as regards ethnicity, the distinctiveness postulate predicts that in racially segregated schools the child's ethnicity should have a very low salience in his/her self-concept, because there ethnicity has low "information" value; but as schools become integrated, racial mix makes one's ethnicity more distinctive and thus enhances the tendency of the children to define themselves (and their classmates) in terms of ethnicity. Ethnicity should be particularly salient in the self-concept of members of the racial minority in the integrated school.

To test these predictions, we studied the spontaneous self-concepts of 560 students drawn from the public schools of a middle-sized manufacturing city in the Northeast. In this study, we used individual interviewing so that the children could respond to the "Tell us about yourself" question orally, enabling us to extend the age range to younger children than is possible with the written responses used in the previous study. We selected 70 boys and 70 girls from each of four grade levels (the first, third, seventh, and eleventh) chosen from a representative set of schools within the city. The oral responses to "Tell us about yourself" were recorded, transcribed, and content analyzed for spontaneous mentions of ethnicity to provide the dependent variable measure. The independent variable score, the child's actual ethnicity, was judged and recorded by the interviewer on the basis of appearance, name, accent, etc. By these criteria, 82% of the children were classified as white English speakers, 9% as Black, and 8% as Hispanic.

The results were in accord with the predictions from the distinctiveness postulate. Among the majority group, the 82% English-speaking whites, only 1%
spontaneously mention their ethnicity in giving their self-concept, whereas
among the other two (minority) ethnic groups, the tendency to describe oneself in
terms of ethnicity was much higher ($p < .01$), 17% of the Black students and 14%
of the Hispanic children spontaneously mentioning their ethnicity in giving their
self-concept. A further prediction from the distinctiveness postulate is that children within any ethnic group will show a lesser tendency to think of themselves
in terms of their race as their own ethnic group comes to constitute a larger proportion of the total student body. For an overall test of this prediction, we partitioned the students of all three ethnicities into two subgroups: an
"underrepresented" condition that included those in classes where their own ethnic group constituted a lesser proportion of the class than their ethnic group constituted within the overall school system versus an "overrepresented" condition
that included children in classes where their own ethnic group constituted a
greater proportion of that class than it did of the total school system. We found
that in the underrepresented condition, 6% of the children spontaneously mention
their ethnicity, whereas only 2% of those whose ethnic group constituted an
atypically large proportion of the class members spontaneously mentioned their
ethnicity ($p < .05$). However, although this tendency obtains for the overall
sample and for the white, English speakers and for the Hispanics separately,
there is a (nonsignificant) reversal for the Blacks, conceivably because the Black
consciousness movement constitutes a social factor that outweighs the
distinctiveness-postulate cognitive factor, and because such consciousness-
raising social forces among Black students arise only if there is a critical mass of
Black students in the school environment (McGuire et al., 1978.).

Salience of Gender in the Self-Concept

We also tested a gender-salience implication of the distinctiveness postulate, implying that one is more conscious of oneself as a male or a female to the extent
that one lives in a social milieu where the other gender is numerically preponder-
ant. We tested this gender-salience prediction using the same data as supplied to
test the ethnicity-salience prediction, that is, the oral responses to "Tell us about
yourself" obtained from 70 boys and 70 girls at the four grade levels, first, third,
seventh, and eleventh. For testing this gender prediction, the recorded and transcribed responses were scored for spontaneous self-descriptions in terms of one's
being male or female.

As the independent variable measure for the gender hypotheses, we could not
use the classroom as the social milieu in terms of which to measure the extent to
which the child's own gender is in the majority or minority because school policy, to have a relatively equal number of boys and girls in each classroom, resulted in little variance from class to class in the boy/girl ratio. Instead, the

independent variable's measure of gender distinctiveness in one's social milieu was calculated in terms of the child's household sex composition. As regards family, there was considerable variance among the children in the extent to which males versus females predominated in their home environment. This being the case, the distinctiveness postulate predicted that boys would be more likely to describe themselves in terms of their maleness to the extent that the number of sisters exceed their number of brothers, and that girls, conversely, would be more likely to describe themselves as being female to the extent that they had more brothers than sisters. To test this prediction, after the children furnished their spontaneous self-concepts, they were interviewed about their household composition so that number of brothers and sisters could be scored. The results confirm the prediction. Boys are progressively more likely to describe themselves in terms of their maleness as we go toward increasing proportion of females in the household and girls are progressively more likely to describe themselves as females to the extent that the proportion of males in the household predominates, the trend for each of the genders being significant beyond the .05 level (McGuire, McGuire, & Winton, 1979).

A further prediction is that father's absence actually increases salience of being male in the boy's self-concept, because the boy's maleness would tend to be more distinctive in a household with father absent. In our sample, 33 of the boys came from fatherless homes (about equal to the national U. S. average) and 18% of these spontaneously describe themselves as boys; on the other hand, only 7% of the 227 boys who had both mother and father present in the home spontaneously mention that they were male, a difference in gender salience significant at the .05 level.

These confirmations of the predictions that ethnicity and gender become more salient in the spontaneous self-concept as they become more distinctive have theory-clarifying implications. Social learning theorists have predicted a deficiency in "masculine" behavior in boys whose fathers are absent or who lack male siblings, basing the prediction on lack of appropriate role models and reinforcers for the boys' carrying out a prescribed "male" behavior when fewer older males are present. The distinctiveness postulate, on the other hand, predicts a contrasting tendency for boys whose fathers are absent or who lack male siblings to be more conscious of their maleness due to its distinctiveness in their social milieu. The results show that these boys from predominantly female households, however poor at carrying out role-prescribed male behavior they may be, are more conscious of themselves as males than are boys from more masculine households.

Confirmation of the distinctiveness-postulate prediction that ethnicity and gender become more salient with distinctiveness has policy as well as theory implications. That people are more likely to think about themselves (and probably others) in terms of ethnicity to the extent that the racial integration of their social milieu makes their ethnicity more distinctive and "informative" raises social policy problems. If one wishes to have an integrated society in school and elsewhere, but one also wishes to have a society where people do not think of themselves or one another primarily in terms of ethnicity, then these findings suggest that one has a conflict of values, because increasing integration will tend to enhance racial salience in self and others. There are also implications for the controversy regarding cross-racial adoption (Ladner, 1977). After cross-racial adoption became increasingly common in the 1960s, some social workers protested that this practice would weaken the racial identity of minority-group children adopted into white households, with the result that policy changes have caused a decline in interracial adoption during the 1970s. Our results suggest, contrary to this social-worker concern, that minority children adopted into white households will be more likely to define themselves in terms of their distinctive ethnicity than will minority children adopted into households of their own ethnicity.

In this chapter we are stressing the advantage of the spontaneous self-concept approach over the more prevalent reactive self-concept procedures, in that it allows us to answer interesting questions about what are indeed the dimensions in which people perceive themselves. Our first series of studies, showing that people tend to think of themselves in terms of their peculiarities, are here described only briefly because detailed reports have already been published elsewhere (McGuire & Padawer-Singer, 1976; McGuire, McGuire, Child, & Fujioka, 1978; McGuire, McGuire, and Winton, 1979; McGuire & McGuire, 1980, 1981). In the remainder of the chapter we describe a newer line of research in more detail because it has not been published elsewhere. This second line of work tests the spontaneous self-concept approach to sex difference and age-trend hypotheses about the "social self," that is, about the ways in which children define themselves in relation to significant other people.

SIGNIFICANT OTHERS IN THE SELF-CONCEPT: HYPOTHESES

People as social beings are highly dependent on and oriented toward other humans and will to a sizable extent define themselves in terms of their relationships to other people. In his most social psychological monograph, Freud (1921) has argued that in the autistic mental acts that are the domain of individual psychology, as well as when one is engaged in interpersonal activities, someone else is invariably involved (as a model, object, helper, opponent, etc.) in one's consciousness, even of one's individual self. Because children's high dependency leaves them particularly immersed and dependent on the social environment, we anticipate that the prevalence of other people in the spontaneous self-concept will be particularly high during childhood and adolescence. In this section we describe our postulates and predictions about the extent and nature of self-definition in terms of significant others, first describing hypotheses about sex differences and then about developmental age trends regarding the place of social self within the total spontaneous self-concept domain.

Sex Differences in the Social Self

The first of our three basic postulates about sex differences in the self-concept is that girls are more people oriented than boys, so that they more than boys will define themselves in terms of significant others. Our second postulate is that girls, leading a more sheltered life, will be more parochial than boys in choosing significant others in terms of whom to define themselves. Thirdly, we postulate that boys and girls will make reciprocal choices in defining themselves in terms of siblings and parents, reflecting the complementary roles to which they are biologically oriented and are being socialized. In the paragraphs that follow, each of these postulates are discussed as regards the theorizing from which it derives and the specific predictions that it yields, and which are tested in the research reported in this chapter.

The Social Self Larger in Girls Than Boys.   Our basic sex-differences postulate is that the social self occupies a greater proportion of total self-space in girls than in boys, girls defining themselves in terms of significant others more than do boys. Operationally, we predict that girls' responses to the open-ended probe, "Tell us about yourself," will contain more self-definitions in terms of significant others than will boys'. Our theorizing here is that for human survival the biological realities of motherhood make social orientation even more important for females than for males, and that this sex difference in nurturant proclivities generalizes to other social relationships; in addition, socialization practices will tend to accentuate any slight biological gender differences in this direction. (Of course, we recognize that in time these sex differences may disappear as society develops more egalitarian roles for men and woman.)

From this first postulate that girls are more people oriented than boys we draw two hypotheses about the self-concept. Firstly and most fundamentally, it is predicted that girls will define themselves in terms of significant others more than will boys. Secondly, it is predicted that girls, being more focused on their social world, will have a more differentiated view of people, defining themselves in terms of specific individuals (e.g., "mother" or "father") rather than general categories of people (e.g., "parents"), whereas the less socially involved boys will perceive significant others in more generic terms (e.g., parents, human beings, etc.).

Girls' Social Selves Less Cosmopolitan Than Boys'.   Our second sex-difference postulate is that girls are more parochial than boys in their self-definition in terms of significant others. Underlying this postulate is the assumption that girls' interests are more channeled toward domestic concerns, and their more sheltered upbringing leaves their interpersonal relations less cosmopolitan than boys', with the result that their self-definitions in terms of others tend to be more concentrated on kin and peers. Specific hypotheses derived from this postulate are that girls' social selves, more than boys', will be formed in terms of family members rather than nonkin persons, and that the girls are more peer oriented (focused on significant others of their own age and gender) than are boys.

Sex Differences in Parent and Sib Orientations.   The third sex-difference postulate deals with self-definition in terms of nuclear family members, asserting that children form their self-concepts in terms of the parent of their own gender and in terms of siblings of the other gender. This postulate follows from the assumption that the child's self-concept development is channeled toward his or her destined role in the procreative family, so that the child focuses on adults (such as parents) of his/her own gender (boys on the father and girls on the mother) for models of the self-image and behavioral patterns that the child must acquire to carry out his or her adult roles. But where age peers (such as siblings) are concerned, the child's destined role in the procreative family involves forging a self-concept in terms of relationships to age peers of the other gender. Hence, the child will focus on peers of the opposite gender, boys developing self-concepts in terms of their relations to their sisters and girls in terms of relations to brothers.

Age Trends in the Social Self

Our hypotheses about age trends in the extent and manner of one's self-definition in terms of significant others are derived from three postulates. The first is that as the child grows and becomes more independent other people occupy a decreasing portion of the self-space. A second postulate is that as the child matures the social self shifts from preoccupations with nurturing adults toward a focus on peers. A third postulate is that as the child grows the significant others for self-definition shift from family members to nonkin. The assumptions underlying these three age-trend postulates and the specific predictions derived from them for testing in the present study are described in the paragraphs that follow.

Contraction of the Social Self with Age.   The first developmental postulate, that as the child grows older his/her self-concept becomes progressively less concerned with other people, is based on the assumption that self-definition in terms of other people is a reflection of dependency; hence, as the child becomes more autonomous (Maccoby & Masters, 1970), self-definition will derive less from one's relationships to other people. Three types of hypotheses are drawn from this postulated age-related desocialization of the self-concept. Firstly, it is predicted that as the child grows, a decreasing proportion of the child's self-descriptions will involve significant others. Secondly, this desocialization will be reflected in a deindividuating of significant others, so that as the child grows older the social self will be defined increasingly in terms of general categories of people rather than specific individuals. A third, somewhat more tenuous derivation is that as the child grows older the social self will involve an increasing proportion of negative-affect significant others.

Increasing Peer Orientation with Age.   The second postulate, that the social self becomes progressively more oriented toward age peers rather than authoritative adults, derives from assumptions about dependency and social roles. It is assumed that because the young child is so dependent on nurturing adults his or her self-definition in terms of significant others will concentrate on these authority figures; as the child develops more autonomy, his or her self-concept will be formed more in the context of relations to socializing peers rather than authoritative adults (Hartup, 1970). A related assumption underlying the second postulate is that there is a shift in social milieu from early childhood confinement to the family of orientation toward greater involvement in peer groups as the child matures. From this postulate are derived predictions that as the child grows older his/her self-definition in terms of family significant others will shift from parents to siblings; and in terms of school significant others, from teachers to students.

Increasing Cosmopolitanism with Age.   Whereas the second developmental postulate regarding shift from adults to peers deals with an across-generational trend in significant others, the third postulate of a shift from kin to nonkin significant others involves a shift regarding within-generation others. It derives from the same assumptions about decreasing dependency and broadening social environment through childhood and adolescence as implied by the second postulate. As regards authority figures, the third postulate predicts that the child's self-definition progressively shifts from relationships with parents to relationships with teachers. As regards the age-peer generation of significant others, it is predicted that self-definition will shift from sibling relationships toward friend and classmate relationships as the child matures.

Nonhuman Animals in the Child's Self-Concept.   In analyzing significant others in the spontaneous self-concept, the present study examines also the salience of nonhuman animals in the child's self-definition. Our prestudies have indicated that among children self-definitions in terms of animals are surprisingly numerous. Perhaps the prevalence of animals in children's self-definitions reflects the child's identifying with small animals (as has been suggested in psychoanalytic theory), and perhaps it is because the child, being so dependent him- or herself, finds in nonhuman animals the social objects needed for expressing nurturing needs.

METHOD FOR STUDYING THE SOCIAL SELF

The empirical study testing these hypotheses about gender and age differences in the salience of significant others in the spontaneous self-concept included two aspects that must be described in order to make the results reported in the next section meaningful, namely, how the children's spontaneous self-descriptions were collected and how these descriptions were content analyzed for mentions of significant others.

Participants

Two aspects of collecting the children's self-concepts call for clarification, namely, the selection of the participants whose spontaneous self-concepts were collected and the procedures used in eliciting and recording these descriptions. The self-concepts were obtained from 70 boys and 70 girls at each of four grade levels in the public school system of a medium-sized, inland city in New England with diversified manufacturing as its economic base. The larger of the city's two high schools was selected to furnish the older schoolchildren. Then two of the junior high schools that fed into this high school were selected to furnish the middle-childhood age groups, and three elementary schools that fed into these two junior high schools were selected to provide the youngest children. We selected this string of schools that fed into one another to increase the likelihood that students at the four grade levels came from similar backgrounds.

Because we were testing developmental hypotheses, we attempted to maximize the age range by choosing first graders and eleventh graders as the two extremes (omitting the twelfth graders because at that level there were appreciable drop-out rates, particularly among boys, that would have reduced the comparability of the twelfth graders). Two intermediate grade levels were also selected, including third graders to pick up any changes that might be occurring during the early malleable years, and seventh graders as falling midway between the third and the eleventh graders. To obtain the 70 boys and 70 girls at each of the four grade levels, we utilized almost all the first and third graders available in the three elementary schools, most of the seventh graders available in the two junior high schools, and most of the eleventh graders in the one high school. We did eliminate from the sample children with special educational problems, and those who had only rudimentary knowledge of English.

The boys and girls at a given grade level were homogeneous in age. The mean age in years of the first, third, seventh, and eleventh graders were 7.0, 9.3, 13.3, and 17.2 years of age, respectively. The standard deviation of the ages within a class averaged 0.54 years.

Procedure

The spontaneous self-concepts were collected by individual interviews of the 560 young people, 140 at each of the four grade levels. The interviewer met each of the elementary school students outside his or her classroom and took the child to the interview room; in the junior high and high schools, the student reported to the interview room after being released by the teacher. When the child arrived at the interview room (improvised from available space within the school, such as the nurse's room), the interviewer demonstrated the recording equipment to the student who was told that general questions would be asked and that the responses would be anonymous, with names not recorded and the recordings not heard by any one at the school or anywhere else who would be able to identify the speaker.

The participants were then told that the question would be a general one without a right or wrong answer, and that he or she should respond with whatever
thoughts came to mind in answer to the question. It was explained that after the
interviewer asked the question the student would then have 5 minutes to reply,
and that the interviewer could not give any more information or answer questions
in that 5 minute period.

The interviewer then asked the spontaneous self-concept eliciting question,
namely, "Tell us about yourself." The student was told to take the next 5 minutes to respond orally with whatever thoughts about the self that came to mind.
With the few participants who said nothing for 10 seconds, the interviewer then
said quietly, "Okay, the tape recorder is on. You can begin to tell us about yourself." If at any point during the 5-minute period the participant paused for more
than 30 seconds, the interviewer said, "We have to wait until the 5 minutes are
up, so if you can think of other things about yourself, just say them aloud." The
following response, fairly typical for an eleventh-grade girl, is presented verbatim (with words scored as significant mentions of significant others *in italics*) to
illustrate the general nature of these spontaneous self-concepts:

"Well, I enjoy *kids* and I like to type and I enjoy coming to school and I like
some subjects but some aren't so hot that I like to go to them. And I really want a
job as a secretary; if I can't get that, I'd like to work with *kids*. And if that's not
possible, I'd like to work in a store. And I like any kind of music that's good. I
like to go out on weekends and have fun. And I really enjoy my *parents; they* try
to understand me when I've got problems and when there's a problem at home, I
try to understand that. If like I can't go where I want, and my *mother* has to yell
at me for some reason, I understand. And, I don't know, I really get along with
my *family* and my *friends* at school. And I really like some of the *teachers* they
have in school, some of *them* are very understanding; *some* are just, I don't
know, you don't understand what *they*'re talking about. And *they* say,'Ask questions,' and when you ask questions, *they* get so pissed. But *Mrs. (name deleted)*
is very nice and *Mr. (name deleted)* and a whole mess of *other teachers;* but
some of *them* just, I don't know, I just can't stand *them*. And I like all of my
friends; they try to help *one another,* you know when *we*'re in trouble. And I like
to help my *friends* if I can; and if I can't, well I try to tell *them* why I can't . . .
and if it's impossible . . .if I can find a way, I always try to help *them;* if *they*
need money if I have it, I give it to *them*. And, I don't know, I guess that's all. I
really enjoy *kids* though."

Content Analysis of the Spontaneous Self-Concept Protocols

The recorded spontaneous self-concept descriptions elicited by the "Tell us
about yourself" probe were transcribed and then subjected to an elaborate content analysis by trained coders. This content-analysis system was worked out on
the basis of extensive analysis of prestudy data in order to preserve as fully as
possible the child's own thoughts, while at the same time translating these

thoughts into a sufficiently standardized language to permit practicable computer analysis. We found that by rewriting the participant's verbatim self-description into a "basic English" the resulting prose could be divided into successive three-unit segments, roughly in the form of "subject/verb/object" format. The content of the three units in any segment could then be translated into four-digit numbers in a dictionary of 777 terms that covered with reasonable specificity all the concepts that occurred in the response protocols. The resulting encoding constitutes a reasonable compromise between preserving fully all the nuances of the child's original prose and achieving a manageable standardization that allows efficient computer storage and analysis. That our complex content analysis system preserves much of the information in the original responses, while at the same time renders it computer storable enables us to do a variety of analyses of these complex self-concept data, including testing the predictions described here about sex differences and age trends in the size and content of the social self.

RESULTS REGARDING THE SOCIAL SELF

Children's self-concepts are quite "social": Of the 30,603 noun concepts (i.e., all contents of the first and third units of all segments produced by the 560 schoolchildren), no fewer than 7170 (or 23% of the total) were mentions of significant others. Almost half (47%) these references to significant others involved mentions of relatives; an additional quarter (24%) were mentions of friends. The remainder included mentions of teachers and students (8%), broad categories of people (adults, women, human beings in general, etc.) (11%), and animals (11%).

Most mentions of relatives referred, as might be expected, to the nuclear rather than extended families. The 47% of mentioned significant others who were relatives was made up of 42% nuclear family (including 20% sibling mentions, 14% parent, and 7% references to the nuclear family in general) plus 5% extended family (including 2% cousin mentions, 1% grandparents, and 1% uncles and aunts). The nonhuman animal mentions, constituting an impressive 11% of all significant-other mentions, are made up of domestic animals (including dogs, cats, fish, birds, other small mammals, and reptiles, in declining order of frequency) plus 2% wild animals. Our next two sections analyze these numerous self-definitions in terms of significant others for what support they give to our predictions about sex differences and about developmental age trends in the social self.

Sex Differences in Salience of Significant Others

Our predictions about sex differences in the comparative salience of significant others in the children's self-concepts derive from three basic postulates: firstly, that girls, being more people-oriented than boys, define themselves in terms of significant others more than do boys; secondly, that girls are more parochial than boys in choice of the significant others in terms of whom to define themselves; and thirdly, that as regards nuclear-family significant others children focus on other-sex siblings and same-sex parents. Each of these three postulates allows derivation of a number of predictions, the results bearing on which are decribed in the next three sections.

Girl's Self-Definition More People-Oriented than Boys.   We postulated that girls are more preoccupied with people than are boys, defining themselves in terms of relations to other people more than do boys. The most obvious test of this postulate is the hypothesis that the number of mentions of other people constitutes a greater proportion of all first- and third-unit content in the self-concepts of girls than of boys. This prediction is strongly confirmed, as can be seen in row A1.1 of Table 3.1. Whereas the self-concepts of both girls and boys are quite "social," with mentions of significant other persons constituting 20% of all noun concepts (or 23% if we include mentions of nonhuman animals), girls are significantly ($p <. 001$) more socially oriented than boys, 24% of all their self-concept nouns being mentions of other people as compared with 17% of boys'.

TABLE 3.1

Results on Hypotheses about Sex Differences in Self-Definitions in Terms of Significant Others Derived from Postulates A (Girls More People Oriented), B (Girls More Parochial), and C (Orientation to Own-Gender Parent and Other-Gender Sibling). Numbers of Cases Are 280 Boys and 280 Girls.

Prediction		Gender of Participants		Significance Level
Number	*Comparison*	*Boys*	*Girls*	
A1.1	Sig.-others nouns ÷ all nouns	.17	.24	<.001
A2.1	"adults," "child" ÷ all categ. others	.05	.35	<.001
A2.2	"males," "females" ÷ all categ. others	.06	.24	<.001
A2.3	specific family members ÷ all "family"	.78	.84	<.001
A3.1	friends ÷ friends and enemies	.87	.94	<.001
B1.1	kin mentions ÷ all human references	.49	.55	<.001
B1.2	nuclear family ÷ all family	.90	.90	not sig.
B1.3	romantic friends ÷ all friends	.11	.14	<.05
B1.4	pets ÷ all animals	.68	.88	<.001
B2.1	sib age peers ÷ all household	.52	.62	<.001
B2.2	student age peers ÷ students & teachers	.48	.66	<.001
B3.1	own gender kin ÷ all kin	.53	.53	not sig.
C1.1	mother ÷ mother and father	.40	.67	<.001
C1.2	brother ÷ brother and sister	.49	.56	<.05

This first postulate, that girls' sense of self focuses more on significant others than does the boys', yields the further, more subtle derivation that girls' preoccupation with other people tends to be more differentiated than boys', focusing on specific individuals, whereas boys tend more to relate themselves to broader categories of people. This derivation is analogous to the argument that, if snow is more significant to the Eskimos than to inhabitants of the Lower 48, Eskimos will have a more differentiated vocabulary and will refer to more specific types of snow. Our coding categories for children's responses allow three tests of this derivation. The first prediction is that when children define themselves in terms of people categorically, girls tend to differentiate people into children and adults, whereas boys tend to refer to "people in general," without regard to their age status. This prediction was strongly confirmed (see row A2.1 in Table 3.1) in that for girls, of the 354 mentions that fell in the three categories of people in general, children in general, and adults in general, 35% were in the latter two, age-distinguished categories; whereas among the 350 mentions by boys in the three categories, only 5% were in the latter two (age-specific) categories. A closely related second prediction is that when defining themselves in terms of people categorically, girls more than boys will differentiate people into males and/or females rather than referring to "people" in general without specification of gender. As shown in row A2.2 of Table 3.1, if we sum all categorical mentions of "people," "males," and "females" and calculate the percent contributed by mentions of the latter two gender-specified categories, we find that for girls 24% were specified by gender as compared to 6% for boys.

A third prediction derived from the hypothesis that girls are more differentiated in their social selves deals with significant others in the nuclear family. The prediction is that in defining oneself in terms of nuclear-family significant others girls are less likely than boys to do so in terms of the nuclear family in general rather than in terms of specific members (mother, father, sister, or brother). This prediction was strongly confirmed, as shown in row A2.3 of Table 3.1. Of the total number of self-definitions in terms of mother, father, sister, brother, and one's nuclear family in general, mentions of the four specific members constituted 84% of all family mentions for girls, whereas for boys they constituted only 78%; that is, self-definition in terms of "my family in general" constituted 22% of all family mentions for boys and only 16% for girls ($p < .001$ for the sex difference).

The postulate that girls are more people oriented in forming their self-concepts yields a third hypothesis (though its derivation is more tenuous than that of the first two), that fewer negatively valenced significant others will enter girls' self-concepts than boys'. The only significant others absolutely identified as disliked within our coding system were those nonrelated age peers translated as "enemies" as opposed to "friends." In terms of these two categories, the hypothesis is confirmed. As can be seen in row A3.1 of Table 3.1, "enemies" furnished only 6% of the total mentions of friends and enemies for girls, whereas for boys, 13% of these mentions were of "enemies" ($p <$ than .001).

Girls Are More Parochial than Boys in Their Social Self-Definition. Our second general postulate about gender differences, that girls would be more parochial than boys in selecting significant others in terms of whom to define themselves, yielded three hypotheses: that for girls the chosen significant others are more likely to be domestic, own gender, and age peers. From the first hypothesis that significant others in terms of whom one defines oneself come disproportionately from the home for girls, four predictions were derived. Firstly, it was predicted that in defining oneself in terms of significant others, girls choose family members more often than do boys. Secondly, when family members are chosen, a greater proportion come from the nuclear household (as compared to extended-family kin) for girls than for boys. Thirdly, it was predicted that when they describe themselves in terms of their friends, girls are more likely than boys to refer to romantic friends. Finally, somewhat metaphorically, it was predicted that when children defined themselves with respect to animals, girls are more likely than boys to think of themselves in terms of domestic rather than wild animals. Three of the four "cosmopolitan" hypotheses receive substantial confirmation as can be seen from the data summarized in rows B1.1, B1.2, B1.3, and B1.4 of Table 3.1. The second prediction is not supported: Family references are concentrated on nuclear family equally for boys and girls.

A third prediction, derived from the postulated greater domesticity of girls' self-definitions, deals with friends. It was predicted and confirmed that when defining self in terms of friends, girls more often than boys would refer to romantic friends. Of the girls' 863 self-definitions in terms of friends, 14% referred to romantic friends; whereas among the 577 self-definitions in terms of friends by boys, only 11% involved romantic friends, a sex difference significant at the .05 level. A fourth, metaphorical implication of greater domesticity in girls' self-concepts, that their self-definitions in terms of nonhuman animals would more often than boys' involve domestic animals (pets), was strongly supported by the data. Partitioning animal self-references between wild and domestic animals (dogs, cats, and other pets), we find that among the 416 references to animals by girls, 88% dealt with pets as compared to 68% of the boys' 352 mentions of animals.

Our postulate that girls are more local and parochial than boys in selecting significant others in terms of whom to define themselves yields a second hypothesis that girls more than boys choose age peers. This hypothesis can be tested by two separate predictions, each applying to one of the two main institutional settings of children, the home and the school. In each setting the prediction that girls are more age-peer oriented than boys is confirmed. Among the 1527 self-definitions in terms of nuclear-family persons (mother, father, brothers, sisters) by girls, 62% of the references are to siblings; whereas among the 939 nuclear family self-definitions by boys, only 52% are to siblings. Similarly, in the school setting, among the 279 schoolperson references by girls, 66% are to students rather than to teachers, whereas of the 308 schoolperson references by boys, only 48% are to students. Rows B2.1 and B2.2 in Table 3.1 show the results relevant to these two predictions drawn from the hypothesis of more pronounced age-peer orientation in the girls.

A third hypothesis derived from the postulated parochialism of girls is that in defining themselves in terms of other people, girls more than boys will choose people of their own gender. We tested this hypothesis in terms of the eight commonest kin terms, using mother, sister, grandmother, and aunt as the female kin terms and father, brother, grandfather, and uncle as the male kin terms. The data do not support the prediction. As can be seen in row B3.1 of Table 3.1, boys and girls showed almost identical 53% preferences for describing themselves in terms of their own gender relatives.

Sex Differences in Gender Models within the Family.   Our third postulate about sex differences in defining the self in terms of significant others is that within the nuclear family children develop their self-definition in terms of their own gender parent and the other gender sibling; that is, boys' self-concepts focus on fathers and sisters, whereas girls are focused on mothers and brothers. Both tendencies have to do with the reciprocal procreative role relationships toward which girls and boys are being socialized. Rows C1.1 and C1.2 in Table 3.1 summarize the results on these two predictions.

As regards orientation toward the senior (parent) generation in developing one's self-concept, we predict that children focus on same-gender parent because boys must learn to model their behavior on their fathers and girls on their mothers in order to play their appropriate adult roles. The results strongly confirm ($p <$ .001) this same-gender orientation toward parent as a model for self-identity. Among the 507 self-definitions in terms of mothers and fathers by girls, 67% are to mothers rather than fathers; whereas among the 398 references in terms of parents by boys, only 40% were to mothers rather than fathers.

As regards children's orientation to the peer generation in the household (brothers and sisters), we predict the reverse interaction tendency such that children of each gender are oriented toward the other-gender siblings, because boys must learn to focus on own-generation females and girls on own-generation males in order to play their appropriate adult roles. This prediction of cross-gender preoccupation with siblings is confirmed ($p <$ .05), though the relationship is less strong than is same-gender preoccupation with the parental generation. Among the 923 mentions of siblings by girls, 56% were to brothers; whereas among the 407 references to siblings by boys, only 49% were to brothers.

Age Trends in the Social Self

Three postulates underlie our predictions about changes with age in the way one defines oneself in terms of significant others. The most basic postulate is that during childhood and adolescence, as the person becomes more autonomous and self-sufficient, the social domain progressively loses importance in determining self-definition. The second postulate is that, as the child grows and becomes pro-

TABLE 3.2
Results on Hypotheses about Age Trends in Salience of Significant
Others in Self-Space Derived from Postulates D (Decreasing
Importance of Significant Others), E (Increasing Peer Orientation), and
F (Increasing Negativity). Each Age Group Includes 70 Boys and 70
Girls

	Predictions	Age Group (in Years)				Significance
Number	Comparison	7	9	13	17	Level
D1.1	sig. others ÷ all items	.29	.27	.24	.16	<.001
D2.1	"humans etc." ÷ all sig. others	.06	.05	.10	.27	<.001
D2.2	"relatives, family ÷ all kin	.11	.18	.22	.29	<.001
D2.3	"students in gen'l ÷ all students	.03	.04	.40	.69	<.001
D2.4	"teach. in gen'l ÷ all teachers	.09	.04	.13	.36	<.001
D3.1	"enemies" ÷ friends + enemies	.04	.08	.09	.13	<.01
E1.1	sibling ÷ sibling + parents	.56	.60	.69	.58	nonmonotonic
E1.2	cousins ÷ all extended family	.40	.38	.54	.32	nonmonotonic
E1.3	students ÷ students + teachers	.66	.65	.26	.58	nonmonotonic
F1.1	parents ÷ parents + teachers	.63	.42	.51	.30	<.001
F1.2	sibs ÷ (friends + students + sibs)	.63	.42	.51	.30	<.001
F1.3	extended family ÷ all nonkin	.19	.11	.07	.02	<.001
G1.1	animals ÷ all sig. others	.09	.19	.10	.03	nonmonotonic

gressively less dependent on nurturing adults, his/her self-concept becomes progressively more peer rather than adult oriented. A third postulate is that, as the
child's social horizon expands during these developmental years, an increasingly
widening and cosmopolitan (nonkin) range of significant others becomes involved in self-definition. Each of these three postulates gives rise to a variety of
predictions, the results regarding which are presented in the sections that follow.

*Decreasing Importance of Significant Others in Self-Definition as the Child
Matures.*   The postulate that as a person matures during childhood and adolescence the social realm becomes decreasingly significant in self-definition derives
from the assumption that, in the highly dependent years of early childhood, one's
phenomenal world is dominated by nurturing others so that one defines oneself in
terms of them. But as one moves through the school years, becoming progressively more autonomous and self-sufficient, other people become less preoccu-
pying in one's view of the world and sense of self. From this postulate we derive
three hypotheses, each yielding a set of predictions as summarized in the "D"
rows of Table 3.2. Firstly and most basic is that mentions of other people as a

part of one's self-description decline progressively over the age span. The second derived set of predictions is that the significant others in self-space become increasingly deindividuated and abstract during this developmental trend. A third prediction is that negatively evaluated others occupy a proportion of the social self that grows over this developmental span.

The first hypothesis is strongly borne out, as can be seen in row D1.1 of Table 3.2. The proportion of all first-and third-unit concepts that involve mentions of significant others declines progressively from .29 for 7-year olds to .16 for 17-year olds. The second "deindividuating" hypothesis, that with age people define themselves in terms of generic categories of people rather than specific individuals, yields four predictions. The results, summarized in rows D2.1 through D2.4 of Table 3.2, significantly ($p < .001$) confirm each of these four predictions. The most general prediction is that mentions of significant others in terms of five broad categories (humans, adults, children, men, women) will constitute an increasing proportion of all social mentions with age. As can be seen in row D2.1 of Table 3.2, references to these five broad categories of significant others increase from .06 of all social mentions for 7-year olds to .27 of all social mentions for 17-year olds. Analogous predictions within more circumscribed social domains are also confirmed. References to one's "family" or "relatives" in general increase as a proportion of all kin references from .11 at age 7 to .29 at age 17; in the school domain, references to "students in general" increase as a proportion of all references to students from .03 at age 7 to .69 at age 17; and references to "teachers in general" increase as a proportion of all teacher references from .09 at age 7 to .36 at age 17.

A final prediction deriving from the postulate of declining importance of the social domain within the maturing self-concept is that there is an increasing mention of negatively evaluated people with age. The results shown in row D3.1 of Table 3.2 support this prediction. Whereas mentions of friends outnumber mentions of enemies at all age levels, mentions of enemies constitute a growing proportion of friend or enemy mentions as age increases, the proportion of enemies mentioned going from .04 at age 7 to .13 at age 17. Hence, our basic developmental postulate receives strong confirmation in that the six predictions derived from its three corollary hypotheses all receive strong confirmation in the form of a fairly monotonic, highly significant age trend in the predicted direction.

Increasing Peer Orientation with Age.   Our second developmental-trend postulate is that the significant others in terms of whom one defines oneself progressively shift from adults to peers through the childhood and adolescent years. Behind the postulate is the thinking that in the early, dependent years of life the child's concept of self is dominated by his or her relationships to nurturing and guiding adults, but that as the child matures toward self-sufficiency his or her self-definitions derive progressively more from friendship ties with age peers. This postulate yields three age-trend predictions: that nuclear-family mentions refer increasingly to siblings; that extended-family mentions refer increasingly to cousins; and that school-people mentions refer increasingly to students. As can be seen in the "E" rows of Table 3.2, none of these second-postulate predictions is confirmed by the data. Conceivably, the obtained nonmonotonic trends could be the complex outcomes of an age trend toward increasing peer orientation, plus the reality that as the child grows older his/her age peers in fact become more adult and he/she has more compelling need to focus on adult role models.

Increasing Cosmopolitanism with Age.   The third postulated age trend is that during childhood and adolescent development children's social self-definitions become progressively more cosmopolitan, with nonkin persons involving an increasing proportion of all those significant others in terms of whom one defines oneself. Underlying this postulate is the assumption that during the early years of childhood the home and relatives supply the social relationships in terms of which the child defines him/herself, but as the child's autonomy and capacity to explore increase as a part of the growth process, he or she is brought into contact with a widening range of significant others, so that his or her self-definition increasingly forms in relation to people outside the immediate domestic environment. Three predictions are derived from this cosmopolitanism postulate, and each of the three is confirmed by the data, as can be seen in the "F" rows of Table 3.2. As the child grows older, his/her self-definition in terms of other people tends to shift away from the family: from parents to teachers, from brothers and sisters to friends and fellow students, from extended-family members to nonkin others.

Self-Definition in Terms of Nonhuman Animals

Prestudies on the spontaneous self-concept indicated a surprising prevalence of nonhuman animals in the self-definitions of children. Hence, our present content analysis of the children's self-concepts was designed to yield detailed information on mentions of nonhuman significant others, and we predicted a high incidence of self-definitions in terms of nonhuman animals. We also expected a declining salience of these animals with increasing maturation. A further prediction, confirmed by the data as discussed earlier in the section on sex differences, is that in defining the self in terms of animals, girls mention a greater proportion of domestic, relative to wild, animals than do boys.

High Salience of Nonhuman Animals in the Self-Concept.   The extent to which children define themselves in terms of nonhuman animals is striking. The substantial 23% of all self-definition items involving mention of significant others is made up of 20% mentions of other human beings and no less than 3% mentions of nonhuman animals. Or using the social self as base line, 11% of all self-definitions in terms of significant others involved mention of nonhuman animals rather than humans. Across the whole age span from 7 to 17 years, the 11%

of significant others supplied by nonhuman animals was exceeded only by the inclusive human categories of friends (24%), siblings (20%), and parents (14%). Even though all the children had mothers and not all had pets, mention of pets (8% of all significant others) substantially exceeded mentions of mothers (7%). And among the particularly animal-oriented 9-year olds, mention of nonhuman animals constituted 19% of all references to significant others, a proportion exceeding that contributed by friends or siblings or parents.

Who are all these animals? Children (especially boys) are clearly "dog" people with 30% of all animal mentions referring to that species of pet, as compared with 23% dealing with cats, 8% with other small mammals (gerbils, etc.), 6% with birds, 5% with horses, and lesser incidence of fish and other pets. All in all, 78% of all animal mentions referred to pets. Among the 22% of animal mentions dealing with nondomesticated species, the most commonly mentioned were fish, birds, and insects. For example, concern about stinging bees is surprisingly prevalent among first graders.

We do not conjecture at length on the deep structural significance of this high salience of nonhuman animals in the child's self-concept. Psychoanalysts have reported a tendency by adults in their fantasies of childhood (for example, as manifested in dreams) to identify with small animals. Our results suggest that in childhood this identification is found in the manifest as well as latent content. This salience of animals in the children's self-concept may also reflect that for children, so dependent and powerless relative to other humans, animals may provide one of the few outlets for nurturing and power needs.

Age Trends in the Salience of Nonhuman Animals. On the assumption that self-definition in terms of nonhuman animals represents rather "primitive" thought content, we predicted that the proportion of the social self occupied by nonhuman animals would decline as the child develops through childhood and adolescence. The results in row G1.1 in Table 3.2 show a rather different developmental trend. It is not the youngest, 7-year-old group whose self-concepts are most concerned with nonhuman animals but rather the 9-year olds. For the 7-year olds, animals furnish only .09 of all self-definitions in terms of significant others, whereas for 9-year olds this proportion more than doubles to .19. Thereafter, the proportion does fall off progressively to .10 among the 13-year olds and .03 among the 17-year olds. This nonmonotonic, inverted U-shaped developmental trend is quite stable across species. It is manifested not only in the Table 3.2 data for all animal species combined but appears with substantially the same shape for each of the four major subclasses of animals (dogs, cats, other pets, and wild animals). For each of the four (as shown in Fig. 3.1), there is the same nonmonotonic trend peaking at age 9. This nonmonotonic inverted U-shaped relationship between salience of nonhuman animals in the self-concept and maturation from ages 7 through 17 may be due to salience of animals' deriving from two mediating factors that show opposite developmental trends. One factor could be maturing needs for power and nurturing, increasing with age; the other could be lack of other human beings toward whom one can exercise these nurturing needs, a lack that declines with age. McGuire (1968) presents a quantitative model demonstrating that under a wide range of parametric assumptions such two-factors models yield a nonmonotonic function, such that the dependent variable (here, salience of animals) peaks at an intermediate level of the independent variable (here, age).

Conclusions

Substantial confirmation was found for numerous predictions derived from each of our three postulates regarding sex differences in defining the self in terms of significant others, as measured by the spontaneous self-concept approach. For girls, the social self occupies a greater proportion of total self-space, and girls are more parochial (domestic and peer focused) in selecting the significant others in terms of whom they define themselves. We also predicted and found that as regards nuclear-family significant others, girls' self-concepts are more focused on mothers and brothers, whereas boys', more on fathers and sisters; that is, children are oriented toward own-gender parent and other-gender sibling in forming their self-concepts, a pattern that facilitates their socialization into prescribed adult sex roles.

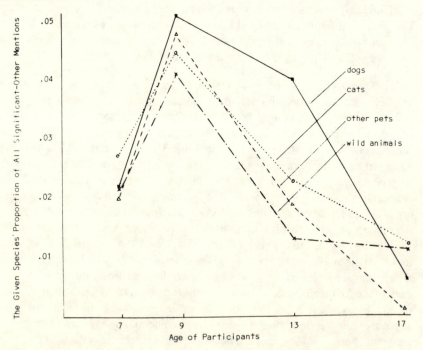

FIG. 3.1.   Nonmonotonic age trend, peaking at 9 years of age, for self-definition in terms of the four major categories of nonhuman animals.

Confirmation was found for multiple predictions derived from two of our three postulates regarding age trends in significant others in the spontaneous self-concept. It was corroborated that as children mature from age 7 through 17 the social self occupies a progressively decreasing proportion of total self-space, and that the selection of the significant others in terms of whom one defines oneself becomes progressively more cosmopolitan. No support was found for predictions derived from a third postulate that children's self-concepts become progressively more peer oriented with age.

It was found, as expected, that nonhuman animals provide a substantial proportion (11%) of all significant others; for example, pets occupy more self-space than do mothers. Rather than the expected monotonic decline with age in the nonhuman animal proportion of significant others, there is clear evidence that preoccupation with animals increases from age 7 to 9 and then decreases progressively from 9 through ages 13 and 17.

Besides its corroborating specific hypotheses about sex differences and age trends in self-definition in terms of relation to significant others, this study shows the utility of the open-ended "spontaneous" rather than the usual constricted "reactive" approach to studying the self-concept. The reactive self-concept approach, where the researcher presents an a priori chosen dimension (usually, self-esteem) on which one is asked to locate oneself, furnishes information only on how one would think of oneself on the dimension if one ever thought of it. The spontaneous "Tell us about yourself" self-concept approach yields additional, often more interesting information regarding what are the dimensions in terms of which one does think of oneself. Our previously published work on the distinctiveness postulate (summarized in the earlier part of this chapter) showed how the spontaneous self-concept approach can be used to test derivations from a cognitive processing theory, that people operate on an information-maximizing strategy, tending to conceptualize themselves in terms of their more peculiar characteristics (physical, gender, ethnic, etc.). The newer line of work on the social self (described in the later part of the chapter) shows how the spontaneous self-concept approach can be used to study predictions focused convergently on a subject-matter area (how people use their relations to other people to define themselves), rather than extending divergently from a theoretical principle (as did the distinctive-theory research). Hence, the spontaneous self-concept approach allows study of both theory-focused and subject matter-focused issues that could not be investigated as appropriately by use of the usual reactive self-concept approach.

ACKNOWLEDGMENTS

This research was made possible by Grant Number 1 RO3 MH32588, received from the Social Science Research Section of the National Institute of Mental Health. The collection of data, content analysis of responses, and computer analyses benefitted greatly from help given by Joyce Ghiroli, Cassandra Appin, and Jason Cheever.

REFERENCES

Bugental, J. F. T.   Investigations into the self-concept: III. Instructions for the W-A-Y method. *Psychological Reports,* 1964 *15,* 643–650.

Freud, S.   *Group psychology and the analysis of the ego.* New York: Norton, 1959 (original edition, 1921).

Hartup, W.   Peer interaction and social organization. In P. H. Mussen (Ed.), *Carmichael's manual of child psychology* (Vol. 2). New York: Wiley, 1970.

Keller, A., Ford, L., & Meacham, J.   Dimensions of self-concept in preschool children. *Developmental Psychology,* 1978, *14,* 483–489.

Kuhn, M. H., & McPartland, T. S.   An empirical investigation of self-attitudes. *American Sociological Review,* 1954, *19,* 68–76.

Ladner, J. S.   *Mixed families: Adopting across racial boundaries.* New York: Anchor, 1977.

Maccoby, E., & Masters, J.   Attachment and dependency. In P. H. Mussen (Ed.), *Carmichael's manual of child psychology* (Vol. 1). New York: Wiley, 1970.

McGuire, W. J.   Personality and social influence. In E. F. Borgatta & W. W. Lambert (Eds.), *Handbook of personality theory and research.* Chicago: Rand McNally, 1968.

McGuire, W. J.   Yin and yang of progress in social psychology: Seven koan. *Journal of Personality and Social Psychology,* 1973, *26,* 446–456.

McGuire, W. J.   Toward social psychology's second century. In S. Koch & D. E. Leary (Eds.), *Psychology Centennial.* NY: McGraw–Hill, 1982, in press.

McGuire, W. J., & McGuire, C. V.   Salience of handedness in the spontaneous self-concept. *Perceptual and Motor Skills,* 1980, *50,* 3–7.

McGuire, W. J., & McGuire, C. V.   The spontaneous self-concept as affected by personal distinctiveness. In A. Norem-Hebeisen, M. D. Lynch, & K. Gergen (Eds.), *The self-concept.* New York: Ballinger, 1981.

McGuire, W. J., McGuire, C. V., Child, P., & Fujioka, T.   Salience of ethnicity in the spontaneous self-concept as a function of one's ethnic distinctiveness in the social environment. *Journal of Personality and Social Psychology,* 1978, *36,* 511–520.

McGuire, W. J., McGuire, C. V., & Winton, W.   Effects of household sex composition on the salience of one's gender in the spontaneous self-concept. *Journal of Experimental Social Psychology,* 1979, *15,* 77–90.

McGuire, W. J. & Padawer-Singer, A.   Trait salience in the spontaneous self-concept. *Journal of Personality and Social Psychology,* 1976, *33,* 743–754.

Montemayor, R., & Eisen, M.   The development of self-conceptions from childhood to adolescence. *Developmental Psychology,* 1977, *13,* 314–319.

Spitzer, S., Couch, C., & Stratton, J.   *The assessment of self.* Iowa City: Sernoll, 1971.

Wylie, R. C.   *The self-concept* (Vol. 1). Lincoln: University of Nebraska Press, 1974.

Wylie, R. C.   *The self-concept* (Vol. 2). Lincoln: University of Nebraska Press, 1979.

4

From the Cradle to the Grave: Comparison and Self-Evaluation Across the Life-Span

Jerry Suls
Brian Mullen
State University of New York at Albany

> *"It is all one to me where I begin; for I shall come back again there"*
>
> —Paramenides

Personal development through the setting of achievement goals—both long and short term—depends largely on one's self-concept. The self-concept, in turn, is a summary of one's evaluations of one's abilities, competencies, successes, and failures. In many instances these evaluations are based on the reactions and opinions of other people, the "reflected appraisals." But equally important are one's own attempts to assess the adequacy of one's own abilities and self-worth. These self-generated attempts at evaluation are the focus of this chapter.

How might one go about evaluating one's own traits and accomplishments? A straightforward way is to compare oneself with objective standards, but such standards are in many, if not most, instances nonexistent. Festinger (1954) observed, if an individual wished to determine whether the temperature outside was below freezing, he or she might look at a thermometer or put a dish of water outside to see if it freezes. But if a person wished to judge, before actually trying to do so, whether he or she could run the Boston Marathon or if he or she possessed the requisite ability to obtain a college degree, objective standards are simply unavailable. However, one does have available the behavior, beliefs, and performances of other people. As a result, interpersonal comparisons are often used to judge the adequacy of one's abilities. This insight led Festinger (1954) to outline a theory of social comparison processes (Latane, 1966; Suls & Miller, 1977).

To be sure, social comparisons are not the only means by which a person judges the adequacy of his or her abilities. Temporal comparisons are another such means: An individual may compare his or her present attainments with past performances of similar tasks to assess improvement or deterioration. The importance of temporal comparison has not always been appreciated by students of the self-evaluation process; recently, however, it has begun to receive attention (Albert, 1977; Bandura, 1977; Veroff, 1969).

Given a situation where objective standards are unavailable, is an individual more likely to make comparisons with other people or with his own past efforts? The present chapter attempts to answer this question, a question that has received little, if any, attention. We argue that the preferred mode of self-evaluation depends to a great degree on the individual's place in the life cycle, and that preferences follow an orderly stage-like course. In the following pages one finds an outline of the stages of the life-span model; then a detailed consideration of processes occurring at each stage. This is followed by a review of evidence from the social, developmental, and gerontological literature relevant to the model. The final section discusses the implications of the model for further research and theorizing on the self. We begin with a discussion of the operations of the social comparison process, because it is the predominant form of self-evaluation for the majority of the life cycle.

Social Comparison

Festinger (1954) was the first theorist to systematically discuss the dynamics of the interpersonal-comparison process. He emphasized the survival value of establishing the bounds of one's capabilities, especially because objective standards are often unavailable or nonexistent, thus making it necessary to employ other people for self-evaluative purposes. He also proposed what is called "the similarity hypothesis"; that is, comparisons are most useful when they are made with people who are similar to oneself. Although this hypothesis is widely accepted, several scholars have noted that there is some ambiguity in Festinger's description of what constitutes "a similar other" (Latane, 1966; Pettigrew, 1967; Singer 1966). Goethals and Darley's (1977) recent restatement of Festinger's hypothesis has helped to clarify the concept of similarity and its role in evaluating ability.

The key to Goethals and Darley's formulation is the treatment of ability evaluation as an attributional process. Stated in its simplest form, what one evaluates via comparison are dispositions (ability) that cannot be observed directly but must be inferred from behavioral manifestations (i.e., performances). Any performance or set of performances is, however, also a function of other nonability factors such as effort and practice. Nonability factors that contribute to performance are called "related attributes." Because ability is only one factor contributing to a performance, it is essential that the individual sort out the contribution of his ability from the contributions of the other factors. If we use other people's performances to gauge our own abilities via social comparison, we must also take into account the related attributes that affect their performances.

This reasoning led Goethals and Darley to propose that the most meaningful comparison information derives from comparisons with others who are similar to us (or matched) on related attributes. For example, suppose a jogger wants to know how much running ability she possesses. Goethals and Darley argue that the most useful comparison information would come from comparing her performance with another runner who is similar in age, sex, experience, fatigue, and so on, that is, with someone who is similar in related attributes. Comparison with those who are dissimilar on related attributes might yield ambiguous information. Why is that so? Assume that a jogger compares herself with someone who is dissimilar in related attributes, for instance with someone who has had more practice. The most likely outcome is that her performance will be inferior. But this says very little about her relative ability, because it is impossible to determine with certainty whether the outcome is due to the other's greater experience or greater ability. In other words, the attributional principal of discounting (Kelley, 1973) comes into play; that is, the role of any given cause cannot be unambiguously evoked when two or more plausible causes (in this case, ability and experience) are present. Consequently, comparing one's performance with the performance of someone who is advantaged (which makes him dissimilar) in attributes related to performance does not allow one to make a meaningful evaluation of one's own ability.

The same ambiguity is present if a jogger compares herself with someone who has less experience as a jogger (dissimilar by virtue of being disadvantaged), because the discounting principle again applies. The most likely outcome is that her performance will be superior, but she cannot be certain whether it is because of her greater degree of ability or because of her greater experience.

On the other hand, if she compares herself with someone who is similar in related attributes (i.e., matched on experience, age, and any other factors or characteristics that make up a performance), the result of the comparison is unambiguous. If her performance is better, she can logically assume she possesses more ability; the related attributes cannot be responsible because she is matched with the other person on these characteristics. By the same token, if her performance is worse, she probably has less ability. If she performs equally well, then she probably has as much ability as the other person. Thus, comparison with others who are similar on related attributes (nonability factors that contribute to performance) will usually yield the most valuable (i.e., unambiguous) information.

The application of attributional concepts to the social comparison process has considerably clarified Festinger's original similarity hypothesis (see Goethals and Darley, 1977, for a more extensive discussion). Furthermore, empirical support for this reformulation has been found in several studies investigating comparison choices (Suls, Gaes, & Gastorf, 1979; Suls, Gastorf, & Lawhon, 1978; Zanna, Goethals, & Hill, 1975) and in studies investigating the effects of comparison on self-evaluations (Gastorf & Suls, 1978; Sanders, Gastorf, & Mullen, 1979).

Although social comparison with similar persons offers the most unambiguous information, there may be situations where comparisons with dissimilar others are used. For example, if the individual does not possess the cognitive sophistication to understand why comparison with similar persons is more useful, then comparisons may be made indiscriminately. The choice of a similar other depends directly on three things: (1) the realization that ability is a hypothetical (inferential) construct; (2) the knowledge that it can be assessed by observing performance; and (3) the cognitive ability to sort out the component factors, of which ability is only one, that jointly determine the performance. As argued later, young children have considerable difficulty with these ideas, and so they should not be expected necessarily to prefer comparison with similar others. They may compare indiscriminately, that is, with similar and dissimilar others, because they fail to appreciate the greater usefulness of the former.

Even persons possessing the cognitive sophistication to appreciate the greater usefulness of similar others may not use them. In some cases it may be difficult to determine which attributes are related to performance, and, therefore, comparison others will be chosen on bases other than related attribute similarity. Also, as discussed later, society may frequently impose comparisons with dissimilars.

In terms of the life-span model we propose, this discussion of social comparison highlights two points. Firstly, there are three major modes of self-evaluation: social comparisons with similar others, social comparison with dissimilar others, and temporal comparisons. Secondly, the choice of a mode may depend mainly on the level of cognitive sophistication of the person seeking information, on the relative complexity of the performance that must be observed, and on situational and societal factors. With these points in mind, we can now address the life-span model.

The Life-Span Model

Like Festinger (1954), we assume that the feedback provided by comparing with objective standards is preferred over other forms of evaluative feedback (temporal or social). When, however, objective standards are unavailable, the individual must resort to social or temporal feedback. The model posits that the individual's position in the life cycle determines which mode of evaluation (temporal, social-similar others, social-dissimilar others) has the greatest influence on self-evaluation.

In the early years (1-3) children should evaluate their capabilities in a very direct way. Because accomplishments like walking and manipulating objects predominate the child's activities, competence is defined by the direct feedback of obvious successes and failures (e.g., "I can catch the ball"; "I cannot tie my shoes"). Objective standards and physical reality dominate the child's world and cognition. Although adults and caretakers are also important for the child's self-appraisals at this stage providing what is obviously social feedback, reverence for adults causes children to equate adult comments with standards of an absolute nature (Piaget, 1965).

After the age of 3, the children gradually begin to acquire a different orientation. Specifically, they begin to gauge their capabilities by comparing their present performances with their past performances (i.e., temporal comparisons). We assume that initially the child's limited memory span permits the use of only recent successes or failures to evaluate present performance. However, as memory processes mature, temporal comparisons can be made with more temporally distant successes or failures. This orientation will continue for a few years, gradually being replaced by an orientation toward social comparisons. Temporal comparisons begin to recede in relative importance, in part because they become less gratifying. In the years 3–5, children typically show rapid advancements in terms of cognitive and physical skills, making temporal comparisons, it would seem, especially pleasurable and satisfying. But as the spurt of development begins to taper off, comparisons with recent and past efforts should yield smaller increments of improvement and thus become less gratifying.

These forces should propel children toward social comparisons. However, because children lack certain critical concepts (i.e., the difference between performance and ability; the discounting principle) necessary to understand and appreciate the greater usefulness of comparison with similar others, they will be relatively indiscriminate in their choices, comparing themselves both with those similar and those dissimilar. When a child understands that ability can only be inferred from performance and that the role of ability must be sorted out from the effects of other factors (related attributes), he or she will appreciate the greater usefulness of similar others. These developments should begin to appear at the age of 8 or so. Once begun, the process of comparing predominantly with similars remains in place, extending from late childhood through adolescence and much of adulthood. We are not contending that temporal comparisons or social comparisons with dissimilar others entirely disappear. Obviously, it is difficult to imagine people perfecting their skills without comparing changes in performance over time (i.e., temporal comparison). However, we argue that social comparison with similar others is weighted more heavily during this period.

At approximately age 40 the process just described begins to change somewhat. At this time, the adult becomes increasingly aware of the finite and vulnerable aspects of physical being and the limits of achievement (Erikson, 1959). It becomes increasingly important to feel that one has made some special contribution and that one is unique. Comparison with others who are dissimilar may serve to highlight one's uniqueness (Fromkin, 1970). Furthermore, comparisons with dissimilar others are frequently encouraged and even imposed in the work place. It is not uncommon for middle-aged persons to find themselves competing with younger as well as older coworkers, competition frequently imposed by one's employers. Both the desire for distinctiveness as well as the imposition of comparisons with dissimilars contribute to an increased tendency to compare with dissimilar others. Comparisons with similar others are still made, however, so there is a mix of comparisons.

With increasing age there is a loss of social and interpersonal contacts as well as cognitive and physical changes, which limits the availability of social comparison. As a result, the individual relies less and less on interpersonal comparisons and more on temporal comparisons; that is, evaluations based on what one could do before and what one can do now. These need not be especially gratifying, but they allow one to relive one's past accomplishments. In a sense, the individual will begin to live in the past. Finally, at extreme age, approaching and expecting the end of life, the individual may disengage from self-evaluation altogether. Figure 4.1 depicts the life-span model described previously.

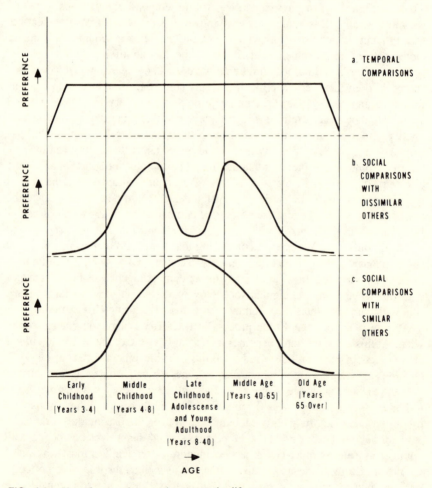

FIG. 4.1.   Use of comparison modes across the life-span.

The three modes of evaluation indicated are temporal comparison (Fig. 4.1a), social comparison with dissimilar others (Fig. 4.1b), and social comparison with similar others (Fig. 4.1c). The figure illustrates only large-scale changes in the use of different modes throughout the life-span. Much more empirical work is necessary before these curves could be superimposed with any precision. For example, we cannot claim that any one mode is twice as influential as any other at any given point in time. Notice that the model is symmetrical with temporal comparisons predominating in the early and late stages of life; social comparisons predominating during the stages of later childhood as well as early and middle adulthood. As already suggested and is discussed in detail in subsequent sections, different processes operate to create this symmetry: The factors that prompt young children to employ temporal comparisons or indiscriminate social comparisons are primarily cognitive, whereas the factors underlying patterns of comparison in older adults are largely socially imposed. A second point is that, whereas some modes of comparison predominate, the other forms are still employed but to a lesser extent. In particular, temporal comparisons remain important throughout the life-span. What changes is the relative weight they are given with respect to the other modes of comparison.

Childhood (Up to 4 Years)

Children under 4 years of age are primarily concerned with immediate physical feedback about success or failure. There are few comparisons that do not involve reasonably objective standards. There are two fundamental reasons why this is so. Firstly, this is a stage of development that is primarily oriented toward action and physical attainments (Piaget, 1952). Secondly, at this stage children are bound to the present, making temporal comparison impossible.

As greater cognitive sophistication develops (increased memory skills, appreciation for past, present, and future), temporal comparison becomes possible. Furthermore, the accelerated development of physical and cognitive skills makes temporal comparison gratifying. With these changes, children begin to gauge their capabilities by comparing present performance with past performances. It is assumed that initially the memory span will allow only comparisons with very recent successes or failures (Brown, 1975). However, as recall abilities expand, a child will be able to gauge present performances against efforts that are temporally more distant.

During this phase of the life-span, social comparisons will not be used in self-evaluation for two reasons. Firstly, the child is egocentric in orientation, preoccupied with his or her own point of view rather than those of others. Secondly, the child lives within a limited social environment that does not yet foster an appreciation of social standards.

Evidence for Temporal Comparisons in Early Childhood

There are several experimental studies that support the proposition that social comparison is not present in very young children. For example, Veroff (1969) reasoned that selecting to perform a task of moderate difficulty was indicative of high social-comparison motivation, because performance of it would provide more information about one's relative standing than would performance on tasks that most peers either could or could not complete. Veroff reported that social-comparison motivation, so defined, was virtually absent in most preschoolers.

Dinner (1976) had children of different ages perform a task in the presence of a coactor and provided them with feedback concerning the success of their performance relative to age peers or adults. Nursery schoolchildren were uninterested in the performance of the coactor and were unaffected by the imposed comparisons with either peers or adults. Ruble, Boggiano, Feldman, and Loebl (1980) conducted two studies in which children of different ages performed with same-aged peers. The results consistently indicated that young children's self-evaluations were little affected by relative comparisons. Finally, McClintock, Muskowitz, and McClintock (1977) studied the choice behaviors of children in three tasks: individualistic, coordinative, and conflictual. Choice options were structured so as to reveal whether children were only concerned with their own outcomes, regardless of the outcome for others. Of special interest was whether young children would prefer to maximize their own rewards or achieve a competitive advantage. McClintock et al. reported that nursery schoolchildren were own-gain oriented and relatively unconcerned with how much they received vis a vis others.

Together, these results strongly indicate that social comparison is not used in social evaluation by young children. In conjunction with these findings, there is evidence that supports the proposition that temporal comparison is the primary mode of self-evaluation in this life-span stage. McClintock and his associates (1977), in the work described previously, reported that the very young children (3 ½), being unconcerned with relative outcomes (social comparisons), were own-gain oriented (temporal comparisons). In addition, Feld, Ruhland, and Gold (1979), employing fantasy measures of achievement motivation, compared temporal and social-comparison strategies of young children. The authors reported that younger children relied proportionately more upon temporal comparisons than did the older children.

Thus, empirical research supports the characterization of very young children as participating in temporal comparisons to the relative exclusion of social comparisons.

Middle Childhood (4 to 8 years)

Temporal comparison begins to recede in relative importance, in part, as it becomes less gratifying. In the years 3 to 5, the child typically shows rapid advancements in cognitive and physical skills. Therefore, temporal comparisons reveal salient improvements in present performance compared to past performances and are very satisfying. However, as the spurt of development begins to taper off, comparisons with recent efforts reveal fewer dramatic improvements in present performance and are less satisfying. As a result, there should be a reduction in the pleasure obtained from temporal comparisons, and children become more concerned with outperforming others. The increased cognitive sophistication at this stage of the life-span also allows the child to decenter and to take on another's perspective. This capacity is a prerequisite for social comparison; an appreciation of one's performance relative to another's requires the ability to refocus attention from oneself to other people.

In addition to changes within the child that facilitate the shift from temporal to social comparisons, there are forces in the child's immediate social environment that contribute to this shift. For example, at this time the child enters formal schooling of some form, a situation that both provides and enforces social comparisons on a regular basis. In conjunction with this, parents probably begin in earnest to communicate to the child the importance of relative standing and of success in terms of competitive excellence.

Thus, social comparison is given more weight than temporal comparison. However, due to various factors, the social comparisons relied upon at this stage are mixed or indiscriminate. Recall the previous discussion of the differences between social comparisons with similar and with dissimilar others. The child of 4 to 7 years of age lacks the cognitive sophistication to separate ability from related attributes and consequently is unable to appreciate the value of information gained from comparison with similar others. Being unprepared to actively seek out social comparisons with similar others, the child simply engages in comparisons with the most salient others available. Such salient others (mother, father, siblings, teacher) are undoubtedly dissimilar on many important related attributes. In many instances, while communicating the values of social comparison, parents are providing and enforcing dissimilar social comparisons (perhaps most dramatically, with older siblings), as well as similar comparisons (with same-age classmates). Given the child's inability to understand the greater usefulness of similar others as well as situational forces that foster dissimilar comparisons, the child engages in social comparisons with both similar and dissimilar others.

As the following section demonstrates, viewing middle childhood as a period of indiscriminate social comparison is supported by empirical evidence.

Evidence for Indiscriminate Social Comparisons in Middle Childhood

There is a considerable body of evidence strongly supporting the proposed development of social comparison during the years from 4 to 8. Veroff (1969) found that social-comparison motivation, demonstrated by the choice of moderately difficult tasks, became more prevalent during this time and peaked between 8 and 9 years of age. Dinner (1976) reported that older children exhibited greater interest in social comparisons than did nursery schoolchildren; further, the self-evaluations of task ability by first, second, and fourth graders were affected by social comparisons, whereas those of the young children were not. McClintock et al. (1977) reported that the tendency for children to show concern for social comparison increased until around 7 years of age. Feld et al. (1979) reported that social comparison increased as children grew older, as have Ruble, Feldman, and Bogiano (1976). Ruble et al. (1980) demonstrated that achievement-related self-evaluations became affected by social comparisons around 7 or 8 years of age.

There are a number of experimental studies indicating that temporal comparisons become relatively less prevalent as social comparisons become more so. The work of McClintock et al. (1977) indicated that between the ages of 4 ½ and 5 social comparisons become increasingly important. Children of this age become increasingly willing to forego success in terms of temporal comparison in order to gain success in terms of social comparison. Similar observations were discussed by Nelson and Kagan (1972) and by Feld et al. (1979).

Given this consistent support for the increase of social comparisons during this stage of the life-span, what does the research suggest about social comparisons being indiscriminate with regard to similarity of comparison others? Empirical evidence strongly supports the proposition that children do not develop the cognitive sophistication required for the appreciation of similar comparisons until 7 or 8 years of age. Karniol and Ross (1976) demonstrated that the discounting principle is not understood until these years. As discussed earlier, the discounting principle is a prerequisite for understanding the importance of related attributes. Similarly, Erwin and Kuhn (1979) have also observed a parallel developmental trend for the recognition that a person's behavior may be determined by more than a single factor.

The work of Kun and of Nicholls demonstrates, even more directly, the inability of children of this age to deal effectively with all the subtleties of social comparisons with similar persons. Kun (1977) had children judge people's ability from information such as task performance and effort. Children under 7 perceived the individual who tried harder as having more ability; Kun referred to this as a halo effect. Older children (7 to 8 years) assumed that greater effort compensated for lower ability to produce the same overall level of performance, indicating an understanding of compensatory relationships. It follows that younger children, relying upon the halo effect, make incorrect inferences regarding their ability if they assume that trying harder always means more ability. Similarly, Nicholls (1978) presented films of two individuals working on a task and had children judge the effort and ability of the two filmed workers under different conditions of reported performance. Four levels of reasoning about effort and ability were derived from responses to the films: The younger children exhibited the lowest levels of reasoning, the older children exhibited the highest levels of reasoning. Consistent with the present framework, the shift toward more advanced levels of reasoning about effort and ability began with children of 7 and 8 years of age.

In addition to studies that demonstrate children younger than 7 or 8 have not developed the cognitive sophistication required to appreciate comparisons with similar others, there are studies that support the prevalence of unselective social comparisons at this age.

Dinner's (1976) work demonstrates this prevalence. Whereas nursery school children were unaffected by comparisons with adults or peers, first and second graders were influenced equally by comparisons with adults and peers. The fact that similar and dissimilar comparisons did not differentially affect self-evaluations in those children just developing social comparison tendencies is entirely consistent with the present framework.

This leads to an additional factor that may contribute, for a time, to the indiscriminance of comparisons during this stage. A variety of dissimilar comparisons are apparent to, if not imposed upon, the child during these early school years. The child looks to nurturant adults (parents or teachers) for standards of evaluation. If the child sets as goals those standards of excellence employed by an adult, the child is in effect creating a situation of social comparison with another dissimilar on important related attributes (age, experience, strength, etc.). Perhaps more frequent, however, is the dissimilar comparison that is inevitable between siblings of different ages. Brown's (1928) discussion of the dynamics of the comparisons that can arise between siblings of different ages provides dramatic documentation of what is probably a relatively common situation in families with two or more children. Brown observed that the younger of two siblings is probably subjected to continual implicit comparison with the older sibling. Leventhal (1970) examined one possible effect of this type of comparison. Examination of men with one sibling indicated that those with older sisters often displayed more masculine behavior than did those with older brothers. A mechanism proposed to account for these results has direct bearing upon the present discussion: The younger of two male children may try to behave differently from his older brother in order to avoid unfavorable comparisons with his more advanced older sibling. This "comparison-prevention strategy" inclines the younger child to perform in (less masculine, more feminine) areas where the older brother does not perform. By the same token, a similar comparison-prevention strategy inclines the younger child to perform in (more masculine, less feminine) areas where the older sister does not perform. The notion of a comparison-prevention strategy is based on the assumption that the younger sibling considers the dissimilar comparison with the older sibling to be a reasonable, legitimate comparison (even if it is extremely unfavorable and dissatisfying). If the comparison were not considered to be legitimate, the younger child would not be inclined to go to such lengths to avoid it. This novel extension of social comparison theory into sex-role acquisition processes leads to an important implication: The comparison-prevention strategy exercised by younger children with regard to comparisons with older siblings would be found at its most intense during the years from 4 to 8.

In any event, empirical research supports the shift from temporal to social comparisons in middle childhood. It also supports the proposition that social comparisons are at this time sometimes with similar others, sometimes with dissimilar others. Neither predominates.

Late Childhood, Adolescence, and Young Adulthood

Social comparisons continue to predominate over temporal comparisons as the child grows older. Moreover, as the child moves into adolescence, several changes facilitate the developing appreciation of social comparison with similar others. An increase in cognitive sophistication, exemplified by the development of concrete operational and then formal operational thought (Inhelder & Piaget, 1958), enables the individual to understand both the discounting principle and the possibility of multiple causes for behavior. Therefore, the individual begins to have the requisite abilities to begin to compare with, and prefer to compare with, similar others. Furthermore, same-age comparisons are increasingly imposed and stressed through spelling bees, test scores, grade levels, and so forth. The child may become discouraged making comparisons with older children or adults, because such comparisons typically show the younger person to be outperformed. Of course, comparisons with younger children may demonstrate one's relative superiority, but any habitual tendencies toward this type of comparison are probably discouraged by parents and teachers. As the child's social world develops and the peer group becomes increasingly significant, adults, such as parents and teachers, and siblings, become less important as standards for comparison. Over time, both cognitive and social factors instill and encourage an orientation toward social comparisons with similar others, especially with one's peers.

Evidence for Similar Social Comparisons in Late Childhood, Adolescence, and Young Adulthood

Evidence for the relative hegemony of social comparisons over temporal comparisons is even more available for this segment of the life-span than it is for earlier segments. Dealing predominately with college-aged subjects, the level of aspiration studies of the 1930s and 1940s revealed the subject's preferences for social rather than temporal performance feedback. For example, Gardner (1939) discussed the reactions of subjects within the level of aspiration paradigm who were provided with temporal-comparison feedback (i.e., repeated objective feedback scores):

> If no percentile scale is provided them, they make an effort to set up their own makeshift scale. They ask "How many got up this high?" or "Am I below aver-

age?'' or "Does anyone ever get way up there?'' . . . If the experimenter refuses such information, the subjects are simply left free to fall back upon hypotheses of their own, all of which . . . have to do not with the absolute goodness of their performance but with the relation of that performance to the group average or some similar reference point (Gardner, 1939, [p. 607].)

Similar observations were made by Hoppe (1930), Frank (1935), Jucknat (1937) and by Gould and Lewis (1940).

The first straightforward demonstration of the priority of social comparison over temporal comparison for this life-span stage was Hertzman and Festinger's (1940) level of aspiration study. College sophomores and juniors performed tasks in two separate situations: firstly with temporal comparison feedback only and then with both temporal- and social-comparison feedback. When subjects received only temporal information, levels of aspiration and feelings of success or failure were gauged, necessarily, in terms of temporal comparison. However, when subjects received both forms of feedback, levels of aspiration and feelings of success or failure were gauged primarily in terms of social comparisons. These results substantiate the hypothesized preference for social comparisons during adolescence and young adulthood.

Similar demonstrations of this trend in college-aged subjects have been reported. For example, in a variant of the level of aspiration paradigm, Simon (1979) found that social-comparison feedback determined whether or not temporal-comparison feedback had an effect on goal setting.

Miller (1977) examined the performance evaluation standards chosen by U. S. Army company commanders in a 1-week leadership training situation. When attraction to the group and importance of the group to the individual were high, subjects preferred to know their relative standing in the group (social comparison) rather than an objective measure of the amount of information they had assimilated during the week's training (temporal comparison).

Given that social comparison is preferred over temporal comparison at this stage, what evidence exists concerning the preference for social comparison with similar rather than dissimilar others? Dinner's (1976) previously discussed research bears directly upon the development of this preference. Nursery schoolchildren were unaffected by comparisons with adults or peers; first and second graders were influenced equally by comparisons with adults and peers; however, fourth graders' self-evaluations were affected only by comparisons with peers; that is, at the age of around 8 or 9 years, the distinction between comparisons with similar and with dissimilar others begins to emerge.

Recent research offers credibility to the argument that this distinction depends on the cognitive processing necessary to separate performance from ability, as well as upon the capacity to use the discounting principle. As noted in the previous section, Kun (1977) and Nicholls (1978) demonstrated consistent and reliable age trends in the development of the capacity to infer ability from effort and task difficulty. Karniol and Ross (1976) reported that the discounting principle is not understood until the age of 7 or 8 years. Kuhn and Ho (1977) as well as Erwin and Kuhn (1979) observed that not until early adolescence are subjects able to recognize two independent causes as simultaneously codetermining an outcome/a person's behavior. These studies all demonstrate the crucial role of cognitive development in the shift to social comparisons with similar others. Apparently, there is a minimum level of sophistication required (e.g., Dinner's fourth-grade subjects) for the emergence of this preference.

It stands to reason that the shifts between the modes of self-evaluation depicted in Fig. 4.1 are not immediately and fully developed at any one age but instead occur gradually. As a result, one should find specific problems inherent in the periods of transition from one stage to another. For example, Flavell (1977) asserted that: "sometimes the reward for a child's information processing skills is a temporary conceptual mistake, a mistake he was previously too cognitively immature to make, and one he will subsequently correct when he matures still further [p. 74]." The same type of error, induced by an inappropriately stringent following of the rules of related attributes, would highlight the developmental trend toward social comparison with similar others. Actually, a study by Graziano (1978) demonstrates just such an error. In this study, 7-year olds (presumably in the transition from indiscriminate to similar comparisons) and 9-year olds (well into the phase characterized by similar comparisons) were asked to distribute rewards to two other children. The relative size, age, and task performance of the two children were independently manipulated. Seven-year olds and 9-year olds were not expected and were not found to perform differently at the task (tower construction). Age and size were thus attributes unrelated to performance. Nonetheless, a significant difference was observed between 7-year olds and 9-year olds in reward allocations. The 9-year olds allocated rewards on the basis of task performance, regardless of the (task-irrelevant) age and size of the performers. Consistent with their presumed level of self-evaluation with similar others, the 9-year olds correctly treated the attributes of age and size as unrelated and ignored them in making reward allocations. However, 7-year olds allocated rewards on the basis of task performance except when the age and size of the performers differed; in this case, 7-year olds allocated rewards that favored the older or larger child. Thus, the 7-year olds treated size and age as related to performance. This curious type of error is important because it occurs at the point in the life-span where the development of appreciation of the concept of related attributes occurs. This is an example of the conceptual mistake that Flavell described and demonstrates the proposed shift in choice of comparison other (or in the use of related attributes) between the age of 7 and 9 years.

Another factor proposed as important in the shift from indiscriminate to similar social comparisons is change through early adolescence in the relative saliences of parents and the peer group. Bronfenbrenner (1970) and Devereux (1970) argued that conformity to peers increases from middle childhood to adolescence; Piaget (1965) and Bronfenbrenner (1970) asserted that conformity to parents declines through this period. Berndt (1979), examining children in grades three through twelve, demonstrated that conformity to parents decreased with age, whereas conformity to peers increased with age, to a point, and then leveled off. These results indicate that those dissimilar others who had previously been salient and important in evaluation (parents) become less important as similar others become more important.

It must be pointed out, though, that the vast majority of social-comparison research has examined the responses of college-age subjects. In these individuals we expect related attributes to most strongly influence the selection of comparison others and the effects of forced comparisons. Individuals providing the most information for the evaluation of abilities (similar others) are indeed most frequently selected as comparison others (Suls, Gaes, & Gastorf, 1979; Suls, Gastorf, & Lawhon, 1978; Suls & Tesch, 1978; Zanna, Goethals, & Hill, 1975). Information concerning the performance of similar others also has more effect on evaluations, satisfaction with performance, or certainty of evaluation than information concerning the performance of dissimilar others (Gastorf & Suls, 1978: Sanders, Gastorf, & Mullen, 1979). Thus, available research on social comparison in college-aged subjects reveals a consistent tendency to appropriately use related attributes and similar others in selecting and using social-comparison information.

There is a recent study from a different context that can also be interpreted as demonstrating that related attribute social comparison takes precedence over temporal comparison in college-age subjects. Brown and Inouye (1978) examined the role of similarity in the modeling of learned helplessness. All subjects had individual experience with highly difficult or insolvable anagrams (temporal comparison). Prior to attempting a second anagram task, all subjects observed a model fail at this task (social comparison). The model was perceived as either similar in competence to the subject (''social-comparison similar'') or inferior in competence to the subject (''social-comparison dissimilar''). Subjects who perceived themselves as similar to the unsuccessful model persisted in the task significantly less than did the control group, whereas subjects who perceived themselves as superior to the unsuccessful model persisted significantly more than did the control group. In the present context, these results suggest that the temporal-comparison information (previous experience with the difficult or insolvable anagrams) was superceded by the social-comparison information (failure of the model). Moreover, the related attributes of the other were appropriately considered by subjects in gauging their own abilities. Brown and Inouye's (1978) results are a clear confirmation of the proposed social comparison processes attributed to this stage of the life-span.

Middle Age

During middle age the tendency to make comparisons with similar others tends to decrease and shift to an increase in comparisons with dissimilar others. However, before identifying the dynamics prompting an increase in social comparisons with dissimilar others during middle age, we must first establish what we mean by middle age. Most people refer to middle age as the years between 40 and 65. Given a population whose average life expectancy is 71 (Butler, 1974), a more precise chronological definition would place middle age between the ages of 24 and 48. As an alternative to tentative chronological classifications, it is more meaningful and more useful to identify this stage in terms of certain specific events that occur within and around the individual (Rosenberg & Farrell, 1976), even though the occurrence of these events is much more variable than the occurrence of events comprising childhood or even adolescence. This alternative is better because it is specifically those events defining middle age that are the major factors that increase the importance of mixed social comparisons, that is, using both similar and dissimilar others.

Two distinct factors can be identified that lead to the relative increase of mixed comparisons at this stage of development. One factor has become a frequent theme of the professional and popular literature on middle age and on the so-called mid-life crisis (Levinson, 1978; Sheehy, 1976); that is, with the realization of one's imminent death, one develops a need to take stock of one's life. In order to feel that it has been worthwhile, one must believe he or she has made some unique contribution. In many instances (discussed at length following), comparison with dissimilar others might better serve to highlight one's uniqueness than comparison with similar others.

A second factor that contributes independently to mixed comparisons among the middle aged involves the dissimilar comparisons that are provided, legitimized, and even enforced by the social world. Competition in the employment market is a common situation in which the middle ager is compared with and forced to evaluate her or himself in terms of someone who might be younger, stronger, better-educated, or otherwise superior on some related attribute.

Before proceeding with our description it is important to note that the mixed comparisons of middle age and the mixed comparisons of middle childhood differ. In middle childhood, social comparisons are indiscriminate; that is, the usefulness of similar comparisons is not appreciated, and so dissimilar others are sought just as much as similars. In middle age, similar comparisons are appreciated; however, dissimilar others become either more valuable for certain types of comparisons or more salient. The comparisons of middle age thus appear to be mixed, although not indiscriminate.

Evidence of Mixed Social Comparisons in Middle Age

With middle age comes a major reassessment of the value of one's life (Bergler, 1954; Butler, 1974; Greenleigh, 1974; Marmor, 1968; Neugarten & Datan, 1974; Thompson, 1955). The need to feel that one's life has been worthwhile stems from perceptions that one's accomplishments were mundane and redundant, that one's time was wasted on trivialities, or that one's life is characterized by the absence of anything particularly special (Greenleigh, 1974; Rosenberg & Farrell, 1976). Erikson (1959), Fromm (1955), and Maslow (1962) suggest that human beings have a need for "uniqueness." Fromkin (1970, 1972) has examined this need at length. When the sense of personal distinctiveness is threatened or damaged, individuals experience less-pleasant affect (Fromkin, 1972); they exhibit greater preferences for scarce experiences than for plentiful experiences (Fromkin, 1970); they emphasize their dissimilarity from an unknown other person, and, most importantly, they show greater attraction for strangers with dissimilar attitudes. Similarity has been demonstrated (see previous section, Evidence for Similar Social Comparisons in Late Childhood, Adolescence, and Young Adulthood) to be superior to dissimilarity for the purpose of consensual validation. By the same token, Fromkin's research has demonstrated that dissimilarity is superior to similarity for the purpose of confirming one's distinctiveness. This leads to the following conclusion: Dissimilar comparisons will be highly valued by the middle-aged individual, who experiences the need for uniqueness that characterizes this stage.

The point is not that middle-aged individuals actively seek out comparisons with individuals who are alien in every way. Rather, individuals dissimilar in some related attributes are treated by the middle-aged person as if they were similar. For example, in examining the value and uniqueness of her life, the middle-aged female executive might compare herself with the up-and-coming junior executive. The middle-aged executive is certainly different from the junior executive on various important related attributes (age, experience, reputation, youthful appearance, stamina, motivation). As a result of these and other differences, the middle-aged executive and the junior executive will almost certainly differ in a variety of comparison dimensions (performance, income, success in interoffice politicking); these differences would satisfy the middle-aged person's need to highlight her sense of uniqueness.

An interesting problem in relativity arises. The objective observers of this hypothetical situation would describe the comparison as being between dissimilar others. The junior executive might in fact agree with this description, whereas the middle-aged executive might describe the comparison as being between two similar persons. In fact, evidence supports this speculation. Tuckman and Lorge (1953, 1954) and Drevenstedt (1976)—examining perceptions of age by young, middle-aged and old-aged adults—reported that older groups perceive middle age and old age to begin significantly later than do the younger groups. In a sense, the middle-aged person perceives herself to be in the same age group as the young adult (and thus similar and comparable). The young adult perceives him or herself to be in a younger age group than the middle-aged person (and thus dissimilar and noncomparable). Thus, those comparisons that best satisfy the middle-aged person's need for uniqueness may be described by others as dissimilar comparisons; however, they may be described by the middle-aged person as similar comparisons.

In addition to this intraindividual factor, various situational factors also contribute to the frequency of dissimilar comparisons. Consider the inevitable comparison between the middle-aged worker and the young adult worker holding the same job position. Bergler (1956), Greenleigh (1974), and Julian (1973) have all observed that the middle-aged worker may develop a sense of obsolescence upon discovering that the company values the younger man (with more recent education or more youthful vigor) as much as, or more than, they value the middle-aged worker. It is possible that management or union would attempt to transfer, retire, or fire the middle-aged employee in order to give younger workers the chance for jobs or promotion (Julian, 1973). This illuminates an important element of this situational factor: The social and especially the employment environment establishes and legitimizes comparisons between middle-aged and young adults. In support of this notion, Goodman (1974) posed that in evaluating one's pay on the job the social context determines the appropriate comparison others. Furthermore, the individual may come to accept as legitimate and agree with the evaluations made by legitimate evaluators in a performance setting. This depicts a situation where the middle-aged worker, *regardless of any possible need for uniqueness,* is compared with, and comes to compare himself with, others who are dissimilar to him.

Billig and Adams (1957) discussed some of the implications of this situation. If the older worker does poorly next to the younger workers, those representing the ascending generation may be seen as a threat. Billig and Adams examined mechanisms whereby the middle-aged worker can handicap, ingratiate, or imitate the younger worker, all in an attempt to bias or diffuse the imposed dissimilar comparsions. The very existence of these defense tactics indicates the import that this type of imposed dissimilar comparison has for individuals at this stage of the life-span. It might be suggested that unfavorable, imposed comparisons of the middle-aged with dissimilars should be eliminated or avoided by social institutions that have legitimized such imposed comparisons. Failure to do so may predispose the middle-aged person to otherwise avoidable stress.

To summarize, dissimilar comparisons become relatively more frequent during middle age because: (1) In some instances dissimilar comparisons can provide specific types of information better than similar comparisons can; and (2) the social context fosters and supports these dissimilar comparisons. Dissimilar comparisons, sought or imposed, can be unfavorable and thus dissatisfying. As the middle-aged individual grows older, he may become increasingly discouraged from making social comparisons if they increasingly provide negative, dissatisfying information. This contributes to the withdrawal from social comparisons and the increasing reliance upon temporal comparisons that characterizes the final stage of the life-span.

Old Age

The transition from middle age to old age is characterized by losses of or, at best, shifts in social and interpersonal contacts. These changes have crucial effects on how elderly individuals will define, perceive, and compare themselves. As noted earlier, the elderly may withdraw from dissatisfying comparisons that serve only to emphasize their incapacity relative to younger, stronger, better educated dissimilar others. Perhaps the most salient characteristic of our stereotype of old age is the idea of isolation. To the extent that an individual is isolated from social interaction, there is a restriction in the opportunities to engage in any type of social comparison.

Changes in the sensory and cognitive apparatus of the elderly also affect the frequency of social comparisons. To the extent that visual and auditory sensitivity diminish, there is a physical impediment to comparing any aspect of oneself with that of others. Similarly, possible declines in operational thought during old age could interfere with the perspective taking required by social-comparison processes.

In the event of reduced opportunity for, or inclination to undertake, social comparison, temporal comparison might still be used to provide some self-definition. The process of reminiscence may be viewed as a special type of temporal comparison. Alternatively, in some instances reminiscing may serve as an attempt to erase the dissimilarity between the older person and some younger-comparison other (in effect, placing the older person back into the same situation that the younger person is in now). These diverse contributions to the increase in temporal comparisons at this stage of the life-span will be considered in terms of empirical evidence.

Evidence of Temporal Comparisons in Old Age

With old age comes retirement, increasingly frequent deaths of acquaintances and intimates, and a general disengagement from society (Julian, 1973; Neugarten, 1968). Some sociologists and social workers are disenchanted with the sterotype of the lonely, isolated elderly individual. Shanus (1963), for example, calls it the "alienation myth" and thinks a view of old people as isolated and neglected has evolved from the professionals' exposure to the socially and economically disadvantaged persons who require help from social agencies. Nonetheless, recently available data still convey a cheerless portrayal of old age (Ferguson, 1975; Julian, 1973). For example, although people 65 years of age and older constitute 10.9% of our country's population, they constitute 41.7% of the total number of people living alone (U. S. Bureau of the Census, 1978). Various factors contribute to the isolation of the aged. For example, only 14% of all elderly people have a driver's license; apparently due to visual impairments, arbitrary age limits, or inability to obtain insurance, or afford a car (Ferguson, 1975). The unique problems of the ecological psychology of the elderly also contribute to their isolation from social contact. For example, even where public transportation exists, facilities seldom accommodate the special needs of the elderly: Entrance and exit from vehicles and terminals can be too high or too steep, schedules are difficult to read, systems are not designed to allow time to wait for a slow-moving elderly passenger. In many cases, the all-encompassing shopping malls exclude many of the elderly due to lack of adequate resting facilities, public toilets, or accessible elevators, and of course, the miles of walking required. It is both safer and simpler for many elderly people to just stay at home.

A very different type of loss that occurs during old age but nonetheless has tremendous import for social-comparison processes is the simple loss of comparison others. Professional groups or work organizations (composed of either similar or dissimilar others) are often lost or abandoned as a result of retirement. Furthermore, longevity can mean that one outlives most of one's previous comparison others. In discussing this situation, Bengston (1973) described an interview with a man who had just turned 104 years of age: "In talking about the problems of growing old, he said, 'You know, I haven't had a friend since I was 77. That's when my last friend died.' Imagine living for 27 years without someone you could term a friend! . . . To what group can this man refer in judging the adequacy of his behavior? [p. 120]."

All these factors can contribute to isolation and are recognized and addressed in the many recent, government-sponsored, paid and volunteer service activities directed toward the elderly (e.g., Foster Grandparent Program, SCORE — Service Corps of Retired Executives, RSVP — Retired Senior Volunteer Program). However, these programs do not appeal to all retirees (Trela & Simmons, 1971); and for those who are interested in participating, there are in many cases few openings offered. Finally, we should note that funding is insecure. The result of these various factors, if not total alienation, is a reduction in the quality and the quantity of social interaction required if social comparison is to occur.

Isolation resulting from physical detachment and seclusion from the social world is compounded by the possibility of physiological and psychological changes occurring during old age. For example, it has been argued that peripheral sensory loss in the elderly has a causal effect on cognitive and behavioral deterioration (O'Neil & Calhoun, 1975). Further, the possibility exists that severe hearing impairment, which strikes at least one out of every four persons of 65 years and older, can result in mental withdrawal and social isolation (Gardner, 1975). Deficits in vision and hearing limit the amount of reading, television viewing, or radio listening in which the elderly could engage (Ferguson, 1975). This means the loss of a secondary means of social contact and information (i.e., the mass media).

On the other hand, apart from physiological declines that may occur in old age, evidence suggests that there may be subtle cognitive shifts that have an impact on social-comparison processes. Data indicating a decline in operational thought (Pabalia & Bielby, 1974; Protinsky & Houghston, 1978) as well as a resurgence of egocentric thought in the elderly (Looft, 1970) suggest that the complex inferences and perspective taking required by social comparisons may become more difficult for the elderly. (We realize that the notion of intellectual decline with age is the subject of some debate [Schaie, 1974]. However, whether changes are due to actual cognitive declines or simply because the elderly live under circumstances that impair their ability to function at a higher level does not affect our basic conclusion that several shifts occurring during old age discourage the use of social comparison.)

These situational and individual elements of old age provide impediments to the capacities and opportunities to engage in social comparisons. Hence, temporal comparisons are probably used in various ways to provide self-definition for the elderly. Consistent with this are Burnside's (1974) observations regarding the increased concern of the elderly with the passage and measurement of time, coincident with their withdrawal from social contacts.

There are data supporting the suggestion that a relative increase in temporal comparison and relative decrease in social comparison occurs during old age. Hutchinson (1974) reported that elderly subjects (mean age = 74) did not, whereas young adults (mean age = 19.7) did, respond to praise and reproof. The relative insensitivity to social reinforcement by the elderly is consistent with the proposed lack of concern for the effects of favorable or unfavorable social comparisons. Two studies in particular provide substantive support for these dynamics. Krugman (1959) had old subjects (70–86 years of age) and young subjects (22–36 years of age) perform in a level of aspiration task with temporal-comparison feedback. Older subjects were more responsive to the temporal feedback (as indicated by setting more extreme goals) than the younger subjects. Davis (1967) also had elderly subjects (mean age = 77.5) and young subjects (mean age = 24.5) perform in a level of aspiration study and then provided these subjects with social-comparison feedback. The results of this study indicated that older subjects were less competitive with a same-age comparison group than were the younger subjects. Davis concluded that the older subjects were disengaged from social comparison. The results of these studies indicate that during this stage of the life-span temporal comparison does indeed have more of an effect on self-evaluative processes than does social comparison.

Reminiscing may also be a form of temporal comparison for the elderly. Reminiscing is usually construed as a meaningless wandering of the mind, indicative of deterioration. A more favorable view is that reminiscing is at least the recall of or at most the actual re-experiencing of personally significant experiences. One would expect, however, that such comparisons would emphasize the discrepancy between the "good old days" and now, and thus result in feelings of discouragement and dissatisfaction. But evidence has accumulated indicating that reminiscing may in fact be beneficial to the elderly. McMahon and Rhudick (1964) found there was a tendency for nondepressed subjects to reminisce more than depressed subjects. In fact, Butler (1961, 1963; Butler & Lewis, 1974) and

Kaminsky (1978) have promoted the use of reminiscing as a therapeutic technique for the elderly. Cumming and Henry (1961) suggested that reminiscing may be useful in adjusting to changes of old age. From the present perspective, recalling one's history of successful instrumentality, of having once been capable and productive, can provide the elderly individual with some modicum of self-worth and a gauge for assessing present abilities. Reminiscing may be such a commonly observed behavior in the elderly (Butler & Lewis, 1974), because it represents a form of temporal comparison and provides a useful and multifaceted means of self-evaluation.

Caveat

In the preceding pages we have described a life-span model of the self-evaluation process and provided supporting evidence from a wide range of research areas. Direct tests of the model described are needed to evaluate its validity; however it is encouraging that, as the preceding pages reveal, so much existing data are consistent with its formulation. It seems appropriate at this point to discuss the implications of the model both for social psychological theorizing about the self and for societal applications. But before doing so let us specify the limitations of our approach. For example, we have focused predominantly on self-evaluation of abilities and have said nothing about opinion evaluation. It seems reasonable that comparable changes in the evaluation of beliefs and values would occur across the life-span. Recent examinations of the social comparison of opinions are also based on the concepts of related attributes, discounting, and similar or dissimilar others (Goethals & Darley, 1977). Developmental and social trends that effect ability evaluation probably exert a parallel influence in opinion evaluations, but this remains for future work and study.

Another, more fundamental problem with any long-range developmental perspective concerns the descriptive nature of the stages and in fact the use of the term *stages*. We provided tentative age ranges for the five stages of the model; however, we do not suggest any cross-cultural or interindividual universality of these age ranges (especially after late childhood). Also the term *stage* is used as a convenience and only for emphasis. We recognize that there may be considerable variability, and that changes are probably more quantitative than qualitative, gradual rather than abrupt. For these reasons the reader may prefer to think of our scheme as a set of phases rather than stages, because the latter implies homogeneity, invariance, and qualitative transformation (Flavell, 1977).

IMPLICATIONS

The present model has many interesting implications, both for social psychological theory and for applications to real-life problems. Perhaps the most important one is that social as opposed to temporal comparison may most appropriately apply to the middle stages of the life cycle. This point may have been overlooked simply because empirical research on comparison processes has predominately been conducted on adults, especially in the 18–25-year-old range. The present model suggests that social comparison should not be assumed to be the dominant mode of self-evaluation across the life cycle; temporal comparisons may have more significance in the very early years and the very late years of life.

A related implication is that several social phenomena believed to be mediated by social-comparison processes may operate only at particular phases of the life cycle. For instance, the polarization effects exhibited in group decision making (the so-called "risky shift") have been shown to be contingent, at least in part, on comparisons between group members (Brown, 1965; Levinger & Schneider, 1969; Sanders, 1979; Sanders & Baron, 1977). Given the present model, the polarization effects should not be demonstrated among very young children or elderly individuals because social comparison (particularly with similar others) is less likely to be important for them. The same implication may apply to other phenomena mediated by social comparisons, such as bystander intervention, group conformity, and feelings of relative deprivation. This seems to indicate the need for future research to examine how these social behaviors may differ at various points in the life cycle.

Of special significance is the implication that certain kinds of performance feedback may be effective only at particular stages of the life cycle. Thus, it may be useful to make salient for children comparisons between their past and present performances (i.e., temporal comparisons), but social comparison feedback may, in the early years, have little impact on self-evaluation. By the same token, if a child has reached the stage where he or she engages in social comparison but makes no distinction between similar and dissimilar others, it may be helpful for parents and caretakers to protect that child by limiting information about others who are dissimilar. Specifically, it may be efficacious to limit comparisons with others who are advantaged in age, experience, or other related attributes, and who will, therefore, typically outperform the child. Only when the child reaches middle childhood and appreciates the difference between similar and dissimilar others will he or she be more able to guard against invidious comparisons.

This point may be extremely relevant to the situation found in the integrated classroom. Black children frequently experience decreases in self-esteem when they first enter integrated schools (Stephan, 1978). Because many of these children come into the school with less preparation, they often initially fall behind their white peers. It is not so surprising that they lose faith in their own capabilities. Compared with their white peers, they may appear to have less academic ability, and such information may have negative effects on their feelings of self-worth and esteem. Only a child who appreciates the fact that the white classmates are advantaged and hence dissimilar on related attributes would be able to discount the comparison. Given this logic and the present model, children in early childhood (5–7 years) should be most adversely affected by being placed in integrated classrooms, because they are likely to compare with others without considering possible differences in the related attributes that contribute to any differences in performance. In contrast, older children who do allow for related attributes should not be as adversely affected by initially performing worse than more advantaged peers.

The same problem may also be found among handicapped children who are mainstreamed and find themselves falling behind compared to their "normal" classmates. The life-span model suggests that children who have not yet attained an understanding of the usefulness of similar others and of the relative inefficacy of dissimilar comparisons may suffer from invidious comparisons. Interestingly, research on mainstreaming reported by Strang, Smith, and Rogers (1978) has reported this pattern.

The present model also has implications about making effective interventions to change modes of self-evaluation. Young children fail to use social comparisons mainly because of their cognitive limits (not understanding the concept of ability; lack of appreciation of the discounting principle). Because attempts to accelerate cognitive development have had some success (Rosenthal & Zimmerman, 1978), it is plausible that children's use of social comparison could be accelerated through training procedures, modeling, etc. In contrast, the elderly's inability to use social comparison is largely socially imposed (e.g., the loss of peers because of isolation or death). These conditions can be altered and such alterations may effectively encourage stimulating and satisfying comparisons with same-aged peers. In fact, elderly citizen's groups and retirement villages may succeed in boosting the spirits and improving the health of senior citizens for just this reason.

The fact that young children do not tend to use social comparison because of cognitive reasons, whereas the elderly show the same tendency but mainly for social reasons, has another implication as well. Because the cognitive skills that underlie social comparison develop in a relatively invariant sequence in young children across all cultures, the life-span model should be applicable across different cultures with respect to at least the first 6 or 7 years of life. After this time there may be considerable variability, because societies may differ in the extent to which they encourage or discourage social comparison and competition. Also, cross-cultural differences in modes of self-evaluation are most likely to appear in older people. Some societies venerate the elderly and keep them in the mainstream of life, where they are active in caring for children and where they serve important roles such as providing leadership and dispensing practical wisdom. To the extent that the elders of some cultures play an important role in their society, they should have readily available social contact, which may cause temporal comparisons to play a lesser role than in cultures where the elderly are shut off and alienated. In any case, these developmental and cross-cultural differences in the modes of self-evaluation need to be studied.

CONCLUSION

In this chapter we have described a life-span model of the self-evaluation process. There are always dangers to such a broad-ranged approach. For instance, we have relied on indirect evidence with respect to certain phases of the model. Only full-scale, longitudinal research can verify or disconfirm the present formulation. Another difficulty is the lack of space necessary for considering the connections and interrelations between our model and other contemporary theories, such as objective self-awareness theory (Duval & Wicklund, 1972), and recent cybernetic models (Carver, 1979). Also conspicuous through its absence is consideration of the effects of reflected appraisals across the life-span. Nevertheless, we have accomplished our aim if we can direct other researchers' attention to the need for considering how self-evaluation operates, not just at a single stage of development but across the life cycle. William James (1890) observed: "A man has as many social selves as there are individuals who recognize him [p. 294]." We would add the individual may also have as many selves as seasons through which he passes.

ACKNOWLEDGMENTS

Preparation of this chapter was facilitated by a grant from the SUNY Research Foundation. The authors are grateful to Albert Bandura, Philip Brickman, Glenn Sanders, Fred Tesch, and Susan Witenberg for their comments and suggestions.

REFERENCES

Albert, S. Temporal comparison theory. *Psychological Review*, 1977, *84*, 485–503.

Bandura, A. *Social learning theory*. Englewood Cliffs, N. J.: Prentice-Hall, 1977.

Bergler, E. *The revolt of the middle-aged man*. New York: Wyn, 1954.

Bergston, V. L. Self-determiniation: A social-psychological perspective on helping the aged. *Geriatrics*, 1973, *28*, 118–130.

Berndt, T. J. Developmental changes in conformity to peers and parents. *Developmental Psychology*, 1979, *15*, 608–616.

Billig, O., & Adams, R. W. Emotional conflicts of the middle-aged man. *Geriatrics*, 1957, *12*, 535–541.

Bronfenbrenner, U. Reaction to social pressure from adults versus peers among Soviet day school and boarding school pupils in the perspective of American sample. *Journal of Personality and Social Psychology*, 1970, *15*, 179–189.

Brown, A. L. The development of memory: Knowing, knowing about knowing, and knowing how to know. In H. W. Reese (Ed.), *Advances in child development and behavior* (Vol. 10). New York: Academic Press, 1975.

Brown, I., & Inouye, D. K. Learned helplessness through modeling: The role of perceived similarity in competence. *Journal of Personality and Social Psychology*, 1978, *36*, 900–908.

Brown, L. G. The development of diverse patterns of behavior among children in the same family. *The Family*, 1928, *9*, 35–39.

Brown, R. *Social psychology*. New York: Free Press, 1965.

Burnside, I. M. Clocks and calendars. In M. H. Browning (Ed.), *Nursing and the aging patient*. New York: American Journal of Nursing, 1974.

Butler, R. N. Reawakening interest. *Nursing Homes*, 1961, *10*, 8–19.

Butler, R. N. The life review: An interpretation of reminiscences in the aged. *Psychiatry*, 1963, *26*, 65–76.

Butler, R. N. Psychiatry and psychology of the middle aged. In A. Freedman, H. Kaplan, J. Sadock (Eds.), *Comprehensive textbook of Psychiatry*. Baltimore: Williams & Wilkins, 1974.

Carver, C. S. A cybernetic model of self-attention processes. *Journal of Personality and Social Psychology*, 1979, *37*, 1251–1281.

Cumming, E., & Henry, W. E. *Growing old*. New York: Basic Books, 1961.

Davis, R. W. Social influences on the aspiration tendency of older people. *Journal of Gerontology*, 1967, *22*, 510–516.

Devereux, E. C. The role of the peer group experience in moral development. In J. P. Hill (Ed.), *Minnesota symposium on child psychology* (Vol. 4). Minneapolis: University of Minnesota Press, 1970.

Dinner, S. H. Social comparison and self-evaluation in children. *Dissertation Abstracts International*, 1976, *37(4-B)*, 1968-1969.

Drevenstedt, J. Perceptions of onsets of young adulthood, middle age, and old age. *Journal of Gerontology*, 1976, *31*, 53–57.

Duval, S., & Wicklund, R. A. *A theory of objective self awareness*. New York: Academic Press, 1972.

Erikson, E. H. Identity and the life cycle. *Psychological Issues*, 1959, *1*, 1–171.

Erwin, J., & Kuhn, D. Development of children's understanding of the multiple determination underlying human behavior. *Developmental Psychology*, 1979, *15*, 352–353.

Feld, S., Ruhland, D., & Gold, M. Developmental changes in achievement motivation. *Merrill–Palmer Quarterly*, 1979, *25*, 43–60.

Ferguson, E. A. *Social Work: An introduction*. Philadelphia : Lippincott, 1975.

Festinger, L. A. A theory of social comparison processes. *Human Relations*, 1954, *7*, 117–140.

Flavell, J. H. *Cognitive Development*. Englewood Cliff, N. J.: Prentice–Hall, 1977.

Frank, J. D. Individual differences in certain aspects of the level of aspiration. *American Journal of Psychology*, 1935, *47*, 119–128.

Fromkin, H. L. The effects of experimentally aroused feelings of undistinctiveness upon valuation of scarce and novel experiences. *Journal of Personality and Social Psychology*, 1970, *16* , 521–529.

Fromkin, H. L. Feelings of interpersonal undistinctiveness: An unpleasant affective state. *Journal of Experimental Research in Personality*, 1972, *6*, 178–185.

Fromm, E. *The Sane Society*. New York: Rinehart, 1955.

Gardner, J. W. Level of aspiration in response to a prearranged sequence of scores. *Journal of Experimental Psychology*, 1939, *25*, 601–621.

Gardner, W. G. Hearing loss, the route to senility? *Audecibel*, 1975, 74–76.

Gastorf, J. W., & Suls, J. Performance evaluation via social comparison: Performance similarity versus related attribute similarity. *Social Psychology*, 1978, *41*, 297–305.

Goethals, G. R., & Darley, J. M. Social comparison theory: An attributional approach. In J. M. Suls & R. L. Miller (Eds.), *Social comparison processes: Theoretical and empirical perspectives*. Washington, D. C.: Hemisphere, 1977.

Goodman, P. S. An examination of referents used in the evaluation of pay. *Organizational Behavior and Human Performance*, 1974, *12*, 170–195.

Gould, R., & Lewis, H. B. An experimental investigation of changes in the meaning of level of aspiration. *Journal of Experimental Psychology*, 1940, *27*, 422–438.

Graziano, W. G. Standards of fair play in same-age and mixed-age groups of children. *Developmental Psychology*, 1978, *14*, 524–530.

Greenleigh, L.   Facing the challenge of change in middle age. *Geriatrics*, 1974, *29*, 61–68.

Hertzman, M., & Festinger, L.   Shifts in explicit goals in a level of aspiration experiment. *Journal of Experimental Psychology*, 1940, *27*, 439–452.

Hoppe, F.   Erfolg and Misserfolg. *Psychologische Forschungen*, 1930, *14*, 1–62.

Hutchinson, S. L.   An investigation of learning under two types of social reinforcers in young and elderly adults. *International Journal of Aging and Human Development*, 1974, *5*, 181–186.

Inhelder, B., & Piaget, J.   *The growth of logical thinking from childhood to adolescence*. New York: Basic Books, 1958.

James, W.   *Principles of Psychology* (Vol. 1). New York: Holt, 1890.

Jucknat, M.   Performance, level of aspiration, and self consciousness. *Psychologische Forschungen*, 1937, *22*, 89–174.

Julian, J.   *Social problems*. New York: Appleton–Century–Crofts, 1973.

Kaminsky, M.   Pictures from the past: The use of reminiscence in casework with the elderly. *Journal of Gerontological Social Work*, 1978, *1*, 19–32.

Karniol, R., & Ross, M.   The development of causal attributions in social perception. *Journal of Personality and Social Psychology*, 1976, *34*, 455–464.

Kelley, H. H.   The processes of causal attribution. *American Psychologist*, 1973, *28*, 107–128.

Krugman, A. D.   A note on level of aspiration behavior and aging. *Journal of Gerontology*, 1959, *14*, 222–225.

Kuhn, D., & Ho, V.   The development of schemes for recognizing additive and alternative effects in a natural experiment context. *Developmental Psychology*, 1977, *13*, 515–516.

Kun, A.   Development of the magnitude covariation and compensation schemata in ability and effort attributions of performance. *Child Development*, 1977, *48*, 862–873.

Latane, B.   Studies in social comparison—Introduction and overview. *Journal of Experimental Social Psychology*, 1966, *Supplement 1*, 1–5.

Leventhal, G. S.   Influence of brothers and sisters on sex-role behavior. *Journal of Personality and Social Psychology*, 1970, *16*, 452–465.

Levinger, G., & Schneider, D. J.   A test of the risk is a value hypothesis. *Journal of Personality and Social Psychology*, 1969, *11*, 165–169.

Levinson, D.   *The seasons of a man's life*. New York: Knopf, 1978.

Lewis, M. I., & Butler, R. N.   Life review therapy: Putting memories to work in individual and group psychotherapy. *Geriatrics*, 1974, *29*, 165–173.

Looft, W. R.   *Egocentrism and its manifestations in young and old adults*. Paper presented at the Gerontological Society Convention, Toronto, Canada, Oct. 22, 1970.

Marmor, J.   The crisis of middle age. *Psychiatric Digest*, 1968, *29*, 18.

Maslow, A. H.   *Toward a psychology of being*. New York: Van Nostrand, 1962.

McClintock, C. G., Moskowitz, J. M., & McClintock, E.   Variations in preferences for individualistic, competitive, and cooperative outcomes as a function of age, game class, and task in nursery school children. *Child Development*, 1977, *48*, 1080–1085.

McMahon, A. W., & Rhudick, P. J.   Reminiscing—adaptational significance in the aged. *Archives of General Psychiatry*, 1964, *10*, 292–298.

Miller, R. L.   Preferences for social versus nonsocial comparison as a means of self-evaluation. *Journal of Personality*, 1977, *45*, 343–355.

Nelson, L. L., & Kagan, S.   Competition: The star-spangled scramble. *Psychology Today*, 1972, *6*, 53–56, 90–91.

Neugarten, B. L.   Awareness of middle age. In B. L. Neugarten (Ed.), *Middle age and aging*. Chicago: University of Chicago Press, 1968.

Neugarten, B. L., & Datan, N.   The middle years. In S. Ariei (Ed.), *American handbook of psychiatry*. New York: Basic Books, 1974.

Nicholls, J. G.   The development of the concepts of effort and ability, perception of academic attainment, and the understanding that difficult tasks require more ability. *Child Development*, 1978, *49*, 800–814.

O'Neil, P. M., & Calhoun, K. S.   Sensory deficits and behavioral deterioration in senescence. *Journal of Abnormal Psychology*, 1975, *84*, 579–582.

Pabalia, D. E., & Bielby, D.   Cognitive functioning in middle and old age adults. *Human Development*, 1974, *17*, 424–443.

Pettigrew, T. F.   Social evaluation theory: Convergence and applications. In D. Levine (Ed.), *Nebraska symposium on motivation*. Lincoln: University of Nebraska Press, 1967.

Piaget, J.   *The origins of intelligence*. New York: International Universities Press, 1952.

Piaget, J.   *The moral judgment of the child*. New York: Free Press, 1965.

Protinsky, H., & Houghston, G.   Conservation in elderly males. *Developmental Psychology*, 1978, *14*, 114.

Rosenberg, S. D., & Farrell, M. P.   Identity and crisis in middle-aged men. *International Journal of Aging and Human Development*, 1976, *7*, 153–170.

Rosenthal, T., & Zimmerman, B.   *Social learning and cognition*. New York: Academic Press, 1978.

Ruble, D. N., Boggiano, A. K., Feldman, N. S., & Loebl, J. H.   A developmental analysis of the role of social comparison in self-evaluation. *Developmental Psychology*, 1980, *16* , 105–115.

Ruble, D. N., Feldman, N., & Boggiano, A. K.   Social comparison between young children in achievement situations. *Developmental Psychology*, 1976, *47*, 990–997.

Sanders, G. S.   An integration of shifts toward risk and caution in gambling situations. *Journal of Experimental Social Psychology*, 1979, *14*, 409–416.

Sanders, G. S., & Baron, R. S.   Is social comparison irrelevant for choice shifts? *Journal of Experimental Social Psychology*, 1977, *13*, 303–314.

Sanders, G. S., Gastorf, J. W., & Mullen B.   Selectivity in the use of social comparison information. *Personality and Social Psychology Bulletin*, 1979, *5*, 377–380.

Schaie, K. W.   Translations in gerontology—From lab to life: Intellectual functioning. *American Psychologist*, 1974, *29*, 802–807.

Shanus, E.   *The unmarried old person in the United States: Living arrangements and care in illness, myth and fact*. Paper presented at International Social Science Research Seminar in Gerontology, Makaryd, Sweden, August, 1963.

Sheehy, G.   *Passages*, New York: Dutton, 1976.

Simon, K. M.   The effects of self-comparison, social comparison, and depression on goal setting and self-evaluation reactions. Unpublished manuscript, Stanford University, 1979.

Singer, J. E.   Social comparison—progress and issues. *Journal of Experimental Social Psychology Supplement 1*, 1966, 103–110.

Strang, L., Smith, M. D., & Rogers, C. M.   Social comparison, multiple reference groups, and the self-concepts of academically handicapped children before and after mainstreaming. *Journal of Educational Psychology*, 1978, *70*, 487–497.

Stephan, W. School desegregation: An evaluation of predictions made in Brown vs. the Board of Education. *Psychological Bulletin*, 1978, *85*, 217–238.

Suls, J., Gaes, G., & Gastorf, J.   Evaluating a sex-related ability: Comparison with same-, opposite-, and combined-sex norms. *Journal of Research in Personality*, 1979, *13*, 294–304.

Suls, J., Gastorf, J., & Lawhon, J.   Social comparison choices for evaluating a sex- and age-related ability. *Personality and Social Psychology Bulletin*, 1978, *4*, 102–105.

Suls, J., & Miller, R. L. (Eds.).   *Social comparison processes: Theoretical and empirical perspectives*. Washington, D. C.: Hemisphere, 1977.

Suls, J., & Tesch, F.   Student's preferences for information about their test performance: A social comparison study. *Journal of Applied Social Psychology*, 1978, *8*, 189–197.

Thompson, L. J.   Stresses in middle life from the psychiatrist's point of view. *Geriatrics*, 1955, *10*, 162–164.

Trela, J. E., & Simmons, W.   Health and other factors affecting membership and attrition in a senior center. *Journal of Gerontology*, 1971, *26*, 45–51.

Tuckman, J., & Lorge, I.   When does old age begin and a worker become old? *Journal of Gerontology*, 1953, *8*, 483–488.

Tuckman, J., & Lorge, I.   Classification of the self as young, middle-aged or old. *Geriatrics*, 1954, *9*, 534–536.

U. S. Bureau of the Census.   *Statistical Abstract of the United States: 1978*. Washington, D. C., 1978.

Veroff, J.   Social comparison and the development of achievement motivation. In C. P. Smith (Ed.), *Achievement-related motives in children*. New York: Russell Sage, 1969.

Zanna, M. P., Goethals, G. R., & Hill, J. F. Evaluating a sex-related ability: Social comparison with similar others and standard setters. *Journal of Experimental Social Psychology*, 1975, *11*, 86–93.

II

THE SELF: ONE OR MANY?

One of the classic questions about the self is whether it is best considered as a single or global entity or is self conception disconnected and multiple? Contemporary psychological research tends to argue for the multiple conception, yet the unity notion still persists. The chapters in this section deal with the one or many, consistent-inconsistent, fluid-stable debate.

Kenneth Gergen, in his chapter "From Self to Science: What Is There to Know?" argues that the scientists' conceptions of themselves as discoverers of objective entities influences the formulations of self theory, particularly classic statements emphasizing the unity and stability of the self. In his discussion Gergen reviews the results of the empirical literature that demonstrate considerable self fluidity and disunity. Reasoning from this base, he argues for a change not only in psychological treatments of the self but in the metaconceptions by which scientists operate in their own enterprise.

In "Is Any*one* in Charge? Personalysis versus the Principle of Personal Unity," Anthony Greenwald attempts to explain the roots of personal disunity by articulating a multisystem analysis of the person (personalysis), based on a computer analogue. According to this approach, the self is a subsystem of the person and is partially independent of body, verbal, and social subsystems. Personalysis is distinguished from psychoanalysis, and special topics in social psychology are discussed within the personalytic context. Special attention is given to the concept of deindividuation, a behavior not mediated by the self system.

5 From Self to Science: What is There to Know?

Kenneth J. Gergen
Swarthmore College

When people set out to discover themselves, to determine their true characteristics, to explore why they behave as they do, what they believe in, what they feel, what constitutes their principles and aspirations, why they can control certain actions and not others, and so on, they are carrying out in an untutored and unsystematic fashion the same line of inquiry guiding the scientific scholar of human behavior. It is traditionally held that the scientific orientation is by far the superior one, following as it does the estimable footsteps of the natural sciences and guided as it is by cannons of logic and observation (Nisbett & Ross, 1980). If the laity could follow the logic of science more assiduously and observe more vigorously, then their attempts at self-understanding might be markedly increased. The layman, it is believed, has much to learn from the more advanced thinking and methods of the behavioral sciences. Although compelling for the scientist, this line of argument depends for its validity on a set of assumptions that generally remain implicit and unexamined, assumptions concerning the character of scientific conduct. In effect, the scientist possesses a concept of self as scientist. It is the concept of self as scientist that furnishes the grounds for concern with the deficiencies of lay self conception; and yet, this concept itself remains beyond question.

This chapter first discusses several key features of the scientist's conception of self and attempts to show how these features influenced theoretical accounts of self-concept formation and change on the lay level. Special attention is given to the scientist's view of self as discoverer of the objective properties of the world, and the way is which this metatheoretical view has shaped traditional theoretical conceptions of self-concept. Lines of research and theory are then examined that point to significant shortcomings in traditional theories of self conception. Informed by this analysis, critical questions are raised concerning the self-concept of the scientist. If metatheory dictates defective theory, there is substantial reason to challenge the metatheory.

Self-Conception in Science and its Impact on Self-Theory

A full account of the behavioral scientist's view of self as scientist is beyond our present scope. Surely, there are wide variations among scientists in such views, and existing views are in a state of continuous alteration. For present purposes it is satisfactory to center on the traditional positivist-empiricist account of the scientist's activity, and, in particular, on two critical aspects of this account. The first central assumption made by the traditional scientist is that he or she is attempting to *discover properties of an objective world*. In this case the scientist generally assumes that the world is composed of objectively isolated entities; it is the scientist's primary task to discover the systematic relations among the observed entities, and to provide an explanatory rationale for such systematic relations. On this account, for example, the scientist might observe and classify various forms of aggressive behavior, isolate those factors to which these forms are systematively related, and provide theories linking observable antecedents with aggressive actions. The scientist in this case serves as a maker of maps reflecting the contours of the physical world.

A second critical aspect of the scientist's self-view within the positivist-empiricist tradition is that *knowledge may be accumulated through the verification or falsification of hypotheses*. For example, the scientist who theorizes that such factors as room temperature, the presence of weapons, or high arousal are related systematically to aggression may, by the traditional account, put such ideas to empirical test. Whether such theoretical statements are correct or incorrect will be indicated by the data. Over time, incorrect theoretical accounts will be eschewed by the scientific process, and theories with a high verification/falsification ratio will remain. The ultimate result of the scientific process should thus be a set of relatively enduring theoretical statements that can enhance one's capacities for adaption to or effective manipulation of the observed world.

It is the view of the present chapter that these conceptions of the scientist's activities have had a strong influence on the formulation of self-theory. Essentially, psychologists have looked at others and seen their own reflection. The view of the scientist as discoverer and mapper of objective entities reappears in the assumption that people develop conceptions of themselves that ideally reflect accurate observations and thus serve as guides to adaptive action. To elaborate, self-concept theorists typically assume that the individual possesses a construct system, or set of conceptual templates that may be compared against his or her behavior. In the observation of self the conceptual templates may be verified or falsified, and they may become increasingly elaborated or differentiated over time as the individual learns more about her or himself. Misperception can occur, but when it does it usually results from some extraneous motivational, emotional, or social source. This line of thinking is first represented in the seminal theories of Kelly (1955) and Rogers (1959). For the former, the individual is viewed as a scientist attempting to improve the validity of his or her construct system. For Rogers, effective therapy was that which brought the individual's self-concept in closer proximity with his or her true feelings or wants. In more recent form, empiricist assumptions emerge in Epstein's influential work (1977, 1980). As Epstein (1980) argues in this theory of self-conception: "We are no less dependent upon a coherent theory for directing our behavior in everyday life than a scientist is for directing his or her activities in a more limited realm. Only by organizing our concepts into an efficient system of higher and lower order generalizations from past experience with implications for future experience can we hope to adjust to the complex social world around us [p. 6]." A similar view underlies much work on self-deception (Gur & Sackheim, 1979; Hilgard, 1949); in order for the individual to be deceived about self, one must be capable of veridical self-perception.

By extension, the empiricist view of science has also had an important impact on theories of causal attribution. Most prominent is Kelley's (1972) account of the individual's search for causal locus. As Kelley proposes:

> Our theory of attribution must be founded in a view of the layman as an 'applied scientist,' that is, as a person concerned about applying his knowledge of causal relations in order to *exercise control* of his world. This proposal is made in the belief that the person's motivation to control has consequences for his attributions and, further, that the process by which attributions are made and the nature of both the accuracies and errors they exhibit can be explained by the problems of control he commonly faces [p. 2].

Similar assumptions underlorly the celebrated assumption of the "fundamental attribution error." As Ross (1977) defines this error it is a: "General tendency to overestimate the importance of personal or dispositional factors relative to environmental influences [p. 184]." It must be presumed on this account that one can objectively assess the extent to which a personal decision, motive, intent, emotion, or conception of self propels behaviors in any given situation.

Because of the assumption that through hypothesis testing people come to form progressively more accurate self-conceptions, modern self-theory has had little difficulty in subsuming traditional symbolic interactionist and psychodynamic views of stabilization of self-conception. One of the most significant lines of argument in such domains is that normal socialization endows the individual with a reasonably stable and enduring conception of who he or she is. This "core conception" remains with people throughout their social life, guiding their actions, providing a needed sense of identity, furnishing a sense of continuity, and essentially acting as a conceptual anchor in an otherwise chaotic social world. For example, in the work of George Herbert Mead (1934) we find the individual learning of his or her identity through taking the role of others toward self. However, for Mead the individual does not adopt all perspectives, but only those of a significant few. It is the views of the significant few that become amalgamated in the concept of "generalized other." Thus, as children grow older, their conception of self becomes increasingly unified and stabilized. For Erik Erikson (1968), the process is different but the end result of the same. The chief accomplishment of a successful adolescence is, from his perspective, a "firm sense of identity." For Erikson, the individual must realize this sense of identity or face severe problems of anxiety and social anomia. In much the same way, Carl Rogers (1959) has spoken of the core set of evaluative experiences forming one's basic sense of worth. If one's socialization is defective, that is to say, dominated by others' "conditional positive regard," then one's adult sense of worth is defective. Many hours of therapy are typically required to alter the defective core. Freud, Sullivan, and Horney have also added weight to the assumption of an enduring sense of self. Such views are quite congenial with those stemming from the projection of positivist-empiricist metatheory onto lay self-processing. In both cases, the endpoint of proper socialization experiences should be a relatively enduring template or concept system with respect to self.

The Unfreezing of Self-Conception

Thus far, we have discussed several major aspects of the scientist's conceptions of his or her own activity and traced the manner in which these conceptions have been manifested in theoretical accounts of normal self-conception. We must now examine the credibility of the normalized account of self-conception. Does it or can it operate in the manner specified? Let us first consider the assumption of stabilization—favored by positivist-empiricist metatheory, early symbolic interactionist, and psychodynamic theorists. This assumption is of particular importance, not only for present purposes, but because its ramifications are so far-reaching. On the theoretical level, for example, the stability assumption is intimately connected to the situationism controversy of long-standing concern (Magnusson & Endler, 1977). The assumption of stabilized dispositions is a virtual requirement for the viability of the trait orientation in personality psychology and furnishes substantial sustenance for attitude study in social psychology. On the more practical level, to argue that early socialization molds life-long patterns of thought is also to argue for highly specialized and individualized programs of caretaking presumably of the kind that only a parent might capably furnish. Both role differentiation within the family and women's participation in the labor force are immediately implicated in the position. Further, if one assumes deeply engrained habits of self-conception, attempts at intervention must be framed accordingly. One must assume that the lowered self-regard of the therapy patient, the self-defeating conceptions of the poor student or the drug addict, or the diminished self-esteem of the target of discrimination will require amelioration programs that are both long-term and intensive. And, on the level of daily life, to assume stabilized self conception is to discourage attempts at self-change. If one believes he or she is "basically inept," he or she is little encouraged to attempt change. "What would be the use?"

Given the significance of the stabilization assumption, there is good reason to attend to murmurings of the recalcitrant minority. For example, William James (1890) has spoken of the many "social selves" adopted by the individual for each significant group in which he is a member. If one continued to shift social groups, would this not threaten the concept of an enduring core of self-conception? James himself argued that, indeed, those who did continue to vascillate in self-conception were "sick souls," who required "straightening our" (James, 1890). Harry Stack Sullivan (1953) also believed in the capacity of the individual to shift in conceptions of self and others during an ongoing relationship. His characterizations of the subtle ways in which people tactically maneuver the impressions made on others and themselves remain classic. From a different stance, Erving Goffman (1959) has described in detail the manner in which people shift performances as they move from one "stage" to another, facing different "audiences" and playing different "roles." And, argues Goffman, people can and do fall prey to the power of their own performance.

Honesty in Multiplicity

Given such demurring voices it seemed auspicious to explore the possibility that the assumption of stabilized self-conception is misleading. Research on this issue was directed toward two major goals. The first was to demonstrate the possibility that alterations in public presentation could take place without disruptions in one's feelings of personal authenticity. If one accepts the traditional view of the stabilized self, then behavior that deviates from this frozen conception should be rapidly recognized, and when recognized, the individual should feel dishonest, self-alienated, or inauthentic. Thus, if one believes that she or he is "Highly principled" and finds her or himself engaging in theft, she or he should feel that behavior and self-conception disagree. Such behavior would appear discrepant with "the real me"; it would seem inauthentic. In contrast, if self-conception is fluid, one should be able to engage in a wide variety of discrepant or contradictory activities without experiencing alienation.

To explore this issue, a variety of experiments were conducted. In the first of these (Gergen,1965), college women were interviewed by what appeared to be a trainee in clinical psychology. During the interview, the attractive female trainee rewarded each subject whenever she evaluated herself in a positive manner. With each positive appraisal of self, the psychologist indicated agreement. She would nod her head, smile, and sometimes murmur some form of support to the subject (e.g., "Yes, I think so, too."). Whenever the subject evaluated herself negatively, the psychologist would indicate some subtle form of disagreement. Often, she would indicate her disagreement through silence. Through this means, the psychologist was able to produce a continuous increase in the positiveness of the subjects' self-presentation. Subjects evaluated themselves in increasingly positive terms as the interview progressed. Such changes were not found in a control group that also evaluated themselves before the interviewer but were not exposed to the psychologist's positive appraisals. In effect, we had been successful in obtaining a pronounced change in self-presentation.

The important question was, however, whether these public alterations in behavior were accompanied by private feelings of authenticity or superficiality. Self-defining behavior had changed overtly, but did the subjects feel the presentation was honest and authentic? To explore this issue, self-esteem tests were given to subjects after the interview. They were completed in private, and subjects were told that they would not be seen by the interviewer. They were further told that honesty was imperative, as the test was being developed and assessed by researchers at the university; their identity was not to be revealed on the test sheet. By contrasting scores on this measure with scores on the same measure taken a month earlier, we found that the interview in which positive appraisals were made had produced a significant increase in subjects' privately rated self-esteem. This increase was not found in the control group. In effect, the subjective self-estimates matched the subjects' altered presentation. Further, in a final questionnaire, subjects almost invariably indicated that they had been very honest and open in the interview, that they had given a true indication of self. This claim to honesty did not differ between experimental and control group. Both felt equally authentic in their presentations. Finally, when subjects in the experimental group were subdivided into those who felt they might have been dishonest versus those who felt most authentic, subjects in the latter group were found to evidence the *most* change in self-evaluation during the interview.

In a second experiment (Gergen & Wishnov, 1965), subjects exchanged information about themselves with another person. The ''other person'' was, in fact, a fictitious individual who was especially prepared for the occasion. In one case this stimulus person presented herself in a most egotistical manner. She described herself in glowing terms, indicated success in all that she did, and looked forward to the future with great optimism. In a contrasting condition, we prepared a stimulus person who was extremely self-critical. She described herself as a miserable person, with very few good qualities, and for whom the future looked very grey. Our first interest was in how subjects would present themselves in response to these contrasting individuals. Dramatic changes were discovered. In response to the egotist, subjects themselves became egotistical. They described themselves in an extremely positive manner, demonstrated their strengths, and seemed to hide whatever weaknesses they may have had. In contrast, subjects who encountered the self-critical stimulus person were far more critical of themselves. They disclosed significantly fewer positive characteristics than subjects encountering the egotist. Essentially, the subjects altered their public appearance to match the presentations of the other person in the relation-ship.

Again, however, the important question for present purposes is whether either of these groups felt a sense of self-alienation. The public presentations were be-ing drawn in opposite directions, one toward the egotistical and one toward the self-critical end of the continuum, but would either of the groups recognize their behavior as false? Through a variety of measures taken in private after the experi-ment, we found that almost all participants felt they had been wholly honest, self-expressive, and open in the exchange. Whether acting egotistically or self-critically, they felt they were wholly authentic in their actions. Their conceptions of self had been apparently violated in neither case.

Momentary Fluctuation in Self-Conception

The results of such research led us into a second line of inquiry. In this case, the principle concern was with the durability of self-conception over time. From the traditional standpoint of frozen conception, we should anticipate essential stabil-ity in self-conception. If people think they are fundamentally "honest," they should manifest this belief at virtually any time—today, tomorrow, or next month. This conception should form part of the "core identity" and should not be easily altered. However, if self-conception is fluid or ephemeral in character, we might anticipate monentary fluctuations in self-conception. Self-appraisal may shift with time and circumstance in a variety of directions, even directions that prove contradictory. Let us consider briefly four sources of momentary alter-ation in self-conception. The first is derived from the traditional symbolic intentionist position (Mead, 1934) and holds that the individual's self-concept is developed through increased cognizance of the views of the *generalized other* to-ward oneself. Identity is shaped through a "social looking glass," which reflects back to the individual information about him or herself (Cooley, 1922). Yet, there seems little important reason to believe that the effects of *social appraisal* are terminated at some early age; there is no obvious point at which one's identity is finally fixed in place. Results of the first study described previously are rele-vant to the point. As shown, those college students whose self-appraisal was ex-posed to the positive reaction of an interviewer systematically increased their positive feelings toward themselves (Gergen, 1965). Social appraisal, then, may possibly continue over the life-span to alter self-conception in a variety of ways.

Although major attention has been given to the process of social appraisal within the self-concept literature, this emphasis may be considered a limited one. A variety of additional processes may also mold self-conception, both in the early years, as well as in the continuous interchange of adult life. For one, it seems apparent that the individual's conception of self may be strongly influ-enced by *self-observation*. From moment to moment most of one's behavior seems to occur spontaneously. One doesn't consider the reasons for each of his or her actions prior to its occurrence, nor indeed does it appear that one possesses access to such processes (Nisbett & Wilson, 1977). Thus, there is a sense in which one is an observer of his or her own actions and may draw conclusions about who he or she is from observing oneself in motion (Bem, 1972). Essentially, one plays roles, and the roles may convince one of who he or she is.

There are now numerous illustrations of the power of role playing techniques in changing attitudes and opinions, and in producing therapeutic insight (Brehm & Cohen, 1962; Kelly, 1955). On the basis of this work, there is good reason to believe that role playing may also be a powerful agent in changing self-conception. To explore this possibility experimentally, young women applying for a job were asked to make up a talk about themselves (Gergen & Taylor, 1969). In this talk, they were to present themselves in the most positive manner possible. They could say anything they wished about themselves as long as it would convince a potential employer of their great value. These positive speeches were subsequently presented into a tape recorder. Later, under differing circumstances, all participants privately completed a standard test of self-esteem. They were asked to be as honest as possible in responding to the items. As the results demonstrated, the role-playing experience was successful in raising self-esteem in significant degree over its level of a month prior to the experiment. This increase in self-esteem was not found in a control group who simply took the self-esteem test twice on both occasions but did not engage in such self-aggrandizing actions.

A third source of momentary change in self-concept is furnished by the *social-comparison* process. As Leon Festinger (1954) reasoned, experience is often frought with ambiguity and difficult to interpret with confidence. As a result, people often compare themselves with others around them. Through social comparison they come to identify their position more clearly and to assess its agreement or disagreement with consensus. Much the same may be true of self-conception. Often, one does not know how to define him or herself—whether a warm and genuine person, or basically cold, whether sincere or fundamentally opportunistic, and so on. Such questions are usually very difficult to answer, and under such circumstances one may well begin to look about and to compare his or her actions with others. If others are extremely warm and one's own behavior is less so, then one may come to view oneself as "not very warm." By the same token, in a group of people who are "cold and distant," the same individual might come to see him or herself as "very warm."

To explore this issue more directly, a study was arranged in which a summer job was advertised (Morse & Gergen, 1970). When each applicant (males) arrived, he was seated in a room by himself and asked to complete several questionnaires. One of these questionnaires contained approximately 30 items from a standardized self-esteem test (Coopersmith, 1967). As the questionnaires were being completed, the secretary entered with a second job applicant. This individual was especially prepared for the occasion. For half the applicants, his appearance was most impressive. He wore well-tailored clothes, carried an attaché case, and, upon being seated at the table across from the subject, opened his case to reveal a philosophy book, a slide rule, and a number of well-sharpened pencils. The other half of the subjects were exposed to a far-different experience. In this case, the secretary entered with a young man of slovenly appearance. His pants were torn at the knees, his shirt was dirty, he had not shaved in days, and he carried a worn copy of a cheap sex novel under his arm. He slumped into a seat across the table from the subject and looked around as if dazed. In neither case were any words exchanged between the subjects and the new arrival. However, the subjects were given additional forms to complete, and among these was the second half of the self-esteem test.

As the results showed, the mere presence of the new arrival had substantial effects on level of self-esteem. The entrance of "bourgeois perfection" precipitated a significant drop in self-esteem; however when the "social failure" entered the room, self-esteem scores moved in the opposite direction. In effect, subjects judged who they were, how much value they should place upon themselves, by comparing themselves with whomever was present.

A fourth process that may contribute to momentary alteration of self-conception is that of *memory scanning*. In this case, people may review certain past memories about themselves and draw a resulting conclusion about their major characteristics. Thus, if asked whether he were an honest person, an individual might remember several instances in which he resisted major temptations to be dishonest, and a minor case in which he did not; he might conclude, "as a general rule, I am an honest person." The more interesting aspect of this process is that its product may be molded in virtually any direction. Because of the immense amount of information stored in memory and the impoverished form in which it is retrieved, it may be possible to find evidence for virtually any self-conception. If people begin with the supposition that they are generally "honest," they can surely find evidence in memory. However, it also appears that a little stimulation of memory would also yield very convincing evidence to the contrary, evidence indicating that their honesty could indeed be thrown into question. The same would be true in judging one's motivation to achieve, intelligence, desire for power, needs for affection, sexuality, and so on.

In one attempt to demonstrate these possibilities, subjects were asked to sit for 20 minutes and to try to develop a positive speech about themselves (Gergen & Taylor, 1969). They were encouraged to think of all the good points they could in order to cause another person to be attracted to them. They were not, as in the earlier described conditions of the study, asked to role play their speech; they merely undertook a cognitive review. Later, these same subjects were given a standardized test of self-esteem. The results showed that in the process of developing arguments to convince another person of their attractiveness, they had succeeded in convincing themselves; that is, their self-esteem scores demonstrated a significant increase, and this increase was not found in a control group that did not participate in the memory-scanning procedure.

In brief, we have argued that the traditional view of stabilized self-conception has serious shortcomings. Firstly, people are capable of marked shifts in their public presentation unaccompanied by private feelings of ''not-self'' or self-alienation. Secondly, they can shift privately from one conception of self to another as a result of appraisals from others, self-observation, social comparison, and memory scanning. There may indeed be other sources of instability in self-conception. The work of McGuire and his colleagues on personal distinctiveness (see Chapter 3) is illustrative. Research on momentary alterations in self-awareness (Wicklund & Frey, 1980) lend additional weight to the argument. Further, the impact of each of these processes may be enhanced by faulty systems of memory (Hastie, Ostrom, Ebbesen, Wyer, Jr., Hamilton, & Carlston, 1980). As demonstrated by Bem and McConnell (1970), people experience great difficulty in accurately recalling their attitudes prior to the moment of change—even with respect to issues of great importance.

Stability Within Change

Thus far, we have seen how certain features of scientific metatheory have insinuated themselves into theories of self conception, and we have begun to raise questions concerning the viability of such theoretical views. In particular, we have attempted to demonstrate shortcomings in the view that self conception in the mature person is stabilized and coherent—a conclusion formed by the hypothesis-testing model of self-conception along with early symbolic interactionist and psychodynamic accounts. Rather, we have painted a picture of the person as possessing a multiplicity of credible self conceptions, often inconsistent, which conceptions may be salient or submerged from moment to moment in ongoing relationships.

It may be countered that in spite of this handful of research demonstrations, common experience cannot be denied. Usually people do recognize a continuity over time in their close friends, in parents, spouses, and children. Their associates do not seem to change in contradictory ways from one moment to the next. ''Rick has not changed in years,'' one hears; ''he may be a little heavier and a little more relaxed, but he is still the same old Rick.'' The same is generally true of oneself. People often believe themselves to be the same over time; they often believe there is a coherence or a continuity about their behavior; they believe that they have always been ''achievement oriented,'' or a ''pretty serious sort of person,'' or ''deeply concerned with humanity,'' ''idealistic,'' or whatever. As Erikson (1968) has pointed out, people don't wake each morning to find they are strangers to themselves.

How is common experience to be reconciled with the picture painted here of momentary multiplicity in self-conception? Three possible solutions bear examination. In exploring them, however, we must pay simultaneous attention to the viability of the view of the person as hypothesis tester. As we see, not only do the solutions to the stability versus process problem fail to vindicate the hypothesis-testing view, they lay the groundwork for questioning the empiricist assumption of an objectively discoverable world of social activity.

The Core Versus the Periphery.   Gordon Allport was one of the first to attempt a reconciliation between the stable and the changing aspects of human personality. As Allport (1966) argued, we must distinguish between those traits that are central to each individual and those that are pheripheral. We may anticipate considerable inconsistency with respect to the periphery, but in terms of the central or core traits, stability across time should be the rule. This is essentially the answer furnished by Bem & Allen (1974) to the question of trait inconsistency. As they reasoned each person may be highly consistent with respect to certain trait dimensions but will manifest situational variability on other, less-significant dimensions. In the same manner, we might say that there are certain self-conceptions that are central to the individual, and others that are more peripheral. The former conceptions are likely to be more frozen, whereas the latter may be more fluid. Thus, people may not generally shift their perceptions of their masculinity or femininity, of their ethical or idealistic concerns; however, they may be quite willing to admit vascillation in their conception of self as a "brisk stroller" or a "tidy lacer of shoes."

Although this solution is entirely reasonable, it is not without limitation. The initial problem is the potential circularity of the concept of "centrality." To what extent are more stabilized conceptions being termed *central* because of their very stability, and the changeable being labeled *peripheral* because of their ephemeral character? Neither Allport not others have managed to isolate the two concepts, and to examine their relationship. Given the unelaborated character of the concept of centrality, it appears to be a synonym for stability. A second reservation with the Allport solution stems from a number of research studies indicating that concepts normally considered central in social life may be changed significantly within relatively brief periods of time. For example, in a controversial study by Bramel (1963), male subjects were given "scientific information" that effectively created doubt concerning their heterosexual preferences. Although the concept of heterosexuality is presumably a central one for most males in late adolescence, Bramel was able to generate such doubt within less than 30 minutes. In the various studies described previously, we have also systematically included items measuring the individual's conception of him or herself as "self-assured," "physically attractive," "warm," "socially effective," and so on. Such characteristics would appear to be resonably central for most people; however, the research studies have consistently demonstrated alterations along all such dimensions resulting from relatively minor changes in social context.

Does the possibility of variations in centrality reinforce the view of the person as objective hypothesis tester? Surely not. Central concepts may be those for which one has received considerable social support—not because they are objectively true but because they are socially appropriate or desirable. There would appear to be no objective criteria, for example, by which a person could be judged valuable, or basically good, or worthy in the Rogerian sense. Yet, parents may sometimes furnish their children with a positive and presumably central view of self as positive. Social comparison may also yield orientations in centrality without an objective basis. A struggling artist may continuously convince himself that his work is superior by contrasting it with the work of those he dislikes. His resulting view of self as a superior artist is not thereby rendered more objective. Let us consider a second possible solution to the stability-change conundrum.

Situational Stability. A second solution to the problem of stability appears less problematic. As we have demonstrated, self-conception seems highly responsive to environmental fluctuation. However, if the environment remains relatively fixed across time, we might anticipate a concommitantly high degree of stability in self-conception. So long as the environmental conditions remain roughly constant, the conception of a "frozen" self may be vindicated. For example, the individual who goes to the same office for 20 years, interacts with roughly the same cast of colleagues, lives with the same spouse, and entertains the same friends may experience little more than slowly evolving changes in self-conception over the years. Should the conditions suddenly shift in radical fashion (e.g., an enemy invader places the individual in a concentration camp), we might anticipate a major alteration in self-conception; otherwise, stability may continue to reign. Stability in self-conception is, from this standpoint, merely a by-product of stabilized social conditions; it is not the result of accumulating evidence about the self.

This line of argument is wholly compatible with our previous discussion of the various sources of self-conception. In each case, situational manipulations were seen to produce change in self-concept. Such argument is further consistent with the entire line of situationist thinking that has been the hallmark of the experimental movement in social psychology. It is also a position that is supported by much recent work in life-span developmental psychology (Datan & Reese, 1977), work that emphasizes the effects of sociohistorical circumstance on life-span trajectories.

Yet, although a compelling means of resolving the stability-change dilemma, this line of argument lends no sustenance to the argument that stability derives from increments in objective knowledge. From the situationist standpoint, self-knowledge is a reflection of social circumstances. If new opinions are confronted, or new standards of comparison are furnished, for example, the individual may experience a shift in what he or she "knows." New inputs in objective information are not required for such change—only shifts in the criterion of opinion.

We can now turn to a third means of resolving the stability-change dilemma, one that confronts us directly with the shortcomings of viewing objective reality as a touchstone for self-conception.

The Social Subjectivity of Self-Description.   We have noted the marked ease with which people seem to shift self-description. Interestingly, this same plasticity appears to prevail in other explorations of person description. In the case of causal attribution, for example, we find that the conception of personal responsibility may be effectively altered according to degree of ego gratification (Bernstin, Stephen, & Davis, 1979; Bradley, 1978; Wortman, Costanza, & Witt, 1973) as one shifts perspective from environment to self or vice versa (Eisen, 1979; West, Gunn, & Chernicky, 1975; Zuckerman, 1979), and as one shifts one's focus over the historical background of an action (Brickman, Ryan, & Wortman, 1975). Similar results have emerged in the study of emotional experience. As research on the reattribution of emotional states indicates, people's conceptions of their pain (Nisbett & Schachter, 1966), fear (Dienstbier, 1972), attraction (Dutton & Aron, 1974), sleepiness (Storms, Denney, McCaul, & Lowery, 1979), and so on may all be altered as environmental conditions shift.

Given the ease with which such modifications in person description are effected, one is moved to inquire into their sources more generally. Why are the anchors upon which person description is suspended not more securely placed? How is such plasticity permitted? To answer such a question requires that we take into account possible sources of stabilization or constraint of such descriptions. Two sources deserve special attention, the one lodged within the social network (social reality) and the other in the realm of objective entities (physical reality).

In the preceding discussion of sources of self-concept change, we have primarily taken the former of these paths; that is, we have viewed self-conception as a socially derived construction. This is most clearly evident in the case for social appraisal. Self conception, on this account, is dependent on the opinion of others, whose opinions, by implication, are also lodged in social milieu. The preceding view of social comparison is quite compatible with Festinger's (1954) early arguments. Social comparison represents a process of decision making employed primarily when physical reality furnishes insufficient judgmental criteria. The social basis for self-observation and memory scanning are more ambiguous. In this case one might argue that one's actions do serve as an empirical basis for self-conception, and that the observations of such actions form the basis of memory. This self-observation may serve as the last bastion against complete social subjectivity in self-knowledge. We take up this possibility shortly.

To tie person description to the social network is not to secure for it a stable base. The patterns of person description within most cultures are hardly univocal, and such patterns may change over time and in various degrees within any given segment of the culture. Thus, the terms that are to be applied to human conduct and the rules of appropriate attribution are not essentially fixed but may evolve within the culture. Thus, within the culture at any given point lies a repertoire of multiple realities (Schutz, 1962), and the individual is essentially free to select from the repertoire as his or her needs dictate. The only major constraint lies in his or her capacities to obtain the agreement or others that indeed the favored interpretation is the accurate one. Thus, the man who beats his wife may be aware that for his working companions the action is seen as "manly," for his children it is "fearsome," for his father it is "the proper way to keep order in the house," for his wife, "a horrible experience," and for his wife's friends, "an act to be avenged." The individual is free to select from the entire range of interpretations. The only essential concern is whether the selected description is negotiable within a given social context.

As should now be apparent, if one accepts the position of a socially constructed self, there is no objective person to be known, discovered, explored, or understood. Rather, there is a shared group of labels or understandings, and these are applied according to common rules within society. There are no traits, intentions, or emotions and the like to be found within persons; these traits, intentions, and emotions form an integral part of a vocabulary of person description. How and when the vocabulary is employed is derived from social practice.

It is within this context that a consideration of the second potential source of stability in person description gains paramount importance. Is it possible that physical reality might furnish a reasonably firm basis for making judgments about persons? For example, do trait terms not refer to reliable patterns of observable behavior, intentional terms to identifiable states of consciousness, and emotional terms to differentiated physiological states? If so, then a shifting vocabulary of person description poses no special difficulty. Changes in person description would be equivalent to alterations in physical theory; although the terms may differ over time, the observation base remains stable. In this case there are entities to be known or discovered; their existence is not created by the descriptive vocabulary. When properly apprehended, such entities or physical patterns should indeed dictate the contours of this vocabulary.

Yet, when closely examined, the possibilities for employing physical reality as a benchmark for person description become minimal. The central problem is not that of defining the units or boundaries of a given action. Although not an insignificant matter, in principle it should be possible to identify with reasonable accuracy certain repeatable movements of the body, vocal sounds, facial expressions, and the like. The critical difficulty lies in the fact that movements, sounds, or expressions are, in themselves, of minimal social significance. The movement of the hand in the air, two consonants and an intervening vowel, or a crease in the forehead are in themselves inconsequential They become important only insofar as they are treated as inferential signals giving a key to the psychological domain—signals of hostility, alarm, affection, and the like. Thus, the same observable pattern of overt activity may signify a variety of different psychological states, and markedly different patterns of observation may all be rendered synonymous in terms of their symbolic goals, intentions, or meanings for the individual. In the former case, a given smile may be categorized as a sign of affection when the individual is in the presence of a lover, but a signal of fear if the individual faces a powerful attacker. In the latter case, the intent to nurture may be expressed in such widely divergent actions as cooking food, ironing clothes, or changing a tire. Any attempt, then, to classify or group human actions on the basis of their observable characteristics seems fundamentally misleading.

The implications of this argument are far-reaching. In-as-much as identification of any given action relies primarily on its capacities to signal psychological states, and these states are in themselves closed for public observation, then the process of person description is essentially liberated from the constraints of observation. Any term may be used to describe any action so long as one can imbed the term in a plausible account of what is taking place (Gergen, 1980). For example, consider a person who describes himself to be humane, warm, and loving of others. You observe this individual beating his children, and suggest to him that perhaps he is not so humane, warm, and loving as he thought he was. "On the contrary," he might reply, "such actions were only for the benefit of the children, a true indication of my deep love for them. I was in far greater pain than they." Later, you observe the same individual striking his mother and suggest that surely he is incorrect in his self-perception. "You don't understand at all," he replies. "I am so deeply drawn to my mother that even her slightest criticisms drive me into a frenzied emotional state. It is, in fact, my deep caring for her that is the source of my seemingly cruel behavior." To return to the argument for social subjectivity, the only significant limit over the individual's interpretation of his actions appears to be that furnished by social convention.

Self-Knowledge and the Challenge to Empiricist Science

At the outset of this chapter, a parallel was drawn between the layman's attempt to understand him or herself and the scientist's attempt to understand the layman. It was noted that scientists typically consider themselves in the superior position, fortified as they are with the traditional empiricist rationale for generating knowledge, along with methods for systematic observation. Further, it was shown how scientists' conceptions of scientific knowledge have shaped their conception of the process by which self-knowledge is acquired. We then went on to challenge two aspects of this latter account, firstly, that because hypotheses about self are tested self-conception tends toward stability, and secondly, that there is an objective grounds against which self-conception can, in principle, be tested. In the first instance it was argued that the individual may more adequately be viewed as possessing a multiplicity of potentially contradictory self-accounts, which may be employed as needed in varying circumstances. In the second case it was ventured that there is no objective yardstick against which self-conception can be tested. So long as the individual can gain social agreement in describing him or herself in a particular manner, this description is rendered legitimate.

In light of this reconstruction of the manner in which people go about the task of self-understanding, what can now be said about the positivist-empiricist metatheory giving rise to the view herein found so objectionable? In particular, questions must be raised concerning the extent to which the social scientist is: (1) exploring or discovering facts about an objective social world; and (2) placing hypotheses about this world under objective test. In the first instance consider how the scientist knows what entities exist for study? How does one determine, for example, that an aggressive act has occurred? It would appear that to make such a determination the scientist must ultimately rely on opinions lodged within the social network. Consider, for example, a student whom we observe tearing a page from a library book. We may all agree that the action is occurring, but how do we determine whether the act is an exemplar of aggression? How can we know whether the action bears on a theory of aggression or the individual's conception of himself as aggressive? It appears virtually impossible to answer such a question without recourse to the opinion of the individual or of others as to the "meaning" of the act. In effect, the entity for study is not essentially objective; what we term *objective experience* may be a necessary input to one's description, but its identification and action implications are essentially products of social invention. The fact that "aggression" constitutes a subject of study depends on its prior existence within the realm of social discourse.

In this light we may consider the issue of theoretical verifiability As argued in our discussion of retaining stability, it is generally possible for the individual to retain a coherent, unified, or stabilized conception of himself because of the ambiguous relationship between concepts and action. Rules for concept application within the culture are difficult to articulate with a high degree of clarity; they may vary from one subculture to another, and they may vary over time. Thus, whether the individual sees himself as aggressive or not depends in large measure on the negotiated relation between concept and action. The meaning of the act is fundamentally open ended. It would appear that the same process of negotiated meaning is endemic to the behavioral sciences themselves. For example, such acts as buffeting a large plastic doll and pressing a button delivering an electric shock to another person have frequently been employed as measures of aggression and used to verify hypotheses in this domain. Yet, can we agree that the term aggression unequivocally applies to such acts? When children strike the plastic doll, are they aggressing, or is this possibly "rough and tumble play," a demonstration to their peers that they are similar to a model, an act of curiosity, or something else? Similarly, in pressing a button to deliver electric shock, can we be certain that the individual is "aggressing" against his peers? Perhaps he is simply "conforming" to instructions, doing his task properly as a subject in order to get paid, following the perceived norms, or trying to teach the recipient a useful lesson. All interpretations of the action are possible and probably would be used by subjects to explain why such actions should not be considered aggressive.

In effect, experimental results serve to verify the theories upon which they are premised primarily to the extent the investigator can negotiate the meaning of the behavior in question in such a way that peer agreement is achieved. If others do not wish to interpret the pattern of confirming actions in the same manner as the investigator, the results cease to serve as confirmations. Thus, the entire edifice of commonly accepted propositions concerning aggression (or any other class of behavior) would not appear to rely on an empirical substructure. All findings are subject to multiple interpretation and add credence to the stated hypotheses only so long as they remain unchallenged (Gergen, 1980).

Self, Science, and the Shaping of Social Conduct

The present chapter has outlined in briefest form a series of arguments raising significant questions not only regarding the function of self-knowledge in daily life but regarding the function of scientific knowledge more generally. From the present standpoint, knowledge at both levels rests not on a firm foundation of objective fact but primarily on the quicksand of social accord. The manner in which people understand their actions, the manner in which concepts are applied to themselves their private ways of making sense of their actions, all are principally dependent on and limited by the particular social support system in which they are enmeshed. Likewise, the manner in which the social scientist interprets behavior, the manner in which data are employed for purposes of defending or criticizing a theory, and one's confidence in the validity of a theory are principally dependent on and limited by the social support systems operating within the sciences themselves. The attempt to develop empirically validated forms of theoretical knowledge, whether in understanding oneself in daily relations, or understanding daily relations from the scientific vantage point, seems misguided.

These conclusions are in no way intended to imply an abandonment of conceptual understanding. Indeed, as creatures whose adaptive capacities are importantly linked to symbolic skills, such prospects would indeed seem perilous. However, it is incumbent upon us to reconsider the function of conceptual understanding, both in daily relations as well as in the sciences themselves. Whether implicit and informal, or explicit and formalized, theories have a variety of important and useful functions quite irrelevant to their state of empirical verification (Gergen, 1980b). Theories may provide intellectual satisfaction, sensitize one to wide-ranging possibilities, provide a means of efficient communication, lend themselves to actuarial enterprise, and challenge common modes of thought. All such functions may be vital to effective social functioning.

At the same time, to assert such functions is not to answer the critical question of theoretical superiority. If the assumption that theories can be differentiated with respect to empirical support is eschewed, then by traditional empirical standards there is lttle reason for selecting one theory over a competitor. Internal logic and aesthetics remain weak criteria for selecting one's form of truth. It is useful in this regard to consider the prospects of value-based selection. Although the traditional attempt in the sciences has been to separate matters of conceptual construction ("clear thinking") from matters of personal value ("the emotions"), it has become increasingly clear that such processes are virtually inseparable (Buss, 1979; Gouldner, 1970: Sampson, 1978; Unger, 1975). In the process of developing and sustaining theory, whether of the self or of social relations more generally, values enter at every juncture. Great effort has been expended thus far in the denial and rationalization of such intimate connection. Both in daily life and within the social sciences more generally, theories are treated as if they represent the pure confluence of fact and intellect; their valuational underpinnings are frequently disguised or distorted and typically remain unelaborated.

The present argument is thus for a reconsideration of valuational criteria in the enterprise. Whether in science or society, the individual might be charged to confront, to indulge, and to sustain the values central to his or her social existence. Theory might be properly harnessed to such values and used in the service of their sustenance. What practical consequences might follow from this position? On the level of daily relations the individual might develop and sustain those forms of self conception that best support his or her sense of well-being. To view oneself in ways that cause one unhappiness (e.g. unlovable, self-centered, unintelligent, powerless, sinful, perverted, useless, and so on,) is often to choose against one's own valuational interests. Such conceptions cannot be adequately supported on factual grounds, no more than their opposites. As the antinomy in each case may provide far more self-satisfaction, the individual might be encouraged in such selection. It may be countered that this is but an invitation to autism. To encourage people to view themselves as intelligent, for example, when others generally view him as dull, is to invite social suicide. However, this latter argument assumes that certain groups are endowed with a superior objectivity. We see from the present standpoint that the individual is wrong only in-so-far as he is unable to locate others who are willing to interpret his or her behavior in a similar manner.

For the social scientist the door might be opened for the development of theory for purposes of social change. Given the fundamental impossibility of accurate representation, the theorist might properly employ his or her theoretical constructions for purposes of altering the character of social life. Contemporary patterns of social conduct owe their existence primarily to commonly shared forms of social understanding. When the scientist transforms this understanding through his or her theoretical efforts, he or she may also affect patterns of social action (Gergen, 1978). When these theoretical efforts are linked to the scientist's own value investments, the resulting change might engender a profound sense of satisfaction.

ACKNOWLEDGMENTS

Support for the present analysis was furnished by a grant from the National Science Foundation 7809393. The author is also grateful to Jerry Suls for his critical reading of an earlier draft of this chapter.

REFERENCES

Allport, G. W.   Traits revisited. *American Psychologist,* 1966, *21,* 1–10.

Bem, D. J.   Self-perception theory. In L. Berkowitz (Ed.), *Advances in experimental social psychology.* (Vol. 6). New York: Academic Press, 1972.

Bem, D. J. & Allen, A. On predicting some of the people some of the time: The search of cross-situational consistencies in behavior. *Psychological Review,* 1974, *81,* 506–5 20.

Bem, D. J. & McConnell, H. K.   Testing the self-perception explanation of dissonance phenomena: On the salience of premanipulation attitudes. *Journal of Personality and Social Psychology,* 1970, *14,* 23–31.

Bernstein, A. M., Stephan, W. G., & Davis, M. H.   Explaining attribution for achievement: A pathanalytic approach. *Journal of Personality and Social Psychology,* 1979, *37,* 1810– 1921.

Bradley, G. W.   Self-serving biases in the attribution process: A reexamination of the fact or fiction question. *Journal of Personality and Social Psychology,* 1978, *36,* 56–71.

Bramel, D.   Selection of a target for defensive projection. *Journal of Abnormal and Social Psychology,* 1963, *66,* 318–324.

Brehm, J. W., & Cohen, A. R.   *Explorations in cognitive dissonance .* New York: Wiley, *1962.*

Brickman, P., Ryan, K., & Wortman, C. B.   Causal chains: Attributions of responsibility as a function of immediate and prior causes. *Journal of Personality and Social Psychology,* 1975, *32,* 1060–1067.

Buss, A. R.   *A dialectial psychology.* New York: Holsted Pres s, 1979.

Cooley, C. H.   *Human nature and the social order.* New York: Scribner, 1922.

Coopersmith, S.   *The antecedents of self-esteem.* San Francisco: Freeman, 1967.

Datan, N.,& Reese, H. Eds.)   *Life-span developmental psychology, dialectic perspectives,* New York: Academic Press, 1977.

Dienstbier, R. A. The role of anxiety and arousal attribution in cheating. *Journal of Experimental Social Psychology,* 1972, *8,* 168–179.

Dutton, D. G., & Aron, A. P.   Some evidence for heightened sexual attraction under conditions of high anxiety. *Journal of Personality and Social Psychology,* 1974, *30,* 510–517.

Eisen, S. V.   Actor-observer differences in information inference and causal attribution. *Journal of Personality and Social Psychology,* 1979, *37,* 261–272.

Epstein, S.   Traits are alive and well, In D. Magnussen & N. S. Endler (Eds.), *Personality at the crossroads: Current issues in interactional psychology.* Hillsdale, N. J.: Lawrence Erlbaum Associates, 1977.

Epstein, S.   The self-concept: A review and the proposal of an integrated theory of personality. In E. Staub (Ed.), *Personality: Basic issues and current research.* Englewood Cliffs, N. J.: Prentice–Hall, 1980.

Erikson, E.   *Identity: Youth and crisis.* New York: Norton, 1 968.

Festinger, L.   A theory of social comparison processes. *Human Relations,* 1954, *7,* 117–140.

Gergen, K. J.   Interaction goals and personalistic feedback as factors affecting the presentation of self. *Journal of Personality and Social Psychology*, 1965, *1*, 413–424.

Gergen, K. J.   Toward generative theory. *Journal of Personality and Social Psychology*, 1978, *36*, 1344–1360.

Gergen, K. J.   Exchange theory: The transient and the enduring. In K. Gergen, M. Greenberg, & R. Willis (Eds.), *Social exchange: Advances in theory and research*. New York: Plenum Books, 1980.a

Gergen, K. J.   Toward intellectual audacity in social psychology. In R. Gilmour & S. Duck (Eds.), *The development of social psychology*. London: Academic Press, 1980.b

Gergen, K. J., & Taylor, M. G.   Social expectancy and self— presentation in a status hierarchy. *Journal of Experimental Social Psychology*, 1969, *5*, 79–92.

Gergen, K. J., & Wishnov, B.   Others' self evaluations and interactions anticipation as determinants of self presentation. *Journal of Personality and Social Psychology*, 1965, *7*, 348–358.

Goffman, E.   *The presentation of self in everyday life*. New York: Doubleday, 1959.

Gouldner, A. W.   *The coming crisis in Western sociology*. New York: Basic Book, 1970.

Gur, R. C., & Sackheim, H. A.   Self-deception: A concept in search of a phenomenon. *Journal of Personality and Social Psychology*, 1979, *37*, 147–169.

Hastie, R., Ostrom, T., Ebbesen, E., Wyer, R., Hamilton, D., & Carlston, D. (Eds.).   *Person memory: The cognitive basis of social perception*. Hillsdale, N. J.: Lawrence Erlbaum Associates, 1980.

Hilgard, E. R.   Human motives and the concept of self. *American Psychologist*, 1949, *4*, 374–382.

James, W.   *The principles of psychology*. New York: Holt, Rinehart Winston, 1890.

Kelley, H. H.   *Causal schemata and the attribution process*. New York: General Learning Press, 1972.

Kelly, G.   *The psychology of personal constructs*. New York: Norton, 1955.

Magnussen, D., & Endler, N. S.   *Personality at the crossroads*. Hillsdale, N. J.: Lawrence Erlbaum Associates, 1977.

Mead, G. H.   *Mind, self and society*. Chicago: University of Chicago Press, 1934.

Morse, S. J., & Gergen, K. J.   Social comparison, self-consistency and the presentation of self. *Journal of Personality and Social Psychology*, 1970, *16*, 148–159.

Nisbett, R., & Ross, L.   *Human influence: Strategies and short-commings of social judgment*. Englewood Cliffs, N. J.: Prentice–Hall, 1980.

Nisbett, R. E., & Schachter, S.   The cognitive manipulation of pain. *Journal of Experimental Social Psychology*, 1966, *2*, 227–236.

Nisbett, R. E., & Wilson, T. D.   Telling more than we can know: Verbal reports on mental processes. *Psychological Review*, 19 77, *84*, 231–259.

Rogers, C. R.   A theory of therapy, personality and interpersonal relationships, as developed in the client-centered framework. In S. Koch (Ed.), *Psychology: A study of a science* (Vol. 3). New York: McGraw–Hill, 1959.

Ross, L.   The intuitive psychologist and his shortcomings: Distortions in the attribution process. In L. Berkowitz (Ed.), *Advances in experimental social psychology* (Vol. 10). New York: Academic Press, 1977.

Sampson, E. E.   Scientific paradigms and social values. *Journal of Personality and Social Psychology*, 1978, *36*, 1332– 1343.

Schneider, D. J.   Implicit personality theory: A review. *Psychological Bulletin*, 1973, *73*, 294–309.

Schutz, A.   *Collected papers* (Vol. 1). The Hague: Nijhoff, 1962.

Storms, M. D., Denney, D. R., McCaul, K. D., & Lowery, C. R.   Treating insomnia. In I. Frieze, D. Bar-Tal, & T. Carrol (Eds.), *New approaches to social psychology*. San Francisco: Jossey-Bass, 1979.

Sullivan, H. S.   *The interpersonal theory of psychiatry*. New York: Norton, 1953.

Unger, R. M.   *Knowledge and politics*. New York: Free Press, 1975.

West, S. G., Gunn, S. P., & Chernicky, P.   Ubiquitious Watergate: An attributional analysis. *Journal of Personality of Social Psychology,* 1975, *32,* 55–65.

Wicklund, R. A., & Frey, D.   Self-awareness theory: When the self makes a difference. In D. M. Wegner & R. R. Vallacher, *The self in social psychology.* New York: Oxford University Press. 1980.

Wortman, C. B., Costanza, P. R., & Witt, T. R.   Effects of anticipated performance on the attributions of causality to self and others. *Journal of Personality and Social Psychology,* 1973, *27,* 372–381.

Zuckerman, M.   Attribution of success and failure revisited: or: The motivational bias is alive and well in attribution theory. *Journal of Personality,* 1979, *47,* 245–2 87.

6 Is Anyone in Charge? Personalysis Versus the Principle of Personal Unity

Anthony G. Greenwald
Ohio State University

> *Unity of personality is only a matter of degree, and we should avoid exaggerating it.* (Gordon W. Allport, 1965)
> *. . . we shall take no account of the soul.* (William James, 1890)

PREFACE

The principle of nonunity of the person, which is developed in this chapter, has many predecessors. Although this principle has received many favorable mentions in psychological literature, there is nevertheless a widespread implicit acceptance of an opposing principle of personal unity. This chapter attempts no systematic survey of previous treatments of personal nonunity. Among the more prominent prior treatments not reviewed is that of Jung, whose work contains a number of ideas that anticipate ones presented here (as well as many that would be quite out of place); similarly, Lewin's theorization about differentiated regions within the person is mentioned only in passing, and Hilgard's (1977) recent presentation of the neodissociationist position is discussed only briefly. I do focus on portions of Freud's psychoanalytic theory, both because of its influence on my ideas and because of its value as an aid to exposition.

A problem encountered in writing the chapter was that of labeling several hypothesized entities. I appropriated suitable terms from everyday language in using *body*, *verbal*, *social*, and *self* as names for partially independent subsystems of the person. In a few places I made up new terms for concepts for which satisfactory old ones did not exist. The new terms are *personalysis* as the designation for the chapter's general approach to nonunity of the person, *personalytic* (pronounced with the stress pattern of "personalistic") as a derivative adjective, and *sociation,* which designates a special type of deindividuation. I ask the reader's indulgence in these attempted enlargements of an already unwieldy psycholexicon.[1] In knowledge that useless terms will be ignored, I have tried to make these useful.

Prospectus

The usefulness of the concept of self in psychology has been limited by psychologists' attempting to deal simultaneously with the self both as an empirical object of study and as the assumed vehicle of conscious experience. This seems an impossible task. A method of divorcing self's content from its consciousness is suggested by an analogy between person and computer as multisystems. In the multisystem analysis of the person (here labeled personalysis), the self is a subsystem of the person and is partially independent of body, verbal, and social subsystems. The independence among these subsystems follows from their using different coding schemes and having limited access to each other's knowledge. This personalytic approach's assumption of independent subsystems stands in contrast to a principle of personal unity that appears as an implicit assumption in many psychological analyses. In this chapter, the conceptual difficulties that are imported into psychology via the implicit principle of personal unity are illustrated by considering six topic areas of social psychology in terms of the contrast between personalysis and personal unity. The multisystem view is developed further by comparing it to Freud's tripartite division of the psyche, and then by using it to resolve paradoxes in the existing conception of deindividuation. The chapter concludes by arguing that the principle of personal unity has dominated psychology because the work of psychology is done by the self-subsystems of scientist-persons.

CONCEPTUAL PROBLEMS OF SELF

"Self" is a very popular term in psychology but is at times an embarrassment. The embarrassment is the difficulty of saying just what is meant by this widely and frequently used term. The problem can be caricaturized by suggesting that the concept of self has been too (self-)conscious, as is apparent from its surrounding itself with mirrors and its unwillingness to appear alone (unhyphenated) in public.

Both the origin of the mirror metaphor for self and a hint of this metaphor's

---

[1]The term, *sociation,* has an existing usage in sociology, but one that has not gained any widespread adoption; the present definition is unrelated to this earlier use. The word, *personalysis,* has been characterized, by some colleagues who first encountered it in an earlier draft of this chapter, as hateful, revulsion inducing, and of impure ancestry. Although I tend to agree, nevertheless I failed in persistent attempts to find a better term, and the term has tended to grow on me with repeated use.

difficulties can be found in the Greek myth of Narcissus, whose fascination with his reflected image led to his metamorphosis into a flower. The virtue of the mirror metaphor is that it captures the dual-faceted conception of self simultaneously as subject and object—just as the person who stands in front of a mirror is both the perceiver and perceived (Cooley, 1902). Interestingly, actual mirrors have seen productive use in empirical studies of properties of the self (especially by Duval & Wicklund, 1972, and Gallup, 1977). Nevertheless, the mirror metaphor is at heart insubstantial and mysterious, as suggested by the following remark by Hilgard (1949): "[The] self-evident character of self-awareness is in fact most illusive. You presently find yourself as between the two mirrors of a barbershop, so that as the self takes a look at itself taking a look at itself, it soon gets all confused as to the self that is doing the looking and the self which is being looked at. [p. 377]."

As for the hyphen, any inspection of psychologists' uses of "self" will show that it is used primarily in combinatorial forms, and only infrequently as a noun. The hyphen is used to connect "self" to a wide variety of abstract nouns, as in *self-concept, self-esteem, self-awareness,* and *self-presentation.* In the index of *Psychological Abstracts* for the second half of 1979, self is used as the first part of a combination with 18 different nouns, covering 16 pages of citations.

The use of self in hyphenated terms and the mirror metaphor both capture the property of reflexiveness—the fusing of subject and object. I don't mean to suggest that it is a mistake to associate the self with the concept of reflexiveness. It is, rather, the insubstantialness of the way the hyphen and the mirror capture the idea of reflexiveness that is a problem. We need, not the pure reflexiveness of the hyphen and the mirror, but rather an embodied concept. Examples of embodied conceptions of reflexiveness are Hofstadter's (1979) appeal to the self-referential structure of Godel's proof and to the self-replicating mechanism of DNA.

The disembodied reflexiveness that is represented by the hyphen and the mirror is also a characteristic of the mental attribute of *consciousness,* a term that has a lengthy past association with the concept of self. Psychologists who have studied the self have often felt obliged to merge their scientific enterprise with their subjective experience of consciousness. The reason for this merger was well-stated by Allport (1965), who may have been speaking more for others than for himself: "The fugitive and undependable nature of consciousness has led some psychologists to deny it any place at all in psychological science . . . And yet the objective method preferred by these psychologists depends completely upon the testimony of their own conscious experience. Of what use are pointer readings unless they are consciously perceived and interpreted [p. 139]?"

William James (1890) provided a brief, but effective, counterargument to the view that psychologists must take subjectivity (consciousness) as a topic of investigation. His point was that the metaphysical status of thoughts and their objects constituted a puzzle that pervaded all science, not just psychology: "About such *ultimate* puzzles he [the psychologist] in the main need trouble himself no more than the geometer, the chemist, or the botanist do, who make precisely the same assumptions as he [p. 184].''

Metaphors and Models for the Self

In addition to the mirror, several more tangible metaphors for the self have been proposed, and these have shown increasing complexity of structure with the passage of time. Hume (1739/1888), in denying self as a special entity, called it: ''nothing but a *bundle* or collection of different perceptions [p. 252, italics indicate the metaphor].'' James (1890) played with metaphors, some borrowed from other philosophers, of a *herd of cattle* (p. 337), a *train* of ideas (p. 355), and *stockings,* the *thread* of which could be replaced without altering the identity of the stockings (p. 372). His preferred metaphor was a *stream* of successive thoughts, with the self identified as the relation of the present thought to those that had preceded it—the present thought is ''the *hook* from which the *chain* of past selves dangles [p. 340].'' Among the more recent models of self are Koffka's (1935) *trace column,* Sherif and Cantril's (1947) organization of *attitudes,* Markus's (1977) trait *schemata,* T. B. Rogers's (1980) self as *prototype,* Epstein's (1973) and Loevinger's (1976) analogy of self to *scientific theory,* and my own (Greenwald, 1980) analogy of self to *totalitarian political organization.*

This sample of metaphors and models helps to introduce the computer as a further metaphor, one that has the special virtue of allowing consideration of complex cognitive aspects of self without concern about consciousness. In the early years of impact of the computer as the dominating model on which cognitive psychology was based, hardware aspects of computers provided the source of theoretical inspiration (Miller, Galanter, & Pribram, 1960, Ch. 14). In such models information was seen as flowing from one location to another within the processing apparatus, and considerations of organizational aspects of the information were subordinated to considerations of organizational aspects of the information-housing apparatus. More recently, there has been recognition of the power of the computer program (rather than the computer itself) as the medium in which psychological processes can be modeled. An essential aspect of such models is that the organization of stored information determines the manner in which new incoming information is processed and stored. The capability of the computer to model an actively functioning organization of knowledge permits the study of cognitive organization to be separated from the phenomenon of consciousness.

The Computer Metaphor in More Detail

The self can be defined as *a protected domain within a larger knowledge system.* The computer metaphor amplifies this definition. ''Domain'' is meant in the sense of an area of dominance, and the protection is not so much against information outside the domain (although self's cognitive biases, see Greenwald, 1980, do indeed provide some such protection), as it is against the loss of mutual access among the portions of the domain. These usages are easily understood by those familiar with computer operating systems. Successful operating systems employ error-detection routines to assure, for example, that the area of memory in which the program operates is the proper domain of the operating system, or that the values of variables retrieved from memory are within ranges that the system's programs are prepared to deal with. Without these protective routines, a runaway condition can readily occur, with potentially disastrous results such as loss of important stored information. A well-designed operating system will protect itself against loss of control by interrupting an errant routine and returning control to an executive (or monitor) routine that reports the error condition and awaits further input. The analogy to the computer's operating system has the virtue of making clear that there need be no homunculus hidden within the conception of self as a protected domain of knowledge. The psychological importance of the protected-domain property of the self system can be appreciated by noting that loss or weakness of this property is likely at the root of a variety of pathological dissociation phenomena such as multiple personality, amnesia, fugue, and depersonalization (Hilgard, 1977).

An important aspect of the protected-domain definition of self is that the self system is contained within a larger knowledge system, from which it is partially independent. This aspect of the definition can be elucidated in terms of the computer metaphor by considering the relation of the computer's operating system to the larger computer system in which it participates. Various portions of the computer system may be independent of the operating system, either by being able to function without the aid of the operating system (e.g., read-only memories and some peripheral devices) or by being unintelligible to the operating system (e.g., data files or programs recorded in an unknown format by another operating system, perhaps a prior and now obsolete version of the current operating system).

Boundaries Between Subsystems

In order for there to be independence among subsystems of an organization, there must be some restrictions on communication between them. Two types of such restrictions are apparent in many large knowledge systems—*language barriers* and *access limits*. Sometimes these two classes of restrictions work together, as when an intelligence agency both encrypts information and prevents access of outsiders to these records. Other examples come readily to mind: The independence of American and Russian scientific establishments, due to different publication languages and to travel and communication restrictions; or the independence between psychological knowledge and lay wisdom due to much of the former being encrypted (in jargon) and hidden (in journals on library shelves and in professors' offices).

The computer metaphor readily provides illustrations of language barriers and access limits as the basis for independence among knowledge systems. A language barrier is apparent when there is an inability to use a program that, although stored in an accessible file, is written in a programing language for which the operating system has no compiler. An access restriction occurs when understandable information on a peripheral medium must be accessed via a directory that is in a format unknown to the operating system. A frequent virtue of access limitations is that they prevent one subsystem from modifying valuable information in another. An access limit that serves this function is the recording of the information needed to invoke the operating system in unmodifiable (read-only) form. One readily thinks of knowledge encoded in the form of reflexes and instincts as a parallel to such read-only computer memories.

PERSONALYSIS VERSUS
THE PRINCIPLE OF PERSONAL UNITY

Many philosophers and psychologists have theorized about the validity of characterizing the person as a unitary entity. Philosophical positions range from Hume's nonunified view of the person as a bundle of perceptions to Kant's unified formulation of the transcendental (or pure) ego. (A review of these early philosophical positions can be found in James's, 1890, chapter on the self.) Psychological positions range from behaviorist views of people as collections of reflexes and habits through the views of various self and ego theorists who regard unity as an accomplishment of the developing ego. (A review of ego-development theories is available in Loevinger, 1976.) An important type of intermediate position is one that considers the person as composed of dissociated subsystems. (See, for example, the review of Jung's position in Hall & Lindzey, 1978, and Hilgard's, 1977, recent statement of a neodissociationist position.)

Lewin (1935) and Allport (1965) devoted chapters to the question of personal unity. Although each of them was reluctant to say outright that the person is nonunitary, their remarks indicate that they saw substantial nonunity in personality. Lewin (1935) suggested that the self was a separate region (system) within the "psychical totality," and that even the self might be conceived as a multiplicity of systems:

> The question of the unity of consciousness is not identical with the question of the unity of the whole region of psychical forms and processes. . . . Further, it is at least questionable whether that which may be called the ego or self, the unity of which is important for many problems, is not merely one system or complex of systems, a functional part region within this psychical totality [p. 56].
>
> It would be natural from Gestalt theoretical considerations to understand the self in terms of the psychical totality perhaps as its structural individuality. . . . A number of facts, however, drive one in the opposite direction to the view that a special region, within the psychical totality, must be defined as the self in the narrower sense [p. 61].
>
> Psychical tensions and energies belong to systems which are in themselves dy-

namic unities and which show a greater or less degree of abscission [i.e., separation] [p. 62].

Allport (1965) viewed unity as an accomplishment toward which personality appeared to be directed, but which was not likely to be fully achieved: "Personality is many things in one—a *unitas multiplex*. . . . For two reasons [the problem of unity] is a preplexing problem: first, because there are many senses in which the term *unity* may be applied to personality; and second, because it is questionable whether unity is ever achieved. Such unification as exists seems to be only a matter of degree [p. 376]."

If there is a position on the unity issue that summarizes the consensus among theorists who have specifically addressed that issue, it is that unity of the person is not to be taken for granted. Yet, that is precisely what we find to have been done by researchers in a number of familiar topic areas of psychology. In the analysis of these topics, unity of the person is never stated as an explicit assumption—yet, the problems chosen for investigation and the manner of stating questions for research show that unity is being assumed implicitly. Perhaps this occurs because psychological researchers, like most lay persons, have a theory of the self (Epstein, 1973) as a unified entity that extends to the boundaries of the person. Before proceeding to document this widespread implicit assumption of personal unity, it is useful to develop concepts and language that make it as easy to talk about the alternative—the person as nonunitary—as it is presently to refer to the person as a unity.

My proposal of a set of designations for subsystems of the person is not intended as a known catalog of the subsystems of the person and their interrelations. This *caveat* is important because it will be easy to assume, when I refer to "the verbal system" or to "body systems," that these terms are intended to have well-defined referents. Rather, these terms are being used in a pretheoretical or metatheoretical sense. They are place-filler terms that should eventually be replaced by better specified concepts. The label for this metatheoretical effort, *personalysis*, designates the general enterprise of characterizing the person as a set of subsystems. The value of this personalytic approach should not stand or fall on the basis of the terms used here as first approximations to designate subsystems.

The label personalysis—deliberately built as a parallel to *psycho*analysis to indicate indebtedness to Freud's approach—also calls attention to one of a few critical differences from psychoanalysis. Freud's theory of the id, ego, and superego was conceived as an analysis of the *psyche* (mind) into functional subsystems. The present approach is conceived instead as an analysis of the *person* into subsystems.[2] Two other critical differences of this personalytic approach from

---

[2]By using a designation, person, that includes both mental and physical systems, I hope to avoid, rather than be trapped by, philosophical mind/body issues. The term *body* is used to name one class of subsystems, but it is not intended for other subsystems therefore to be interpreted as *mind*. The term, person, is additionally preferable to *individual*, which can be seen (from its derivation) to prejudge the personal unity question.

psychoanalytic theory are: (1) the conception of subsystem boundaries in terms of language barriers and access limitations (adapted from the computer metaphor); and (2) a stronger emphasis on the independence among the subsystems.[3]

Any demarcation of the person into subsystems can be specified only to the extent that we know the nature of languages (codes) used and patterns of knowledge access within the person. Because such knowledge is presently far from complete, the Fig. 6.1 specification of four subsystems—body, self, verbal, and social—is no more than a speculation that is subject to revision. Some justification for using these four as an initial set of subsystems follows.

Body (nonverbal) Systems. We know enough of biology, physiology, and psychology to know that there exist distinct codes for genetic information, several channels of sensory information, various channels of nonverbal behavioral communication, and affective or emotional information. For the most part, we don't know the details of these codes. (It is only this ignorance that justifies lumping these various nonverbal systems into the catchall category of "body" systems.) These several nonverbal codes have widely varying functions. The genetic code is a remarkably stable language (across time and species) that ties all life forms on the planet into one large system. Nonverbal behavior (e.g., gestural) codes serve a social communication function, even permitting some interspecies communication. Sensory codes are strictly for intrapersonal use and are extensively verbally translated. Affective codes appear also to serve largely intrapersonal functions and have translations into the verbal system that are probably far from perfect (Schachter & Singer, 1962).

The Verbal System. This may be the central subsystem of the person because of its potential for providing the common language that can permit access to the knowledge of all the other subsystems—that is, its potential for providing what unity the person can achieve. Figure 6.1 indicates that a portion of the verbal system lies outside the self system. This portion of the verbal system is especially significant psychologically and corresponds in part to the psychoanalytic conception of the unconscious (some differences are noted later). Another interesting overlap is that of the verbal and social systems *outside* the self system. This suggests the existence of some verbal social communications that do not involve the the self system, such as unremembered conversations with a hypnotist

---

[3]Erdelyi and Goldberg (1979) present an impressive argument to the effect that Freud would have used a computer metaphor had one been available in the early 20th century. In a personal communication, Erdelyi has further suggested that Freud's theories, elaborated with the aid of the computer metaphor, might closely resemble the multisystem view that I am presenting here. Even though the point is necessarily hypothetical, I am inclined to agree—which may explain why I have the feeling of having used the computer metaphor more to enable me to understand, rather than to disagree with, Freud.

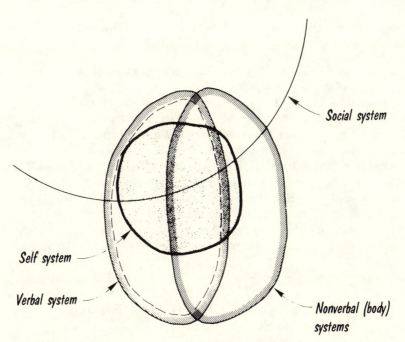

FIG.6.1   Representation of subsystems of the person. The hint of a cerebral-hemisphere structure, with the verbal system located in the left hemisphere, is based on much evidence of verbal specialization of the left hemisphere. The biasing of self and social systems toward the left hemisphere is sensible, if one assumes that the verbal system is crucial to these other two systems. The potentially misleading aspect of the hemispheric representation is the appearance that the subsystems of the person are confined to the cerebrum. However, the systems potentially include not only other parts of the brain but also the remainder of the physical person.

or verbally mediated mass behaviors in which the participants appear to be deindividuated (see section, "Behavior Without Self: Deindividuation").

The Self System.   The special character of the self system is the protected-domain property that was described earlier in terms of the computer operating system as a metaphor. The protected-domain property is assumed to be associated with a set of cognitive biases that also characterize other protected knowledge systems such as governmental propaganda and scientific theory (Greenwald, 1980), and with a capacity to retrieve long-established memories. Other subsystems of the person may also have learning or memory capacities, but those capacities must be rudimentary in comparison with those of the self system. This view of the special role of the self system in memory was central to the theorizing of the gestalt psychologist, Koffka (1935). Recent views of the role of the self system in memory can be found in Greenwald (1981b) and Rogers (1980), as well as in the chapter by Markus and Sentis in this volume.

The Social System.   In Fig. 6.1 the social system is shown as one of the subsystems of the person. This manner of depiction is intended only to capture an emphasis in this chapter; it is also indicated that the social portions of person systems can be represented as subsystems of a social system. It is in keeping with the personalytic approach to suggest that social roles (Sarbin & Allen, 1968) can be construed as subdivisions of the overlap of the social and self systems, an idea that can be related to James's (1890) suggestion about the multiplicity of ''social selves'': ''Properly speaking, a man has as many social selves . . . as there are distinct groups of persons about whose opinion he cares. He generally shows a different side of himself to each of these groups [p. 294].''

The relation of the self and the social system is considered further in the section following on deindividuation (see section ''Behavior Without Self: Deindividuation'').

APPLICATIONS OF PERSONALYSIS TO SOCIAL PSYCHOLOGY

Theoretical analysis of a number of topics in social psychology has been more troublesome than necessary because of researchers' implicit assumption of personal unity. The personalytic orientation of Fig. 6.1, which avoids the assumption of unity of verbal, nonverbal, social, and self systems, is illustrated for six topic areas—verbal and nonverbal communication, attitude–behavior consistency, relation of affect and cognition, accuracy of introspection, the attribution of consistent dispostions, and sociobiological versus cognitive interpretations of social behavior. In each of these cases, I try to show the subtle and sometimes obstructive manifestations of the implied unity principle.

Before proceeding to these battlegrounds between the forces of unity and nonunity, it is useful to mention some cases for which the principle of nonunity is fairly well-accepted. The disjunction between autonomic and voluntary response systems provides a good illustration. Although there are plausible claims of the possibility of gaining voluntary control over many autonomic nervous system and endocrine functions, few would oppose the hypothesis that control over circulation, digestion, etc. is *usually* independent of verbal process. Similarly, reflexive actions that are organized subcortically are usually assumed to operate independently of verbalization. The evidence from patients commisurotomized for the treatment of epilepsy (Gazzaniga, 1970) suggests a large degree of independence between functions that are respectively localized in the left (e.g., verbal) and right (e.g., affective) cerebral hemispheres. As a final example, it is commonplace for people to have cognitive abilities that are not matched by bodily abilities. There are many would-be athletes who have verbal knowledge of some skill—such as serving a tennis ball—but this verbal knowledge is independent of (i.e., not translatable into) the body system. Correspondingly, there are highly skilled athletes who are incapable of expressing verbally the knowledge that is encoded in their bodily performances. These last examples are specially interesting because such bodily-verbal independence is widely believed to be remediable by practice. In the multisystem (personalytic) view, such practice serves to develop translations between verbal and motor systems.

Communication Discrepancies Between Verbal and Nonverbal Channels

Taking their inspiration from the conclusions of Mehrabian (Mehrabian & Wiener, 1967) and Ekman and Friesen (1969), many textbook writers make the point that when verbal and nonverbal channels communicate discrepant evaluative messages, it is the nonverbal channel that can be expected to convey the true or accurate message (Berkowitz, 1980, p. 148; Freedman, Sears, & Carlsmith, 1978, p. 95; Schneider, 1976, p. 113; Worchel & Cooper, 1979, p. 275). A perhaps-abused example from popular novels and films is the woman whose words are presumably not to be believed when her mouth says "no," while her body says "yes." (But should those words be disbelieved?)

As others have noted (Krauss, Apple, Morency, Wenzel, & Winton, in press), the conclusion of nonverbal dominance derives from research settings that have used artificial tasks, such as instructing subjects to dissimulate. Nevertheless, secondary reporters have used these findings to conclude that nonverbal communications provide a pipeline to an underlying truth that characterizes the person as a whole. This conclusion—which subjects in bogus pipeline experiments (Jones & Sigall, 1971) seem also to accept willingly—shows the implicit principle of personal unity in operation. In contrast, the personalytic (subsystem independence) approach permits the interpretation that *inconsistent truths can be communicated simultaneously by verbal and nonverbal systems of the same person.* The epistemological status of discrepant verbal and nonverbal messages thus resembles that of discrepant responses to a survey question by two members of the population being surveyed. The aim of characterizing the person's knowledge by a single state of truth is accordingly no more (or no less) achievable than that of characterizing a population of voters as having a single preference among competing candidates.

Some other illustrations may help to make this point. Suppose you are asked if you are afraid of snakes and you say, with the conviction of belief, that you aren't. Surreptitiously, the questioner arranges for a harmless snake to appear crawling toward you on the arm of your chair—and you leap in haste out of the chair. Does this mean that you were lying when you said you weren't afraid of snakes? Not necessarily—it could be that your verbal knowledge included no fear of snakes, whereas your bodily reaction was controlled emotionally and reflexively by genetically transmitted knowledge. (Continued experience with people who arrange for snakes to crawl toward you might alter your verbal knowledge, but the naive situation of independence of verbal and bodily knowledge is not at all implausible.) A related example is based on the assumption that some bodily knowledge is sex-specific—which is to say, it has been transmitted by sex-linked genes. One's verbal knowledge may well not have good access to sex-linked nonverbal knowledge. Thus, our verbal reports concerning the way our personal interactions are contingent on our own or others' gender may truthfully reflect verbal knowledge, even though they may be contradicted by our nonverbal behavior. This example shows how asking the question as to whether a given *person* discriminates among others on the basis of their sex implies the questioner's assumption of personal unity. From the personalytic perspective, the question about sexual discrimination can be asked and answered separately for verbal, nonverbal, and social subsystems of the person.

Attitude–Behavior Consistency and the Three-Component Definition of Attitude

Following first LaPiere (1934) and later Wicker (1969), social psychologists have frequently observed that attitudes are poor predictors of behavior (Goldstein, 1980, p. 106; Schneider, 1976, p. 390; Worchel & Cooper, 1979, p. 70; Wrightsman, 1977, p. 342). Although this argument has lost some of its force as a consequence of recent reporting of conditions that can produce greater consistency (especially Fishbein & Ajzen, 1974; see also Dillehay, 1973), still there are many circumstances in which verbally measured attitude and overt behavior disagree by implying different evaluations of the same social object. The problem, stated this way, can be recognized as a close relative of the problem of verbal-nonverbal communication discrepancy. As before, these discrepancies need be troublesome only to a theory that assumes that there is a unified system in control of all behavior.

The problem of evaluative consistency between verbal attitude and nonverbal overt behavior should be (but is not often) distinguished from that of consistency between verbally measured attitude and *verbal reports* of behavior. The latter discrepancies, unlike the former, are problematic to the personalytic approach. Fortunately, it appears that these discrepancies within the verbal system are more apparent than real. When verbal measures are selected on the basis of reasonable psychometric criteria, high levels of consistency can generally be achieved (Fishbein & Ajzen, 1974; see also Ross, McFarland, & Fletcher, 1981). Additional available evidence shows that consistency between verbal attitude and nonverbal overt behavior is greater for people who have prior experience in overt behavioral interaction with the attitude object (direct experience) than for those who do not (Regan & Fazio, 1977). This result suggests that direct experience provides the verbal system with information that is otherwise unavailable to it (presumably due to independence among systems—cf. the snake example on pp. 161–162).

This discussion of attitude-behavior consistency can be extended readily to the problem of consistency among the affective, cognitive, and behavioral components of attitudes (Krech, Crutchfield, & Ballachey, 1962). The possibility of independence among these three attitude components has generally been regarded as a viable theoretical alternative to the assumption of a unitary attitude underlying the three components. The best evidence for consistency among the three components comes from studies in which the components have all been assessed in verbal form (Ostrom, 1969). From the present view, this verbal measurement approach can well give a much-inflated picture of intercomponent consistency. It is much more difficult to do the needed study with affect and behavior measured nonverbally—particularly when the unreliability and possible invalidity of single observations necessitate multiple observations for each component (Fishbein & Ajzen, 1974). Nevertheless, until such a definitive study is done it is inappropriate to conclude that the unity of the attitude construct is well-founded on an empirical basis.

Relation of Affective and Cognitive Processes

Zajonc (1980) has recently reviewed evidence in support of the position that affective reactions to stimuli occur more rapidly than, and may be independent of, cognitive reactions. The evidence reviewed by Zajonc is consistent with the multisystem personalytic view developed here, in which affect and cognition can be regarded as outputs of independent systems.

The conclusion that the affective (body) system responds more rapidly than the cognitive (verbal) system has interesting implications. If we add the assumption that the cognitive system is capable of detecting the affective system's reactions with at least partial accuracy, we may anticipate the frequent occurrence of a situation in which a person who is asked to report affective reactions to a stimulus employs the verbal (cognitive) system to describe a reaction that originated outside that system. Psychologists are likely to assume, however, that the system that reports the result is the system that was directly influenced by the stimulus. (Bem's [1967] self-perception analysis of this situation is an important exception to this generalization.)

Psychologists who take seriously the conclusion of affective-cognitive independence might advocate affective change techniques that operate directly on the affective system rather than ones—such as verbal persuasion—that operate on the cognitive system. Possibly the technique that Zajonc (1968) has pioneered—mere (repeated) exposure to a stimulus—is one such technique that operates directly on an affective system, even though its results may be (and are necessarily in experiments) reported via the verbal system. In support of that interpretation, Zajonc and his colleagues (reviewed in Zajonc, 1980) have shown that verbal reports of affective reactions to stimuli are influenced by repeated exposure under conditions in which subjects cannot reliably report effects of repeated exposure on verbal measures of familiarity or recognition.

The result of an affective consequence of a stiumlus being manifest in the absence of ability of the verbal system to report the occurrence of the stimulus is familiar from research on perceptual defense (Dixon, 1971; Erdelyi, 1974). In the present multisystem view, such independent effects of the same stimulus on verbal and nonverbal systems are expectable. The preference of some prominent reviewers (Eriksen, 1960; Goldiamond, 1962) to dismiss perceptual defense results as artifacts of experimental procedures reflects, perhaps, some mixture of astute criticism with predilection toward the principle of personal unity.

The assumption of affective-cognitive independence has implications also for theories of emotion that postulate an important cognitive contribution to emotional experience. The influential analysis by Schachter and Singer (1962), for example, proposes that emotions are relatively undifferentiated in physiological terms and depend on cognitive interpretive processes to acquire distinctive characteristics. In the personalytic view, Schachter and Singer's conclusion can be regarded as a plausible characterization of the verbal system that reports emotions, but does not require an assumption that emotions are physiologically undifferentiated. Rather, emotional events in the body system may be well-differentiated (Winton, Putnam, & Krauss, unpublished), but these differentiations may be only weakly accessible to the verbal (cognitive) system. When asked to report the body's emotional state, the verbal system may provide its best hypothesis. Such hypotheses are more than idle speculation, not only because they may accurately reflect the body system, but also because the verbal system's hypotheses can influence behavior independently of their accuracy.

Accuracy of Attributions and Introspections

In the last few years there has been renewed and vigorous attention to a problem that is methodologically fundamental to much of psychology—the validity of verbal explanations of behavior. The method of introspection foundered early in the 20th century when behaviorists undermined the belief that verbal report data could be taken at face value. The occasion for the renewed interest in this problem (Ericsson & Simon, 1980; Nisbett & Wilson, 1977) has been the heavy reliance of contemporary psychologists on methods that assume validity of verbal reports about behavior-mediating processes. Areas of recent research that rely heavily on verbal explanations of behavior include attribution, cognitive response analysis of persuasion, and complex problem solving. It should not be assumed from these uses of verbal report data that contemporary psychologists are simply mining old veins with obsolete tools. The gain over introspectionism is well represented in the position taken by Ericsson and Simon (1980)—specifically, that the processes underlying verbal reports are now understood to the point at which some conditions associated with valid reports can be specified.

In terms of the multisystem interpretation of Fig. 6.1, verbal reports are most likely to be accurate when the processing between stimulus and response occurs largely within the verbal system. On the other hand, verbal reports are likely to be less accurate in explaining behavior that is mediated by nonverbal systems.

Attribution of Consistent Dispositions to Self and to Others

Psychologists, as well as lay persons, are prone to assume that behavior is under the control of cross-situationally and temporally stable dispositions. Psychologists' predilections for such dispositional interpretations are evidenced in the extensive effort invested, over many years, in developing measures of dispositions. They are indicated in quite another way by the flurry of empirical and theoretical responses that were elicited by Mischel's (1968) critique of the adequacy of dispositional constructs in personality research. By now, there are many supports for the conclusion that cross-situational consistency can be found when suitable subsets of persons and situations are samples (Bem & Allen, 1974; Epstein, 1979; Kenrick & Stringfield, 1980; Markus, 1977). By assuming that the major locus of consistency within personality is the self system (cf. Epstein, 1980; Greenwald, 1980; Greenwald & Ronis, 1978), personalysis provides a plausible framework for interpreting the variable efficacy of dispositional interpretations; that is, evidence for cross-situational consistency should be expected to be strong only when the measures being used in different situations all tap the operation of the self system (cf. Allport, 1943). Further, because the structure of the self system need not be the same across persons, it should not be expected that one could specify a set of situations and measures that should yield strong evidence of consistency for all persons.

Although it requires a mild digression, this is a convenient place to comment on a point of some recent confusion concerning the attribution of stable dispositions. Jones & Nisbett (1971) have hypothesized that people typically perceive others' behavior as being responsive to features of the situation in which the behavior occurs. Although this *situation/disposition hypothesis* has received adequate empirical support, the theoretical conclusion that people are loathe to attribute dispositions to themselves cannot be regarded as justified. The point is relevant to personalysis because it concerns the extent to which people perceive unity in their own behavior. Two comments can make clear that people are as susceptible to assuming unity in their own behavior as they are in the behavior of others.

Firstly, there is no justification for extending the situation/disposition hypothesis to a conclusion that people tend to see their own behavior as *caused* by external influences, rather than as being internally controlled. This extension of the situation/disposition hypothesis is based on the faulty assumption that the phrases, ''responsive to features of the situation,'' and ''externally controlled,'' are psychologically equivalent. To the contrary, people may see their behavior as being fully under internal control, in the sense that they feel *responsible for* their actions, even though they also see their behavior as properly *responsive to* the situation in which it occurs. For example: The person who gives the ''situational'' attribution, ''I helped because the other person needed help,'' cannot be interpreted as denying internal control over—that is, personal responsibility for—the act of helping.[4]

Secondly, explanations of very recent behavior are affected by self-presentational concerns that can suppress description of oneself in terms of stable dispositions. It is well-established that subjects generally seek to present themselves in a favorable light in their interactions with experimenters (Rosenberg, 1969; Weber & Cook, 1972). When asked to explain an action that has just occurred, subjects can expect to appear more intelligent if they claim to have responded to appropriate features of the situation (e.g., I helped because the other person was in need of help, not because I am always helpful). On the other hand, when subjects are asked to explain a comparable action that occurred some time ago, a favorable impression may best be generated by giving the appearance of consistent responding to similar situations (e.g., I generally help people in need, it was nothing about that particular person). As can be seen from the examples just used, the explanation of the action from the subject's perspective has not really changed—in both explanations, help was given because the other person needed help. However, the emphasis contained in the statement of the reason nevertheless shifted dramatically from the stimulus properties of the situation to the stable dispositional properties of the actor. Experimental findings showing just this shift in emphasis as a function of temporal distance from the event being explained have been reported by Moore, Sherrod, Liu, and Underwood (1979; cf. Funder, 1980).

We can conclude that the tendency to attribute consistent dispositions to persons characterizes not only psychologists administering personality inventories and lay persons viewing others' behavior, but also people perceiving their own behavior over time. All of these tendencies to attribute stable dispositions reveal the widespread tendency to assume personal unity. As noted a few paragraphs back, the unity assumption may be well-justified for selected situations and behaviors that tap fundamental dimensions of the person's self system.

Instinct and Purpose: Sociobiology Versus Cognitive Social Psychology

During the last decade social psychology has become strongly cognitive. At the same time that academic social psychology has moved toward a cognitive approach, there have been important developments toward a noncognitive approach to social behavior in the emerging field of sociobiology (Alexander,1979; Dawkins, 1976; Wilson, 1978). These competing developments have not been integrated, with the result that students often are compelled to choose sides. With a multisystem analysis, however, the two approaches can readily coexist. This

---

[4]In the case of one's actions causing undersired outcomes, then attributions "to the situation" *are* often meant as a denial of responsibility or intentionality. However, when one's actions cause desired outcomes, there is no reluctance to accept personal responsibility (Greenwald, 1980, pp. 605–606).

coexistence depends on a recognition that cognitive social psychology applies most to the self and verbal systems, whereas sociobiology deals with physiological, nonverbal (body) systems.

The conflict between sociobiological and cognitive approaches may be nowhere more apparent than in the clash between instinctive and purposive accounts of aggressive behavior. In contemporary (cognitive) social psychology texts, it is customary to define aggression as behavior that has the purpose or goal of harming another. In contrast, the sociobiological approach defines aggression in terms of overt behavior, without reference to purpose. From the personalytic perspective, there is no reason to confine the meaning of aggression to just one of these two definitions. Further, in order for the analysis of aggression to be responsive to the needs of society to control injurious behavior, neither the cognitive nor the sociobiological approach should be excluded. Harming behavior, that is, can be deliberate and purposeful (guided by the self system), but it can also be emotional and impulsive (controlled outside the self system). The multisystem approach thus supports and provides added justification for treatments such as that of Buss (1961), who has distinguished between instrumental (goal-directed) and angry (emotional) aggression. Zillmann (1979) makes a parallel distinction between incentive-motivated and annoyance-motivated aggression but does so in the context of a perhaps overly strong attack on sociobiological views of human aggressive behavior.

The justification for analyzing aggression in terms of multiple systems that may achieve similar effects (harming, in the case of aggression) applies with equal force to several other topic areas of social psychology—such as altruism, attraction, affiliation, and sexual behavior.

PERSONALYSIS COMPARED TO PSYCHOANALYSIS

Freud's analysis of the psyche into id, ego, and superego was a multisystem view, in that he did not oblige these three systems to function as a unity. Given the force with which Freud justified this multisystem view in his own writings, and the influence of those writings on major segments of world culture, it is surprising that the personal unity principle remains so deeply entrenched, albeit implicitly, in both lay and psychological thought. Perhaps one reason that Freud's multisystem theoretical theme did not take stronger root was that Freud and his followers focused more on the coordination among psychic systems than on their independence. Indeed, Freud's treatment of the *unconsious* did not make full theoretical use of the possibility that the psyche's subsystems could function independently. The present view that knowledge subsystems are separated by language barriers and access limits—that is, that some information available to one system may not be translatable by or accessible to another system—provides a basis for reconsidering the Freudian notions of repression and the unconscious.

The Equestrian Metaphor

The present conceptions of body and self systems have clear antecedents in Freud's conceptions of id and ego. Freud (1923/1961) likened the relation between id and ego to that between a horse and its rider. This metaphor is a powerful one that helps to develop the present multisystem approach:

> The functional importance of the ego is manifested in the fact that normally control over the approaches to motility devolves upon it. Thus in its relation to the id it is like a man on horseback, who has to hold in check the superior strength of the horse; with this difference, that the rider tries to do so with his own strength while the ego uses borrowed forces. The analogy may be carried a little further. Often a rider, if he is not to be parted from his horse, is obliged to guide it where it wants to go; so in the same way the ego is in the habit of transforming the id's will into action as if it were its own [p. 25].

The horse-rider metaphor effectively captures the concept of systems that have both relation and independence. Perhaps the only fault in the metaphor is that one expects the horse and rider to separate periodically, whereas the subsystems housed within the human organism must necessarily keep each other company throughout their existences. Try the thought experiment of obliging the horse and rider to be perennial companions. Among the results I get from this experiment are:

1. Despite the lack of direct neural interconnections, the rider develops great sensitivity to the actions of the horse, and vice versa. (The metaphor leads one to wonder where the reference to intuition as "seat of the pants" knowledge originated.)

2. The rider acquires the ability to influence many of the horse's movements and to anticipate others. In this sense the rider gains "control over the approaches to motility." It would not be surprising if the rider developed the illusion that it was directly "willing" the actions of the horse (and perhaps vice versa also).

3. When asked to explain the behavior of the horse, the rider readily produces answers, but these may have little validity, unless the rider has managed to form a theory of the separateness of the horse's nervous system.

Perhaps I have biased the results of this thought experiment, but it is apparent that my results suggest that the equestrian pair has many of the properties of human behavior and cognition.

Repression and the Unconscious

Freud was much less concerned with the independence of the id from the ego than he was with their interdependence. Indeed, he made such strong assumptions about their interdependence that he effectively treated the two systems as a unit. This assumption of close interrelation required a cumbersome account of repression and the unconscious. He asserted (1923/1961):

"The repressed merges into the id . . . and is merely a part of it. The repressed is only cut off sharply from the ego by the resistances of repression; it can communicate with the ego through the id [p. 24]."

Freud thereby assumed that ego lacked access to certain knowledge (the unconscious) because of an active force (repression) that prevented access. The inaccessible knowledge consisted of: (1) the primitive id; (2) the repressed; and (3) the agency of repression within the ego. Freud (1923/1961) acknowledged that the necessity of postulating the third aspect of the unconscious was especially troublesome:

> When we find ourselves thus confronted by the necessity of postulating a third *Ucs.* [Ucs. is the dynamic unconscious, consisting of all inaccessible knowledge], which is not repressed, we must admit that the characteristic of being unconscious begins to lose significance for us. It becomes a quality which can have many meanings, a quality which we are unable to make, as we should have hoped to do, the basis of far-reaching and inevitable conclusions [p. 18].

Personalysis uses the concepts of coding differences and access limitations in place of psychoanalysis's concepts of the unconscious and repression. The portions of the body system that are unintelligible or otherwise inaccessible to the self system correspond to the primitive id portion of the psychoanalytic unconscious. Corresponding to the repressed portion of the unconscious are portions of the verbal system that are outside the self system.[5] Personalysis needs no counterpart of the troublesome third portion of the psychoanalytic unconscious—ego's agency of repression.

Interestingly, personalysis allows readily for phenomena corresponding to the notion of the collective unconscious that was developed as a variant of psychoanalytic theory by Jung (1936/1959). In Fig. 6.1 the verbal and body systems are shown as having an overlap with the social system *outside* the self system. This overlap comprises socially shared knowledge that is inaccessible by the self system. (Of course, the present analysis provides no new evidence regarding the existence of such socially shared knowledge.)

A legitimate criticism of this personalytic account is that the assumption of subsystem independence provides enough degrees of freedom to enable it to ac-

---

[5]Although explanations of the nature of the barrier between portions of the verbal system that lie within versus outside the self system is not attempted in this chapter, it is sufficiently important a task to warrant a few remarks that suggest its possible accomplishment within the personalytic framework. Part of the explanation can make use of an analogy to the evolution of natural language systems, in which contemporary speakers cannot understand ancestral forms of their own language. Thus, the person's evolving use of verbal codes amounts to a dialect change that prevents access by the user of the current dialect (the self system) to verbal information encoded early in life. (This explanation may be recognized as equivalent to Schachtel's, 1959 explanation of amnesia for childhood experiences.) The dialect-evolution analogy cannot, however, explain lack of access to recently established knowledge. This important residual problem may best be addressed by building on recent analyses of retrieval failures (Loftus & Loftus, 1980; Watkins & Tulving, 1975).

count for virtually anything. Indeed, personalysis has been described here in a fashion that renders it (like psychoanalysis) difficult to disprove. Nevertheless, personalysis and psychoanalysis do differ in the way that they direct researchers' attention. Psychoanalysis orients researchers to look for antecedents and indicators of motivational conflict, and to seek evidence for an active barrier (the agency of repression) that restricts access to knowledge. Personalysis, on the other hand, suggests a search for evidence of independent operation of person subsystems and suggests that important general research tasks for psychologists are to seek and to decipher the codes that define subsystems within the person.[6]

BEHAVIOR WITHOUT SELF: DEINDIVIDUATION

The multisystem personalytic approach provides for analysis of behavior that is *not* mediated by the self system. In social psychology, the study of deindividuation is concerned with just such behavior. Deindividuation is widely understood to mean loss of individuality, although, as we shall see, there are disagreements about just what happens when individuality is lost. Before showing how personalysis can resolve these disagreements, let us examine the variations in social psychologists' treatments of deindividuation.[7]

Paradoxical Aspects of Deindividuation

In the initial laboratory investigation of deindividuation, Festinger, Pepitone, and Newcomb (1952) defined deindividuation:

> as a state of affairs in a group where members do not pay attention to other individuals *qua* individuals, and, correspondingly, the members do not feel they are being singled out by others.[This] results in a reduction of inner restraints in the members and . . . the members will be more free to indulge in behavior from which they are usually restrained . . . . This is a satisfying state of affairs and its occurrence would tend to increase the attractiveness of the group [p. 389].

Since the Festinger et al. article, the concept of deindividuation has expanded

---

[6]This difference in the way psychoanalysis and personalysis direct researchers' attention can be illustrated in the domain of ordinary errors—of the sort that Freud analyzed in *The Psychopathology of Everyday Life* (1901/1938). Personalysis seeks explanations in terms of inadequate linkage between intention (verbal) and performance (body) systems, whereas psychoanalysis searches for hidden intentions that can explain the precise form of the error. A strong form of personalysis that excluded the possibility of hidden intentions or self-deceptions (Gurs, Sackeim, 1979) cannot be justified. Therefore, it might be best to characterize the personalytic approach as encouraging the discrimination of within-system errors (symptoms) from between-system errors (slips).

[7]Deindividuation is the only topic of social psychological study (to my knowledge) in which there is an apparent willingness to oppose the implicit assumption of personal unity. The increasing recent interest in this topic, as evidenced in the literature reviews by Diener (1977) and Dipboye (1977), may presage some readiness to overthrow the unity principle.

progressively with the research contributions of others. Ziller (1964) introduced the idea that deindividuated group members might become perceptually indistinct to themselves at the same time that they were becoming indistinguishable to others. He did not regard the result of such "ego diffusion" as necessarily satisfying: "Under conditions of ego diffusion, the individual has difficulty in distinguishing his uniqueness; contrasts and similarities between the self and others fail to be perceived and the result is an amorphous, diaphanous, or obscured self portrayal [p. 342]."

An article by Singer, Brush, and Lublin (1965) reported two experiments that were guided by the initial Festinger et al. formulation. However, Singer et al., like Ziller, interpreted deindividuation from the self's perspective: "Deindividuation is a subjective state in which people lose their self-consciousness. . . . The hallmark of deindividuation is the performance of a socially disapproved act and the attendant liking for the deindividuated setting. [pp. 356, 376]."

In a review that encompassed a broad sweep of contemporary events as well as imaginative original laboratory and field experiments, Zimbardo (1969) amplified earlier treatments by formulating deindividuation as a "minimization of: 1. self-observation-evaluation [and of] 2. concern for social evaluation [leading to] weakening of controls based upon guilt, shame, fear, and commitment [and] lowered threshold for expressing inhibited behaviors [p. 253]."

A new and problematic perspective on deindividuation was introduced by Maslach (1974), when she commented on the close relation between deindividuation and a common social strategy for establishing *uniqueness*. Her description of such "collective attempts at individuation" is reminiscent of Sherif and Cantril's (1947) interpretation of ego-involvement in terms of adopting the attitudes and other characteristics of reference groups: "By being part of a group that is singled out by others, the individual receives some sort of personal identity or sense of uniqueness . . . In collective individuation, the individual group member must first become very similar to some people in order to become very different from others [p. 424]."

In his recent review Dipboye (1977) drew explicit attention to the inconsistencies in the evolving conception of deindividuation. He noted the contrast "between deindividuation as a release of restraints and deindividuation as a search for identity," suggesting that the former was mediated by "a momentary reduction in self-awareness [whereas] the latter seems to be mediated by a threat to the uniqueness and/or stability of the person's important self-conceptions [p. 1072]." Paradoxically, as he pointed out, the search for identity associated with deindividuation could take the form either of conformity or nonconformity: "Conformity should result from a threat to the stability of self-conceptions, whereas anticonformity to group norms should result from a threat to uniqueness [p. 1071]."

Another recent reviewer (Diener, 1977, 1980) has noted the paradoxical aspects of deindividuation—particularly the fact that it may sometimes by sought and sometimes avoided—but has otherwise followed more closely in the line of development that includes the work of Festinger et al. (1952), Singer et al. (1965), and Zimbardo (1969). Diener (1980 asserts: ''People who are deindividuated have lost self-awareness and their personal identity in a group situation. . . . Prevented from self-attention and self-monitoring by the group situation, they become more reactive to immediate stimuli and emotions and are unresponsive to norms and to the long-term consequences of their behavior [p. 210].''

In sum, *deindividuation is sometimes associated with loss of identity but other times with acquisition of identity via a distinctive group (of which one is an indistinguishable member); it is sometimes sought but other times avoided; and it is sometimes associated with chaotic, norm-violating behavior but other times with conforming, uniform behavior.*

Resolving the Paradoxes: Deindividuation Versus Sociation

The concept and phenomena of deindividuation can be analyzed into two usages that, from the multisystem perspective of personalysis, are mutually antithetical. These two usages agree in conceiving deindividuation as a loss of control over the person's behavior by the self system, but they differ sharply in the nature of control that replaces the self system. In what appears to be the more common usage, both the self and the social system as sources of control are inoperative. It is with this form of deindividuation that one can associate antinormative behavior, such as riot, panic, and revelry, and perhaps also certain other forms of unrestrained behavior that call less attention to themselves, such as sleep and vigorous exercise. The second form of deindividuation entails a high degree of social control and organization, such as military action, congregational prayer, organized cheering, and a variety of more intricate organized group efforts, such as ballet and orchestral performances, athletic teamwork, and more mundane social coordinations like driving an automobile in traffic.

Although the single term, deindividuation, may be a proper designation for both of these categories—in the sense that each involves reduction of the controlling role of the self system—nevertheless it is obviously useful to be able to distinguish the form that lacks social control from the one that is characterized by a high degree of social organization. The former category seems best to warrant the original label of deindividuation. The latter form, in which the person is subordinated to the social system, can be referred to as *sociated deindividuation.* or more simply as *sociation*. The basis for distinguishing deindividuation from sociation is summarized in Table 6.1.

Most of the conclusions summarized in Table 6.1 are drawn from the reviews of deindividuation by Zimbardo (1969), Dipboye (1977), and Diener (1977, 1980). The recent analyses of self-awareness by Buss (1980) and by Scheier and

Carver (1980), and my integration of their concepts with phenomena of ego-involvement (Greenwald, 1981a) provide the bases for the table's reference to I-type (intrapersonally-oriented) and S-type (socially oriented) settings. As defined in Greenwald, (1981a): "The essence of I-type situations is that they focus the subject's attention on evaluation of self in relation to personal standards. In contrast, the essence of S-type settings is that they focus others' attention onto evaluation of the subject [p. 132]."

I-type settings are ones that involve self-confrontation, such as looking in a mirror, reading one's diary, listening to the sound of one's voice, or seeing a photograph or videotape of oneself (cf. Buss's, 1980, list of inducers of *private* self-awareness). S-type situations involve confrontation with an audience of others, including symbolic self-confrontations such as the presence of a camera (Buss's discussion of inducers of *public* self-awareness).

A Sometimes Subtle Distinction.   Despite the fact that the antecedents of deindividuation and sociation are conceptual opposites, the situational differences associated with these opposites are sometimes subtle—which makes it understandable that these processes have not been differentiated in previous treatments. Loud music, for example, may sometimes be perceived as strong unstructured stimuli, sometimes as structured rhythmic stimulation. People in uniforms may perceive themselves as separate and anonymous or, alternately, as

TABLE 6.1
Deindividuation Versus Sociation

Deindividuation	Sociation
ANTECEDENTS	
1. Strong unstructured stimuli	1. Strong structured (e.g., rhythmic) stimuli
2. Privacy (also anonymity)	2. Uniformity in group
3. Absence of self-control inducers (absence of I-type evaluative settings)[a]	3. Presence of social controls or authorities (presence of S-type evaluative settings)[a]
4. Intoxicating drugs	4. Tranquilizers?
CONSEQUENCES	
1. Norm violation (independence)	1. Norm adherence (conformity)
2. Enhanced responsiveness to nonsocial stimuli	2. Enhanced responsiveness to nearby others
3. Social chaos	3. Collective organization

[a]I-type and S-type are summary labels developed in Greenwald (1981a) and also described further in the text.

participants in a well-defined social structure (Johnson & Downing, 1979). In such circumstances, the effect on the person (deindividuation versus sociation) may depend critically on other situational features, such as use of drugs and presence or absence of social controls. It may also depend importantly on personality differences, which are now considered further.

Because the difference between induction of deindividuation and of sociation can depend on the way a situation is perceived, and because different people may perceive the same situation differently, it might often happen that some people are deindividuated, whereas others are sociated, in the same setting! A nightclub with loud music may house a mixture of drunk and deindividuated revelers together with sober and sociated dancers. A lynch mob may include sociated organizers and followers,[8] together with more disorderly and deindividuated participants.

Predisposition to Vacate the Self System?   Personalysis offers a suggestive interpretation of the nature of personality differences associated with predispositions to enter states of deindividuation and sociation. Figure 6.2 shows the segments of the person's multisystem that should be involved in the four states defined by combining the presence or absence of individuation with the presence or absence of sociation.[9] The four states are assumed, that is, to correspond to a temporary dominance of different subsystems. An initial, and admittedly speculative, suggestion is that self-esteem, in combination with the I-type and S-type predispositions that I have described elsewhere (Greenwald, 1981a), may predict differential predispositions to enter the four states.

The proposed role of self-esteem draws on Hoffer's (1951) conception of "the true believer": "to be one thread of the many which makes up a tunic; one thread not distinguishable from the others. No one can then point us out, measure us against others and expose our inferiority [pp. 29-30]." More specifically, we may extend Hoffer's conception by proposing that self-esteem in effect measures the capacity of the self system to retain dominance. Persons with low self-esteem, then, should have self systems that are predisposed to vacate control, in the direction of *either* deindividuation or sociation.

What determines whether the self system, in giving up control, will yield in the direction of (unsociated) deindividuation versus sociation? Here, the analysis of differential predispositions to engage in the socially oriented (S-type) task of impression management may be useful. People who are high in this S-type orien-

---

[8]Description of lynch-mob organizers and followers as sociated obviously considers only their relation to the mob, which temporarily establishes norms that violate those of the larger community.

[9]The use of deindividuation and sociation and their complements in four combinations presents a nomenclature problem that had best be treated explicitly. In order to avoid having to use many compound expressions, such as "unsociated deindividuation" or "deindividuated sociation," I suggest the convention of assuming the negative value of a term that is not specified. The only compound term that is needed, then, is sociated individuation (or, equivalently, individuated sociation). The solitary term, sociation, thus replaces both "sociated deindividuation" and its equivalent "deindividuated sociation,"etc.

tation may be predisposed to enter the sociated, rather than the deindividuated state, and those low in the S-type orientation may be more susceptible to becoming deindividuated. (The I-type and S-type orientations correspond approximately to, and may prove to be measurable by, Fenigstein, Scheier, & Buss's, 1975, scales of *private* and *public* self-consciousness, respectively.)

As indicated in Fig. 6.2, individuation and sociation need not be regarded as mutually exclusive. Among the settings in which one may be simultaneously individuated and sociated are various types of public performances by groups. The

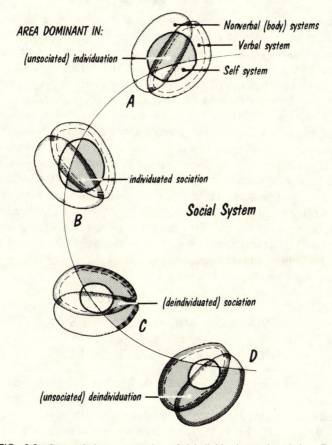

FIG. 6.2 Personalytic representation of deindividuation and sociation. Four members of the social system are shown with different "sizes" of self and social systems. Persons with "small" self systems (C and D) should be most prone to deindividuation, but C should be more likely to show the sociated form of deindividuation than D because of C's larger social subsystem. Similarly, having "large" self systems both A and B should show individuation (i.e., resist deindividuation), but, because of B's larger social subsystem, B should be more predisposed than A to show the sociated form of individuation.

members of athletic teams, theater companies, dance troupes, and musical groups are often sociated by virtue of their uniform dress and the need to coordinate their performances—but at the same time they can retain personal identifiability. (The recent trend for athletes' names to be printed in large letters on their uniforms is a sign of the individuation that can accompany sociation.) People who are simultaneously high in the S-type orientation *and* in the predisposition to engage in the intrapersonally oriented (I-type) task of self-image management may be prone to the combined sociated-individuated state.

Applications of the Deindividuation-Sociation Analysis

The foregoing multisystem analysis is undisguisedly speculative. A justification for this extent of speculation in the absence of specifically supporting data is the practical significance of the theoretical topics being considered. One example is automobile driving. Because driving in traffic at high speeds calls for a high degree of social coordination, it is obviously not desirable for drivers to be deindividuated. Some of the stimulus characteristics of driving, however, may produce deindividuation. These include the anonymity afforded by the masking exterior of the automobile and the infrequency of encounters with controlling agents (highway police) in ordinary driving. Additionally, use of drugs by drivers is an important concern, not just because of direct effects of intoxicants on the motor and perceptual skills needed for driving, but because of the likely effect of drugs in producing deindividuation and concomitant disregard for norms. This analysis of driving can be applied by suggesting the desirability of reducing the anonymity afforded by automobiles (perhaps by using much larger license-plate identifications), of increasing the symbolic or actual presence of control agents, and of designing driver education programs in consideration of the deindividuating effect of intoxicants.

SUMMARY AND CONCLUSIONS: SOCIAL PSYCHOLOGY FROM THE PERSPECTIVE OF SELF

The twist on this book's title that is used in the heading of this concluding section is to be taken in two senses. The straightforward meaning suggests that the concept of self can provide an organizing basis for many of the major phenomena of social psychology. The less obvious meaning—but the one that is more in keeping with the content of this chapter—is that much of social psychology reflects the (incomplete) perspective of the (psychologist's) self system on the behavior of the person.

The chapter has reviewed a variety of manifestations of an implicit assumption of personal unity in social psychological theory. This implicit assumption may best be accounted for by observing that it is the self system of the psychologist that does the work of formulating theories. The person *does* appear to be a unified system from the self's perspective, because the self lacks ready access to evidences of nonunity. From the personalytic perspective of person as multisystem, this theory-formulating enterprise becomes questionable when the implicit unity assumption generates a search for an assumed single, coherent, consistent structure underlying all appearances of nonunity. Included in the class of such questionable theory are:

1. Analyses of the relative truth of verbal and nonverbal communications (from the multisystem perspective, both channels can be true even when in conflict because they can reflect the operation of different knowledge bases).

2. Protection of the integrity of the attitude concept by using verbal measures of its components (from the multisystem perspective, these efforts observe the integrity of the verbal system and suppress genuine independence of affective, verbal, and behavioral responses to the same object).

3. Attempts to provide coherent accounts of phenomena such as aggression, attraction, and altruism either from an exclusively cognitive perspective or from an exclusively sociobiological perspective (from the multisystem view, such behaviors are influenced by verbal, body, self, and social systems, with these influences not being fully accountable from the perspective of any one of these).

The tendency for social (and other) psychologists to perceive the world through their own self systems is a variety of what William James (1890) called "the psychologist's fallacy":

> The great snare of the psychologist is the confusion of his own standpoint with that of the mental fact about which he is making his report [p.196].
> Crude as such a confusion of standpoints seems to be when abstractly stated, it is nevertheless a snare into which no psychologist has kept himself at all times from falling and which forms almost the entire stock-in-trade of certain schools [p. 197].

Even Freud—whose methods for discovering knowledge that was not accessible to the self system allowed him to lead others around one set of snares—was not completely immune. His struggles to formulate the concepts of repression and the unconsious, and the complexities of the resulting formulations, suggest that he accepted a principle of personal unity that he held to be more fundamental than his tripartite division of the psyche into id, ego, and superego.

The present multisystem analysis has used the metaphor of language barriers and access restrictions to characterize independence among the subsystems of the person. Each subsystem, it is assumed, possesses significant knowledge that is unavailable to other subsystems because they use different coding systems, they lack exact translations, and/or they lack access to the knowledge. The notion of an exact translation of codes between systems corresponds to the idea of "direct knowledge" passing between systems. It is this lack of direct knowledge between the verbal system and other systems that makes the introspective method, at best, an unreliable device for psychological analysis of nonverbal processes.

Perhaps more germane to psychology than the fact that knowledge subsystems of the person do not possess exact translations of each others' codes is the fact that psychologists do not possess translations of these codes either. This situation has been characterized in part by Simon (1980):

> While an enormous amount of knowledge has been gathered about brain structures and functions at chemical and neurological levels, we still do not even know the physiological basis for long-term or short-term memory—whether it involves macromolecules, neuronal circuits, some combination of these, or something entirely different. We are in a position similar to that of 19th-century chemistry, which had developed an extensive theory of chemical combination long before that theory could be linked to the physics of atoms [p. 77].

It seems obvious that identifications and translations of the codes for knowledge in the different subsystems of the person will be among the major contributions to be produced in the future of behavioral science. Further, those discoveries can have profound impact if they can be applied to dissolve the language barriers among verbal and nonverbal subsystems of the person. The presently unjustified assumption of personal unity could become a justified assumption.

ACKNOWLEDGMENTS

Work on this chapter was aided substantially by grants MH 31762 and MH 32317 from the National Institute of Mental Health. I am also greatly indebted to the colleagues—Steven Breckler, Deborah Davis, Ed Diener, Seymour Epstein, Matthew Hugh Erdelyi, David C. Funder, Ernest R. Hilgard, Alice M. Isen, Robert M. Krauss, Anthony R. Pratkanis, Harold A. Sackeim, M. Brewster Smith, Jerry Suls, and Robert B. Zajonc—who commented on an earlier draft of this chapter. I hope the readers of this final version escape some of the confusion to which they were subjected.

REFERENCES

Alexander, R. D.   *Darwinism and human affairs.* Seattle: University of Washington Press, 1979.

Allport, G. W.   The ego in contemporary psychology. *Psychological Review,* 1943, *50,* 451–478.

Allport, G. W.   *Pattern and growth in personality.* New York: Holt, Rinehart, & Winston, 1965.

Bem, D. J.   Self-perception: An alternative interpretation of cognitive dissonance phenomena. *Psychological Review,* 1967, *74,* 183–200.

Bem, D. J., & Allen, A.   On predicting some of the people some of the time: The search for cross-situational consistencies in behavior. *Psychological Review,* 1974, *81,* 506–520.

Berkowitz, L.   *A survey of social psychology* (2nd ed.). New York: Holt, Rinehart, & Winston, 1980.

Buss, A. H.   *The psychology of aggression.* New York, Wiley, 1961.

Buss, A. H.   *Self-consciousness and social anxiety.* San Francisco: Freeman, 1980.

Cooley, C. H.   *Human nature and the social order.* New York: Scribner's, 1902.

Dawkins, R.   *The selfish gene.* New York: Oxford University Press, 1976.

Diener, E.   Deindividuation: Causes and consequences. *Social Behavior and Personality,* 1977, *5,* 143–155.

Diener, E.   Deindividuation: The absence of self-awareness and self-regulation in group members. In P. Paulus (Ed.), *The psychology of group influence*. Hillsdale, N. J.: Lawrence Erlbaum Associates, 1980.

Dillehay, R. C.   On the irrelevance of the classical negative evidence concerning the effect of attitudes on behavior. *American Psychologist*, 1973, *28*, 887–891.

Dipboye, R. L.   Alternative approaches to deindividuation. *Psychological Bulletin*, 1977, *84*, 1057–1075.

Dixon, N. F.   *Subliminal perception: The nature of a controversy*. London: McGraw–Hill, 1971.

Duval, S., & Wicklund, R. A.   *A Theory of objective self awareness*. New York: Academic Press, 1972.

Ekman, P., & Friesen, W. F.   Nonverbal leakage and cues to deception, *Psychiatry*, 1969, *32*, 88–108.

Epstein, S.   The self-concept revisited: Or a theory of a theory. *American Psychologist*, 1973, *28*, 404–416.

Epstein, S.   The stability of behavior: I. On predicting most of the people much of the time. *Journal of Personality and Social Psychology*, 1979, *37*, 1097–1126.

Epstein, S.   The self-concept: A review and the proposal of an integrated theory of personality. In E. Staub (Ed.), *Personality: Basic issues and current research*. Englewood Cliffs, N. J.: Prentice–Hall, 1980.

Erdelyi, M. H.   A new look at the new look: Perceptual defense and vigilance. *Psychological Review*, 1974, *81*, 1–25.

Erdelyi, M. H., & Goldberg, B.   Let's not sweep repression under the rug: Toward a cognitive psychology of repression. In J. F. Kihlstrom & F. J. Evans (Eds.), *Functional disorders of memory*. Hillsdale, N. J.: Lawrence Erlbaum Associates, 1979.

Ericsson, K. A., & Simon, H. A.   Verbal reports as data. *Psychological Review*, 1980, *87*, 215–251.

Eriksen, C. W.   Discrimination and learning without awareness: A methodological survey and evaluation. *Psychological Review*, 1960, *67*, 279–300.

Fenigstein, A., Scheier, M. F., & Buss, A. H.   Public and private self-consciousness: Assessment and theory. *Journal of Consulting and Clinical Psychology*, 1975, *43*, 522–527.

Festinger, L., Pepitone, A., & Newcomb, T.   Some consequences of de-individuation in a group. *Journal of Abnormal and Social Psychology*, 1952, *47*, 382–389.

Fishbein, M., & Ajzen, I.   Attitudes toward objects as predictors of single and multiple behavioral criteria. *Psychological Review*, 1974, *81*, 59–74.

Freedman, J. L., Sears, D. O., & Carlsmith, J. M.   *Social psychology* (3rd ed.). Englewood Cliffs, N. J.: Prentice–Hall, 1978.

Freud, S.   *The psychopathology of everyday life*. In A. A. Brill (Ed. & transl.), *The basic writings of Sigmund Freud*, New York: Random House, 1938 (original German publication, 1901).

Freud, S.   *The ego and the id*. In *Standard edition* (Vol. 19). London: Hogarth Press, 1961 (first German edition, 1923).

Funder, D. C.   *On the accuracy of dispositional versus situational attributions: A comment on the paper by Moore, Sherrod, Liu, & Underwood*. (Unpublished ms., Harvey Mudd College, Claremont, California, 1980.)

Gallup, G. G.   Self-recognition in primates: A comparative approach to the bidirectional properties of consciousness. *American Psychologist*, 1977, *32*, 329–338.

Gazzaniga, M. S.   *The bisected brain*. New York: Appleton-Century-Crofts, 1970.

Goldiamond, I.   Perception. In A. J. Bachrach (Ed.), *Experimental foundations of clinical psychology*. New York: Basic Books, 1962.

Goldstein, J. H.   *Social psychology*. New York: Academic Press, 1980.

Greenwald, A. G.   The totalitarian ego: Fabrication and revision of personal history. *American Psychologist*, 1980, *35*, 603–618.

Greenwald, A. G.   Ego task analysis: An integration of research on ego-involvement and self-awareness. In A. Hastorf & A. M. Isen (Eds.), *Cognitive social psychology*. New York: Elsevier North Holland, 1981(a).

Greenwald, A. G.   Self and memory. In G. H. Bower (Ed.), *Psychology of learning and motivation* (Vol. 15). New York: Academic Press, 1981(b).

Greenwald, A. G., & Ronis, D. L.   Twenty years of cognitive dissonance: Case study of the evolution of a theory. *Psychological Review*, 1978, *85*, 53–57.

Gur, R. C., & Sackeim, H. A.   Self-deception: A concept in search of a pheonomenon. *Journal of Personality and Social Psychology*, 1979, *37*, 147–169.

Hall, C. S., & Lindzey, G.   *Theories of personality* (3rd ed.). New York: Wiley, 1978.

Hilgard, E. R.   Human motives and the concept of the self. *American Psychologist*, 1949, *4*, 374–382.

Hilgard, E. R.   *Divided consciousness: Multiple controls in human thought and action*. New York: Wiley, 1977.

Hoffer, E.   *The true believer*. New York: Harper, 1951.

Hofstadter, D. R.   *Godel, Escher, Bach: An eternal golden braid*. New York: Basic Books, 1979.

Hume, D.   *A treatise of human nature* (L. A. Selby-Bigge, Ed.). London: Oxford University Press, 1888 (original edition, 1739).

James, W.   *Principles of psychology* (Vol. 1). New York: Holt, 1890.

Johnson, R. D., & Downing, L. L.   Deindividuation and valence of cues: Effects on prosocial and antisocial behavior. *Journal of Personality and Social Psychology*, 1979, *37*, 1532–1538.

Jones, E. E., & Nisbett, R. E.   The actor and the observer: Divergent perceptions of the causes of behavior. In E. E. Jones, D. Kanouse, H. H. Kelley, R. E. Nisbett, S. Valins, & B. Weiner (Eds.), *Attribution: Perceiving the causes of behavior*. Morristown, N. J.: General Learning, 1971.

Jones, E. E., & Sigall, H.   The bogus pipeline: A new paradigm for measuring affect and attitude. *Psychological Bulletin*, 1971, *76*, 349–364.

Jung, C. G.   The concept of the collective unconscious. In *Collected works* (Vol. 9, Part I). Princeton, N. J.: Princeton University Press, 1959 (originally published in English, 1936).

Kenrick, D. T., & Stringfield, D. O.   Personality traits and the eye of the beholder: Crossing some traditional philosophical boundaries in the search for consistency in all of the people. *Psychological Review*, 1980, *87*, 88–104.

Koffka, K.   *Principles of gestalt psychology*. New York: Harcourt, Brace, 1935.

Krauss, R. M., Apple, W., Morency, N., Wenzel, C., & Winton, W. M.   Verbal, vocal and visible factors in judgments of another's affect. *Journal of Personality and Social Psychology*, in press.

Krech, D., Crutchfield, R. S., & Ballachey, E. L.   *Individual in society: A textbook of social psychology*. New York: McGraw–Hill, 1962.

LaPiere, R. T.   Attitudes versus actions. *Social Forces*, 1934, *13*, 230–237.

Lewin, K.   *A dynamic theory of personality: Selected papers*. New York: McGraw–Hill 1935.

Loevinger, J.   *Ego development*. San Franciso: Jossey-Bass, 1976.

Loftus, E. F., & Loftus, G. R.   On the permanence of stored information in the human brain. *American Psychologist*, 1980, *35*, 409–420.

Markus, H.   Self-schemata and processing information about the self. *Journal of Personality and Social Psychology*, 1977, *35*, 63–78.

Maslach, C.   Social and personal bases of individuation. *Journal of Personality and Social Psychology*, 1974, *29*, 411–425.

Mehrabian, A., & Wiener, M.   Decoding of inconsistent communications. *Journal of Personality and Social Psychology*, 1967, *6*, 109–114.

Miller, G. A., Galanter, E., & Pribram, K. H.   *Plans and the structure of behavior*. New York: Holt, Rinehart, & Winston, 1960.

Mischel, W.   *Personality and assessment*. New York: Wiley, 1968.

Moore, B. S., Sherrod, D. R., Liu, T. J., & Underwood, B.   The dispositional shift in attribution over time. *Journal of Experimental Social Psychology*, 1979, *15*, 553–569.

Nisbett, R. E., & Wilson, T. D.   Telling more than we can know: Verbal reports on mental processes. *Psychological Review*, 1977, *84*, 231–259.

Ostrom, T. M.   The relationship between the affective, behavioral, and cognitive components of attitude. *Journal of Experimental Social Psychology*, 1969, *5*, 12–30.

Regan, D. T., & Fazio, R.   On the consistency between attitudes and behavior: Look to the method of attitude formation. *Journal of Experimental Social Psychology*, 1977, *13*, 28–45.

Rogers, T. B.   A model of the self as an aspect of the human information processing system. In N. Cantor & J. F. Kihlstrom (Eds.), *Cognition, social interaction and personality*. Hillsdale, N. J.: Lawrence Erlbaum, Associates, 1980.

Rosenberg, M. J.   The conditions and consequences of evaluation apprehension. In R. Rosenthal & R. L. Rosnow (Eds.), *Artifact in behavioral research*. New York: Academic Press, 1969.

Ross, M., McFarland, C., & Fletcher, G. J. O.   The effect of attitude on the recall of personal histories. *Journal of Personality and Social Psychology*, 1981, *40*, 627–634.

Sarbin, T. R., & Allen, V. L.   Role theory. In G. Lindzey & E. Aronson (Eds.),   *Handbook of social psychology* (2nd ed., vol. 1). Reading, Mass.: Addison-Wesley, 1968.

Schachtel, E. G.   *Metamorphosis*. New York: Basic Books, 1959.

Schachter, S., & Singer, J.   Cognitive, social and physiological determinants of emotional state. *Psychological Review*, 1962, *69*, 379–399.

Scheier, M. F., & Carver, C. S.   Private and public self-attention, resistance to change, and dissonance reduction. *Journal of Personality and Social Psychology*, 1980, *39*, 390–405.

Schneider, David J.   *Social Psychology*. Reading, Mass.: Addison-Wesley, 1976.

Sherif, M., & Cantril, H.   *The psychology of ego-involvements*. New York: Wiley, 1947.

Simon, H. A.   The behavioral and social sciences. *Science*, 1980, *209*, 72–78.

Singer, J. E., Brush, C. A., & Lublin, S. C.   Some aspects of deindividuation: Identification and conformity. *Journal of Experimental Social Psychology*, 1965, *1*, 356–378.

Watkins, M. J., & Tulving, E.   Episodic memory: When recognition fails. *Journal of Experimental Psychology: General*, 1975, *104*, 5–29.

Weber, S. J., & Cook, T. D.   Subject effects in laboratory research: An examination of subject roles, demand characteristics, and valid inference. *Psychological Bulletin*, 1972, *77*, 273–295.

Wicker, A. W.   Attitude versus actions: The relationship between verbal and overt behavioral responses. *Journal of Social Issues*, 1969, *25*, 41–78.

Wilson, E. O.   *On human nature*. Cambridge, Mass.: Harvard University Press, 1978.

Winton, W. M., Putnam, L. E., & Krauss, R. M.   *Phasic autonomic correlates of facial and self-reported affective responses*. Unpublished manuscript.

Worchel, S., & Cooper, J.   *Understanding social psychology* (2nd ed.). Homewood, Ill.: Dorsey, 1979.

Wrightsman, L. S.   *Social psychology* (2nd ed.). Monterey, Calif.: Brooks/Cole, 1977.

Zajonc, R. B.   Attitudinal effects of mere exposure. *Journal of Personality and Social Psychology*, 1968, *9*, (Monograph), 1–27.

Zajonc, R. B.   Feeling and thinking: Preferences need no inferences. *American Psychologist*, 1980, *35*, 151-175.

Ziller, R. C.   Individuation and socialization: A theory of assimilation in large organizations. *Human Relations*, 1964, *17*, 341–360.

Zillmann, D.   *Hostility and aggression*. Hillsdale, N. J.: Lawrence Erlbaum Associates, 1979.

Zimbardo, P. G.   The human choice: Individuation, reason, and order versus deindividuation, impulse and chaos. In W. J. Arnold & D. Levine (Eds.), *Nebraska symposium on motivation* (Vol.17.). Lincoln: University of Nebraska Press, 1969.

III

THE SELF IN SOCIAL INTERACTION

How does self-conception influence behavior in the social setting, and how does the social setting influence self-conception? These are the questions considered by the chapters in this section.

In "Self-Monitoring: The Self in Action," Mark Snyder and Bruce Campbell distinguish between two implicit theories individuals might endorse with respect to their self-conceptions. One might be considered a pragmatic theory by which persons perceive themselves as flexible and adaptive individuals who tailor their social behavior to be situationally appropriate. Such individuals are identified by their higher scores on the Self-Monitoring Scale. The other theory stresses a principled conception of the self in which identity is construed in terms of congruence between action and underlying attitudes and dispositions. Individuals who are low scorers on the Self-Monitoring Scale can be characterized in this way. Taking these two types as a starting point, Snyder and Campbell formulate a set of hypotheses about the influence of the two different self-conceptions on cognitive, behavioral, and interpersonal activities. The authors then review the results of a wide range of investigations testing these notions. The review cogently demonstrates that people demonstrate a meaningful cogruence between their global conception of self (pragmatic or principled) and the events of their lives.

In recent years psychology has seen the development of theory and research on self-awareness by Wicklund, Duval, and their associates. The focus of this work has primarily been on how inward-directed attention affects subsequent behavior. In his chapter, Robert Wicklund takes a somewhat different approach and considers "How Society Uses Self-Awareness." He discusses by referring to theory and research how self-focus can be a civilizing state and of benefit to society, as well as ways in which it can be disruptive to social functioning.

It is well-appreciated that people employ strategies to establish and maintain certain impressions of themselves in the eyes of others, but that there has been little attempt to provide a taxonomy of such situations. In "Toward a General Theory of Strategic Self-Presentation," Edward Jones and Thane Pittman redress this gap and describe five distinct strategies of self-presentation—ingratiation, intimidation, self-promotion, exemplification, and supplication. Employing an attributional framework, the authors discuss the aims of each strategy and the manner in which they are carried out. In a concluding section, Jones and Pittman consider how stable aspects of the self may influence strategic self-presentations and in turn be influenced by them.

7

Self-Monitoring: The Self in Action

Mark Snyder
Bruce H. Campbell
University of Minnesota

The quest for knowledge of ourselves, the desire for a meaningful identity, the search for answers to the questions "Who am I?" and "How can I be me?" are experiences familiar to all who share our cultural heritage. Parents and teachers draw upon the wisdom of poets and philosophers as they exhort us to "Know thyself" and "Unto thine own self be true." Authors of self-help books offer techniques for discovering ourselves, for liking ourselves, for respecting ourselves, and for asserting ourselves. And, rare indeed is the individual in this culture who even questions the existence of a self that is uniquely his or her own, that distinquishes him or her from all others, that gives meaning to his or her experiences, and that gives continuity to his or her life.

The concept of self is one of the oldest and most enduring in psychological and philosophical considerations of human nature. For centuries, students of the self have been concerned with the processes by which individuals gain knowledge about themselves; in particular, they have sought to understand how individuals identify and define those attributes of their behavior and their experience that they regard as "me." Within this tradition, social psychologists concerned with the self have focused primarily on the social origins and the interpersonal antecedents of self-conceptions; in particular, they have examined the extent to which self-conceptions are products of social interaction and of interpersonal relationships. Indeed, both classical (Cooley, 1902; James, 1890; Mead, 1934) and contemporary (Bem, 1972; Gergen, 1977) treatments of self and identity have emphasized the social, interpersonal, and societal determinants of self-conceptions.

In the context of the considerable attention that social psychologists have directed at understanding the social *origins* and interpersonal *antecedents* of self-conceptions, it is noteworthy that comparatively little attention has been directed to considerations of the *consequences* of self-conceptions. Of what consequence are self-conceptions for what individuals subsequently think, feel, and do? How do beliefs about the self influence those processes of thought by which individuals organize and interpret self-relevant material? How are beliefs about the self translated into patterns of social behavior that are meaningful reflections of these self-conceptions? How do beliefs about the self channel and constrain the unfolding dynamics of social interaction and interpersonal relationships? More generally, how are the conceptions of self possessed by individuals reflected in the lives that they live? Clearly, theoretical and empirical answers to these fundamental questions are central to any inquiry into the nature and processes of the self. Accordingly, it is the cognitive, behavioral, and interpersonal *consequences* of self-conceptions that are the central concerns of this chapter.

Our strategy in conducting this inquiry into the nature and processes of the self is a straightforward one. First, we will specify a global domain of self-conceptions within which it is possible to identify categories of individuals who differ meaningfully in their beliefs about their characteristic selves within that domain. Then, we will articulate a set of theoretical propositions about the influences of these conceptions of self on the cognitive, behavioral, and interpersonal activities of these categories of individuals. Finally, we will examine a set of empirical investigations that are relevant to evaluating these theoretical propositions. In so doing, we hope to document the manner in which conceptions of self can and do meaningfully channel and influence the worlds within which individuals live.

THE PRAGMATIC SELF AND THE PRINCIPLED SELF

Of necessity, our inquiry into the nature and consequences of self-conceptions begins with the choice of a domain of self-conceptions within which to conduct this inquiry. In making this critical choice, we sought a domain of self-conception that was sufficiently broad and global in scope that it would encompass individuals' global beliefs about their own personal characteristics, the situations within which they live their lives, and their actions within these situations. We sought a domain of self-conception of sufficient breadth that it would capture individuals' "theories" of their own human nature.

In terms of what general theories might individuals conceive of their personal characteristics, the situations of their lives, and their actions? One can readily imagine at least two theories that individuals might endorse within this global domain of self-conception. Some individuals may regard themselves as rather flexible and adaptive creatures, who shrewdly and pragmatically tailor their social behavior to fit situational and interpersonal specifications of appropriateness. Such individuals may be said to endorse a rather *pragmatic* conception of self—a theory that construes their identities in terms of the specific social situations and interpersonal settings of their lives. By contrast, other individuals may regard themselves as rather principled beings who value congruence between their actions in social situations and relevant underlying attitudes, feelings, and dispositions. Such individuals may be said to endorse a rather *principled* conception of self–a theory that construes their identities in terms of their personal characteristics and psychological attributes.

How might one identify those individuals who endorse the pragmatic theory of self and those individuals who endorse the principled theory of self? We suggest that such theories of self are intimately associated with the social psychological construct of self-monitoring and may be readily identified with the Self-Monitoring Scale (Snyder, 1974, 1979a, b). The Self Monitoring Scale is a set of 25 true-false self-descriptive statements that describe: (1) concern with social appropriateness of one's self-presentation (e.g., "At parties and social gatherings, I do not attempt to do or say things that others will like"); (2) attention to social comparison information as cues to situationally appropriate expressive self-presentation (e.g., "When I am uncertain how to act in social situations, I look to the behavior of others for cues"); (3) the ability to control and modify one's self-presentation and expressive behavior (e.g., "I can look anyone in the eye and tell a lie [if for a right end]"); (4) the use of this ability in particular situations (e.g., "I may deceive people by being friendly when I really dislike them"); and (5) the extent to which one's expressive behavior and self-presentation are tailored and molded to fit particular social situations (e.g., "In different situations and with different people, I often act like very different persons"). For details of the psychometric construction and validation of the Self-Monitoring Scale, as well as its items and instructions for its administration and scoring, see Snyder (1972, 1974).[1]

Does the Self-Monitoring Scale capture differences in the extent to which individuals endorse either the pragmatic theory of self or the principled theory of self? An examination of the patterns of responses to the items of the Self-Monitoring Scale reveals that high-self-monitoring individuals (that is, individuals with relatively high scores on the Self-Monitoring Scale) claim to prossess decidedly pragmatic conceptions of self, and that low-self-monitoring individu-

---

[1]For information about the internal structure of the Self Monitoring Scale, see Briggs, Cheek, and Buss (1980) and Gabrenya and Arkin (1980). The factor analyses reported by Briggs, Cheek, and Buss (1980) yielded three factors: Acting, Extraversion, and Other-Directedness. The factor analyses reported by Gabrenya and Arkin (1980) yielded four factors: Theatrical Acting Ability, Sociability/Social Anxiety, Other-Directedness, and Speaking Ability. To our knowledge, no systematic attempts have been made to define the domains of predictive utility of each of the factors that have been identified by these factor analyses. Accordingly, it is not possible to determine the extent to which these individual factors can, on their own, account for any of the findings reported in this chapter, all of which are the outcomes of research in which individuals were classified as high-self-monitoring or low-self-monitoring individuals on the basis of their scores on the entire 25-item measure of self-monitoring. Nevertheless, we do recognize that some researchers may wish to examine the extent to which scores on the entire 25-item measure and scores on each of the factors may perform differently as predictors of relevant criterion variables. Presumably, their efforts will contribute to the further theoretical and empirical refinement of the construct and the measure of self-monitoring.

als (that is, those with relatively low scores on the Self-Monitoring Scale) claim to possess markedly principled conceptions of self.

The Pragmatic Selves of High-Self-Monitoring Individuals

Based upon their endorsement of items on the Self-Monitoring Scale, it appears that high-self-monitoring individuals regard themselves as rather flexible and adaptive individuals, who shrewdly and pragmatically tailor their social behavior to fit situational and interpersonal specifications of appropriateness. For example, they claim that:

> "When I am uncertain how to act in a social situation, I look to the behavior of others for cues.":
> "In different situations and with different people, I often act like, I often act like very different persons.";
> "In order to get along and be liked, I tend to be what other people expect me to be rather than anything else."

Moreover, high-self-monitoring individuals report that what they say and do need not, and often does not, necessarily reflect what they think and believe. Furthermore, high-self monitoring individuals regard themselves as sufficiently skilled actors to effectively and convincingly adopt whatever self presentation seems to be appropriate to the requirements of their current situations. It appears, from the self-portrait that they paint with their responses to the items of the Self-Monitoring Scale, that the sense of self for high self-monitoring individuals is a flexible "me for now in this situation." It is as if they endorse the pragmatic conception of self.

The Principled Selves of Low-Self-Monitoring Individuals

Based upon their endorsement of items on the Self-Monitoring Scale, it appears that low-self-monitoring individuals seem to cherish images of themselves as rather principled individuals, who value congruence between "who they think they are" and "what they try to do." They claim that:

> "My behavior is usually an expression of my true inner feelings, attitudes, and beliefs.";
> "I can only argue for ideas that I already believe.";
> "I would not change my opinions (or the way I do things) in order to please someone or win their favor."

Moreover, low-self-monitoring individuals tend not to perceive themselves as possessing the self-presentational skills that would permit them to adopt any orientation other than "being themselves." It appears, from the self-images that they reveal with their responses to the items of the Self-Monitoring Scale, that the sense of self for low-self-monitoring individuals is an enduring "me for all times and places." It is as if they endorse the principled conception of self.

The Selves in Action

Of what consequence are the pragmatic selves of high-self-monitoring individuals and the principled selves of low-self-monitoring individuals? Are these conceptions of self reflected in the personal and interpersonal lives that these individuals actually live? Or, are the pragmatic and principled conceptions of self simply theories that individuals believe, or claim to believe, but do not translate into action? To answer these questions, let us examine the ways in which the pragmatic and principled conceptions of self may be manifested in the cognitive, behavioral, and interpersonal activities of individuals high and low in self-monitoring.

THE PRAGMATIC SELF AND THE PRINCIPLED SELF IN ACTION: THE COGNITIVE DOMAIN

If, as we have suggested, high self-monitoring individuals and low self-monitoring individuals do hold the fundementally different conceptions of self that we have characterized as the pragmatic self and the principled self, then it ought to be possible to predict and to document the impact of these theories of self on individuals' processing of information about themselves and others. What then are the cognitive consequences of these theories of self?

Location of Identity

High-self-monitoring individuals regard themselves as pragmatic creatures of their situations. One cognitive consequence of operating with this pragmatic theory of self might be that these individuals may come to define their personal identities to a large degree in terms of features of their external environments. Low-self-monitoring individuals claim that their actions are principled expressions of their own feelings, beliefs, and dispositions. One cognitive consequence of operating with this principled theory of self might be that these individuals may come to define their personal identities primarily in terms of enduring attributes that reside within themselves. An empirical investigation by Sampson (1978) provides support for these predictions.

Sampson presented participants with a set of "identity characteristics." Half of these were *externally located* features of a person's environment and surroundings (e.g., "memberships that I have in various groups"). The other half of these characteristics were internally located features typically thought to exist within the person (e.g., "emotions and feelings"). When participants judged the importance of each of these characteristics for their personal identities, or their "sense of who I am," a clearly defined pattern emerged. High-self-monitoring individuals considered externally located identity characteristics to be particularly important to their personal identities. By contrast, low-self-monitoring individuals judged internally located identity characteristics to be particularly important to their personal identities.

Attributional Processes

If the pragmatic theory of self leads high-self-monitoring individuals to regard externally located characteristics as particularly important to their identities, should it not also lead these individuals to offer relatively situational attributional explanations for their actions? And, if the principled theory of self leads low-self-monitoring individuals to regard internally located characteristics as particularly important to their identities, should it not also lead these individuals to offer relatively dispositional attributional explanations for their actions? Indeed, the converging results of diverse measures of attributional processes suggest ''yes'' answers to these questions (Brockner & Eckenrode, 1978; Gutkin & Suls, 1979; Snyder, 1976; Snyder & Tanke, 1976).

In one investigation of self-monitoring and attributional processes, participants judged what behavior they would display in each of a variety of situations differing in situational and contextual factors relevant to the display of generosity, honesty, and hostility (Snyder, 1976). These judgments are readily interpretable in attributional terms. Those individuals who believe that their behavior is a reflection of underlying dispositions should report little cross-situational variability in their behavior. Those who consider their behavior to be a reflection of situational factors should report considerable cross-situational variability in their behavior. Accordingly, high self-reported variability in this attributional task is an operational definition of situational self-attribution; low self-reported variability is an operational definition of dispositional self-attribution. And, in accord with their pragmatic conceptions of self, high-self-monitoring individuals offered relatively situational attributions for their own behavior. By contrast, low-self-monitoring individuals, in accord with their principled conceptions of self, offered relatively dispositioned attributions for their own behavior.

Organizational Processes

If the pragmatic and the principled theories of self are reflected in the processes of location of identity and attribution of cause, perhaps those theories also are reflected in the processes by which individuals organize and store information about themselves and other people. To live one's life according to the pragmatic theory of self would require high-self-monitoring individuals to pay studious attention to the behavior of other persons in order to appropriately manage and regulate their own self-presentation. Accordingly, we might expect that, in the long run, this attention to other people ought to provide high-self-monitoring individuals with extensive stores of knowledge about various types of other people and their typical behavior in a wide variety of social situations, knowledge that may be abstracted and organized into a set of constructs of ideal types of persons who typify particular trait domains (e.g., the prototypic extravert, the prototypic good samaritan, etc.; for elaboration of this argument, see Snyder & Cantor, 1980). To live one's life according to the principled theory of self, on the other hand, would require low-self-monitoring individuals to pay studious attention to their own internal states, dispositions, and personal characteristics in order to guide their social behavior. Accordingly, we might expect that continuing efforts to act in terms of their own true attributes may provide low-self-monitoring individuals with extensive and well-organized knowledge of their characteristic dispositions in diverse trait domains, knowledge that may be organized into a set of schematic constructs of one's characteristic and personal standing within particular trait domains (for elaboration of this argument, see Snyder & Cantor, 1980).

If this line of reasoning is correct, it ought to be possible to demonstrate empirically that low-self-monitoring individuals have richer and more accessible images of their characteristic selves in diverse trait domains than do their high-self-monitoring counterparts. Furthermore, it ought to be possible to demonstrate that high-self-monitoring individuals have richer and more accessible images of the types of individuals who are prototypic examples of a wide variety of trait domains than do low-self-monitoring individuals. Indeed, Snyder and Cantor (1980) have found that high-self-monitoring individuals are particularly skilled at constructing informative images of other people who are prototypic examples of a wide variety of trait domains (e.g., independence, sociability, conscientiousness, creativity); at the same time, low-self monitoring individuals are particularly adept at constructing meaningful images of themselves and their characteristic actions in the same set of trait domains.

These outcomes are readily interpretable as manifestations of the pragmatic and principled theories of self in action. To be particularly knowledgeable about the types of other individuals who are prototypes or best examples of particular trait domains is precisely the predicted cognitive consequence of the pragmatic theory of self (endorsed by high-self-monitoring individuals) in the domain of social knowledge. To be particularly knowledgeable about one's own characteristic self in particular trait domains is precisely the predicted cognitive consequence of the principled theory of self (endorsed by low-self-monitoring individuals) in the domain of self-knowledge. These outcomes, as well as the empirical investigation of location of identity and attribution of cause, suggest the breadth and scope of the manifestations of the pragmatic and principled theories of self in the cognitive worlds of high-self-monitoring and low-self-monitoring individuals.

THE PRAGMATIC SELF
AND THE PRINCIPLED SELF IN ACTION:
THE BEHAVIORAL DOMAIN

As we have seen, the pragmatic and the principled theories of self appear to be reflected systematically in how individuals think about themselves and about other people. Are these theories of self also reflected in the actual social behavior of individuals high and low in self-monitoring? To the extent that high-self-monitoring individuals can and do behave in ways that reflect the pragmatic theory of self, their actions ought to manifest marked situation-to-situation shifts. They literally ought to act like different persons in different situations and with different people. To the extent that low-self-monitoring individuals can and do behave in ways that reflect the principled theory of self, their actions ought to be accurate and meaningful expressions of their own enduring attitudes, traits, and dispositions. They literally ought to manifest the behavioral consistency that they claim to value so dearly. Indeed, empirical investigations of the behavioral consequences of self-monitoring suggest that high-self-monitoring individuals do act as if they were attempting to live their lives according to the pragmatic theory of self, and that low-self-monitoring individuals do act as if they were attempting to live their lives according to the principled theory of self.

The Pragmatic Self and Situational Specificity

Are high-self-monitoring individuals actually the pragmatic creatures that they believe themselves to be? Do they successfully translate their pragmatic theories of self into patterns of social behavior that embody the situation-to-situation specificity of self-presentation that would reflect their pragmatic conceptions of self? In one investigation of self-monitoring and the situational specificity of self-presentation, group discussion conditions sensitized individuals to different reference groups that could provide cues to social appropriateness of self presentation (Snyder & Monson, 1975). In the *public* condition, the experimenter led the group members to a room furnished with two videotype cameras, a microphone, a videotape monitor, a table, and chairs. Participants in the public condition then signed release forms to allow their discussions to be videotaped for possible presentation to their own undergraduate psychology class. The videotape cameras, the feedback on the monitor, and the explicit consent form all highlighted the public nature of the group members' behavior and helped make salient membership in the larger reference group of undergraduate students with its norms favoring autonomy in response to social pressure. In the *private* condition, the discussions took place in a room furnished only with a table and chairs. In these discussion conditions, the most salient social comparison cues to normative appropriateness of self-presentation most likely were provided by the group. Accordingly, in the private condition, group consensus probably would seem to be the most socially appropriate self-presentation.

High-self-monitoring individuals were keenly attentive and sensitive to the differences between the situations in which the discussions occurred. They were conforming in the private discussion condition, where conformity was the most appropriate interpersonal orientation and nonconforming in the public discussion condition, where reference group norms favored autonomy in the face of social pressure. Low-self-monitoring individuals were virtually unaffected by these differences in social settings. Presumably, their self-presentations were more accurate reflections of their personal attitudes, dispositions, and self-conceptions within the domain of conformity.

In these social contexts, high-self-monitoring individuals appear to have translated their pragmatic conceptions of self into patterns of behavioral self-presentation that were molded and tailored pragmatically to their social surroundings (also see Rarick, Soldow, & Geizer, 1976). Moreover, there are good reasons to believe that high-self-monitoring individuals manifest this same pronounced situation-to-situation variability in their social behavior in such diverse behavioral domains as altruism, honesty, and self-restraint (Snyder & Monson, 1975), as well as within the domain of nonverbal behaviors expressive of, for example, sociability, anxiety, and sex-role identity (Lippa, 1976, 1978a, b; Lippa & Mash, 1979). When it comes to their behavior in social situations, high-self-monitoring individuals very well may be the pragmatic creatures that they conceive themselves to be.

The Principled Self and Behavioral Consistency

Are low-self-monitoring individuals actually the principled beings that they believe themselves to be? Do they successfully translate their principled theories of self into patterns of social behavior that manifest the behavioral consistency that would reflect their principled conceptions of self? In fact, it appears that low-self-monitoring individuals typically do enforce and display substantial consistency between their private attitudes and intentions and their public behaviors and actions (Becherer & Richard, 1978; Lutsky, Woodworth, & Clayton, 1980; Snyder & Kendzierski, 1982; Snyder & Swann, 1976; Snyder & Tanke, 1976; Zanna, Olson, & Fazio, 1980; Zuckerman & Reis, 1978).

In one investigation of self-monitoring and consistency between attitudes and behavior, Snyder and Swann (1976) examined the relationship between measured attitudes toward affirmative action and verdicts rendered 2 weeks later in a mock court case involving alleged sex discrimination. Overall, the relationship between general attitudes toward affirmative action and verdicts in this specific sex discrimination case was, at best, modest. However, when the relationshop between attitudes and behavior was considered separately for low-self-monitoring and for high-self-monitoring individuals, this pattern emerged: Covariation between measured attitudes and actual behavior was substantially larger for low-self-monitoring individuals than for high-self-monitoring individuals.

Moreover, not only is it possible to predict accurately the future behavior of low-self-monitoring individuals from measures of their present attitudes, but also it is possible to forecast the attitudes that they will express in the future from knowledge of their current actions (Snyder & Tanke, 1976). And, beyond the domain of social attitudes, low-self-monitoring individuals also display marked correspondence between inner states and self-presentation (Ickes, Layden, &

Barnes, 1978), as well as between various personality attributes and corresponding expressive behaviors (Lippa, 1978a,b; Lippa, Valdez, & Jolly, 1979). Evidently, when it comes to correspondence between the private realities of
attitudes, feelings, and dispositions and the public realities of words and deeds,
low-self-monitoring individuals do seem to be the consistent, principled beings
that they conceive themselves to be.

THE PRAGMATIC SELF AND
THE PRINCIPLED SELF IN ACTION:
THE INTERPERSONAL DOMAIN

Not only are the pragmatic self and the principled self reflected in the domain of
thought and in the domain of action, but also these conceptions of self are reflected within the domains of social interaction and interpersonal relationships.
Empirical research has identified links between self-monitoring and the activities
associated with the initiation and the development of social relationships. And,
these links are precisely the ones that the operation of the pragmatic self and the
principled self would be expected to generate within the interpersonal domain.

The Initiation of Social Relationships

Even before individuals actually become involved in social relationships, they
often engage in the cognitive activities of thinking about and anticipating the
events of their forthcoming interactions. With few exceptions, most students of
social cognition have endorsed the view that cognitive activities serve to stabil-
ize, make predictable, and make manageable the individual's view of the social
world (Brunswik, 1956; Heider, 1958; Kelley, 1972). From this perspective,
there is clear functional value to individuals in construing others with whom they
anticipate social interaction largely in terms of traits and dispositions. To do so
implies that their social behavior will be consistent across diverse situations and
stable over time. These characteristics would facilitate prediction and potential
influence of the behavior of these others in the course of forthcoming interactions. To do so also would allow those who are so motivated to use their beliefs
about other people as cues to managing and regulating their own self-
presentational behaviors in these forthcoming social relationships. "Those who
are so motivated" most likely are those individuals who operate with a pragmatic
comception of self. For those high-self monitoring individuals, perceiving the
behavior of other people with whom they anticipate social interaction as
dispositionally organized would facilitate the use of their perceptions of other
people as cues to pragmatically monitoring and tailoring their own expressive
self-presentation in their anticipated social interactions. By contrast, these same
cognitive activities would be of considerably less utility to those individuals

(i.e., low-self-monitoring individuals) who operate with a principled conception of self.

The empirical work of Berscheid, Graziano, Monson, and Dermer (1976) provides support for this theoretical analysis that joins the pragmatic and principled conceptions of self associated with self-monitoring propensities to the cognitive activities associated with the initiation of social relationships. Given the opportunity to observe another person whom they expected to date socially, men and women high in self monitoring were more likely than their low-self-monitoring peers to notice and accurately remember information about that person, to infer her or his traits and dispositions, and to think favorably of and express liking for their prospective dates. Evidently, for high-self-monitoring individuals, the prospect of social interaction may initiate perceptual and cognitive activities that predictably channel the search for potentially relevant information, the interpretation of that information, and the form and substance of the images constructed of those with whom they anticipate further social relationships.

That high-self-monitoring individuals actively invest cognitive time and effort in attempting to "read" and understand others in the service of planning and guiding their own behavior in social relationships is manifested further in their keen attention to the subtle interplay between an actor's behavior and its context, and their use of this information in inferring that actor's intentions (Geizer, Rarick, & Soldow, 1977; Jones & Baumeister, 1976; Krauss, Geller, & Olson, 1976) and in predicting that actor's behavior (Kulik & Taylor, 1981). Moreover, at times, high-self-monitoring individuals actually will go so far as to "purchase"—at some cost to themselves—information that may aid them in guiding and managing their own self-presentation in forthcoming social interaction with another person (Elliott, 1979).

It appears, then, that the cognitive activities by which high-self-monitoring individuals seek and acquire knowledge in the initiatory phases of their social relationships are well-suited to adopting the strategic orientation to interpersonal relationships that would reflect their pragmatic conceptions of self. As a consequence of these activities, high-self-monitoring individuals may provide themselves with precisely the stable and predictable images of other people that would be most useful to them in their strategic attempts to regulate the course of their interpersonal relationships.

The Development of Social Relationships

Having initiated social relationships, individuals then may find the events of their social relationships to be a rich source of opportunities to act upon their conceptions of self. In fact, the reflections of the pragmatic and principled selves are readily observable in the unfolding dynamics of social interactions involving individuals high and low in self-monitoring (Barnes & Ickes, 1979; Dabbs, Evans, Hopper, & Purvis, 1979; Ickes & Barnes, 1977, 1978). In one investigation of the role of self-monitoring in the development of social interaction and acquaintance processes, Ickes and Barnes (1977) arranged for pairs of strangers to spend time together in a room. They then surreptitiously audio and video recorded the verbal and nonverbal behaviors of both individuals over a 5-minute observation period. They then scrutinized these tapes for evidence of the impact of self-monitoring on the interactional dynamics of these spontaneous encounters between strangers.

The channeling influences of self-monitoring on the unfolding patterns of social interaction were considerable. Early in the course of social interaction, individuals high in self monitoring actively took an initiatory and regulatory role in the conversations: The higher-self-monitoring members of the dyads were inclined to talk first and to initiate subsequent conversational sequences. They also felt, and were seen by their partners to have, a greater need to talk. Their partners also viewed them as having been the more directive member of the dyad. It was as if high-self-monitoring individuals were particularly concerned with managing their social behavior in order to create, facilitate, and maintain a smooth and pleasing flow of conversation throughout the course of the social interaction. In the service of these goals, high-self-monitoring individuals took an active and continuing role in initiating and maintaining the conversations. And, by adopting a regulatory role, high self-monitoring individuals very well may have enhanced their ability to influence the subsequent course of the interaction in ways that would promote the display of whatever ''selves'' they chose to project in the interaction.

The consequences of the differing orientations that high self-monitoring and low-self-monitoring individuals adopt in their social interactions and interpersonal relationships may be profound ones. Their differing behavioral orientations, coupled with the initiatory cognitive activities in which they engage, may ensure that both high-self-monitoring individuals and low-self-monitoring individuals succeed in constructing for themselves social worlds in which their interpersonal relationships not only are well-suited to expressing and living out their pragmatic or principled conceptions of self but also are well-suited to bolstering, preserving, maintaining, and perpetuating these conceptions of self.

THE PRAGMATIC SELF AND
THE PRINCIPLED SELF IN ACTION:
THE STRUCTURE OF THE SOCIAL WORLD

High-self-monitoring individuals regard themselves as rather flexible and adaptive creatures who shrewdly and pragmatically tailor their social behavior to fit situational and interpersonal specifications of appropriateness. Low-self-monitoring individuals seem to cherish images of themselves as rather principled and consistent beings who value congruence between ''who they think they are'' and ''what they actually do.'' To what extent might the social worlds within which individuals high and low in self-monitoring live actually reflect their characteristically pragmatic or principled conceptions of self?

To the extent that an individual resides in a social world that reflects his or her characteristic conceptions of self, it ought to be possible to provide relatively precise specifications about the population of an individual's social world, the activities, competences, and dispositions of the members of that individual's social world, the nature of the social relationships that exist between the individual and the other members of his or her social world, the settings within which the individual and those other members interact and conduct their social relationships, and so on. What then are the characteristics of the social worlds that would be well-suited to expressing and maintaining the characteristic conceptions of self of high-self-monitoring and low-self-monitoring individuals? By what processes might high-self-monitoring and low-self-monitoring individuals create for themselves social worlds that would be reflections of their characteristic conceptions of self?

One might predict that the social worlds of high-self-monitoring individuals should be structured in ways that allow them to be the different persons in different situations demanded by their pragmatic conceptions of self, to adopt a wide variety of identities specific to particular social settings and interpersonal relationships; that is, high-self-monitoring individuals ought to live in highly partitioned, differentiated, or compartmentalized social worlds, in which they engage in specific activities with specific members of their social worlds. Members of a high-self-monitoring individual's social world may be chosen because they each bring out one of a wide variety of "selves" in that high-self-monitoring individual. Similarly, the social settings of a high-self-monitoring individual's social world may be chosen because they have clearly defined characters; that is, because they provide clear specifications of the type of person that one ought to be in those situations.

By contrast, one might predict that the social worlds of low-self-monitoring individuals should be structured in ways that allow them to "be themselves," to guarantee the high level of congruence between private dispositions and public actions demanded by their principled conceptions of self. Members of a low-self-monitoring individual's social world may be chosen because they have personalities and characters similar to, and supportive of, that of this low-self-monitoring individual. The social settings of a low-self-monitoring individual's social world may be chosen because they call for personalities or characters of the type possessed by that low-self-monitoring individual. Thus, low-self-monitoring individuals may live in social worlds that are, in comparison with those of high-self-monitoring individuals, relatively homogeneous and undifferentiated, in terms both of the population and of the settings of these social worlds.

To what extent do these characterizations accurately capture the social worlds of high-self-monitoring and low-self monitoring individuals? Two empirical investigations provide support for these characterizations.

The Population of the Social World

Do high-self-monitoring individuals, more so than low-self monitoring individuals, live in highly partitioned and differentiated worlds in which they engage in specific activities with specific members of their social worlds? To answer this question, we recruited college undergraduates, known:to be relatively high or low in self-monitoring, to participate in a study of ''social networks.'' When participants arrived for their individual appointments, the experimenter asked each participant to generate a list of the ''population'' of his or her ''social world.'' The first seven people (excluding family members, if any) who appeared on each participant's list subsequently served as the targets of his or her ratings. The participant next selected the one specific social activity (e.g., ''going to a fancy French restaurant,'' ''playing tennis,'' ''going to the ballet'') that was most representative of his or her actual social life within each of eight global categories of activities that the experimenter described (e.g., ''going out to dinner,'' ''competitive recreational activity,'' ''attending live entertainment'').

When this was done, the experimenter explained that each cell of the 56 cells in a 7 X 8 matrix (now labeled with the seven people and with the eight activities nominated by the participant) represented engaging in a particular social activity with a particular person. For each activity, the participant then estimated how likely it would be that he or she would choose each of the people listed in the matrix as a partner for that activity. Subsequently, each participant estimated how much he or she would enjoy engaging in each of these activities with each of these people, assuming that such an interaction were to take place.

Was there evidence in these ratings of greater differentiation or segmentation in the social worlds of high-self-monitoring individuals than in those of their low-self-monitoring counterparts? Was the patterning of choices and preferences of high-self-monitoring individuals highly affected by properties of specific person-situation pairings? And, was the patterning of social choices of low-self-monitoring individuals comparatively uniform or homogeneous (both within and between persons) across activities?

To answer these questions, a statistic reflecting the amount of variation present in each participant's ratings that could not be independently accounted for by differences due to targets or by differences due to activities was calculated. Specifically, the data in each individual matrix were analyzed in a 7(persons) X 8(activities) analysis of variance with one observation per cell. The residual sum of squares calculated for each matrix in this fashion represents, for each participant, the amount of variation in the ratings that was *not* predictable from differences among persons or from differences among activities independently; that is, it represents the person X activity interaction. As predicted, high-self-monitoring individuals showed significantly more nonadditive variation (i.e., differentiation, partitioning, segmentation) in both their likelihood ratings and their enjoyment ratings than did low-self-monitoring individuals.

Evidently, the social worlds of high-self-monitoring individuals are characterized by greater partitioning, differentiation, and segmentation than those of low-self-monitoring individuals. No doubt, segmentation makes it easier for high-self-monitoring individuals to adopt different identities with different members of their social worlds, to display the many selves that they pragmatically conceive themselves to be. Low-self-monitoring individuals appear to live in relatively more homogenous social worlds, in which they typically engage in the majority of their social activities with primarily the same set of other individuals who are most preferred as interaction partners across a wide range of situational contexts. As a consequence, they may live in social worlds well-suited to being the single coherent selves that they conceive themselves to be.

The Settings of the Social World

Not only is it possible to specify the populations of the social worlds of individuals high and low in self-monitoring, but also it is possible to specify the interpersonal settings within which individuals high and low in self-monitoring choose to conduct their social relationships. In the course of their lives, individuals typically have considerable freedom to choose where to be, when, and with whom. Accordingly, the interpersonal situations in which individuals find themselves may be partially of their own choosing. It has been suggested that these choices of interpersonal settings may reflect relevant features of one's conceptions of self (Snyder, 1981). How then might the pragmatic and principled conceptions of self be reflected in the choices of interpersonal situations within which to conduct social relationships made by high-self-monitoring and low-self monitoring individuals?

Behavioral enactment of the pragmatic conception of self ought to be facilitated in interpersonal settings that provide clearly defined situational guidelines for high-self-monitoring individuals to use in molding and tailoring their social behavior to their situations. Therefore, we might expect that high-self monitoring individuals would choose, whenever possible, to spend time in social situations with which there are associated clearly defined images of the type of individual who would be ideally suited for that situation. These clearly defined images of the prototypic individual called for by the situation may then provide the operating guidelines for enacting a pattern of self-presentation that allows high-self-monitoring individuals to "become" the persons called for by their situations. By contrast, behavioral enactment of the principled conception of self would be facilitated in interpersonal settings that permit low-self-monitoring individuals to "be themselves." Therefore, we might expect that low-self-monitoring individuals would choose, whenever possible, to spend time in social situations and interpersonal settings that provide information indicating that it will be appropriate to engage in behaviors that express and reflect whatever traits and dispositions low-self-monitoring individuals regard as relevant to those situations.

Are the interpersonal settings of the high-self-monitoring individual's social world chosen because they provide clear specifications of the type of character one ought to be in those situations? Are those of the low-self-monitoring individual chosen because they call for personalities of the type possessed by that low-self-monitoring individual? To answer these questions, Snyder and Gangestad (1982) allowed individuals to choose to enter or not to enter a social situation that called for the expression of social extraversion. For some individuals, the extraverted character called for by the situation was defined in clear, precise, and unambiguous fashion. For other individuals, the extraverted character called for by the situation was defined in only the vaguest of terms. High-self-monitoring individuals were highly responsive to this difference between the two situations: they were particularly eager to enter the situation of clearly defined extraverted character but relatively unwilling to enter the situation of vaguely defined extraverted character. Low-self-monitoring individuals were virtually unaffected by the clarity of the character of the situation: They were equally willing to enter the situations of clearly defined and of vaguely defined character. However, the willingness of low-self-monitoring individuals to enter either situation was a direct reflection of their own personalities: extraverted low-self-monitoring individuals were particularly eager to enter either extraverted situation; introverted low-self-monitoring individuals were distinctly unwilling to enter either situation.

Of what consequence are the differing choices of situations of high-self-monitoring individuals and low-self-monitoring individuals? To the extent that high-self-monitoring individuals gravitate toward situations of clearly defined character, they may provide themselves interpersonal settings ideally suited to acting out their pragmatic conceptions of self. And, to the extent that low-self-monitoring individuals gravitate toward situations that call for personalities or characters of the type possessed by them, they may provide themselves interpersonal settings ideally suited to acting upon their principled conceptions of self.

Strategies and Tactics for Structuring the Social World

Empirical investigations of the populations and the interpersonal settings of the social worlds of individuals high and low in self-monitoring suggest that their social worlds are reflections of their characteristically pragmatic or principled conceptions of self. By what strategies and tactics might individuals high and low in self-monitoring actively create for themselves these very different kinds of social worlds? Tentative answers to this question emerge form an integration of the pragmatic and principled theories of self with Goffman's (1959) analysis of self-presentational activities. In particular, Goffman's concepts of audience segregation, selective interaction, and front are particularly relevant to this integrative effort.

Audience Segregation.   Audience segregation refers to efforts on the part of actors to see that those individuals before whom they have presented one self-image will not witness them fostering an incompatible self-image before other individuals. The situation-to-situation tailoring of self-images characteristic of high-self-monitoring individuals may require them, more often than low-self-monitoring individuals, to practice the strategy of audience segregation. Thus, high-self-monitoring individuals who present a very different image of themselves at work than they do in their bowling leagues actively might seek to avoid social situations where they would be forced to interact simultaneously with members of both groups. For example, they might decline invitations to social events to be attended by members of both groups. Low-self-monitoring individuals, by contrast, might tend to initiate and encourage social contact between well-liked individuals from different spheres of their social worlds.

Selective Interaction.   Selective interaction refers to choosing *only* specific kinds of other individuals as interaction partners for particular types of social occasions. In keeping with their pragmatic conceptions of self, high-self monitoring individuals may employ this strategy to facilitate their efforts to present the most appropriate self-image for each particular type of social situation. Thus, high-self-monitoring individuals might be expected to select as interaction partners those individuals whose knowledge, experience, skills or resources would facilitate their own efforts to appear to be precisely the type of person called for by particular situations. By contrast, and in keeping with their principled conceptions of self, low-self-monitoring individuals may employ the strategy of selective interaction to keep company, across a wide range of situations and contexts, with those individuals whose own personality traits, attitudes, tastes, preferences, and overt behavior characteristically support and facilitate the projection of the particular images of self that they strive to foster in all situations. Thus, for example, we might expect that low-self monitoring individuals who characteristically regard themselves as "strong, take charge" types will habitually choose as interaction partners (for even markedly different social situations) other people who characteristically acquiesce to, and even actively elicit, dominant behaviors from them.

Front.   Front consists of aspects both of the setting (i.e., scenery and stage props) in which an interaction takes place as well as aspects of the actor's personal appearance (e.g., clothing, personal effects, hairstyle, cosmetics, etc.). Because the pragmatic conception of self engenders situation-to situation tailoring of self-images, we might expect that high self-monitoring individuals would select carefully and display precisely those items of front most supportive of the optimal self-image for each specific occasion. By contrast, low-self-monitoring individuals ought to show considerably less variability in the items of front displayed from situation to situation.

In the domain of clothing and personal effects, we would expect high-self-monitoring individuals to be particularly sensitive to and aware of the potential "messages" carried by these aspects of personal front; moreover, they ought strategically to employ this knowledge in choosing particular items of clothing and personal accessories to display in specific contexts. The choices of low-self-monitoring individuals may be considerably more dependent on global and abiding personal preferences. Thus, for example, when deciding whether to wear a three-piece suit or a sports jacket, the high-self-monitoring individual may ask himself "Would the suit or the sports jacket be more appropriate to wear tonight?," whereas the low-self-monitoring individual may ask himself "Which would I rather wear tonight?," or "Which do I like better?," etc.

In the domain of the furnishing and decoration of one's house, apartment, or office, we might expect high-self-monitoring individuals would choose such items, not so much on the basis of their own tastes and preferences but instead on the basis of the potential implications of these choices for the creation of situationally appropriate self-images. Furthermore, the wardrobes, books, records, and magazines owned by high-self-monitoring individuals may generally tend to be more heterogeneous or eclectic than would those of their low-self-monitoring counterparts. After all, efforts to play the part of the "right person" for each of a wide variety of social situations would seem to require a more diversified set of "costumes" and "props" than would seeking to be one's "true self." By contrast, the collections of such items owned by low-self-monitoring individuals may tend to be relatively homogeneous, internally coherent reflections of their own personal tastes and preferences.

Finally, it is perhaps not unreasonable to expect that even an individual's choice of occupation or profession may reflect principled or pragmatic conceptions of self. Low-self-monitoring individuals may choose occupations or professions that require and support the enactment of behaviors that express their true personalities, traits, or dispositions. Thus, low-self monitoring individuals who consider themselves to be warm, compassionate, and relatively nonmaterialistic individuals, for example, might tend to choose careers in relatively low-paying social service or "helping" professions. And, low-self-monitoring individuals who consider themselves to be assertive and aggressive, and who value material possessions, might tend to choose careers in business, law, or real estate. High-self-monitoring individuals may choose occupations or professions that permit or even demand the portrayal of a wide range of roles. Thus, high-self-monitoring individuals may be attracted to careers in fields such as theatre, public relations, law, politics, sales, or diplomacy, precisely because these careers provide them ample opportunity to exercise their self-presentational and expressive skills. And, whatever their career choices, the potential success of high-self-monitoring individuals in their chosen occupations may be substantially less dependent on a good match between the "personality" required by the job and their own personal traits and dispositions than typically may be true for low-self-monitoring individuals.

CONCLUSIONS

We began our inquiry into the nature and consequences of the self—the self in action—by asking a fundamental question that has been conspicuously absent in psychological considerations of the self: Of what *consequence* are self-conceptions for what individuals subsequently think, feel, and do? In attempting to answer this question, we sought a domain of self-conception sufficiently broad and global in scope to capture the essence of individuals' sense of "me" and found it in individuals' theories about their own personal characteristics, the situations within which they live their lives, and their actions within these situations. Individuals who endorse the pragmatic theory of self (identified by their relatively high scores on the Self-Monitoring Scale) regard themselves as rather flexible and adaptive creatures who shrewdly and pragmatically tailor their social behavior to fit situational and interpersonal specifications of appropriateness. Individuals who endorse the principled theory of self (identified by their relatively low scores on the Self-Monitoring Scale) regard themselves as rather principled beings who value congruence between their actions in social situations and relevant underlying attitudes, feelings, and dispositions. We then examined the manner in which these pragmatic and principled conceptions of self manifest themselves in the cognitive, behavioral, and interpersonal activities of individuals high and low in self-monitoring.

Within the cognitive domain, the pragmatic self and the principled self are reflected in the thought processes by which individuals organize and interpret self-relevant material. In accord with their pragmatic conceptions of self, high-self-monitoring individuals are particularly likely to define their identities in terms of externally located features, to offer situational self-attributions, and to be particularly knowledgeable about the types of other individuals who are prototypes or best examples of diverse trait domains. And, in accord with their principled conceptions of self, low-self-monitoring individuals are particularly likely to define their personal identities in terms of internally located features, to offer dispositional self attributions, and to be particularly knowledgeable about their own characteristic selves in diverse trait domains.

Within the behavioral domain, the pragmatic self and the principled self appear to be translated into patterns of social behavior that are meaningful reflections of these global conceptions of self. Not only do high-self-monitoring individuals regard themselves as pragmatic creatures of their situations, but also their social behavior displays the marked situation-to-situation specificity that the behavioral enactment of their pragmatic selves would generate. Similarly, low-self-monitoring individuals manifest the substantial consistency between their behavior and their underlying personal attributes that the behavioral enactment of their principled selves would generate.

Within the interpersonal domain, the pragmatic self and the principled self channel the initiation and development of social interaction and interpersonal relationships. In the initiatory phases, self-monitoring processes are reflected in cognitive processes that predictably channel the search for potentially relevant information about other people, the interpretation of that information, and the form and substance of the images constructed of the people. In the developmental phases, self monitoring processes are reflected in the unfolding dynamics of social relationships.

Moreover, the pragmatic self and the principled self are reflected in the very structure of the social worlds within which individuals live. High-self-monitoring individuals live their lives in social worlds well-suited to their pragmatic conceptions of self: highly partitioned, differentiated, and compartmentalized social worlds in which they engage in specific activities with specific other people. Moreover, the interpersonal settings of their social worlds appear to be chosen because they have clearly-defined characters; that is, because they provide clear specifications of the type of person one ought to be in those situations. Low-self-monitoring individuals live their lives in social worlds well-suited to their principled conceptions of self: social worlds that are relatively homogeneous and undifferentiated both in terms of their populations and their settings, social worlds that are structured in ways that allow them to maintain the high level of congruence between private dispositions and public actions that permits them to "be themselves."

Evidently, the lives of high-self-monitoring individuals appear to be meaningful reflections of the pragmatic sense of self that they express in their responses to the items of the Self-Monitoring Scale. Similarly, the lives of low-self-monitoring individuals appear to be meaningful reflections of the principled sense of self that they express in their responses to the items of the Self-Monitoring Scale. That is, for all individuals, whatever their self-monitoring propensities. there appears to be clearly defined and readily detectable congruence between their conceptions of self and lives that they live.

Nevertheless, to witness this definite congruence it was necessary for us to consider conceptions of self at the *global* level of individuals' general theories of the pragmatic self and the principled self. Had we considered conceptions of self at the more *molecular* level of specific traits and attitudes that individuals conceive themselves to possess, we would have reached a somewhat different conclusion about the links between self-conceptions and activities within the cognitive, behavioral, and interpersonal domains. At the level of specific traits and attitudes it is only low-self-monitoring individuals who, in accord with their principled theories of self, appear to manifest consistency between specific self-conceptions and social behavior. By contrast, at the level of specific traits and attitudes, the behavior of high-self-monitoring individuals appears to be less a reflection of these personal attributes than it is a reflection of the features of their immediate situations. It is only by realizing that this pattern of situation-to-situation specificity at the molecular level very well may reflect faithfully the influence of global conceptions of oneself as a pragmatic creature of one's situations that it becomes clear that high-self-monitoring individuals are manifesting definite congruence between their global pragmatic conceptions of self and their situationally specific patterns of social behavior.

From this perspective, it becomes understandable why empirical searches for consistency between measured traits and behavior (Mischel, 1968) and for consistency between measured attitudes and behavior (Wicker, 1969) have produced little evidence of pervasive consistencies. For, to the extent that one employs measures of specific traits and specific attitudes in this endeavor, one is employing a strategy that is well-suited for detecting the directive influence of self-conceptions on social behavior in low-self-monitoring individuals (who, in keeping with their principled global conceptions of self, *do* display congruence at the molecular level of specific self-conceived traits and attitudes), but poorly-suited for detecting the directive influence of self-conceptions on social behavior in high-self-monitoring individuals (who, in keeping with their pragmatic global conceptions of self, only display congruence at the level of global conceptions of self).

In contrast, by examining global conceptions of the pragmatic self and the principled self, we were employing a strategy well-suited to understanding not only low-self-monitoring individuals but also high-self-monitoring individuals. By adopting this strategy, we were able to see that both high-self monitoring individuals and low-self-monitoring individuals may demonstrate meaningful congruence between global conceptions of self and the events of their lives. As different and distinctive as their cognitive, behavioral, and interpersonal orientations may be, both high-self-monitoring individuals and low-self-monitoring individuals may succeed in living their lives in ways that are true to their own conceptions of self.

More generally, as a strategy for understanding the nature of the self, considerations of the consequences of conceptions of self sensitize us to the processes by which beliefs about the self are translated into and become embodied in the cognitive, behavioral, and interpersonal activities of individuals. Indeed, in this realization may lie the key to understanding the true importance of the conceptions of self possessed by individuals. Conceptions of self may be important precisely because of their pervasive manifestations in the lives that individuals live. Such may be the nature of the self in action.

ACKNOWLEDGMENTS

This research and the preparation of this manuscript have been supported in part by National Science Foundation Grant BNS 77–11346, "From Belief to Reality: Cognitive Behaviorial, and Interpersonal Consequences of Social Perception" to Mark Snyder. Portions of this manuscript were prepared while Mark Snyder was a Fellow of the Center for Advanced Study in the Behavioral Sciences.

REFERENCES

Barnes, R. D., & Ickes, W. J. *Styles of self-monitoring: Assimilative versus accommodative.* Unpublished manuscript, University of Wisconsin, Madison, 1979.

Becherer, R. C., & Richard, L. M. Self-monitoring as a moderating variable in consumer behavior. *Journal of Consumer Research,* 1978, *5,* 159–162.

Bem, D. J. Self-perception theory. In L. Berkowitz (Ed.), *Advances in experimental social psychology* (Vol. 6). New York: Academic Press, 1972.

Berscheid, E., Graziano, E., Monson, T., & Dermer, M.   Outcome dependency: Attention, attribution, and attraction. *Journal of Personality and Social Psychology,* 1976, *34* , 978–989.

Briggs, S. R., Cheek, J. M., & Buss, A. H.   An analysis of the Self-Monitoring Scale, *Journal of Personality and Social Psychology,* 1980, *38,* 679–686.

Brockner, J., & Eckenrode, J. Self-monitoring and the actor-observer bias. *Representative Research in Social Psychology,* 1978, *9,* 81–88.

Brunswik, E. *Perception and the representative design of experiments.* Berkeley: University of California Press, 1956.

Cooley, C. H. *Human nature and the social order.* New York: Scribner, 1902.

Dabbs, J. M., Evans, M. S., Hopper, C. H., & Purvis, J. A.   Self-monitors in conversation: What do they monitor? *Journal of Personality and Social Psychology,* 1980, *39,* 278–284.

Elliott, G. C. Some effects of deception and level of self monitoring on planning and reacting to a self-presentation. *Journal of Personality and Social Psychology,* 1979, *37* , 1282–1292.

Gabrenya, W. K., Jr., & Arkin, R. M.   Factor structure and factor correlates of the Self-Monitoring Scale. *Personality and Social Psychology Bulletin,*1980, *6,* 13–22.

Geizer, R. .S., Rarick, D. L., & Soldow, G. F.   Deception and judgment accuracy: A study in person perception. *Personality and Social Psychology Bulletin,* 1977, *3,* 446–449.

Gergen, K. J.   The social construction of self-knowledge. In T. Mischel (Ed.), *The self: Psychological and philosophical issues.* Totowa, N. J.: Rowman & Littlefield, 1977.

Goffman, E. *The presentation of self in everyday life.* Garden City, N. Y.: Doubleday-Anchor, 1959.

Gutkin, D. C., & Suls, J.   The relation between the ethics of personal conscience—Social responsibility and principled moral reasoning. *Journal of Youth and Adolescence,* 1979, *8,* 433–441.

Heider, F. *The psychology of interpersonal relations.* New York: Wiley, 1958.

Ickes, W. J., & Barnes R. D.   The role of sex and self-monitoring in unstructured dyadic interactions. *Journal of Personality and Social Psychology,* 1977, *35,* 315–330.

Ickes, W. J., & Barnes, R. D.   Boys and girls together—and alienated: On enacting stereotyped sex roles in mixed-sex dyads. *Journal of Personality and Social Psychology,* 1978, *36,* 669–683.

Ickes, W. J., Layden, M. A., & Barnes, R. D.   Objective self awareness and individuation: An empirical link. *Journal of Personality,* 1978, *46,* 146–161.

James, W. *The principles of psychology* (Vols. I & II). New York: Henry Holt, 1890.

Jones, E. E., & Baumeister, R.   The self-monitor looks at the ingratiator. *Journal of Personality,* 1976, *44,* 6 54–674.

Kelley, H. H.   Attribution of social interaction. In E. E. Jones, D. Kanouse, H. H. Kelley, R. E. Nisbett, S. Valins, & B. Weiner (Eds.), *Attribution: Preceiving the causes of behavior.* New York: General Learning Press, 1972.

Krauss, R. M., Geller, V., & Olson, C. *Modalities and cues in perceiving deception.* Paper presented at American Psychological Association, Washington, D. C., 1976.

Kulik, J., & Taylor, S. E.   Self-monitoring and the use of consensus information. *Journal of Personality,* 1981, *49,* 75–48.

Lippa, R. Expressive control, and the leakage of dispositional introversion-extraversion during role-played teaching. *Journal of Personality,* 1976, *44,* 541–559.

Lippa, R. Expressive control, expressive consistency, and the correspondence between expressive behavior and personality. *Journal of Personality,* 1978, *46,* 438–461. (a)

Lippa, R. *Self-presentation and the expressive display of personality.* Paper presented at American Psychological Association, Toronto, 1978. (b)

Lippa, R., & Mash, M. *The effects of self-monitoring and self reported consistency on the consistency of personality statements made by strangers and intimates.* Unpublished manuscript, California State University, Fullerton, 1979.

Lippa, R., Valdez, E., & Jolly, A. *Self-monitoring and the consistency of masculinity-femininity cues.* Paper presented at American Psychological Association, New York, 1979.

Lutsky, N., Woodworth, W., & Clayton, S. *Actions-attitudes/actions: A multivariate, longitudinal study of attitude-behavior consistency.* Paper presented at Midwestern Psychological Association, St. Louis, 1980.

Mead, G. H. *Mind, self, and society.* Chicago: University of Chicago Press, 1934.

Mischel, W. *Personality and assessment.* New York: Wiley, 1968.

Rarick, D. L., Soldow, G. F., & Geizer, R. S. Self-monitoring as a mediator of conformity. *Central States Speech Journal,* 1976, *27,* 267–271.

Sampson, E. E. Personality and the location of identity. *Journal of Personality,* 1978, *46,* 552–568.

Snyder, M. Individual differences and the self-control of expressive behavior (Doctoral dissertation, Stanford University, 1972). *Dissertation Abstracts International,* 1972, *33,* 4533A–4534A.

Snyder, M. The self-monitoring of expressive behavior. *Journal of Personality and Social Psychology,* 1974, *30,* 526–537.

Snyder, M. Attribution and behavior: Social perception and social causation. In J. H. Harvey, W. J. Ickes, & R. F. Kidd (Eds.), *New directions in attribution research* (Vol. 1). Hillsdale, N. J.: Lawrence Erlbaum Associates, 1976.

Snyder, M. Cognitive, behavioral, and interpersonal consequences of self-monitoring. In P. Pliner, K. R. Blankstein, & I. M. Spigel (Eds.), *Advances in the study of communication and affect (Vol. 5): Perception emotion of self and others.* New York: Plenum Press, 1979. (a)

Snyder, M. Self-monitoring processes. In L. Berkowitz (Ed.), *Advances in experimental social psychology* (Vol. 12). New York: Academic Press, 1979. (b)

Snyder, M. On the influence of individuals on situations. In N. Cantor & J. G. Kihlstrom (Eds.), *Personality cognition, and social interaction.* Hillsdale, N. J.: Lawrence Erlbaum Associates, 1981.

Snyder, M., & Cantor, N. Thinking about ourselves and others: Self-monitoring and social knowledge. *Journal of Personality and Social Psychology,* 1980, *39,* 222–234.

Snyder, M., & Gangestad, S. Choosing social situations: Two investigations of self-monitoring processes. *Journal of Personality and Social Psychology,* 1982, in press.

Snyder, M., & Kendzierski, D. Acting on one's attitudes: Procedures for linking attitudes and behavior. *Journal of Experimental Social Psychology,* 1982, in press.

Snyder, M., & Monson, T. C. Persons, situations, and the control of social behavior. *Journal of Personality and Social Psychology,* 1975, *32,* 637–644.

Snyder, M., & Swann, W. B., Jr. When actions reflect attitudes: The politics of impression management. *Journal of Personality and Social Psychology,* 1976, *34,* 1034–1042.

Snyder, M., & Tanke, E. D. Behavior and attitude: Some people are more consistent than others. *Journal of Personality,* 1976, *44,* 510–517.

Wicker, A. W. Attitudes versus actions: The relationship of verbal and overt behavioral responses to attitude objects. *Journal of Social Issues,* 1969, *25,* 41–78.

Zanna, M. P., Olson, J. M., & Fazio, R. H. Attitude-behavior consistency: An individual difference perspective. *Journal of Personality and Social Psychology,* 1980, *38,* 432–440.

Zuckerman, M., & Reis, H. T. A comparison of three models for predicting altruistic behavior. *Journal of Personality and Social Psychology,* 1978, *36,* 498–510.

8 How Society Uses Self-Awareness

Robert A. Wicklund
University of Texas at Austin

Characteristic questions about self-awareness, at least in recent history, have been directed toward the psychology of the self-aware *individual*. Theoretical thought and accompanying research have been concerned with individual morality, achievement, self-criticism, emotion, and a variety of other processes that have only nebulous connections to group or societal functioning. The pervading question has been, "How are individual thought, idiosyncratic values, and personal goals brought to affect behavior when the person's attention takes a reflexive form?". But one may ask an equally important question, one that shifts the focus to society: What is the function for others of the individual's self-awareness? Independent of the long-range benefits for the individual (or short-range, which we discuss momentarily), how are the partner, the small group, and the broader society benefitted by the self-aware condition of any particular member?

This question had a fairly simplistic answer in the terms of the symbolic interactionists (Cooley, 1902; Mead, 1934), who defined self-awareness solely in terms of reflecting on oneself through the perspective of others. Thus, one has the immediate group in mind while being self-aware. A common and simplistic interpretation of this theme holds that the self-aware person is more attuned to, and thereby conforming to, the immediate social perspective. This interpretation is, of course, incorrect. As early as Cooley (1902), the symbolic interactionist school recognized that the immediate social group doesn't define the dominant value, or rule for action, of the self-aware person. To be sure, the hero, the creative person, and the deviate can all bring representations of the perspectives of *other* groups with them to the present situation; thus, they might even act contrary to the immediate group's interests.

How Is the Person Controlled Through Self-Awareness?

The important question to begin with, stemming out of the symbolic interactionist perspective, is this: How is the organism constructed such that the community stands to gain control by making that one person self-aware? The human is often conceived of as an organism whose behaviors are dictated by certain internalized values, or personal rules. These may also be called self-components, after James (1890). These behavioral standards, however they come to be incorporated (Aronfreed, 1964; Hoffman, 1975; Mead, 1934), are presumed to have a relatively constant impact upon behaviors.

Value-Consistent Behavior. But it turns out that the preceding statement is simply not true, even though taken for granted by much of psychology for decades. In answering a questionnaire, a person might manifest high sex guilt, high punitiveness, or high creativity; yet, such traits are not invariably or automatically reflected in behavior (Wicklund, 1979b). Rather, it has recently been found that the person must be made to think about these value dimensions, in a self-conscious way, before the trait becomes manifest in behavior. Without such a self-conscious orientation, the high-sex-guilt person shows no special reluctance to express pleasure at pornography, relative to a person with low sex guilt (Gibbons, 1978). Similarly, the difference between self-rated high-punitive and low-punitive perople doesn't show up in actual punishing behavior unless self-awareness is introduced (Carver, 1975). And the same for the trait of creativity: Even with a well-established creativity measure, the differences in creative behaviors of low-and high-creative people (as assessed by questionnaires) are minimal, given insufficient self-reflection (Hormuth, 1979). Another useful way of saying this is that the person who is not very self-focused engages in sex-related, punitiveness-related, and creativity-related behaviors in a way *un*mediated by the value that provides a point of orientation for those behaviors. The self-component (i.e., the personal value) is bypassed unless one is self-aware with respect to that self-component.

This is an important finding because much of what has been written about the self is misleading. The self is not a bundle of habits that is manifested in overt behavior by principles of learning. Rather, the self is a bundle of behavioral guides, strainers, or defining characteristics that must be reflected upon in order that they are manifested in behavior. Without that self-reflection, the behavior is dictated by a multiplicity of other causes, unmediated by those elements that constitute the self.

Self-Reports. A very similar process seems to occur when people are asked to discribe themselves, which often times is tantamount to asking them to retrospect about their own behavior. For example, a person might be asked "How sociable are you?" or "How much do you like to play Monopoly?". Quite astonishingly, people who are not very self-aware are not terribly adept at making their answers correspond with their actions. Thus a non-self-aware person seems as likely to say "sociable" as "not very sociable," even though this same person shows a very high degree of overt sociability. And the non-self-aware person is just as likely to say "I like that game" as "I don't like it," even though the person plays with that game more than any other games.

What does this mean? The most immediate kind of interpretation says that the self is bypassed when the person is not self-conscious. This means that self-knowledge is bypassed. A certain measure of self-consciousness is prerequisite to reporting on oneself with any degree of accuracy. The organism to be discussed here has the quality of possessing self-components that lie dormant until activated by self-reflected attention. Actions in a variety of realms, and reports about previous actions or qualities, will be made quite independent of those self-components unless self-awareness is brought to bear on the actions or self descriptions. This means, very simply, that a person's behaviors can be brought under the influence of the self-components—(i.e., the values, internalized norms, chronic personality differences)- provided the individual can be made to be self-aware. Without that self-awareness, behavior will be determined by other influences, such as habits or basic drives, and not by those self-components.

So this is where we begin. To be sure, we may speak of the human as being controllable by self-awareness, and perhaps ideally, we may speak of the human as being in a position, via the self awareness mechanism, of being made increasingly civilized. It turns out that there is much more to the picture, but we begin with this simple tentative thesis, that society can bring the person under control by forcing the person to attend to the self.

SOCIETAL STANDARDS:
SELF-AWARENESS AS A CIVILIZING AGENT

Since the theorizing of Shibutani (1961), it has been recognized that the self-reflective condition is one of falling under the control of social norms. By Shibutani's reasoning self-awareness is a very social process: The onset of self-awareness is a social occasion, and the nature of the behavioral rules enacted during self-awareness are highly social in nature.

Consider firstly the onset of self-awareness. By Shibutani's reasoning, developed directly out of Mead (1934), socially disruptive happenings force the person into a self-reflective condition. Anything that breaks the individual's harmony with the group (i.e., breaks the individual's deindividuated state) will cause the person to become self-reflective. Operationalized, this would mean that any characteristically embarrassing event would set off self-reflection—accidentally cursing in front of the priest, lowering one's necktie into the soup, introducing someone by the wrong name, or perhaps just being "different"—are all sufficient to engender self-awareness. What happens then is our second step: The self-aware person will come to think of others' points of view. Now the statement "come to think of others' points of view" is a very tricky one. This doesn't necessarily mean that the self-aware person is thereby paranoid, imputing motives into those in the immediate milieu. Nor does it mean that the person is even motivated to try to figure the others out. For that matter, it doesn't even have to mean that the person is thinking about the thoughts, opinions, or judgments of anyone present. The crucial thing, by Shibutani's symbolic interactionist perspective, is that the self-aware person comes to be increasingly aware of *some other* point of view. As it turns out, this other point of view can often be an abstraction from individual viewpoints—an abstraction that takes the form of an internalized value; that is, the person doesn't have to be thinking of individual minds, present or not present, but may be described as thinking of some set of values that has been dominant in his past.

And then what? Shibutani refers to the next step as self-control. As the self may be described as the embodiment of these collected values, or points of view abstracted from others, we can say that the self-aware person's behavior becomes controlled by the self (i.e., by the generalized opinion of some group).

If Shibutani is right, this already tells us something rather important about self-awareness. Perhaps it is a tool for bringing the individual into line. If everyone in a society has been socialized to dwell on such virtues as punctuality, fidelity, or honesty, all we need to do is create socially disruptive conditions for some individual member, who will then—in the resulting self-aware state—start to react in more punctual, faithful, or honest ways.

A number of questions remain about this analysis, primarily because Shibutani didn't provide us with a handle for his scheme, in the sense of an empirical system or research tradition. So it becomes necessary to become more detailed at this point. For the remainder of this chapter we move on from Shibutani's starting point and consider self-awareness processes in light of a theory specifically written around the concept of self-focused attention (Duval & Wicklund, 1972; Frey, Wicklund, & Scheier, 1978; Wicklund, 1975, 1978, 1979a, 1980; Wicklund & Frey, 1980).

The theory of self-awareness views the onsets of self focused attention somewhat more broadly than Shibutani. In particular, there is no special reason why socially disruptive conditions should be the exclusive onset of self-focused attention. Such conditions no doubt function rather well, but, more generally, any symbol of the self should suffice to bring attention increasingly onto the self. People who see their images in reflecting pools, who hear their voices played back, or who see their images on a screen, or who view photographs of themselves should become increasingly self-aware. Thus, such simple self-focusing devices should be added to the Shibutani method, which implicitly includes all types of social disruptions, including minority status. To be sure, there is already direct evidence that some of these manipulations can effect an increment in self-directed attention. Carver and Scheier (1978) have shown that the person's mirror image, as well as a small attentive audience, can heighten subjects' preoccupation with the first person, thus presumably with oneself. Davis and Brock (1975), somewhat earlier, showed that a camera's presence can increase preoccupation with the self, and that a mirror image had the same effect.

Self-awareness theory views the self-focused condition as a state of motivation. The individual is said to engage in self evaluation to the extent that attention is directed toward a within-self discrepancy, for instance, a discrepancy between a moral principle and morally relevant actions. To be sure, there is evidence that focused attention upon a discrepancy is uncomfortable and carries affective consequences, no matter whether assessed through physiological measures (Sackeim, 1974), subjective affect ratings (Archer, Hormuth, & Berg, 1979; Brockner, in press) or attempts to flee the self-aware condition (Duval, Wicklund, & Fine, in Duval & Wicklund, 1972; Gibbons & Wicklund, 1976; Greenberg & Musham, 1981). Under the category of "fleeing self-awareness" is an intriguing set of studies by Wolff (1932), who conducted the first-known experimental investigations of self-awareness phenomena. His studies dealt with the curious human propensity not to recognize one's own voice, profile, and hands. These sorts of refusals to acknowledge reflections of the self have again been documented by Sackeim and Gur (1978), who have written in detail on self-deception and self-confrontation.

As a motivated state, self-awareness is presumed to move the individual to close the gap between behavior and ideals. The result should be attempted achievements, morally consistent behaviors, and generally, greater internal consistency where the self is involved.

If we may elaborate upon Shibutani's thinking in terms of the previously mentioned arsenal of self-awareness onsetters, the social milieu suddenly gains power in its ostensible control over the person via shared societal values. It should now be possible to steer the person's behavior into socially desired directions by mirrors, T V cameras, and audiences, as well as by social disruptions. Beaman, Klentz, Diener, and Svanum (1979) set out to show how making groups of trick-or-treaters self-aware can bring their behavior into line with the commonly accepted norm of not cheating (or honesty). On the evening of Halloween a number of homes had been set up such that the lady of the house was actually an experimenter. She asked the children to step into the foyer, told them that they could each take one piece of candy from a bowl on a table, then excused herself and went into the interior of the house. This left the behavior of the children to be dictated by whim, habit, or perhaps even by a component of the self, such as an internalized value. As it turned out, a rather large percentage of the children cheated, particularly those at least 9-years old. For instance, in the first experiment (of two), 46% of the children 9–12-years old took more than one candy, and a seemingly psychopathic 73% of the trick-or treaters over 12 years violated the one-candy rule. Such effects would lead one to think that their behavior was being dictated by forces other than the moral constraint of not cheating. Such forces could presumably have been as simple as the habitual tendency to commit petty theft, or perhaps deep-seated aggressive urges.

For some of the groups of trick-or-treaters a mirror had been placed behind the table, allowing the children a plain view of themselves as they reached into the bowl. From self-awareness theory, the mirror should create a general orientation toward the self, with a resultant focus on whatever aspect of self is most salient in the situation. The salient aspect in Beaman et al.'s situation was the question of how many candies to take. Or in the language of morals, the issue was the question of whether or not to be dishonest. It turned out that the mirror seemed to have the effect of bringing subjects' attention to bear on the moral issue: The cheating rate of 9–12-year olds dropped dramatically to less than 10%, and the adolescents (over 12) who were made self-aware showed no cheating whatever.

A very similar effect was found by Diener and Wallbom (1976) among college students. When given full opportunity to cheat on a test, the students cheated (worked beyond the time limit) at the rate of about 70%; if they were confronted with their mirror images while working, this rate dropped to a mere 7%.

From these results it is tempting to conclude something complex about the workings of societal values. The values that we like to think are such an integral part of our mental life do not function 100% of the time. There is a certain faltering in their effectiveness in guiding behavior, and the periods of faltering can be traced to those times during which the person is relatively un-self-aware. Even though the subjects of Beaman et al., and of Diener and Wallbom, obviously possessed the necessary moral rules to refrain from cheating when self-aware, these rules were almost completely bypassed in the control conditions of these experiments. Shibutani may have been right: The residue from others' perspectives seems to come into play, in the form of self-control, when self-awareness is generated.

It also turns out that Shibutani was correct regarding social disruptions as one specific cause of self-reflection. Wegner and Schaefer (1978) showed that more helping could be obtained from people who thought they were in the minority, suggesting that finding oneself to be on the perimeter of the group serves to engender self-awareness, with consequent acting upon a norm of social responsibility or helpfulness. Earlier, Duval (1976) showed that people are much more susceptible to influence, regarding estimating the number of dots projected onto a screen, when they first find that they have minority status with respect to their opinions. This experiment is particularly congruent with Shibutani's observations, as finding oneself to be at odds with the surrounding group is obviously a source of social disruption. And on the dependent variable side, Shibutani's prediction of increased control over the individual is clearly realized in the conformity effect.

In the realm of the more individualized (less social) bases of self-awareness, it has been possible to use subjects' mirror images to make them work harder (McDonald, in press; Wicklund & Duval, 1971), and to increase conformity by playing back subjects' voices (Wicklund & Duval, 1971).

IDIOSYNCRATIC VALUES

What happens when a value isn't necessarily shared throughout a society? Does

Shibutani's reasoning still hold? Perhaps this is a stupid question, in that the symbolic interactionist answer would obviously be that the self-aware person would take the perspective of those who happen to embody the values by which he abides. Said otherwise, we incorporate values from certain segments of society, and these are likely to be the values upon which we act, even when people representing other values (or nebulous values) are present.

The question of societal controls, however, our major concern here, becomes slightly more complicated. If a group wants to bring someone's behavior into line via self-awareness-inducing tactics, it must realize that the resulting behavior won't necessarily please the group. The research to date would suggest that as long as the person's preexisting value is strong, dominant, or highly salient, self-awareness will bring that value to influence behavior, even if the immediate milieu doesn't condone that kind of behavior (Carver, 1977). Therefore, control of the individual's behavior, given the possibility that values can vary between extremes or opposites, means knowing first the direction in which the person's value is likely to lead. We might take an experiment by Gibbons (1978) as an example.

Subjects were first measured on something called a "sex guilt" inventory (Mosher, 1968). The values implicit in the scale items had a good deal to do with whether one would approve of pornographic or other sexual literature. A reading of the scale would lead us to think that someone scoring high in sex guilt would not enjoy pornographic literature, whereas someone low in sex guilt might be rather interested in the same literature.

Having measured the subjects' sex guilt, Gibbons then let them read a passage from a pornographic novel and asked them to rate how much they enjoyed it. In the control condition (no self-awareness induction) there was practically no relationship at all between sex-guilt score and enjoyment of the sexual passage. But, if subjects were confronted with their mirror images while reading, their rated enjoyment of the pornography then came to fit their sex-guilt scores. In other words, self-reflection brought the sex-related value to influence overt behavior.

We should now return to our theme: What does it mean, in this case of diverse values, to use self-awareness to control others? The group is likely to want the individual member to act the same as other group members, thus would be interested in using the individual person's values to bring behavior closer to an ideal promoted by the group. Suppose, for instance, that the group is constituted by a group of college-age men who spend much of their leisure time trading jokes and pictures clipped out of *Playboy*. If a potential new member were to be introduced into the group, it might make very good sense to force that person into self-awareness—especially if the members know that he holds a value of low-sex guilt. Self-awareness should then promote behavior consistent with not feeling guilty about sex, as in Gibbons' experiment. But if the same person harbored Puritanical values, self-awareness may not serve the group's purposes at all, as the self-control set off by self-focused attention would tend to move behavior toward the pole of antisex and antipornography. Thus, using self-awareness to control members' fit to the group mode can be a tricky matter.

But there is a second sense in which we might talk about gaining control. A group has some measure of control over an individual member if it can simply predict the member's behavior—even if the behavior doesn't coincide with the ongoing behaviors of the group. The results of Gibbons' experiment imply that we gain a definite predictive power over others' actions when the actions are performed while the people are self-aware. It has to be added that these striking effects of Gibbons are not isolated events: Gibbons reports two other experiments with comparable results, and Carver (1975), who performed the first research of this type, showed in two separate experiments that values about punitiveness are better reflected in behavior when subjects are self-aware. Finally, Hormuth (1979) followed a comparable procedure in showing that creativity scores and creativity behaviors can be brought into better correspondence with self-awareness.

THE INDIVIDUAL'S SELF-DESCRIPTIONS

Thus far, we have talked about exerting control over individuals only in the sense of making people self-aware while they behave. To be sure, the values that make up the self are better manifested in behavior when the behaving individual is self-focused. But the group also stands to control the individual by having knowledge of the person's characteristics, and it turns out that overt knowledge of one's self is much improved by momentarily slipping into self-awareness.

This is a rather important use of self-awareness principles. For instance, take the case of a new group member who is a relatively unknown entity. It would be normal for the person to be questioned about different aspects of the self, and it is adaptive for the group to obtain accurate answers regarding that person's personality. If they ask "How sociable are you?" "How aggressive are you?" or "Do you like such and such pastimes?", they will be able to handle the new member much more easily.

This may seem like an area in which there is no apparent problem. Why shouldn't a new group member tell the truth? As it turns out, self-reports in these kinds of situations have extremely low correspondence with actual behavior, a point documented in a very thorough review by Wicker (1969). Surprisingly, when we ask someone, "Are you of the Introverted Type?," the answer we get is typically not going to be very useful for predicting that person's behavior. Said in other words, we don't gain much predictive control by asking these kinds of questions.

And why should this be? Among the several possible reasons, one fairly dominant one is that the person actually seems to bypass the nature of the self when answering. The answer often comes in the form of an overrehearsed (Kimble & Perlmuter, 1970; Langer, 1978) or perhaps socially acceptable response, and unfortunately is not based in a thorough digging into the components of the self. A priori, this reasoning may seem a bit unlikely; after all, when we ask someone, "Do you have high introversion?", we might be hard pressed to imagine where the answer would come from except to be predicated on the nature of the self. But as the following illustration makes clear, people seem to be rather adept at basing self-reports on something *other* than the self.

The first of the three studies by Pryor, Gibbons, Wicklund, Fazio, and Hood (1977) asked male subjects to fill out a simple, face valid measure of sociability. After a few days wait they returned, had to wait 3 minutes in a small room with an attractive female, and during that time their overt sociability was assessed. Not only was it possible to count the quantity of verbiage the subject addressed toward her, but the female (an accomplice) also made a subjective rating of his sociability. When these two criteria were combined into one behavioral index of sociability and then correlated with the subject's self-reported sociability (taken from the scale he filled out earlier), the correlation proved to be practically insignificant ($r = .16$). If we are using scales to predict people's behavior, it's not terribly impressive when only 2 ½% of the variance can be accounted for.

In another condition subjects had a mirror before them as they completed the scale, and by the preceding reasoning, the resulting self-awareness should have caused their self-reports about sociability to be based more on the self and less upon extraneous factors. As it happened the correlation rose to an r of .62. Or in other words, a relatively high 38% of the variance was accounted for by using the scale. Thus, it was not the testing format, the nature of the items, or a faulty behavioral criterion of sociability. Rather, subjects in the control condition were not drawing upon the nature of the self in producing answers.

Similar kinds of findings were reported in two subsequent experiments by Pryor et al. (1977), as well as in a study on self-reports of hostility by Scheier, Buss, and Buss (1978), and also in self-reports of creativity (Hormuth, 1979).

The underlying principle thus far is simple. Society has control over the individual member in-so-far as the person's self-awareness can be maximized. The self-focused condition pushes the individual to act in accord with incorporated standards, whether those standards are generally accepted or highly idiosyncratic. Self awareness also has a marked impact on self-reports, such that descriptions of the self are more likely to be based on the nature of the self. So for the group, self-awareness incurred by any one member is highly beneficial. As we have treated the issue thus far, the group incurs all advantages and no disadvantages by rendering individuals self-aware. But the issue becomes complex: The first trouble spot has to do with what aspect of self the self-focused person might be expected to act upon.

WHICH ENDPOINT?

By *endpoints* we mean goals, ends, or purposes toward which the person is behaviorally oriented. Thus far, the self-aware person has been described as possessing just one kind of endpoint—a value, or standard, by which to guide behavior. And thus far, we have also talked about situations in which the endpoint was well-defined and unequivocal. For instance, in Gibbons' sex-guilt experiment there was little question about which end point people were likely to pursue. Given the setting, in which their behavior was confined to rating what they had read, it seemed very clear that their values regarding pornography would dictate the direction they would take.

But there are exceptions. For one, how about the instance of conflicting values? Vallacher and Solodky (1979) were clever enough to arrange a setting in which standards about cheating (Beaman et al., 1979; Diener & Wallbom, 1976) and achievement (McDonald, in press; Wicklund & Duval, 1971) were in conflict. The situation in which their subjects were working allowed and enticed a certain amount of cheating, and two elements were varied: The attractiveness of successful performance was varied, and subjects' self-awareness was also experimentally manipulated. If desire to perform well was relatively low, self-awareness had the same effect as in the experiments reported previously. The amount of cheating declined given self-awareness. But if achievement needs had been brought to the fore experimentally, self-aware subjects began to disregard the norm against cheating *in the interest of* making better progress in their achievements. This is to say that the achievement ethic won out over the noncheating ethic as self-awareness rose.

There is another kind of situation in which standards about correct behavior may be pushed aside. Scheier (1976), as well as Scheier, Carver, and Gibbons (1981) found that strong states of affect are exaggerated in subjective import among self-aware people. And in the process, behaviors that are normally governed by such standards as personal values about aggression, or by humanitarian values, are then determined more by the level of emotion. In short, the emotion seems to come to supplant the value and plays the dominant role as an endpoint in guiding behavior.

Further instances of conflicts among endpoints have been documented by Wicklund (1978, 1979a, b, 1980) and Wicklund and Frey (1980), and a principle has been devised that indicates when one endpoint will come to dominate over another. Those endpoints such as emotions, or strong motivational states, generally take precedence over the more static aspects of self (values, logical thinking), thus the lesson for the group that is trying to control individual behavior through self-awareness is clear. If the group sets out to guide the individual's behavior, it should first insure that the person is not experiencing a strong emotion, and that the person is also not experiencing a strong sense of threat to the ego. Only when the person comes into the self-aware state relatively devoid of passions, ongoing defenses, and emotions will the relatively static values have a clear impact on behavior. This analysis comes directly from some remarks on the relative centrality of parts of the self, by James (1910). It was James' thesis that the more dynamic aspects of self (he names emotional states and "volitional decisions") take precedence in their effects over the more static aspects of self, such as perceptual processes.

A SECOND STAGE: THE INDIVIDUAL MUST PERFORM

The preceding sections have dealt with the advantages for society of the individual's self-awareness. That entire analysis, however, was predicated on the assumption that the particular individual, who may or may not be self-aware, was a potential threat to group functioning. The individual we discussed implicitly had the character of being relatively unknown, not totally trustworthy, not completely predictable. The commitment of this individual to the group—to the people who might be interested in controlling that individual—was viewed as questionable. Thus, self-awareness was discussed as an instrument of refining the individual's orientation toward the group. The self-awareness process was depicted as something that would bring the group better control over the person in the sense of knowing the person's idiosyncrasies, predicting the person, and directly controlling the person's behaviors. But is it wise to hold the individual continually in a state of self-focus? Once one is beyond that first phase (i.e., once the person's allegiances are assured), once the group knows that the person is headed in the "right" direction, we might wonder whether it serves the group's purposes to hold that member continually in self-awareness.

Suppose, for instance, that the individual member is a tightrope walker. Although there have been no systematic investigations of self-awareness among tightrope walkers, common sense would dictate that it would be better to concentrate on where one is walking, rather than engaging in the self-evaluative and self corrective exercises that are brought on by self-focused attention. Or consider the public orator. The group has accepted a new member and now wants the person to hold forth before large crowds. Whereas self-awareness might motivate the speaker to try especially hard, one should have serious doubts about the beneficial impact of self-focus on the quality of public speaking.

The general idea here is that society should not attempt to hold total evaluative control, via self-awareness, over individual members. Once the group can rest assured that the member is committed in a prosocial direction, there are numerous general kinds of circumstances under which an absence of self-focus would be more beneficial for everyone. Thus, we probably should speak of a trade-off, whereby society must grant the individual a certain liberty—a freedom from self-examination—in order to gain the maximal productivity or quality from each person. What are some of the general kinds of performances or acts that gain no benefit from self-focused attention? We might talk with some confidence about two kinds of settings: One consists of any sort of *complex task,* requiring great attention to the elements of the actual work as one proceeds along. A pilot negotiating an emergency landing with the radar not functioning would be executing a complex task, as would a symphony conductor who is in the midst of leading an intricate work for orchestra.

Complex Tasks

The principle involved here is a very simple one. The more demanding the components of the task, the more attention that is required in order to bring it to completion. If one's attention is diverted, no matter whether by other tasks, freezing temperatures, a barking dog, or self-focus, there is simply less time remaining for task performance.[1] One of the first illustrations of the task-interfering impact of self-focused attention came from Liebling and Shaver (1973), who used a complex task involving a test of speed in copying Swedish prose. They manipulated self-focused attention in two ways. In addition to the presence or absence of a mirror, they also varied whether or not subjects felt evaluated—presuming that the subjects who were led to feel self-evaluative would direct more attention inward. The effects were intriguing: A minimal degree of self-awareness served to increase performance, an effect also observed by Wicklund and Duval (1971) under nonevaluative conditions. But when the mirror was placed into conjunction with evaluative instructions, there was a sharp decline in performance. Thus, we are inclined to think that self-awareness has motivating properties, in that subjects did work faster given some degree of self-focus. But an overflow of the self-directed attention, although leaving the person well-motivated, will not allow sufficient attention for the details of an involving task.

A very similar phenomenon was found repeatedly by Brockner (Brockner 1979; Brockner & Hulton, 1978). The task was indeed complex, taken from Schrauger (1972). The subjects' tasks was to examine 32 individual squares, attempting to abstract a certain concept from them. Clearly, such a task required the utmost attention, and one would expect that any kinds of distracting conditions would have impaired that performance. In fact, no matter whether self-awareness was brought about through a mirror and video camera, an audience and a mirror, or defined through an individual difference measure of self-focus (Fenigstein, Scheier, & Buss, 1975), Brockner (1979) and Brockner and Hulton (1978) were able to show decrements in performance.

The opposite end of this task complexity continuum should also be considered. For example, a number of the effects described earlier required virtually no "performance" in the usual sense. Subjects could behave consistent with their standards or values just by checking a point on a scale, or by pressing a button at a specified time (Gibbons, 1978; and Carver, 1975, respectively). The self-awareness threshold would be considerably higher for such tasks, in that the individual who is almost totally self-aware will not be prevented from behaving effectively in a manner consistent with the value or moral. The task at hand requires practically no attention.

The general issue of "How much self-awareness if beneficial?" is something of a balancing act. There is ample evidence that the self-aware person is at the same time a motivated person, thus some degree of self-focus will have positive effects (Liebling & Shaver, 1973—copying of Swedish prose; Wicklund &

---

[1]An explanation for the debilitating effects of test anxiety has been formulated by Wine (1971), and the thesis centers around an attentional explanation akin to that proposed here. Heckhausen (in press) has taken this notion a step further, in discussing the kinds of task-irrelevant cognitions that are especially conducive to task interference.

Duval 1971—copying of German prose). But the more complex the task, the less self-awareness one can introduce without danger of disrupting performance. Thus, the practical question for the group is how to deal with the individual from whom a complex performance is required. That person must be motivated but, at the same time, not diverted.

Automatic Acts

There is an important second kind of setting in which self awareness serves a definite debilitating function on performance. This setting is the one in which the individual is called upon to perform automated acts. Such acts (Kimble & Perlmuter, 1970; Langer, 1978) are to be viewed as highly overlearned, carried out without the necessity of conscious reflection, and normally constructed from a series of molecular, component acts. "How do you do today?" is a perfect illustration. The utterance is composed of molecular components, it is an automatic, non-thought-out response to meeting someone, and its performance requires no reflection on the nature of the task or the self. The response simply rolls off. The veteran automobile driver and smoker has no doubt noticed that it is possible to carry on a seemingly intelligent and creative conversation, all the time shifting gears, operating the clutch and brake pedals and accelerator, while chain smoking. This is because the acts of driving and smoking are overrehearsed, requiring no thought, and no conscious decision points once the acts are initiated. Once it is decided to drive 3 miles down the road to Point X, the precise movements required to make the car function receive practically no attention.

Ironically, it is these overrehearsed, automated behaviors that are most easily upset by self-directed attention. When typists think precisely about what they are doing they begin to make mistakes. When someone reciting a poem is self-aware during recitation, the presentation falters (Wicklund, Morris, & Dorflinger, in Wicklund, 1975). The presence of an audience, which is a well-established source of self-awareness (Carver & Scheier, 1978), can be shown to raise feelings of anxiety among performers (Jackson & Latané, 1979) and to reduce fluency among speakers (Porter, 1939; Storms & McCaul, 1976). And more generally, it is entirely possible to make the case that the kinds of evaluative conditions conducive to self-awareness are a general source of speech disfluency (Bloodstein, 1969).

The analysis of such disfluencies by Kimble and Perlmuter (1970) is quite straightforward. The idea is that attention directed toward the act serves to make one think of the component actions that make up the entire overrehearsed performance. As a result, the components effectively break apart, destroying the unit of the action. The idea proposed here, then, is that self-awareness while performing would lead one to begin thinking about the individual component acts that make up the more general act, and the effect would be an overall debilitation of action.

There is a hint in the experimental literature that performers sense the maladaptiveness of self-awareness while performance is underway. Take, for instance, the case of someone who is just on the verge of responding during a conversation. Such a person may realize, at some level, that self-awareness cannot serve the effectiveness of the performance and should try especially hard to minimize self-focus at the onset. Thus, one should expect people to avoid making eye contact with a conversation partner as utterances are begun, an effect reported by Kendon (1967). In a similar vein, habitual kinds of motor movements may generally be thought to serve the function of reducing self-awareness (Duval & Wicklund, 1972; Wicklund, 1975). To be sure, there is already evidence that engaging in a simple motor activity can reduce attributions to the self, in a context where a mirror has the impact of *increasing* those same attributions. In short, whereas mirrors increase self-focused attention, repetitive motor movements seem to decrease it. Thus, someone who is trying to keep an automated act from falling apart might be expected to engage in motor activities, particularly at the start of an act, in an effort to divert attention outward. Dittmann and Llewellyn (1969) offer some interesting evidence for this point. During pauses and also immediately following disfluencies, speakers are inclined to make hand or head movements almost as if they are trying to insure that self-reflection won't interfere with the automated nature of the act of speech. And finally, there is an idea that stems from speech therapy that has been in existence for a long time: Stutterers often try to get their speech underway by using "starters," a variety of motor movement that seems to affect the flow of speech. Swift and Hedrick (1917) list a number of such starters, compiled from several stutterers. Approximately a third of the stutterers showed definite starters such as throwing the head to one side,[2] long closing of eyes,[3] pounding the fist, and various other body motions. The subjects described these devices as "instant helps," according to Swift and Hedrick, but not as permanent cures.

It is easy to see that the group can defeat its own purposes by forcing individual members into excessive self-awareness. Once the group recognizes that the actions are "appropriate" or "necessary," it would do well to remove the individual from self-awareness-generating situations, because performance stands only to suffer. And perhaps here lies a genuine conflict for society: Some of the acts that are most valued are by nature the highly practiced, overrehearsed performances, and these are exactly the kinds of acts that everyone attends to. Thus, the more refined an individual's automated performance, the more likely it is that that performance will be met with audiences, evaluations, competition, reviews, and all possible sources of self-focused attention.

And now comes the question—When should society *not* cease with its in-

---

[2]This resembles what the nonstutterers of Dittmann and Llewellyn (1969) did following disfluencies.

[3]This is directly analogous to the lowering of eye contact among the nonstutterers of Kendon (1967).

stilling of a self-reflective attitude? From all of the preceding discussion one would gather that the prompting of self-focusing is especially invaluable in two kinds of domains: (1) The untrained person requires a certain measure of self awareness in order to guide individual movements into coordination with designated standards. In short, the entire process of learning is furthered by the self-critical piecemeal approach taken in the activities of self-focused individuals; (2) There is the difficult question of bringing the person to be a responsible member of the group. Just as with task performance, we would suppose that normative behavior, and the sense of acting for the group, can eventually become automated—but until the point of automaticity, the steering function implicit in the self-reflective orientation would seem a necessity from the perspective of society.

NARCISSISM: THE INDIVIDUAL VERSUS THE GROUP

One of the major tenets of self-awareness theory is the thesis that self-awareness is experienced subjectively as uncomfortable, as a condition that the individual would prefer not to enter into (Archer et al., 1979; Brockner, in press; Gibbons & Wicklund, 1976; Sackeim, 1974). This discomfort is said to occur to the extent that a negative within-self discrepancy is the salient aspect of the self-awareness. And to be sure, all we have discussed thus far is the individual who falls short of standards or ideals and the role of self-awareness in motivating movement toward those endpoints.

But there is a flip side to the potentially aversive character of self-awareness—namely, if a success experience is salient, the person may well enjoy dwelling on that aspect of self (Wicklund, 1975). At least two findings in the literature attest to this idea.

For one, subjects in one condition of a study by Gibbons and Wicklund (1976) first found that they were sought after by an attractive member of the opposite sex. Then, when they subsequently had the opportunity of listening either to their own voice or to the voice of another male, they tended to prefer their own voice. Said otherwise, they preferred a stimulus that reminded them of themselves. A similar finding with stronger results is reported by Greenberg and Musham (1981). Subjects with a variety of opinions on the issue of women's rights were asked to engage in behaviors that were variously in keeping with that of their own opinions, somewhat discrepant, or else very discrepant. Subsequently, all subjects were given the choice of sitting directly before a mirror or else away from the mirror. Interestingly, the subjects who had shown no hypocrisy whatever (their behaviors were in accord with their opinions) generally chose to sit before the mirror, thus heightening their self-awareness.

The issue from the standpoint of this chapter is whether this narcissism is appreciated by society. The implicit assumption in the preceding discussion has been that society has a utilitarian view of individuals and wants maximal obedience, conformity, honesty, and performance from each member. From such an assumption one would almost be forced to conclude that no one benefits from narcissism except the narcissist, for the narcissist is by definition in a resting state—nonproductive, and not thinking of the future. It is a special case of the self-aware person's being oriented not toward self-criticism and self-improvement, but rather toward an egotistical status quo.

Summary

We see that society's creation of self-awareness-provoking conditions can serve to bring the individual orientation more in the direction of norms, thus rendering the person more acceptable and useful to the functioning group. Parallel to this behavioral implication of self-awareness is the knowledge function: The group should have a more accurate sense of the person when that person is self-aware. Self-reports are more accurate, and overall consistency is greater. At the same time, the group as controlling agent will not invariably profit by instituting self-awareness. In particular, the special problems include: (1) not fully understanding which endpoint the self-aware individual will act upon; (2) creating too much self-awareness when complex behaviors must be enacted; (3) interfering with automated actions; and (4) having to tolerate narcissism. Thus, we see that the society's use of the individual's self-awareness is a multifaceted phenomenon. Although instrumental in producing a civilized individual, self-awareness can serve at the same time to overcontrol the individual, to the long-range detriment of society.

ON THE SOCIETAL IMPLEMENTATION OF SELF-AWARENESS

There remains a vital issue. For the sake of simplicity, we have talked about society's control over the individual as if society possessed an intimate knowledge of the antecedents and processes of self-awareness. This is a bit naive. In fact, the issue of whether society knows that it is controlling through the means of self-awareness is probably a moot issue. The psychological condition of self-aware individuals might be labeled variously by society. For instance, the child who is forced to look the adult in the eye following some transgression is likely to be self-focused,[4] but from the adult's perspective the state is not described precisely as *self-awareness*. Attention, shame, embarrassment, contrition, and a variety of other terms might be used to characterize the state of the person whom we would like to call self-aware. Another way of saying this is that the label is of no consequence. As long as society is generating self-awareness-producing conditions, it is important to know just that, but much less important to know whether the social unit knows exactly what is transpiring.

---

[4]Eye contact has been shown to play a central role in the social instigation of self-awareness (Scheier, Fenigstein, & Buss, 1974).

That issue aside, what then are the sources of societal control over the self-awareness process? Here an important dichotomy must be drawn. One class of self-awareness inducers is intentionally brought forth by society in the course of trying to civilize or change; the other class is incidental, accidental, or ongoing.

Intentional Control

When society needs to bring someone under control, meaning to gain a better knowledge of the person or insure that the person is oriented correctly in behaviors, it gives a good deal of attention to that person. The parent insists on eye contact when lecturing on a moral principle, the deviate is singled out and shamed or otherwise evaluated in the group's effort to create homogeneity, and perhaps more subtlely, those who don't abide by the norms are labeled as "weird," "different," or "nonconformists." The effect of such labeling should be one of heightening the person's self-awareness, simply by his sense of uniqueness and nonfit (Duval, 1976; Wegner & Schaefer, 1978).

In a more sophisticated realm of behavior change, self-awareness is generated in ways that resemble laboratory manipulations. Psychotherapy entails direct introspection, where the individual is in the spotlight and distractions are pushed aside. And such training techniques as video feedback (Sackeim & Gur, 1978) have increased in frequency—these obviously being identical to laboratory antecedents of self-focus. Interestingly, this literature also illustrates the kinds of self-improvement effects that we would expect from the theoretical ideas on self awareness.

Incidental Control (and Lack of Control)

Much of day-to-day self-awareness is produced independent of any specific societal effort at behavior control. One of the most common sources is simply the feeling of being unique, or different. Take the traveller, for instance. The American who visits a European country, or a European who visits another European country, should very likely feel estranged. This would be especially true at first, when the sense of differentness is the most imposing. Wicklund and Frey (1980) interviewed a number of such tourists, and measuring self-focus with a simplified version of the Fenigstein et al. (1975) private self-consciousness scale, found that travellers were more self-aware if they were making their first visit to a given country.

This uniqueness, or estrangement notion, also has an opposite side to it. Psychology has long talked about a concept called "deindividuation" (Diener, 1980; Festinger, Pepitone, & Newcomb, 1952; Singer, Brush, & Lublin, 1965; Zimbardo, 1969), wherein the individual's personal boundaries are subsumed by the sense of groupness. The phenomenon is especially to be noticed in cohesive groups in which members are devoid of special identifying charactistics. Interestingly, when a small group stands before a mirror, a sense of group self-focus seems to predominate over the sense of "I", self-focus, a phenomenon recently examined by Pennebaker (1978) and Wegner (1979). In other words, the person who is submerged in the group loses the sense of being an individual that is crucial in the instigation of self-awareness. This phenomenon was reflected in another aspect of the study on European travellers by Wicklund and Frey. There was a distinct difference between people travelling alone and those in groups, such that the lone travellers experienced significantly more self-swareness on the modified Fenigstein et al. (1975) scale.

The deindividuation theme may be carried one step further. Society, as a collection of individuals, also has its needs vis-a-vis self-awareness, and one of these is the avoidance of self-focus, a theme that opened this chapter. A very similar point is to be found in a theoretical statement by Bassos (1973):

> All in all, the culture and the individuals in it work against realization of separateness. To be so separate is also to be responsible for one's own behaviors and to cope with the aloneness and isolation the existentialists see as central to man's experience. In addition to the normal developmental predisposition, the cultural values and the semantic and linguistic meanings which foster nonseparation, it is also the case that the child because of early experiences, may itself resist ego differentiation [p. 18].

To the extent that individuals collect in deindividuated units, thus transforming the unit of analysis from the "I" to the "we," the potential of each individual member for the discomfort of self-focus is thereby reduced. One would suspect that this is a strong, ongoing tendency, which effects a reduction in potential awareness, hence lowered control via values and personal standards.

When control over individual members is not the foremost goal, it is likely that a condition just opposite to self-awareness will arise—that of deindividuation—which entails the relaxing of standards and morals. Deindividuation may well be an index of a secure society or group, one with no concerns about individual members' obedience and allegiance, that can afford the happy escape from self-awareness.

SUMMARY

To place the individual into self-focused attention is a powerful tool of society. By virtue of the self-focused state, the individual member of society abides more by cultural prescriptions, behaves more consistently with individual morality, and is known more fully and accurately to the community. At the same time, society's placing the individual in a self-aware state can backfire: The person may come to act on moral principles that run against the grain of the immediate society, or circumstances may turn the self-aware condition into what is commonly called narcissism. Even more serious is the debilitating impact of self-awareness on individual performances. The very acts that society most prizes—the mastery of intricacte tasks, and the display of overrehearsed, automated performances—stand to be upset by instituting self-focused attention. Thus, self-awareness may be seen as a tool of bringing the individual into line with societal expectations, and as such might be treated as an instrument of training. Once the individual is oriented in a prosocial direction, and once highly trained in valued activities, self awareness becomes more an instrument of disruption and distress.

And a final moral note. From the research illustrations and examples the reader may well have gathered that the "group" or "society" described here is virtually panic stricken at the idea that particular members would not behave fully in accord with norms or the status quo. The functioning of self-awareness appears to serve such an impatient, intolerant attitude toward individuals. This, there is a danger beyond those already described. Whatever is idiosyncratic, creative and even temporarily outlandish is obviously endangered when we find the unique individual in the self-awareness-promoting group setting, and here is where the reader needs to make a value judgment. What is it about the human's unsocialized acts that we value particularly, and what is it about the norm-abiding human that makes us think the person is valuable or worth knowing? The self-reflexive, civilized human is a valued entity only through some eyes, whereas from another perspective the impulsive and seemingly more instinctive being encompasses ultimate human status.

ACKNOWLEDGMENTS

The author wishes to thank Daniel M. Wegner for his creative observations on an earlier version of this chapter.

REFERENCES

Archer, R. L, Hormuth, S. E., & Berg, J. H.   *Self-disclosure and self-awareness*. Paper presented at the annual meeting of the American Psychological Association, New York, 1979.

Aronfreed, J.   The origin of self-criticism. *Psychological Review*, 1964, *71*, 193–218.

Bassos, C. A.   *The duality of the shame experience*. Paper presented at the annual meeting of the American Psychological Association, Montreal, Canada, 1973.

Beaman, A. L., Klentz, B., Diener, E., & Svanum, S.   Self-awareness and transgression in childrens: Two field studies. *Journal of Personality and Social Psychology, 1979, 37,* 1835–1846.

Bloodstein, O.   *A handbook on stuttering*. Chicago: National Easter Seal Society for Crippled Children and Adults, 1969.

Brockner, J.   Self-esteem, self-consciousness, and task performance: Replications, extensions, and possible explanations. *Journal of Personality and Social Psychology*, 1979, *37*, 447–461.

Brockner, J., & Hulton, A. J. B.   How to reverse the vicious cycle of low self-esteem: The importance of attentional focus. *Journal of Experimental Social Psychology*, 1978, *14*, 564–578.

Brockner, J.   The effects of self-esteem, success-failure, and self-consciousness on task performance. *Journal of Personality and Social Psychology*, in press.

Carver, C. S.   Physical aggression as a function of objective self-awareness and attitudes toward punishment. *Journal of Experimental Social Psychology*, 1975, *11*, 510–519.

Carver, C. S.   Self-awareness, perception of threat, and the expression of reactance through attitude change. *Journal of Personality*, 1977, *45*, 501–512.

Carver, C. S., & Scheier, M. F.   Self-focusing effects of dispositional self-consciousness, mirror presence, and audience presence. *Journal of Personality and Social Psychology*, 1978, *36* , 324–332.

Cooley C. H.   *Human nature and the social order.* New York, Scribner's , 1902.

Davis, D., & Brock, T. C.   Use of first person pronouns as a function of increased objective self-awareness and prior feedback. *Journal of Experimental Social Psychology*, 1975, *11*, 381–388.

Diener, E. Deindividuation: The absence of self-awareness and self-regulation in group members. In P. B. Paulus (Ed.), *Psychology of group influence*, Hillsdale, N. J.: Lawrence Erlbaum Associates, 1980.

Diener E , & Wallbom M.   Effects of self-awareness on antinormative behavior. *Journal of Research in Personality*, 1976, *10*, 107–111.

Dittmann, A. T., & Llewellyn, L. G.   Body movement and speech rhythm in social conversation. *Journal of Personality and Social Psychology*, 1969, *11*, 98–106.

Duval, S.   Conformity on a visual task as a function of personal novelty on attitudinal dimensions and being reminded of the object status of self. *Journal of Experimental Social Psychology*, 1976, *12*, 87–98.

Duval, S., & Wicklund, R. A.   *A theory of objective self awareness.* New York: Academic Press, 1972.

Fenigstein, A., Scheier, M. F., & Buss, A. H.   Public and private self-consciousness: Assessment and theory. *Journal of Consulting and Clinical Psychology*, 1975, *43*, 522–527.

Festinger, L, Pepitone, A., & Newcomb, T.   Some consequences of deindividuation in a group. *Journal of Abnormal and Social Psychology*, 1952, *47*, 382–389.

Frey, D., Wicklund, R. A., & Scheier, M. F.   Die Theorie der objektiven Selbstaufmerksamkeit. In D. Frey (Ed.), *Kognitive Theorien der Sozialpsychologie.* Bern, Switzerland: Huber, 1978.

Gibbons, F. X.   Sexual standards and reactions to pornography: Enhancing behavioral consistency through self-focused attention. *Journal of Personality and Social Psychology*, 1978, *36* , 976–987.

Gibbons, F. X., & Wicklund, R. A.   Selective exposure to self. *Journal of Research in Personality*, 1976, *10*, 98 –106.

Greenberg, J., & Musham, C.   Avoiding and seeking self-focused attention. *Journal of Research in Personality*, 1981, *15*, 191–200.

Heckhausen, H.   Task-irrelevant cognitions during an exam: Incidence and effects. In H.W. Krohne & L. Laux (Eds.), *Achievement, stress, and anxiety.* Washington, D. C.: Hemisphere, in press.

Hoffman, M. L. Moral internalization, parental power, and the nature of parent-child interaction. *Developmental Psychology*, 1975, *11*, 228–239.

Hormuth, S. E.   Self-awareness, internal standards, and response dominance. *Unpublished doctoral dissertation*, University of Texas at Austin, 1979.

Jackson J. M., & Latané, B.   All alone in front of all those people: Stage fright as a function of number and type of coperformers and audience. *Unpublished manuscript*, Ohio State University, 1979.

James, W.   *The principles of psychology* (Vol. I). New York: Henry Holt, 1890.

James, W.   *Psychology: The briefer course.* New York: Holt, 1910.

Kendon, A.   Some functions of gaze-direction in social interaction. *Acta Psychologica*, 1967, *26*, 22–63.

Kimble, G. A., & Perlmuter, L. C.   The problem of volition. *Psychological Review*, 1970, *77*, 361–384.

Langer, E.   Rethinking the role of thought in social interaction. In J. H. Harvey, W. Ickes, & R. F. Kidd (Eds.), *New directions in attribution research* (Vol. 2). Hillsdale, N. J.: Lawrence Erlbaum Associates, 1978.

Liebling, B. A., & Shaver, P.   Evaluation, self-awareness, and task performance. *Journal of Experimental Social Psychology*, 1973, *9*, 297–306.

McDonald, P. J.   Reactions to objective self-awareness. *Journal of Personality*, in press.

Mead, G. H.   *Mind, self, and society*. Chicago: University of Chicago Press, 1934.

Mosher, D. L.   Measurement of guilt in females by self-report inventories. *Journal of Consulting and Clinical Psychology, 1968, 32,* 690–695.

Pennebaker, J.W.   Group self-awareness. *Unpublished manuscript*, Univeristy of Virginia, 1978.

Porter, H.   Studies in the psychology of stuttering, XIV. Stuttering phenomena in relation to size and personnel of audience. *Journal of Speech Disorders, 1939, 4,* 323–333.

Pryor, J. B., Gibbons, F. X., Wicklund, R. A., Fazio, R. H., & Hood, R.   Self-focused attention and self-report validity. *Journal of Personality, 1977, 45,* 513–527.

Sackeim, H. A.   A theory of the self-confrontation experience. *Unpublished manuscript*, Oxford University, 1974.

Sackeim, H. A., & Gur, R. C.   Self-deception, self-confrontation, and consciousness. In G. E. Schwartz & D. Shapiro (Eds.), *Consciousness and self regulation*. New York: Plenum, 1978.

Scheier, M. F.   Self-awareness, self-consciousness and angry aggression. *Journal of Personality,* 1976, *44,* 627–644.

Scheier, M. F., Buss, A. H., & Buss, D. M.   Self-consciousness, self-report of aggressiveness and aggression. *Journal of Research in Personality, 1978, 12,* 133–140.

Scheier, M. F., Carver, C. S., & Gibbons, F. X.   Self-focused attention and reactions to fear. *Journal of Research in Personality, 1981, 15,* 1–15.

Scheier, M. F., Fenigstein, A., & Buss, A. H.   Self-awareness and physical aggression. *Journal of Experimental Social Psychology, 1974, 10,* 264–273.

Shibutani, T.   *Society and personality: An interactionist approach to social psychology*. Englewood Cliffs, N. J.: Prentice–Hall, 1961.

Shrauger, J. S.   Self-esteem and reactions to being observed by others. *Journal of Personality and Social Psychology, 1972, 23,* 192–200.

Singer, J. E., Brush, C. A., & Lublin, S. C.   Some aspects of deindividuation: Identification and conformity. *Journal of Experimental Social Psychology, 1965, 1,* 356–378.

Storms, M. D., & McCaul, K. D.   Attribution processes and emotional exacerbation of dysfunctional behavior. In J. H. Harvey, W. Ickes, & R. F. Kidd (Eds.), *New directions in attribution research.* (Vol. 1). Hillsdale, N. J.: Lawrence Erlbaum Associates, 1976.

Swift, W. B., & Hedrick, J.   Sidetracking of stuttering by "starters." *Journal of Applied Psychology, 1917, 1,* 84–88.

Vallacher, R. R., & Solodky, M.   Objective self-awareness, internal standards, and moral behavior. Journal of Experimental Social Psychology, 1979, *15,* 254–262.

Wegner, D. M.   From individual self-awareness to group self awareness. Unpublished manuscript, Trinity University, 1979.

Wegner, D. M., & Schaefer, D. The concentration of responsibility: An objective self-awareness analysis of group size effects in helping situations. *Journal of Personality and Social Psychology,* 1978, *36,* 147–155.

Wicker, A. W.   Attitudes versus actions: The relationship of verbal and overt behavioral responses to attitude objects. *Journal of Social Issues, 1969, 25,* 41–78.

Wicklund, R. A.   Ogjective self-awareness. In L. Berkowitz (Ed.), *Advances in experimental social psychology* (Vol. 8). New York: Academic Press, 1975.

Wicklund, R. A.   Three years later. In L. Berkowitz (Ed.), *Cognitive theories in social psychology*. New York: Academic Press, 1978.

Wicklund, R. A.   The influence of self-awareness on human behavior. *American Scientist,* 1979, *67,* 187–193. (a)

Wicklund, R. A.   Die Aktualisierung von Selbstkonzepten in Handlungsvollzügen. In S. H. Filipp, (Ed.), *Selbstkonzept Forschung: Probleme, Befunde, Perspektiven*. Stuttgart: Klett-Cotta, 1979. (b)

Wicklund, R. A.   Objektive Selbstaufmerksamkeit: Ein theoretischer Ansatz zur Persönlichkeits- und Sozialpsychologie. In S. E. Hormuth (Ed.), *Sozialpsychologie der Einstellungsänderung*. Konigstein /Ts., Germany: Athenäum Hain, 1979. (c)

Wicklund, R. A.   Group contact and self-focused attention. In P. B. Paulus (Ed.), *Psychology of group influence*. Hillsdale , N. J.: Lawrence Erlbaum Associates, 1980.

Wicklund, R. A., & Duval, S.   Opinion change and performance facilitation as a result of objective self-awareness. *Journal of Experimental Social Psychology*, 1971, *7*, 319–342.

Wicklund, R. A., & Frey, D.   Self-awareness theory: When the self makes a difference. In D. M. Wegner & R. R. Vallacher (Eds.), *The self in social psychology*. New York: Oxford, 1980.

Wine, J.   Test anxiety and direction of attention. *Psychological Bulletin*, 1971, *76*, 92–104.

Wolff, W.   Selbstbeurteilung und Fremdbeurteilung im wissentlichen und unwissentlichen Versuch. *Psychologische Forschung*, 1932, *16*, 251–328.

Zimbardo, P.   The human choice: Individuation, reason, and order versus deindividuation, impulse and chaos. In W. J. Arnold & D. Levine (Eds.), *Nebraska symposium on motivation* (Vol. 18). Lincoln: University of Nebraska Press, 1970.

9

Toward a General Theory of Strategic Self-Presentation

Edward E. Jones
Princeton University
Thane S. Pittman
Gettysburg College

We hope that the initial word of our title diminishes its pretentiousness. The present chapter is offered as a preliminary formulation that will obviously be modified to accommodate new data. Nevertheless, we believe that the self-presentation area has been slow to develop in social psychology because of the lack of comprehensive theorizing (as well as the difficulty of doing theory-based experimental research). Self-presentational phenomena are ubiquitous in social life, and yet we have no conceptual framework to relate and understand these phenomena. The present chapter attempts to outline such a framework to facilitate the organization—and indeed the identification—of self-presentation research.

A DEFINITION AND SOME EXCLUSIONS

One problem in coming to terms with self-presentation is its very omnipresence. No one would seriously challenge the general idea that observers infer dispositions from an actor's behavior or that actors have a stake in controlling the inferences drawn about them from their actions. Goffman crystallized one viewpoint on impression management with his classic dramaturgical account in 1959, one that essentially gave us the label of *self-presentation* and provided enough descriptive variety and richness to convince us that here was an important area for social psychological analysis. Goffman's emphasis, however, was on the subtle ways in which actors project or convey a definition of the interaction situation as they see it. Attempts on the part of the actor to shape others' impressions of his personality received only secondary emphasis. Jones (1964), and Jones and

Wortman (1973), focused on our interest in getting others to like us and developed a theoretical framework that combined motivational, cognitive, and evaluative features.

A number of experiments have since addressed the determinants and social consequences of "self-disclosure" (Cozby, 1973; Jourard, 1964; and others). Solid conclusions in this area have proved hard to come by. All the while we have been occasionally edified, sometimes amused, and often appalled by a popular literature dealing with power, manipulation, and self-salesmanship (Carnegie, 1936; Korda, 1975; Ringer, 1973; Webb & Morgan, 1930).

Impression management concerns have found their way into many areas of social psychology. Tedeschi, Schlenker, and their associates (1971) have argued that such concerns can explain most of the phenomena that others have attributed to cognitive dissonance reduction. Orne (1962), Rosenthal (1966), Rosenberg (1965), and others have written at length about the concerns of experimental subjects with how they will be evaluated by an experimenter.

And yet, in spite of the volume of seemingly relevant literature and research, the topic of self-presentation suffers from an amorphous identity with insecure underpinnings in motivational and cognitive theory. Our intent is to provide such underpinnings and demarcate the area of concern more clearly than previous treatments.

To these ends we start with definitions first of the phenomenal self and then of what we mean by strategic self-presentation. The *phenomenal self* was defined by Jones and Gerard (1967) as: "a person's awareness, arising out of interactions with his environment, of his own beliefs, values, attitudes, the links between them, and their implications for his behavior [page 716]." We accept this view that each of us has a potentially available overarching cognition of his or her interrelated dispositions. The notion of a phenomenal self implies that memories of past actions and outcomes are available in integrated form to clarify current action possibilities. The evolution of this overarching phenomenal self is greatly facilitated by the fact that other people, in their attempt to render *their* social environment more predictable, endow us with stable attributes and respond to us as enduring structures. It is not surprising that we learn to take ourselves as definable social objects and become concerned with the consistency of our actions over time.

But the words "potentially available" are important in approaching the phenomenal self. The phenomenal self is not always salient; we are not always self-focused or preoccupied with self-consistency. A consequence of being socialized in a particular culture is that sequences of action become automatic, triggered off by contextual cues in line with past reinforcements. We are often, in effect, "mindless" (Langer & Newman, 1979). In many of the routine social interchanges of everyday life, therefore, the phenomenal self is not aroused, does not become salient. Conflict and novelty do, however, give rise to mindfulness and self-salience. When we do not have preprogrammed response sequences, the phenomenal self becomes a reference point for decision making as we review the implications of our beliefs and values for action. Pressures toward self-consistency (and long-range adaptation) may then compete with pressures toward shorter-range social gains in creating the conflicts and dilemmas of social life. These dilemmas are often cast in moral terms as the individual assesses the relative virtues of integrity, consistency, and authenticity on the one hand, as against the virtues of adaptive effectiveness and personal security gained through power augmentation on the other. Jones and Wortman (1973) have argued, however, that this conflict is often avoided as adaptive social responding becomes automatic in the face of well-established recurrent cues. Thus, the contextual cue that defines our momentary social position as "dependent" may trigger off ingratiating actions or other attempts at impression management without necessarily evoking the phenomenal self.

A vital point to stress is that in spite of certain pressures toward self-stability and consistency over time, the phenomenal self: (1) shifts from moment to moment as a function of motivational state and situational cues, and (2) is constantly evolving and changing in ways that incorporate or come to terms with one's actions or one's outcomes. The impact of self presentation on the self-concept receives our recurrent attention throughout this chapter.

But, now, what exactly do we mean by strategic self-presentation? Most would agree that self-presentation involves an actor's shaping of his or her responses to create in specific others an impression that is for one reason or another desired by the actor. Most, if not all, of these reasons can be subsumed under an interest in augmenting or maintaining one's *power* in a relationship. The actor uses his behavior to convey something about him or herself, regardless of what other meaning or significance the behavior may have.[1]. Formally, we define strategic self-presentation as *those features of behavior affected by power augmentation motives designed to elicit or shape others' attributions of the actor's dispositions.* "Features" of course include the most subtle aspects of style and nonverbal expressions, as well as the contents of overt verbal communications. The definition also makes clear that we are unlikely to find a given response or set of responses that are intrinsically or universally self-presentational. Rather, self-presentation is likely to be intimately intertwined in social responses that have other significances as well. It is also by no means implied that strategic self-presentational features are necessarily false, distorted, or seriously discrepant from the phenomenal self. As we subsequently argue in more detail, such features typically involve selective disclosures and omissions, matters of emphasis and toning rather than of deceit and simulation.

In view of the difficulties created by the intertwining of self-presentational and other features of behavior, about the only way to identify the presence of strategic self-presentation is to arouse particular impression-management motives experimentally, and to observe the features that distinguish ensuing responses from behavior without such implanted motivation. This is easier said than done,

---

[1]The pronouns *he, his,* and *him* are used throughout this chapter to refer to both sexes.

but at least it provides a starting point for ostensive definition and is more or less the prescription followed in the ingratiation area (Jones 1964; Jones & Wortman, 1973).

It may be helpful to continue this definitional discussion by paying some attention to those conditions likely to inhibit self-presentational concerns. In other words, let us list some examples of settings in which strategic self-presentation behaviors are absent or minimal:

1. Behavior under conditions of high task involvement. This essentially refers to those settings that arouse "subjective self-awareness" in Duval & Wicklund's (1972) terms. The individual is absorbed by physical or intellectual challenge that, to use a Freudian image, totally captures the libidinal cathexis. The demands of the task (whether it involves hem stitching, observing, reading, or involvement in an athletic contest) preclude self-consciousness. Even lecturers and actors, though addressing an audience, may be so engrossed in their material as to elude momentary concern with its response.

2. Purely expressive behavior—anger, mirth, joy—may escape self-presentational shaping at or near the moment of provocation. Some emotions apparently overwhelm the concerns of impression management, if only for a brief moment before we start to worry whether our reactions are "appropriate" to the occasion.

3. We would also set aside as *not* self presentational a large class of overlearned, ritualized social interchanges. Actors are often apt to forgo the self-presentational possibilities of divergent ways of conducting routine commercial transactions, driving through traffic, or checking out library books—though the opportunities for impression management are very much available in these instances for the person who is constantly obsessed with his public image.

4. Finally, for psychological completeness, we might include those occasions when persons are above all concerned with the integrity or authenticity of their actions. They want their actions to be self-fulfilling and self-disclosing. They reach inward for available traces of beliefs, values, and feelings, which they try to capture in self-revealing comments or nonverbal expressions. Therapy sessions, encounter groups, and intimate relationships often motivate us to portray the phenomenal self with maximum fidelity, concealing and distorting as little as possible. This is not, however, to suggest that such contexts normally preclude a concern with managing the attributions of others. What we sincerely believe is "authentic" may vary with our audience and our purpose.

We would emphasize that self-presentation is an important subcategory of social behavior, but, nevertheless, it is a *sub*category. To summarize, our actions in the presence of others are relatively unaffected by our concern with their impressions of us to the extent that the behavior in question is task centered, spontaneously expressive, normatively ritualized, or deliberately self-matching. On the other hand, self-presentational features will be intertwined with behavior whenever the actor cares, for whatever reasons, about the impression others have of him. We now move on to show what some of the reasons are, and how some of them are linked to recognizably different self-presentational strategies.

A TAXONOMY OF ATTRIBUTIONS SHAPED BY SELF-PRESENTATIONAL STRATEGIES

We believe strongly that a theory of strategic self-presentation must be anchored in identifiable social motives. Self presentation involves the actor's linkage of particular motives to his or her strategic resources. In short:

1. *A* wants to make secure or to augment his power to derive favorable outcomes from *B*.

2. The desired growth or consolidation of power may or may not be directed toward these outcomes in the immediate future. *A* may invest his stategic outcomes in a "power bank," whose resources may be tapped in unspecified future encounters with *B*.

3. *A*'s getting the kind of power he wants will be facilitated if *B* has a certain impression of *A*.

4. Creating that impression will be easy or difficult depending on *A*'s resources, which in turn are defined by *A*'s cognitive and behavioral capacities within the settings available for interaction with *B*.

5. The linkage of a particular power motive with the self presentational features of social behavior is mediated by cognitive processes in the self-presenting actor. The behavior is further shaped by evaluative or moral constraints. The complex interaction of motive, cognition, and morality determines the choice of self-presentational strategies.

Hoping that the reader keeps these assumptions in mind, we offer a taxonomy of five classes of self-presentational strategies. The defining feature of each class is the particular attribution sought by the actor. The taxonomy consists of ingratiation, intimidation, self-promotion, exemplification, and supplication. In our view these rubrics, although not entirely exhaustive, encompass most instances of strategic self-presentation.

Ingratiation

Ingratiation is undoubtedly the most ubiquitous of all self presentational phenomena. Much of our social behavior is shaped by a concern that others like us and attribute to us such characteristics as warmth, humor, reliability, charm, and physical attractiveness. The ingratiator's goals may shift back and forth among these specific attributional foci, but by definition the ingratiator seeks to achieve the *attribution of likability*. Consistent with this orientation, ingratiation has been formally defined by Jones and Wortman (1973) as: "a class of strategic behaviors illicitly designed to influence a particular other person concerning the attractiveness of one's personal qualities [p. 2]." Ingratiating actions are illicit because they are directed toward an objective that is typically not contained in the implicit contract underlying social interaction. In fact, the very success of ingratiation usually depends on the actor's concealment of ulterior motivation or of the importance of his stake in being judged attractive. The illicit nature of ingratiation may also lead ingratiators to deceive themselves concerning either the importance of being judged attractive or the relationship between this desired goal and the strategic features invading their action decisions. A tantalizing conspiracy of cognitive avoidance is common to the actor and his target. The actor does not wish to see himself as ingratiating; the target wants also to believe that the ingratiator is sincere in following the implicit social contract.

A considerable volume of research has been conducted in the ingratiation area, much of it summarized by Jones and Wortman (1973). Such prominent subclasses as conformity, other enhancement, doing favors, and various forms of direct and indirect self description have been dealt with extensively. The general finding is that placing an actor in a position of dependence vis a vis a more powerful target person, in comparison to control conditions in which actor and target person have equal power, gives rise to greater conformity (Jones, 1965), self-enhancement (Jones, Gergen, & Davis, 1962), and other enhancement (Jones, Gergen, & Jones, 1963). Typically, however, the dependent actor's behavior is complicated to increase credibility (Jones, 1965). Bystanding observers react negatively to conformity and other ingratiating overtures, when such overtures are obvious or excessive and the power discrepancy between the actor and the target is great (Jones, Jones, & Gergen, 1963). It is also true, however, that target persons respond more positively to a highly agreeable actor dependent on them than do bystanders watching the interchange on film (Jones, Stires, Shaver, & Harris, 1968). A number of more subtle considerations qualify these findings, but the broad outlines of ingratiation research basically show that people are responsive to ingratiation "incentives"; they tend to avoid the more blatant forms of ingratiating behavior, and if an actor's overtures are blatant, he is readily identified by outside observers as responding to ulterior motives—and less readily charged with ulterior motivation by the high-power target person himself.

The theoretical treatment of ingratiation has been more fully developed than the theoretical bases of other self-presentational strategies. The particular form that ingratiation will take (conformity versus favors versus other enhancement versus self-enhancement) is no doubt determined in complex ways by the ingratiator's resources and the nature of the setting. It is easier for the applicant to be self-enhancing than conforming in an employment interview situation. It is easier to be flattering after observing a performance or meeting an offspring of the target than in an informal discussion of world affairs. High status persons with a low-status target are more likely to use flattery to gain attraction than conformity or agreement. Thus, the time, the place, and the nature of the relationship promote the likelihood of particular attraction-seeking strategies. Individual difference factors undoubtedly also play a role both in the generation of ingratiating behavior and in bystander evaluations of ingratiation (Jones &

Baumeister, 1976). Nevertheless, a general theoretical account of the ingratiation process is plausible and consistent with known data. Such an account stresses three underlying determinants of attraction-seeking overtures:

1. Incentive value—the importance of being liked by a particular target. This varies directly with the dependence of the actor on the target and inversely with the degree of his power over the target. In most nonritualized, nontransient relationships, the incentive value is greater than zero, because the actor is unlikely to be indifferent toward others' evaluations of his attractiveness as a person.

2. Subjective probability—the choice of a particular ingratiation strategy is also determined by the subjective probability of its success and the inverse probability that a boomerang effect (decreased attraction) will occur. Thus, the motivational determinant, incentive value, is qualified or constrained by the cognitive determinant, subjective probability, in its effects on behavior. The *ingratiator's dilemma* is created by the fact that as the actor's dependence on the target goes up, his motivation to ingratiate goes up, whereas the subjective probability of its success goes down. This occurs because dependence makes salient to the target as well as any bystanding observers the possibility of ulterior purposes in actions that are commonly seen as eliciting attraction. The dilemma for the ingratiator is that the more important it is for him to gain a high-power target's attraction, the less likely it is that he will be successful. Attempts to avoid or minimize the effects of this dilemma can lead to the complication of strategic overtures already noted previously. The actor must go out of his way to establish his credibility, especially in those settings where extreme dependence might make his credibility suspect. Matters of timing are also important. We have already noted that individuals may invest the profits from strategic overtures in a power bank for use on future occasions. The far-sighted ingratiator may thus avoid the greater risks of failure attendant upon maneuvers specifically linked to those times when his dependence is most apparent and his need for approval the most imperative.

3. Perceived legitimacy—in addition to the contribution of motivational and cognitive factors, ingratiation is further shaped and constrained by moral or evaluative factors. We have already noted that the forms of ingratiating behavior vary with opportunity and resources, including appropriateness within a setting. Perceived legitimacy adds another dimension of appropriateness: the extent to which one's presentations of self are consistent with the phenomenal self and with the norms governing acceptable departures (for reasons of kindness or courtesy) from candor. Each of us internalizes a set of moral standards defining the reprehensibility of dissimulation and deceit in human relations. The moral situation is complicated, however, by the inculcation of other values favoring the promotion of self-interest and the legitimacy of self-salesmanship. Thus, out of a complex mixture of moral forces pushing here for "authenticity" and there for "impression management," the individual must decide on the best strategic combination in his dealings with others.

Because of various ambiguities connected with the "business ethic," many would-be ingratiators can find considerable freedom of movement in their strategic choices. The press to perceive ingratiation as legitimate undoubtedly increases with other features defining the relationship: Ingratiation is likely to be perceived as legitimate in settings where self-salesmanship is sanctioned by the individualistic norms of the business world, where the target is not respected by the actor, in the absence of bystanders, and where the actor feels that his dependence is unfair or inequitable. Other possibilities are discussed by Jones (1964; Jones & Wortman, 1973). Many of these reflect the importance of consensus or perceived consensus. What "everybody does" is all right for one to do. Other factors stress the readiness of actors: (1) to deny that their behavior was insincere; and (2) to insist that their intentions were benign and socially supportive.

The theory of ingratiation does not specify clearly how these three major determinants interact. Perhaps they combine multiplicatively because if any factor is zero, ingratiation will presumably not occur. Though normative factors undoubtedly shape the form as well as the occurrence of ingratiation, it may turn out that perceived legitimacy is more a dichotomous variable than either incentive value or subjective probability. Moral decisions tend to have an either-or quality about them. This would suggest that incentive value and subjective probability multiply to produce a strong or weak tendency to ingratiate. Legitimacy then plays its role as a threshold factor, providing a go or stop signal depending on the strength of incentive value and subjective probability. Thus, a person may flatter or ingratiate even though he knows this behavior is not entirely legitimate, once the importance and the likelihood of obtaining a benefit reach a certain combined value.

Intimidation

Whereas the ingratiator attempts to convince a target person that he is likeable, the intimidator tries to convince a target person that he is *dangerous*. Whereas successful ingratiation reduces or blunts the target person's power by causing him to avoid doing anything that would hurt or cost the actor, the intimidator advertises his available power to create pain, discomfort, or all kinds of psychic costs. The actor seeks to receive the attribution that he has the resources to inflict pain and stress *and* the inclination to do so if he does not get his way. Quite unlike the ingratiator, the intimidator typically disdains any real interest in being liked; he wants to be feared, to be believed.

The intimidation prototype is the sidewalk robber who extracts money from a pedestrian by brandishing a gun or a knife. The robber is successful when the pedestrian believes the threat: If I do not give him my money, he will kill or maim me. A more benign, and more psychologically interesting prototype is an older person in some position of authority within an organization. He is gruff, austere, impatient with shoddy performance. He does not suffer fools gladly. Underlings do his bidding because they fear the consequences of his response to failure or inadequate performance. In some cases he may not even make his expectations or desires clear, thus leaving his dependent subordinates in an uncomfortable position of edgy anxiety. In any event, it is clear in these cases that the intimidator has managed to project and elicit an attribution from others that supports his continuing social control.

Though it is perhaps more common for intimidation to flow from high-power to low-power persons, than vice versa, relationships without some element of counterpower are almost inconceivable in contemporary society. And where there are elements of counterpower, there is the opportunity for intimidation. It is by no means farfetched to speak of the power of children to intimidate adults. In fact, we suggest that the occurrence of filial intimidation is indeed common. Children learn in infancy the rewards of tears and tantrums. Especially as they progress into adolescence, our offspring can blunt the exercise of parental power by having previously established that they are quite capable of making a "scene." The anticipated likelihood of such scenes can deter the most conscientious mother from asking her son to clean his room or to do the company dishes. Parents will sometimes go to great lengths to avoid the disharmony that follows in the wake of demands on their children for services that are reasonable and equitable.

The counterpower resource of making a scene is also available to otherwise impotent employees, students, servants, or prisoners. There are, of course, a number of self-abnegating variants such as hunger strikes and passive resistance. Of especial importance in the attributional context is the threat, usually created quite unwittingly, of emotional breakup or collapse. An otherwise impotent person can gather considerable power by acquiring the reputation of one who cannot stand stress or disappointment without responding with hysterical weeping, coronary distress, or suicidal depression. The costs of acquiring such a reputation may be too great for most of us, but there are milder variations on this theme of manipulation that have considerable controlling power in many organizational contexts. The employer who fails to criticize the inept performance of an emotionally unstable employee, in the interests of avoiding a breakdown on his part, may end up unable to fire him because the employer has never given him fair warning. Similarly, it is natural for one spouse to avoid actions and conversational topics that upset the other. It is just as natural for a spouse to signal through incipient distress those mannerisms or topics that he or she wishes to eliminate from the repertory of the other spouse.

When the potential intimidator has enough power to be a credible aggressive threat, incipient anger is a very common controlling device in his relations with others. A man with a short fuse can often dominate a relationship or a group, especially if his ultimately provoked overt anger is likely to be explosive or consequential. President Eisenhower had a very mobile face whose expressions ranged from the famous grin to a dark and forbidding glower. The latter often appeared when a particular line of questioning began in a press conference, and we are tempted to speculate concerning the controlling potential of such "incipient rage," especially in view of our knowledge of his blood pressure problem.

The concept of threat is obviously central to a discussion of intimidation, but we would stress the implicit nature of most interpersonal threats and note that their effectiveness depends on the manipulation of attributions to the actor by those he desires to control. We may summarize this descriptive account of intimidation variants by suggesting some of the more common alternative attributional goals:

Attribution 1. I cannot tolerate much stress, and if I am placed under stress I will develop symptoms or engage in behaviors that will cost or embarrass you.

Attribution 2. I am willing to cause myself pain or embarrassment in order to get my way with others.

Attribution 3. I have a low threshold for anger, and when angered I behave unpredictably and irrationally.

Attribution 4. I have a low threshold for anger, and when angered I have the resources to be effectively vindictive.

Attribution 5. I am not likely to be deterred in my actions by sentiment, compassion, or the wish to be liked by others.

In theoretical terms, intimidation is in many respects the obverse of ingratiation. Intimidating gestures are likely to make the intimidator less, rather than more, attractive. As such, intimidation drives people apart and creates pressures toward withdrawal and avoidance by the target person. This is why we have stressed that intimidation most commonly occurs in relationships that have nonvoluntary status: families, marriages, student-teacher relationships, employers and employees, and military service. It is important that the intimidator have a clear conception of the strength of nonvoluntary bonds. Because intimidation generates avoidance pressures, miscalculations can result in divorces, delinquency, disinheritance, job switching, and various forms of sabotage and insurgency.

A glance at the preceding list of alternative attributions also suggests that intimidation is limited in other respects. The high-power intimidator must often forego affection and a number of attributions that are highly prized in our society. The low-power intimidator must often undergo humiliation or pain in order to carry out such threats as "making a scene," getting drunk, or becoming ill, to say nothing of carrying out such ultimate threats as suicide.

But we must also remember that much of the intimidation range is rather benign and involves transitory sequences in relationships that are otherwise stable and even, on balance, affectionate. Rather than destroy a relationship, patterns of intimidation may redefine it so that certain kinds of interaction are avoided. Thus, marital adjustments may involve a considerable amount of mutual intimidation within a framework of affection and love.

To summarize this introductory view of intimidation, interpersonal power may be exerted by credible threats that create fears of negative consequences for a target person. As a class of self-presentational strategies, intimidation involves the manipulation of attributions that support the credibility of such threats of negative consequences. The threats may be exceedingly vague or implicit. The intimidator may or may not be aware of the strategic goals of his self-presentations. His actions may, as in the case of the ingratiator, represent an overlearned response to a particular pattern of social conditions, rather than a self-conscious strategy of manipulation. There are almost no empirical data concerning the conditions favoring intimidation as currently defined. From the preceding discussion, however, we may extract the following suggestions about the antecedent conditions under which intimidation is most likely to occur:

1. When relationships are nonvoluntary, involve commitments difficult to abrogate, or when alternative relationships are unavailable to the target person.

2. When the potential intimidator has readily available resources with which to inflict negative consequences (weapons, wage control, sexual availability).

3. When the potential target person has weak retaliatory capacities (inhibitions regarding direct aggression toward the young or less fortunate, small stature, lack of confidence in capacity to make verbal rejoinders).

4. When the potential intimidator is willing to forego affection and the attributions of compassion, generosity, and humility—either because he has "given up" on such attributions or can obtain them in alternative relationships.

Self-promotion

Although using self-descriptions to enhance one's attractiveness was originally presented (Jones, 1964) as one form of ingratiation, we would like to separate out an important class of self descriptive communications that seek the attribution of competence rather than likability. For such communications we reserve the name self-promotion. Within the overall self-presentation taxonomy, then, we speak of an actor as "self-characterizing" when he describes himself with the ulterior goal of increasing his personal attractiveness. We speak of the actor as "self promoting" when he seeks the attribution of competence, whether with reference to general ability level (intelligence, athletic ability) or to a specific skill (typing excellence, flute-playing ability).

At the outset it should be noted that self-promotion partakes of certain features of both ingratiation and intimidation. In fact, the fusion or combination of attributional goals is common in all forms of self-presentation. We may wish to be both liked for our attractive personal qualities and respected for our talents and capacities. Or we may wish to appear competent so that we gain the social privilege of being intimidating: so that, for example, we can "get away with" depriving others for inferior performance. There is a sense in which competence itself is intimidating. We defer in awe to Einsteins, Horowitzes, and Borgs. The projection of a competent image is often an important part of the intimidator's baggage. But self-promotion is not equivalent to intimidation. We can convince others of our competence without threatening them or striking fear in their hearts.

A brief digression may delineate the difference. In 1973, R. Ringer wrote a best seller called *Winning Through Intimidation*. By the current taxonomy, this book actually said very little about intimidation and a great deal about self-promotion. Ringer describes again and again various ploys and mannerisms for convincing others that you are worthy of their time, their attention, their business. In describing his own success as a real-estate broker, he notes the importance of flying to the potential client's city in a private Lear jet and sweeping into the office with expensive portable dictating equipment and a personal secretary. But these "trappings of power" seem less designed to threaten the client than to reassure him that the broker knows what he is doing. If he were an incompetent broker, after all, he could hardly afford a Lear jet or a traveling secretary.

There are obviously many contexts in which we are eager to impress others with our competence. Some of the more obvious ones are students confronting teachers, applicants being interviewed for professional schools or jobs, actors trying out for a play, and athletes trying to make a team. But for many of us, self-promotion is almost a full-time job. The phenomenal self is typically organized in such a way that some talents, some areas of competence, are clearly more important than others. We laugh at our own ineptitude at music, bridge, or ping pong, but we are deadly serious about our ability to diagnose an ailment, or to design a house, or to raise a family. Many self-promoters parade their ineptitude in minor areas to establish the credibility of their claims of competence in crucial areas (Jones, Gergen, & Jones, 1963).

The ingratiation strategist must cope with the problems of establishing sincerity and authenticity. The intimidator must cope with the costs and potential dangers of his threatening behavior. The self-promoter must cope with the apparent ease with which many areas of competence may be objectively diagnosed. One might wonder if a person can get away with claims of competence for very long before being observed in some form of diagnostic performance. Within long-range relationships among spouses, academic colleagues, or business associates, competence claims can ordinarily be tested against the data of performance.

An experiment by Baumeister and Jones (1978) demonstrates how people cope with diagnostic information about them to which others have access. Subjects took a personality test, the (bogus) results of which were shown to them and (so they believed) to a fellow subject with whom they were later to interact. When subjects were then given the opportunity to communicate further information about themselves to the other subject in the form of self-ratings, these ratings depended crucially on the particular personality profiles allegedly in the other subjects' hands. If the profile was generally negative, subjects rated themselves negatively on traits disparaged by the profile but strongly compensated by positive self-descriptions on dimensions not specifically mentioned. If the profile was positive, on the other hand, subjects were typically modest on all their communicated self-ratings. The relevance of these data for the current discussion of self-promotion lies in the fact that these same self-description tendencies were absent when only the subjects themselves (and not the "other subject") saw their personality profile. The compensation effect noted in the negative profile case (positive self-descriptions on traits unrelated to the profile) was not present when only the subject was the recipient, and the notable modesty in the positive profile case also disappeared when the subject thought he was describing himself to someone who knew nothing as yet about him. It is apparent, then, that people develop fairly standard ways of coming to terms with self referent information that is publicly known. They manage their self-presentations so as not to contradict directly any known information that is negative in implications. When the information others have is generally positive, however, people apparently strive for the extra social rewards that accompany modesty, without the risk of appearing incompetent.

It is relatively easy to think of instances where the data of performance or other diagnostic information are not readily available to contradict self-promoting claims. One example is the claim of an older man that he was a star athlete, or an older woman that she was a polished dancer. There are certain crucial decisions of selection or admission that are often based largely on claims alone, though some information about previous performance is typically available as well. Nevertheless, the admissions committee or the selection officer is usually aware of the fact that prior performance in one setting may be a poor predictor of good performance in the setting to which they control access. Finally, some people may claim important attributes like a high IQ without fearing that their IQ will ever by publicly assessed. Thus, there are occasions when all we can go by in judging another's competence are his claims, and many more occasions when the claims can be only indirectly tested and never totally refuted if false.

This leaves most of us with considerable freedom to maneuver, but if there is ''an ingratiator's dilemma'' (see earlier), there is also a ''self-promoter's paradox.'' Most of us learn that many people exaggerate their abilities, and therefore their competence claims can often be at least partly discounted. In fact, the paradox arises because it is often the case that competence claims are *more* likely when competence is shaky than when it is high and securely so (as evident in Baumeister and Jones's modesty findings). Even if direct competence claims are credible, the attribution of competence may be achieved along with less favoring attributions of arrogance, insecurity, or at least dreariness.

However, the gifted self-promoter will not be totally inhibited by this paradox. He will seek indirect ways to enable the target person to reach the conclusion that he is competent in the desired respects. The adroit social climber is not likely to claim membership in the upper class to establish his aristocratic origins. He will do so by subtle patterns of consumption (clothing, house, cars, furniture) that convince others he is not just a pretentious or gauche nouveau arrivé. Similarly, college, job, and professional school applicants can establish the *likelihood* that they will succeed if accepted by noting factors that would normally be expected to facilitate success: middle-class family background, educated parents, previous entry to a prestigious school, diverse summer employment experiences, elections to leadership positions, etc.—and noting them in the most matter-of fact way.

Quattrone and Jones (1978) investigated self-presentational priorities in a role-playing experiment in which subjects either did or did not have the opportunity for a diagnostic performance. In one vignette, for example, subjects were to imagine themselves trying out for a coveted dramatic role and were told to be motivated to convince the director that they were versatile actors, suitable for roles in future plays as well. Some subjects were to assume that they impressed the director with a highly relevant performance audition. Others were to assume that no such audition took place. In the latter case, as predicted, subjects chose to disclose to the director those designated facts about themselves that were evaluatively positive and would normally facilitate the likelihood of doing well in the part (e.g., they chose to disclose readily that they had acted the same part previously). When an audition occurred and the subject's performance was applauded by the director, however, subjects chose to assign disclosure priority to facts that would normally make it *less* likely that they could perform the particular role (e.g., they had received good notices in a play where their role was the opposite kind of person from that in the role to be currently filled). Thus, when correspondent, diagnostic behavior is possible and successful, the individual will present *inhibitory* background factors to augment the significance of his general ability or his perseverance or his innate courage. When there is not an opportunity for correspondent performance, on the other than, the individual will disclose features that normally are seen to *facilitate* the likelihood that subsequent performance will be successful.

This study has several strategic implications and especially suggests that we often do not merely wish to establish that we are competent at X, Y, or Z. Beyond this, whenever possible, we want to convince the target person that our talents stem from causal conditions that enhance our attractiveness or respectworthiness. We may wish our competence as a musician to be attributed to great natural ability rather than hard work and, thus, fail to disclose the long practice hours in our past. We may for similar reasons conceal that we have taken lessons in golf. On the other hand, if we are a member of a seminar in which the appraisal of our performance is very much a matter of the instructor's subjective judgment, we may go out of our way to impress him that we have worked harder than other seminar members in preparing papers for the course. Though he may influence the instructor to give him a higher grade in this particular course, however, the seminar member who follows this strategy also runs the risk of being evaluated as a little too limited and overconscientious for consideration as a top candidate for subsequent academic positions. Following the line of reasoning developed by Quattrone and Jones, the appropriate graduate student strategy might be to marshal all the relevant facilitatory factors for presentation to the department before admission, and to emphasize the inhibitory factors once having been admitted. The applicant might, for example, stress his Yale education prior to admission but talk much more about growing up in Appalachia once in graduate school.

To summarize the subclass of self-presentation strategies that we have labeled here as self-promotion: Individuals commonly have a stake in convincing particular target persons that they are competent in one or more areas where there are no readily available, highly criterial competence tests. Their success may be an important factor in gaining access to such important goals as prestigious school admission and responsible jobs. There are strategic problems associated with straightforward competence claims, however, in that the most persistent claimants are often the most insecure about the talents being claimed. For this reason it is a superior strategy for the self-promoter to arrange for others to make claims in his behalf, but even these can range in impact because the outside claimant may be far from an objective judge. Professors often have a stake in the success of their students and are unlikely to be ruthlessly candid in their letters of reference for a mediocre protégé. On the whole, there is no substitute for diagnostic performance itself—especially if this can be managed under conditions that implicate desirable causal origins for the demonstrated competence. The individual who wants her professional success to be attributed to her natural brilliance will obviously behave in a different way than one who wants others to attribute her success to hard work and self-denial. Self-promotion thus has a property of being multitiered, with attributions underlying attributions. It is desirable to be seen as competent, but it is even more desirable to be seen as competent for the most admired causal reasons—whatever they may be in a particular culture or situational context.

Exemplification

The ingratiator wants to be liked and the intimidator wants to be feared. The self-promoter and the exemplifier both want to be respected, to be admired, but there are subtle and important differences in the attributions they seek. Whereas the self promoter wants to be seen as competent, masterful, olympian, the exemplifier seeks to project *integrity and moral worthiness*. Once again, we emphasize that there is nothing mutually exclusive about these goals. Many of us would love to be seen as simultaneously competent, likable, and morally worthy. Nevertheless, we single out exemplification because of its distinct strategic qualities and its special relationship to the behavior of emulation and the internal conditions of guilt and shame.

The exemplifier (in Western society at least) typically presents himself as honest, disciplined, charitable, and self abnegating. He is the saint who walks among us, the martyr who sacrifices for the cause. But to be successful he must not cross over the line into self-righteousness. For appropriate social effect he must exemplify morality and not merely claim it. But what *is* the appropriate social effect? Exemplary actions may be sincere and self-consistent: The actor may have so strongly internalized the ideal values of a society that his consistently virtuous behavior is unaffected by the response of others to its expression. In-so-far as this is true, we are not dealing with strategic self-presentation as we have defined it earlier. There may be such people. We suspect that totally autonomous, self consistent, and self-expressive exemplifiers—true "exemplars"—are rare.

In keeping with our interests in strategic behavior, we turn to the more common everyday self-presenter who wants others to perceive, validate, and be influenced by his selfless integrity, even though he might vigorously deny such motivation and, indeed, be unaware of it.

The prototype for the exemplifier is, of course, the religious leader who lives a life of apparent Christian (Buddhist, Moslem, etc.) virtue in return for persuasive power. In celebrated and unusual cases, the exemplifier seeks martyrdom or, at least, passively accepts incarceration, torture, institutionalized deprivation. Examples such as Ghandi, Martin Luther King, the Ayatollah Khomeini come to mind. The power that may accrue from such dramatic exemplifiers may be used for a variety of specific objectives: recruiting a following, raising funds, changing a law, fomenting a revolution.

A variant of exemplification is ideological militancy, though the relationship of militancy to self-presentation is undoubtedly complex because militancy is typically more a collective than an individual phenomenon. Nevertheless, individuals may, in the service of an ideological belief, exploit self-deprivation to influence such institutionalized power sources as employers, legislators, judges, and government executives. This self-deprivation may often be coupled with violent confrontation. This is obvious in the case of ''prolife'' advocates who vandalize abortion clinics, or student militants who take over administration buildings. Antinuclear and proenvironmental forces seem to have similar potential. In all such cases the exemplifier attempts to trade on the worthiness of his cause and not solely on the physical power of his coalition with like-minded colleagues. We would label him an exemplifier, because he attempts to arouse guilt in those who otherwise have the power to control the possibilities of physical confrontation. He presents himself as taking an exclusively worthy stand for which he is willing to undergo abstinence, arrest, expulsion, and so on. The target persons to whom he presents this selfless image can reduce their resulting guilt by, if not undergoing the same deprivations, at least supporting the same cause and implicitly recognizing the worthiness of the militant advocate.

Such confrontations have a less-dramatic counterpart in many instances of social influence and self-presentation. Parental socialization of children relies heavily on exemplification. Most parents attempt to put their best foot forward in front of their children. They attempt to exemplify the values of the culture in the hopes that their children will model these values and feel guilty when falling short of parental standards. We refer here not so much to the kinds of response modeling discussed by Bandura (1971) and other social-learning theorists but rather to the sequence of self-presentation, eliciting an attribution of moral worth, providing the conditions for potential guilt in a target person, who in turn is motivated to emulate or model the exemplifier. Even in the context of socialization, the sequence implies that the child has clearly acquired a sufficient ''feel'' for idealized cultural values, so that he can recognize and appreciate the exemplary status of his parents.

Exemplification as a self-presentational strategy is probably as ubiquitous as the other strategies we have discussed (and is often fused with them). The fellow alumnus who calls for a contribution to the college class fund is exemplifying because *he* is making the kind of sacrifice he wants and expects you to make. The neighbor who bicycles to the train station arouses our guilt as we climb into our commodious gas guzzler. The housewife who eats peanut butter sandwiches for lunch and wears clothes from the 60s can have a decisive moral edge over her self-indulgent husband with his three-martini lunch. Employers and supervisors who arrive early and leave late may exert exemplifying pressure on their subordinates, even though they may take long lunches, play midday tennis, or seclude themselves for an afternoon nap. In general, to practice what you preach is to give the preaching that much more force,but exemplification may also be effective when the preaching is not explicit.

In summary, aside from wanting others to think of us as competent and likable, we usually want them to think of us as morally worthy: honest, generous, self-sacrificing. Furthermore, attributed worthiness may provide considerable strategic leverage when asking others for support or self-sacrifice. Most would agree that President Carter was more prone to use exemplification as an influence strategy than were Presidents Johnson or Nixon. It is difficult to assess the extent to which this helped to alert the nation to the virtues of physical exercise or the need for self-sacrifices in the energy sector.   The present discussion merely scratches the surface of a complex subject, but we believe that the attribution of worthiness is often sought for strategic purposes, and that "worthy" persons often find it difficult to avoid exploiting the power inherent in their own apparent virtue.

Supplication

A final self-presentational strategy may be available to those who lack the resources implied by the preceeding strategies: A person may exploit his own weakness and dependence. When the wolf feels overwhelmed by superior fighting power, it displays its vulnerable throat. This appears to evoke some form of instinctive inhibition in the attacker so that the supplicant wolf is spared. We venture to suggest an analogy in interpersonal relations. By stressing his inability to fend for himself and emphasizing his dependence on others, the human supplicant makes salient a norm of obligation or social responsibility (Berkowitz & Daniels, 1963) that is more or less binding on target persons with greater resources. Supplication— the strategy of advertising one's dependence to solicit help— works best when there appears to be an arbitrary or accidental component in the power differential (Schopler & Matthews, 1965). If through an accident of birth one enjoys such resources as physical strength, intelligence, natural beauty, or money, and another is born handicapped in some physical or mental way, social responsibility norms impose an obligation on the former to care for the latter. Matters may be somewhat different when the "self-made" man confronts the "indolent"welfare applicant, but even here there are general if less-imperative norms, that those who need have some claim over those who have more than they need. The prototype of the self-presenting supplicant is the sexist female paired with the sexist male. The classic female supplicant (against ERA to the core) is nearly helpless in coping with the physical world. She cannot change a tire, understand algebra, read a legal document, carry a suitcase, or order wine. Her classic male counterpart, of course, rushes in to fill the breach. His vanity is touched by the indispensability of his contributions to her survival in the world. Regardless of the ultimate psychological or social consequences of this symbiosis, the supplicant female influences the male to expend energy on her behalf; to do things for her that she would like to have done. She accomplishes this at the small cost of being considered totally incompetent by her vain and dedicated husband or suitor.

We hasten to reaffirm that not all females are supplicants; nor, we now add, are all supplicants females. One suspects that many children exaggerate their ineptitude at common household chores in order to influence their parents to complete the chores themselves. Similarly, husbands often avoid learning to sew, iron, or change diapers, in order to ensure that their wives will continue to perform these functions for them, or instead of them. In a typical job setting, A may entreat B for substantial help on a project for which A gets the credit. A may then pay B with an expression of gratitude, but the more important hidden payment may be A's implicit acknowledgment of B's superiority. Such exchanges of help for competence validation are undoubtedly common in group life, whether they involve students, siblings, or job colleagues. Even more common, however, are relationships sustained by mutual dependence in which A is better than B in some areas, and B is better than A in others. Complementary aid in such cases can result in a stable and satisfactory division of labor, expertise, or advice.

The exploitation of one's dependence is a risky strategy and presumably one that is normally of last resort. There may be heavy costs to one's self-esteem in acknowledging or even advertising one's helplessness and incompetence. And there is always the good possibility that the resource-laden target person is insensitive to the social responsibility norm. Even if he responds initially with a helpful or noble gesture, he may arrange to avoid getting entrapped by the supplicant in the future by breaking off the relationship ("tell him I'm not in"). It is not too difficult for an impoverished graduate student to wangle a free lunch from his professor at a campus restaurant; it is substantially more difficult to bring about such an event a second time. The professor may start bringing sandwiches to work or eat at odd hours to avoid further exploitation by the student—who may feel that the economic deprivation that goes with student status entitles him to trade on noblesse oblige from the more affluent professor.

Summary

We have introduced a taxonomy of self-presentational strategies classified in terms of the kinds of attributions sought by the presenter. In all cases we conceive of the underlying goal as the augmentation or protection of the strategist's

	attributions sought	negative attributions risked	emotion to be aroused	prototypical actions
1. Ingratiation	likable	sycophant, conformist, obsequious	affection	self-characterization, opinion conformity, other enhancement, favors
2. Imtimidation	dangerous (ruthless, volatile)	blusterer, wishy washy, ineffectual	fear	threats, anger (incipient), breakdown (incipient)
3. Self-promotion	competent (effective, "a winner")	fraudulent, conceited, defensive	respect (awe, deference)	performance claims, performance accounts, performances
4. Exemplification	worthy (suffers, dedicated)	hypocrite, sanctimonious, exploitative	guilt (shame, emulation)	self-denial, helping, militancy for a cause
5. Supplication	helpless (handicapped, unfortunate)	stigmatized, lazy, demanding,	nurturance (obligation)	self-deprecation, entreaties for help

FIG. 9.1 A taxomony of self-presentational strategies classified primarily by attribution sought.

power to influence and control his social environment. The ingratiator augments his power by reducing the likelihood that the target person will deliver negative outcomes and increasing the prospects for positive ones. The intimidator more directly enhances his power by increasing the likelihood that he will use the negative part of the range of outcomes that he can deliver to the target person. The self promoter enhances his putative instrumental value as a problem solver for the target person. Because he obviously has something to offer, he may extract money or other outcomes in exchange. The exemplifier trades on the power of recognized social norms undergirded by the judged consensus about proper values and aspirations. He influences by successfully reflecting these norms. The supplicant also gains the power provided by the sheltering norm of social responsibility. By relinquishing his claims to more immediate personal power, he places himself at the mercy of more powerful others who are, he hopes, sensitive to the dictates of noblesse oblige.

We have in passing noted that these five strategies need not be mutually exclusive, though some combinations may be more plausible and therefore more likely than others. There is a certain imcompatibility between ingratiation and intimidation, though self-promotion may fit nicely with either. The exemplifier may be intimidating if he can arouse guilt and fear simultaneously. Supplication is the obverse of self-promotion, though the supplicant can obviously be ingratiating and even, in a certain sense, intimidating. And so on. It is also undoubtedly the case that the same act can serve different functions for different audiences. The militant picketer may intimidate management, while being an exemplifier to passersby. We separate the strategies in our taxonomy not to segregate personal types or behavior episodes but rather to distinguish the particular attributional goal, the "self" presented in the strategic act. Figure 9.1 presents a summary of the taxonomy in terms of the attribution sought, negative attributions risked, the emotion aroused, and prototypical actions.

THE IMPLICATIONS OF THE PHENOMENAL SELF
FOR STRATEGIC SELF-PRESENTATION—
AND VICE VERSA

We now consider the relations between self-presentation and the phenomenal self. We ultimately want to know both how strategic self-presentations are influenced by the immediately salient features of the phenomenal self, and how the phenomenal self is altered or shaped by particular self-presentational strategies. It is perhaps self-evident that socially oriented actions should in some way reflect the phenomenal self, though there is surprisingly little evidence on this point. We here deal with the issue very briefly.

The Phenomenal Self as a Determinant of Strategy Choice

We have already commented on the existence of various social norms that support and give social value to personal consistency. The concept of "integrity" is tied in with an individual's capacity to avoid being different things to different people—in effect, to avoid being overly influenced by strategic concerns. These norms coalesce in the concept of perceived legitimacy, which constrains the circumstances under which strategic self presentations take place. We have not discussed the role of perceived legitimacy in determining the most acceptable *form* of strategic behavior once it takes place, but such considerations obviously relate to the current concern with how the phenomenal self influences the presented self. It seems likely, for example, that a person who (momentarily or characteristically) sees himself as tough and competitive is more likely to be intimidating or self-promotive than supplicating or ingratiating. Someone who has just given to charity or helped a friend move, and whose worthiness is therefore phenomenally salient, is more likely than others to adopt the strategies of exemplification. Clearly, there is a wide-open field of study involved in charting the role that individual differences play in preferences for particular forms of strategic behavior. Immediate prior experiences may also affect strategic choice, however, and this avenue of experimentation should not be ignored.

Self-Enhancement, Approval, and Self-Esteem

We ultimately want to know both how strategic self-presentations are influenced by the immediately salient features of the phenomenal self, and how the phenomenal self is temporarily affected by a particular choice of self-presentational strategy. Turning to effects of self-presentation on the phenomenal self, research on this question has been largely restricted to the consequences of ingratiation for the actor's self-esteem. We review this research briefly and then speculate concerning the consequences for the phenomenal self of self-presentations involving the remaining strategies.

Let us begin by picturing an actor who is asked to characterize himself in a setting where he has a stake in gaining attraction from a target person. Typically, ingratiation research shows an actor in such a setting will be more self-enhancing than one in more neutral settings where attraction is less of an issue (Gergen, 1965; Jones, Gergen, & Davis, 1962; Jones, Gergen, & Jones, 1963). Self-enhancement will be reduced and self-characterization will be more modest to the extent that the actor's dependence on the target person is salient (Stires & Jones, 1969). If we could subsequently gain access to the undistorted phenomenal self, would it reflect in any way the preceding self-characterization? What circumstances might augment and what might lessen the impact of such self-characterization on the phenomenal self?

First of all, it is abundantly clear that if an actor is positively reinforced for characterizing himself in a very enhanced way, his phenomenal self will subsequently shift in the direction of the characterized self. Indirect evidence on this point is presented by Jones, Gergen, and Davis (1962). Subjects instructed to play the role of fellowship applicants with an interviewer were considerably more self-enhancing than control subjects instructed to present themselves accurately to a counselor trying to help them. Half the subjects in each condition then learned that they had impressed the interviewer favorably; the other half learned that the interviewer was unfavorably impressed. Regardless of whether subjects were in the ingratiation or control (accuracy) conditions, those with positive feedback rated their behavior in the interview as "more representative" of their true selves than those with negative feedback.

More direct evidence along the same lines comes from Gergen's (1965) experiment, in which subjects in an ingratiation condition were instructed to make a positive impression on an interviewer, and those in an accuracy condition were instructed to help the interviewer get to know them. All subjects in the ingratiation condition and half the accuracy condition subjects were then reinforced by the interviewer's head nods and expressions of agreement each time they characterized themselves in a positive way on a special triads test. The remaining accuracy subjects were not reinforced at all. Finally, all subjects filled out a self-esteem scale for the experimenter to gauge the extent to which the reinforcement generalized. The results showed a considerable elevation of self-esteem scores in the reinforcement conditions. Although ingratiation subjects were significantly more self-enhancing in the interview than accuracy subjects, both groups ultimately showed approximately the same degree of self-esteem elevation. This seems to indicate that even though subjects in the ingratiation condition realized that their self-characterizations were somewhat unrealistic, as measured by the decline in self evaluation from the interview situation to the final self ratings in a more neutral setting, they nevertheless did not lower their self-esteem back to its original level. In both Gergen's experiment and the earlier one of Jones, Gergen, and Davis, positive feedback was an important factor in determining resultant self-esteem levels.

Recent studies by Jones, Rhodewalt, Berglas, and Skelton (1981) took a different approach to the question of the impact of self-presentation on the phenomenal self. If subjects can be induced to characterize themselves positively without explicit instructions to fabricate or distort their characteristics, this may be sufficient to elevate subsequent self-esteem, even in the absence of positive feedback. Why might this be so? Two possibilities suggest themselves: dissonance reduction and biased scanning. If we were to assume that actors have stable phenomenal selves and that ingratiation incentives induced them to describe their characteristics in ways that differ from this stable self-picture, dissonance would be aroused. If the dissonance could not be reduced by attributing responsibility for the discrepancy to experimental instructions, it could most conveniently be reduced by a change in the phenomenal self in the direction of the ingratiating self-characterization. This would be yet another instance of attitudes reflecting behavior in a situation where the actor has some choice and responsibility for his actions (Wicklund & Brehm, 1976).

The biased-scanning approach (Janis & Gilmore, 1965) assumes that the selves phenomenally available to the same person over time are highly variable in many respects, including favorability; that is, situational cues and immediate past experiences elevate the salience of certain self-features more than others. It follows that inducing a subject to describe himself in a highly favorable way is not necessarily dissonant with some of the phenomenally available selves and will not motivate the subject to *change* his stable self-concept in the direction of a new phenomenal self. Instead, the biased-scanning hypothesis assumes selective attention to those aspects of the phenomenal self that are most consistent with the actor's strategic goals. A subject induced to characterize himself very favorably, for example, will typically do this without clear dissimulation or misrepresentation. He will put his best foot forward, but it is nevertheless *his* foot. Subsequently, because of the recent biased scanning of favorable instances and self-appraisals, the actor will show the kind of elevated self-esteem observed in Gergen's study.

Jones and Berglas (Experiment I in Jones, et al., 1981) set out to explore some of the conditions under which self presentation produces a shift in subsequent self-esteem. They invited prospective college-student subjects to participate for money as members of small teams that would be observing high-school student encounter groups. (This activity was selected as a highly desirable one for most undergraduates.) Subjects were informed, however, that selection as an observer team member was contingent on: (1) doing well on a social sensitivity test; and (2) impressing the team leader with their attractive qualities during an interview. The social sensitivity test involved looking at videotaped excerpts of three previous interviewees responding, allegedly, to the same ingratiation-promoting instructions. The subject was asked to indicate which of the three received the highest attraction ratings by the interviewer. This observation and rating task provided a means of varying the perceived legitimacy of highly favorable versus rather modest self-characterizations. Half the subjects saw tapes of highly self-enhancing behavior in all three interviewees. For the remainder, the interviewees were uniformly modest and self-deprecating. Crosscutting this variation in the direction of the consensus about how to be ingratiating, the order of events was varied. Some subjects were exposed to the taped interview segments before their own interview; others saw the tapes after the interview. The interview itself included a series of items from which a self-enhancement score could be derived.

After the two procedures, whatever their order, all subjects were asked as an incidental afterthought to fill out some questionnaires for a colleague of the experimenter at another university. Their responses would be anonymous and would be mailed directly to him. This afterthought questionnaire provided a measure of self-esteem in a totally different format than that used for the behavioral measure in the interview, and the setting was itself neutral, nonstrategic, and anonymous. Results showed a striking carry over from self-presentation to subsequent self-esteem. Subjects who saw the consensus tapes prior to their interviews were much affected by them; those exposed to the self-enhancing consensus were themselves much more self-enhancing than those exposed to the self-deprecating consensus. These differences continued to be reflected in highly significant differences on the supposedly unrelated self-esteem task. Subjects exposed to the tapes *after* their interview were unaffected by the apparent consensus. Thus, the self-esteem carry-over is more than a simple effect of what is perceived to be legitimate or normative in a situation. It depends crucially on whether the actor has been induced to modify his behavior.

Although powerful carry-over effects were obtained in this study, their bearing on the dissonance biased-scanning controversy is not clear. The results are very compatible with the biased scanning hypothesis, because subjects presented a selective pattern of strengths or weaknesses that could easily have made salient either an optimistic or pessimistic view of the self. Dissonance theory would have more trouble handling the results, because it is not clear why dissonance should have been aroused by the procedures—at least by those in the self enhancing conditions. Why should there be dissonance when a subject describes himself positively in the same setting in which he has seen others describing themselves positively as well? Presumably, self-enhancement should have high perceived legitimacy in such a setting. Dissonance arousal would be prevented by the presence of a consensus justifying any exaggerations or distortions in characterizing the self.

In a follow-up study (Experiment III in Jones, et al., 1981) subjects were instructed to present themselves either in a self-enhancing or a self-deprecating way in a contrived interview situation. The interviewer supposedly did not know the situation was contrived. Half the subjects were explicitly told that they could withdraw from the experiment at this point. The remaining subjects were given no such option. This intended manipulation of cognitive dissonance produced variations in self-esteem carry-over, but only in the self-deprecating conditions. Thus those who, in effect, chose to participate in an interview under self-deprecation instructions later rated their self-esteem lower than those who deprecated themselves without being told they had the option to withdraw.

Although the choice manipulation had no effect on self-esteem carry-over in the self-enhancing interviews, a biased scanning manipulation did. Half the subjects generated their own responses to the interview instructions; the remaining subjects were yoked to these so that their responses in the interview were specified for them. This variation in the degree of self reference had no effect on self-esteem carry-over in the self-deprecation conditions but clearly affected carry-over after the self-enhancing interviews. Those who had generated their own self-enhancing interview responses later showed higher self-esteem than yoked subjects constrained to make exactly the same responses.

These results are complex but comprehensible. Jones, et al. (1981) suggest that the self-concept is not inflexibly structured. Like other attitudes it has a latitude of acceptable attributes—things that the individaul is willing to believe about himself—and a latitude of rejection. Subjects in the self-enhancing condition are basically operating within the latitude of acceptable attributes. Therefore, following the proposal of Fazio, Zanna, and Cooper (1977), self concept changes should be explainable in terms of self perception theory (Bem, 1972).

According to this theory, subjects' self concepts should be heavily influenced by their recent behavior, as long as that behavior is seen as self-relevant. Presumably, subjects in the yoked conditions do not see their behavior as self-relevant since the specific content is specified by someone else. Self-deprecating subjects, on the other hand, are acknowledging self attributes that fall in the latitude of rejection. Thus, again according to Fazio, Zanna, and Cooper (1977), dissonance is created to the extent that there is perceived choice to describe oneself in a self-deprecating way.

The results of this final experiment in the series reported by Jones, et al., (1981) suggest that self presentation can influence the phenomenal self both through biased scanning and dissonance reduction processes, depending importantly on the conditions and the content of the self presentation episode.

Performance Authenticity, Self-handicapping, and Social Feedback

The effects of other presentational tactics on the phenomenal self are contingent both on the social feedback they elicit and the "authenticity" of the presented self. The ingratiator wants to be liked, but it is especially rewarding if he is viewed as attractive having not misrepresented himself. Jones (1964) refers to this as the "signifying" value of feedback, noting each actor's interest in verifying or validating his self-concept by reading the social responses of others and also noting that the signification value of approval is less meaningful to the extent that the actor has gone out of his way to achieve it. As Lord Chesterfield (1774) proposed, futhermore, approval is especially valued if we are uncertain about whether we deserve it. We believe that very similar points could be made with regard to self-promotion and the desire for respect. It is nice if someone believes we are competent, it is better if the same person confirms our own beliefs in our competence, and it is even better if someone convinces us we are competent in an area where we were previously uncertain.

The fact that approval is especially valuable following an authentic or representative performance puts pressures on the actor that have consequences for the phenomenal self. On the one hand, perceived legitimacy considerations constrain his self-presentations so that they are at least loosely tethered to the phenomenal self. On the other hand, given the fact that some self-presentations occur in settings that tempt the actor to make questionable claims, we can imagine pressures on the individual to bring his phenomenal self in line with these claims. Only in this way can he maximize the signification value of any approval received.

The desire for self-validating approval may become especially strong when events conspire to threaten cherished features of the phenomenal self. Thus, the rejected suitor may try especially hard to be charming and likable around his female friends; the solid citizen arrested for speeding might decide to increase his community service work. In such cases threats to the phenomenal self lead to self-presentations designed to secure restorative feedback. To the extent that the threatened actor sustains his counteractive behavior or to the extent that the counteractive behavior involves effortful and costly commitments, social confirmation will have the restorative power sought.

Such validation-oriented self-presentations involve a kind of "positioning" to optimize the value of self-presentational success. An observer's respect for a self-promoting actor is more valuable when it confirms the actor's own image of self competence. And the actor's subjective competence image may itself evolve from, or be protected by, self-handicapping strategies. Jones and Berglas (1978) used this term to denote a widespread tendency to avoid unequivocal information about one's own abilities when that information might suggest incompetence. To this end people may arrange performance circumstances that create impediments in the path of optimal performance (thus, the word *handicapping*). In this way responsibility for success may be triumphantly internalized and for failure, discounted. Berglas and Jones (1978) present the data from two experiments to show subjects will protect ill-gotten performance gains (in their experiments a "success" derived from luck or chance) by choosing a performance-inhibiting rather than a performance-facilitating drug prior to retest. The notion of self-handicapping fits into a more general framework of "egotism" in self-attribution (Snyder, Stephan, & Rosenfield, 1978). From the present point of view, self-handicapping and other egotistic maneuvers may be seen as one way to position one's self so that signs of respect from others for one's competence will not be dismissed as ill-gotten or undeserved gain. At the same time, such maneuvers reduce the impact of failure or disparaging criticism.

Other Carry-Over Effects

Intimidation. To what extent must the intimidator come to terms with his potential to hurt others and his willingness to exploit that potential? We have noted that intimidation requires a relationship that is to some extent nonvoluntary. This fact has the important consequence that the intimidator may seldom receive the attributional feedback that his actions deserve. Instead of learning that he is ruthless or dangerous or violence prone, he may receive signals of admiration and fealty. Thus, intimidation can elicit ingratiation or supplication often enough for the intimidator to be quite misled concerning the attributions he has actually elicited in those who do his bidding. This is reminiscent of the tyrant's dilemma noted by Thibaut and Riecken (1955): A tyrant may exert successful control over his subjects, but the more he applies his power the less information he receives concerning their spontaneous goodwill and affection. Thus, the intimidator may bask in the unwarranted inference that people are doing things for him because they like him or respect him, rather than because they are afraid not to.

On the other hand, there may be circumstances that shatter such illusions and leave the intimidator with the realization that his power is truly based on his willingness to apply negative sanctions. Here, perhaps, the intimidator can and does protect his phenomenal self from the negative implications of his behavior by one of a number of justifications: The world is a jungle, it's for your own good, it's my neck if we fail, war is hell.

Exemplification.   It is an intriguing fact that exemplifiers often present themselves as mediators or spokesmen for external agencies. Thibaut (1964) has written of the paradoxical mixture of activism and fatalism in the lives of great exemplars: "In many cases there appears to be a strong dependence on a powerful external agency of control, which may sometimes be a form of deity, an ineluctable historical force, an institution (the army), etc. It is as though the man belonged to a coalition that gave him greater strength to strive or to resist than could be commanded by any single individual [p. 87]." Thibaut suggests a number of reasons why such an imagined coalition with a powerful agency might lead to a high level of striving and influence and accomplishment. In the present context, however, we are more interested in some of the paradoxical consequences for the phenomenal self of acting on behalf of an all powerful force. One's immediate associations might suggest that servile "humility" would be the self-image most compatible with exemplification. But there are many conflicting data that involve instances of arrogance and exploitation, even if we avoid the totally fraudulent cult leaders and evangelists who deliberately dissimulate for power or cash. There are enough cases in which initially humble, selfless exemplifiers were transformed into arrogant exploiters to pose a challenge for social psychological analysis. Perhaps because of the coalition with an omnipotent agency mentioned previously, the exemplifier may come to believe in his own moral invulnerability and lose contact with normally effective social and legal sanctions. The case of Jim Jones and his voracious sexual exploitations seems pertinent here, along with the ultimate homicidal behavior of Charles Hedrick, the founder of Synanon. There are doubtless other cases in which the exemplifier gets carried away with his own moral authority. Such transformations seem to be extreme instances of the impact of a self-presentational strategy on the phenomenal self.

Turning to the more casual everyday exemplifier, we suspect that there is considerable strain inherent in maintaining an impeccable moral posture. The exemplifier may find himself on a perpetual treadmill, for behavioral departures from worthiness claims can elicit ridicule and contempt. Here, perhaps, it might seem important to distinguish between the implicit exemplifier and the more explicit claimant to worthiness. To the extent, however, that the actor attempts to trade on his worthiness in the market of social influence, he becomes a claimant whether or not this is made explicit. Implicit or explicit worthiness claims place a greater burden on the exemplifier than competence claims do on the self-promoter. To overestimate one's competence may be seen as part of the game of life; to parade one's worthiness is at the very least to heighten one's vulnerability to charges of hypocrisy, self-righteousness, or fraudulent piety. There is something paradoxical about expressing pride in one's humility, or exerting influence through self-denial. In addition, whereas one can be competent at x but not at y or z, worthiness is a more either/or quality, a more indivisible whole.

A consequence of the constant pressure on the exemplifier may be the use of "time-outs" or the segregation of on-stage from back-stage performances (Goffman, 1959). Thus, the exemplifier may be able to maintain a consistent moral posture in front of one audience, whereas behaving differently in private or with other audiences. The priest may be a secret heavy drinker or visit brothels in a neighboring city. The father may be profligate and self-indulgent at a convention, although emphasizing the virtues of self-denial to his children.

Supplication. The phenomenal self of the supplicant is by definition incomplete. The supplicant's self-esteem must be threatened by his cultivation of dependence and ineptitude. We speculate that this might be countered by a form of "identification with the aggressor" that may provide psychological sustenance. To take pleasure in the outcomes and achievements of those who control your fate may be an important form of vicarious gratification that gives closure to the self-concept. An emphasis of the team, the organization, the family, the ethnic group may perhaps be a saving feature of the supplicant's phenomenal self. If one is dependent on others, it may be comforting to think in terms of larger symbiotic units when reflecting on one's identity.

An alternative possibility is that the supplicant can view himself as deserving the largesse of others more fortunate than he. This may coincide with a broader ideological conviction that those who have gained more should be expected to give more. Equity, not equality is the watchword. Or the dependent supplicant may feel that the system let him down; therefore, the conviction that the system "owes him" is woven into an ideology of embittered and peevish passivity.

SUMMARY AND CONCLUSIONS

The strategic self-presentation rubric encompasses much, though by no means all, of interpersonal behavior. The present essay has drawn attention to five distinct strategies designed to manipulate a target person's attributions to an actor. The attributions sought are in the ultimate interest of power maintenance or augmentation. It should be emphasized that most of the time these strategies are not self-consciously pursued. We assume that because power-reducing actions are maladaptive for the person, he learns—indeed overlearns—those ways of behaving that have power-augmenting implications for the self. By and large these ways of behaving become semiautomatic reactions triggered by interpersonal threats and opportunities.

The strategy of *ingratiation* is undoubtedly the most ubiquitous as well as the most highly researched. It is hard to imagine a person who is totally indifferent to the affective reactions he induces in others; we all would rather be liked than ignored or disliked. And efforts to be liked are presumably boosted when we find ourselves in a dependent or low-power position. Research has highlighted the dilemma facing the would-be ingratiator; the greater or more obvious the dependence, the greater the target person's defensive sensitivity to ingratiating overtures. Nevertheless, target persons are often trapped by their own vanity.

Just as the ingratiator wants to believe in his own sincerity, the target person wants to believe in the sincerity of the compliments or agreements he receives. This clearly mutes the ingratiator's dilemma. Nevertheless, establishing credibility is a major task for the ingratiator—precisely in those settings where he most wants to be liked.

Intimidation is a second strategy and one quite distinct from ingratiation in emphasizing threat and the manipulation of fear rather than the more positive emotions associated with affection. Intimidation also requires credibility for its effectiveness, but even credible intimidation may be a self defeating strategy in relationships that may be easily abrogated or avoided. However, the more subtle forms of intimidation are often woven through relationships that are basically founded on affection, respect, and other positive emotions. Subtle intimidation pressures may shape the flow of behavior and lead to consistent conversational omissions or diversions. Intimidators are generally (though not necessarily) in positions of high power relative to their targets. To the extent that this is true, the intimidator is not likely to learn that the target's compliances are based on fear. In such settings of clear differential power intimidation often breeds ingratiation and thus provides the intimidator with misleading feedback concerning the attributions actually suggested by his actions.

Self-Promotion, the third strategy discussed, is a close cousin to ingratiation with the emphasis on competence and respect rather than personal attractiveness and affection. A distinctive feature is the potential availability of independent evidence concerning ability. This raises the danger of false claims with which the self-promoted may be discredited. But the lines of inference from performance to attributed ability are usually tenuous enough to permit considerable strategic maneuvering. Self-handicapping strategies are not only useful for deceiving oneself; they can be very important in arranging one's self-presentations before influential audiences. The self handicapper can always make sure that his performances are given under less than optimal circumstances, thus guaranteeing that poor performance will be attributionally ambiguous, and that good performance will yield high competence attributions. In addition, research has shown that people are well aware of the relative attractiveness of certain causal factors underlying competence, and we assume that they will arrange their self-presentations to suggest the existence of these attractive causal factors. Most of us would rather be considered as relaxed but brilliant, for example, than as plodding overachievers. There are occasions, however, when the latter attribution might be acceptable or even preferred.

Exemplification, the fourth strategy, runs the gamut from the explicit manipulations of muckrakers and religious leaders to the subtleties of serving as a modest moral model in the parent or teacher role. Attempting to exemplify virtue or culture-defined worthiness has different implications for the actor than attempting to promote one's competence image. Worthiness is a more seamless whole attribute than competence. A man who has been a model of virtue all his life, but who one day is caught with his hand in the till, is suddenly but a parody of virtue, a fraudulent hypocrite. A performer who occasionally fails to live up to expectations is easily excused as having a bad day.

The final strategy, *supplication,* may be considered a strategy of last resort, but it may nevertheless be a highly effective way of avoiding the negative reaches of others' power when one's own power resources are limited. By throwing himself at the mercy of the high-power target person, the supplicant counts on social responsibility norms to reduce the risk of being even further exploited because he has advertised his dependence. His reading of the target person's susceptibility to such normative pressure is obviously very important.

We propose that these five strategies are interwoven in much of social behavior, though the behavior almost always serves other purposes as well as power augmentation. We do not propose that this is somehow a typology of persons, even if for expositional purposes we have written about intimidators, exemplifiers, and supplicants. Though we do not think much would be gained by a psychometric individual-difference approach to self-presentational strategies, it would not be altogether surprising to find that certain experiences and certain personal resources would make one strategy much more prominent than others in a particular actor's repertoire. It is clear also that the strategies are often linked or fused so that one precedes or gives way to another. This is particularly true of the trio, ingratiation, self-promotion, and exemplification. On the other hand, ingratiation and intimidation seem to be rather incompatible strategies, as are self-promotion and supplication. Finally, one actor's strategy may trigger counterstrategies in the target person. We have noted that intimidation can lead to ingratiation, but the opposite may also be true if target persons rise to take advantage of those who appear to like them. Self-promotion might in some cases give rise to competing self-promotion in the target, or in other circumstances it could evoke supplication or ingratiation. All of which makes it extremely difficult to think of promising research strategies for pinning down determinants and conditions. We hope and suspect, however, that the provision of the present taxonomy will not only stimulate such research but provide a framework for a fair amount of existing research that was produced under different labels for different theoretical purposes. We ourselves intend to pursue these possibilities in our future work.

ACKNOWLEDGMENTS

Preparation of this chapter was greatly facilitated by grants from the National Science Foundation to each author. We are greatly appreciative of comments and criticisms from many students and from Roy Baumeister, Jerome Bruner, Nancy Cantor, Joel Cooper, John Darley, Reid Hastie, Albert Hastorf, Arthur Miller, George Miller, George Quattrone, David Schneider, and Barry Schlenker.

REFERENCES

Bandura, A. (Ed.), *Psychological modeling: Conflicting theories.* Chicago: Aldine-Atherton, 1971.

Baumeister, R. F. & Jones, E. E.   When self-presentation is constrained by the target's knowledge: Consistency and Compensation. *Journal of Personality and Social Psychology,* 1978, *36,* 608–618.

Bem, D.   Self-perception theory. In L. Berkowitz (Ed.), *Advances in experimental social psychology* (Vol. 6). New York: Academic Press, 1972.

Berglas, S., & Jones, E. E.   Drug choice as a self-handicapping strategy in response to noncontingent success. *Journal of Personality and Social Psychology,* 1978, *36,* 405–417.

Berkowitz, L., & Daniels, L. R.   Responsibility and dependency. *Journal of Abnormal and Social Psychology,* 1963, *66,* 664–669.

Carnegie, D.   *How to win friends and influence people.* New York: Simon Schuster, 1936.

Chesterfield, Earl of (Philip Darmer Stanhope).   *Letters to his son.* (Walter M. Dunne, ed.) Wiley, 1901. Original Publ. 1774.

Cozby, P. C.   Self-disclosure: A literature review. *Psychological Bulletin,* 1973, *79,* 73–91.

Duval, S., & Wicklund, R. A.   *A theory of objective self awareness.* New York: Academic Press, 1972.

Fazio, R. H., Zanna, M. P., & Cooper, J.   Dissonance and self perception: An integrative view of each theory's proper domain of application. *Journal of Experimental Social Psychology,* 1977, *13,* 464–479.

Gergen, K. J.   The effects of interaction goals and personalistic feedback on the presentation of self. *Journal of Personality and Social Psychology,* 1965, *1,* 413–424.

Goffman, E.   *The presentation of self in everyday life.* Garden City, N. Y.: Doubleday and Company, 1959.

Janis, I. L., & Gilmore, J. B.   The influence of incentive conditions on the success of role playing in modifying attitudes. *Journal of Personality and Social Psychology,* 1965, *1,* 17–27.

Jones, E. E.   *Ingratiation: A social-psychological analysis.* New York: Appleton-Century- Crofts, 1964; Irvington, 1975.

Jones, E. E. Conformity as a tactic of ingratiation. *Science,* 1965, *149,* 144–150.

Jones, E. E., & Baumeister, R.   The self-monitor looks at the ingratiator, *Journal of Personality,* 1976, *44,* 654-674.

Jones, E. E., & Berglas, S. Control of attributions about the self through self-handicapping strategies: The appeal of alcohol and the role of underachievement. *Personality and Social Psychology Bulletin,* 1978, *4,* 200–206.

Jones, E. E., & Gerard, H. B.   *Foundations of social psychology.* New York: Wiley, 1967.

Jones, E. E., Gergen, K. J., & Davis, K. E.   Some determinants of reactions to being approved or disapproved as a person. *Psychological Monographs,* 1962, *76,* (2, Whole No . 521).

Jones, E. E., Gergen, K. J., & Jones, R. G.   Tactics of ingratiation among leaders and subordinates in a status hierarchy. *Psychological Monographs,* 1963, *77,* (3, Whole No. 566).

Jones, E. E., Jones, R. G., & Gergen, K. J.   Some conditions affecting the evaluation of a conformist. *Journal of Personality,* 1963, *31,* 270–288.

Jones, E. E., Rhodewalt, F., Berglas, S., & Skelton, J. A.   Effects of strategic self-presentation on subsequent self-esteem. *Journal of Personality and Social Psychology,* 1981, *41 ,* 407–421.

Jones, E. E., Stires, L.K., Shaver, K. G., & Harris, V. A.   Evaluation of an ingratiator by target persons and bystanders. *Journal of Personality,* 1968, *36,* 349–385.

Jones, E. E., & Wortman, C.   *Ingratiation: An attributional approach,* Morristown, N. J.: General Learning Press, 1973.

Jourard, S. M. *The transparent self.* Princeton, N. J.: Van Nostrand, 1964.

Korda, M.   *Power: How to get it, how to use it.* New York: Random House, 1975.

Langer, E., & Newman, H. M.   The role of mindlessness in a typical social psychology experiment. *Personality and Social Psychology Bulletin,* 1979, *5,* 295–298.

Orne, M. T.   On the social psychology of the psychology experiment. *American Psychologist,* 1962, *17,* 776–783.

Quattrone, G. A., & Jones, E. E.   Selective self-disclosure with and without correspondent performance. *Journal of Experimental Social Psychology,* 1978, *14,* 511–526.

Ringer, R. J. *Winning through intimidation.* Los Angeles: Los Angeles Book Publishers Company, 1973.

Rosenberg, M. J.   When dissonance fails: On eliminating evaluation apprehension from attitude measurement. *Journal of Personality and Social Psychology,* 1965, *1,* 28–42.

Rosenthal, R. *Experimenter effects in behavioral research.* New York: Appleton-Century-Crofts, 1966.

Schopler, J., & Matthews, M. W.   The influence of the perceived causal locus of partner's dependence on the use of interpersonal power. *Journal of Personality and Social Psychology,* 1965, *2609–612.*

Snyder, M. L., Stephan, W. G., & Rosenfield, D.   Attributional egotism. In J. H. Harvey, W. J. Ickes, & R. F. Kidd (Eds.), *New directions in attribution research,* (Vol. 2). Hillsdale, N. J.: Lawrence Erlbaum Associates, 1978.

Stires, L. K., & Jones, E. E.   Modesty vs. self-enhancement as alternative forms of ingratiation. *Journal of Experimental Social Psychology,* 1969, *5,* 172–188.

Tedeschi, J. T., Schlenker, B. R., & Bonoma, T. V.   Cognitive dissonance: Private ratiocination or public spectacle? *American Psychologist,* 1971, *26,* 685–695.

Thibaut, J. W.   The motivational effects of social dependence on a powerful agency of control: In W. W. Cooper, H. J. Leavitt, & M. W. Shelley II (Eds.) *New perspectives in organization research.* New York: Wiley, 1964.

Thibaut, J. W., & Riecken, H. W.   Some determinants and consequences of the perception of social causality. *Journal of Personality,* 1955, *24,* 113–133.

Webb, E. T., & Morgan, JJ. B. *Strategy in handling people.* Garden City, L. I.: Garden City Publishers, 1930.

Wicklund, R. A., & Brehm, J. W. *Prespectives on cognitive dissonance* Hillsdale, N. J.: Lawrence Erlbaum Associates, 1976.

Author Index

Page numbers in italic indicate complete bibliographic information

Kopp, R. E., 13, *36*
Korda, M., 232, *261*
Krauss, R. M., 161, 164, *180, 181,* 195, *206*
Krech, D., 41, *68,* 163, *180*
Krugman, A. D., 117, *123*
Kuhn, D., 106, 109, *122, 123*
Kuhn, M. H., 73, *96*
Kuiper, N. A., 53, 55, 56, 57, 58, *68, 69*
Kulik, J., 195, *206*
Kun, A., 106, 109, *123*
Kurtines, W., 18, *36*

L

LaBerge, D., 66, 67, *70*
Ladner, J. S., 79, *96*
Landers, D. M., 26, *35*
Langer, E. J., 25, *36,* 215, 221, *228,* 232, *261*
LaPiere, R. T., 162, *180*
Latane, B., 97, 98, *123,* 221, *228*
Latham, G. P., 10, *36*
Launier, R., 26, *36*
Lawhon, J., 97, 99, 111, *124*
Layden, M. A., 193, *206*
Lazarus, R. S., 26, *36*
Lefcourt, H. M., 22, *36*
Lepper, M. R., 8, *36,* 53, *69*
Lerman, D., 9, *39*
Leventhal, G. S., 107, *123*
Levinger, G., 119, *123*
Levinson, D., 112, *123*
Lewin, K., 9, *36,* 156, *180*
Lewis, H. B., 108, *122*
Lewis, M. I., 4, *38,* 117, *123*
Lichtenstein, S., 32, *38*
Liebert, R. M., 8, *37*
Liebling, B. A., 220, *228*
Lindzey, G., 156, *180*
Lingoes, J. C., 54, 56, *68*
Lippa, R., 193, *206*
Litrownik, A. J., 11, *37*
Liu, T. J., 166, *181*
Llewellyn, L. G., 222, *228*
Locke, E. A., 10, 13, *37*
Loebl, J. H., 104, 106, *124*
Loevinger, J., 154, 156, *180*
Loftus, E. F., 169, *180*
Loftus, G. R., 169, *180*
Looft, W. R., 116, *123*
Lord, C. G., 56, 58, *68*

Lorge, I., 113, *125*
Lowery, C. R., 141, *148*
Lublin, S. C., 171, 172, *182,* 225, *229*
Lutsky, N., 193, *206*

M

Maccoby, E., 81, *96*
Magnusson, D., 4, *35,* 132, *148*
Mahoney, M. J., 7, 8, 11, 14, 17, *34, 37*
Mailer, J., 8, *36*
Malone, T. W., 5, *39*
Mann, L., 21, *36*
Mantell, D. M., 20, *37*
Markus, H., 50, 52, 53, 54, 55, 56, 59, 60, *68, 69, 70,* 154, 165, *180*
Marlatt, G. A., 26, *37*
Marmor, J., 112, *123*
Marston, A. R., 8, *36*
Mash, M., 193, *206*
Maslach, C., 5, *39,* 171, *180*
Maslow, A. H., 112, *123*
Masters, J. C., 8, 11, *37,* 81, *96*
McCall, G. J., 8, *37*
McCaul, K. D., 141, *148,* 221, *229*
McClintock, C. G., 104, 106, *123*
McClintock, E., 104, 106, *123*
McConnell, H. K., 138, *147*
McDonald, P. J., 214, 218, *229*
McDougall, W., 41, *69*
McFarland, C., 162, *181*
McGuire, C. V., 72, 73, 74, 75, 79, *96*
McGuire, W. J., 71, 72, 73, 74, 75, 79, 94, *96*
McMahon, A. W., 117, *123*
McMains, M. J., 8, *37*
McPartland, T. S., 73, *96*
Meacham, J., 73, *96*
Mead, G. H., 131, 135, *148,* 185, *206,* 209, 210, 211, *229*
Mehrabian, A., 161, *180*
Meichenbaum, D. H., 26, *37*
Menlove, F. L., 16, *34*
Messick, D. M., 49, *69*
Milgram, S., 20, 21, *37*
Miller, D. T., 49, *69*
Miller, G. A., 43, *69,* 154, *180*
Miller, R. L., 8, 30, *39,* 97, 109, *123, 124*
Miller, S. M., 26, *37*
Mischel, T., 3, *37*
Mischel, W., 12, *37,* 165, *180,* 204, *206*

Subject Index